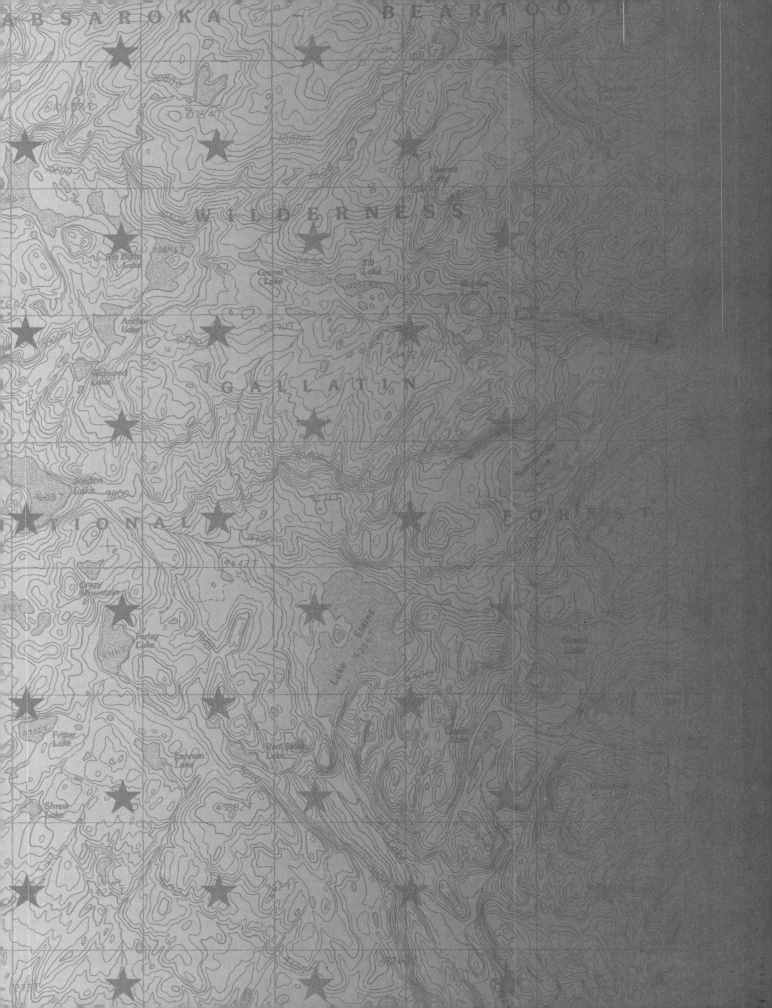

# HOUGHTON MIFFLIN

# SOCIAL STUDIES

## ★ STATES AND REGIONS ★

Visit **Education Place®**
www.eduplace.com/kids

 HOUGHTON MIFFLIN                    BOSTON

## ★AUTHORS★

**Senior Author**

Dr. Herman J. Viola
Curator Emeritus
Smithsonian Institution

Dr. Cheryl Jennings
Project Director
Florida Institute of
    Education
University of North
    Florida

Dr. Sarah Witham Bednarz
Associate Professor,
    Geography
Texas A&M University

Dr. Mark C. Schug
Professor and Director
Center for Economic
    Education
University of Wisconsin,
    Milwaukee

Dr. Carlos E. Cortés
Professor Emeritus, History
University of California,
Riverside

Dr. Charles S. White
Associate Professor
School of Education
Boston University

**Consulting Authors**

Dr. Dolores Beltran
Assistant Professor
Curriculum Instruction
California State University, Los Angeles
(Support for English Language Learners)

Dr. MaryEllen Vogt
Co-Director
California State University Center
for the Advancement of Reading
(Reading in the Content Area)

HOUGHTON MIFFLIN

# SOCIAL STUDIES

**★ STATES AND REGIONS ★**

 HOUGHTON MIFFLIN　　　BOSTON

## Consultants

**Philip J. Deloria**
Associate Professor
Department of History
and Program in
American Studies
University of Michigan

**Lucien Ellington**
UC Professor of Education
and Asia Program
Co-Director
University of Tennessee,
Chattanooga

**Thelma Wills Foote**
Associate Professor
University of California,
Irvine

**Stephen J. Fugita**
Distinguished Professor
Psychology and Ethnic
Studies
Santa Clara University

**Charles C. Haynes**
Senior Scholar
First Amendment Center

**Ted Hemmingway**
Professor of History
The Florida Agricultural &
Mechanical University

**Douglas Monroy**
Professor of History
The Colorado College

**Lynette K. Oshima**
Assistant Professor
Department of Language,
Literacy and Sociocultural
Studies and Social Studies
Program Coordinator
University of New Mexico

**Jeffrey Strickland**
Assistant Professor, History
University of Texas Pan
American

**Clifford E. Trafzer**
Professor of History and
American Indian Studies
University of California,
Riverside

## Teacher Reviewers

**Kristy Bouck**
Mullenix Ridge Elementary
Port Orchard, WA

**Martha Eckhoff**
Mullanphy ILC Elementary
St. Louis, MO

**Melanie Gates**
John Burroughs Elementary
Long Beach, CA

**Jo Ann Gillespie**
Argonaut Elementary
Saratoga, CA

**Sharon Hawthorne**
Milton H. Allen Elementary
Medford, NJ

**Martha Lewis**
Lawton Elementary
Oviedo, FL

**Tammy Morici**
Piñon Hills Elementary
Piñon Hills, CA

**Andrea Orndorff**
Triadelphia Ridge
Elementary
Ellicott City, MD

**Theresa Powell**
Harbor View School
Charleston, SC

**Kay Renshaw**
Leila G. Davis Elementary
Clearwater, FL

**Kristin Roemhildt**
Pinewood Elementary
Moundsview, MN

**Cathy Stubbs**
Martin Luther King
Elementary
Ft. Lauderdale, FL

**Tonya Torres**
Madie Ives Elementary
North Miami Beach, FL

**Kristen Werk**
Parkside Elementary
Pittsburg, CA

Printed in the U.S.A.

ISBN: 978-0-618-83092-3

1 2 3 4 5 6 7 8 9 DW-13 12 11 10 09 08 07 06

# Contents

Bringing the world to your classroom!

# References

## Citizenship Handbook

## Resources

# Extend Lessons

Connect the core lesson to an important concept and dig into it. Extend your social studies knowledge!

# Skill Lessons

Take a step-by-step approach to learning and practicing key social studies skills.

Apply Critical Thinking

# Visual Learning

Become skilled at reading visuals. Graphs, maps, and fine art help you put all of the information together.

## Charts and Graphs

## Diagrams and Infographics

## Timelines

## Interpreting Fine Art

# About Your Textbook

## ➊ How It's Organized

**Units** The major sections of your book are units.

Each starts with a big idea.

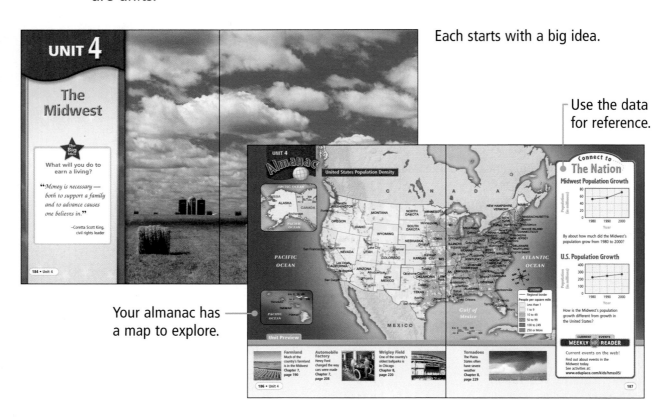

Use the data for reference.

Your almanac has a map to explore.

Get ready for reading.

**Chapters** Units are divided into chapters, and each opens with a vocabulary preview.

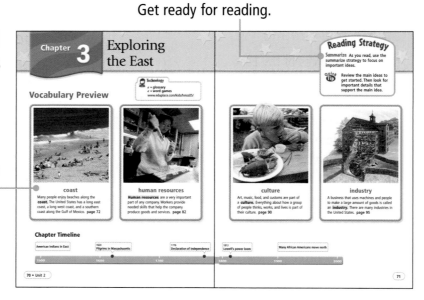

Four important concepts get you started.

# ② Core and Extend

**Lessons** The lessons in your book have two parts: core and extend.

### Core Lessons
Lessons bring social studies to life and help you meet your state's standards.

Core Lesson 3

### Extend Lessons
Go deeper into an important topic.

Extend

Primary Sources

---

## Core Lesson

Vocabulary strategies help with word meanings.

Before you read, use your prior knowledge.

Reading skills support your understanding of the text.

Practice summarizing the lesson.

Studying social studies means asking why ideas are important to remember.

After you read, pull it together!

---

Core Lesson 1

# Land and Climate

**Build on What You Know** Does wind seem harsher out in the open than in a forest? The Midwest has lots of flat, open plains. What might the wind feel like there?

### Land and Water of the Midwest

**Main Idea** The Midwest is a central region of wide open plains, thick woods, and huge waterways.

The Midwest lies in the middle of the country. Canada lies to the north. The Rocky Mountains and the Appalachian Mountains lie on either side of it.

The eastern part of this region features the Great Lakes. The land is mostly flat, with some hilly areas. The rainfall ... the north ca... has a mix o...

West of ... climate is d... land. A **prai**... trees. People... Much of the...

**Iowa Farmla**... grasslands int...

190 • Chapter 7

**VOCABULARY**

prairie
tributary
levee
lock

**Vocabulary Strategy**

tributary

**Tributary** and **contribute** have the same root. **Contribute** means to give or add to something. A **tributary** adds water to a larger stream or river.

**READING SKILL**
**Cause and Effect**
How did waterways affect settlement in the Midwest? List causes on the chart.

| Cause | Effect |
|-------|--------|
|       |        |

Main ideas for sections state what is important.

---

### Midwestern Plants and Animals

Plants and animals have adapted to the region's climate extremes. For example, some prairie grasses have deep roots. They help the plants find moisture. Pine trees keep their needles for years. This saves energy and helps the trees survive harsh weather.

Animals have also adapted. Some birds migrate to warmer places. Prairie dogs dig underground dens that protect them from severe weather. A prairie dog is a rodent that belongs to the squirrel family.

Millions of bison, or buffalo, once roamed the Great Plains. Thick coats of fur kept them warm. Hunters wanted this fur. By 1885, they had killed all but a few hundred bison. Then people started protecting bison. Today, about 150,000 bison live in the United States.

**REVIEW** How have people and wildlife adapted to the climate of the Midwest?

### Lesson Summary
- Landforms of the Midwest include prairies, hills, and forests.
- The two main waterways are the Great Lakes and the Mississippi River system.
- The Midwest is very hot in summer and very cold in winter.

### Why It Matters ...
People, plants, and animals have adapted to the Midwest's climate and made it their home.

**Prairie Dog** The prairie dog, found in the Midwest, is not really a dog. It is a rodent.

### Lesson Review

❶ **VOCABULARY** Write a paragraph showing that you know what **levee** and **lock** mean.

❷ **READING SKILL** Explain one **cause** of the growth of Chicago.

❸ **MAIN IDEA: Geography** Name the major midwestern landforms.

❹ **MAIN IDEA: Geography** How does location affect climate in the Midwest?

❺ **CRITICAL THINKING: Evaluate** In what ways might the Midwest be different without its large rivers and tributaries?

**WRITING ACTIVITY** Suppose a student from Florida was moving to the Midwest. What clothes should the student bring? Write a letter explaining what the student should pack.

193

**Extend Lesson**  Learn more about an important topic from each core lesson.

Dig in and extend your knowledge.

Look closely. Learn more about geography.

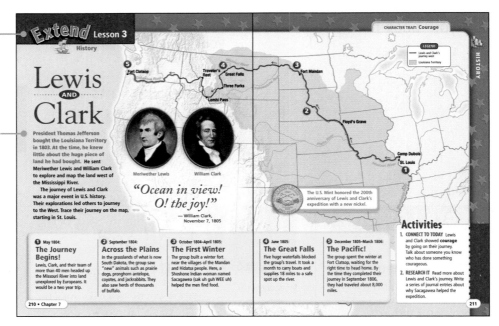

Look for literature, readers' theater, geography, economics— and more.

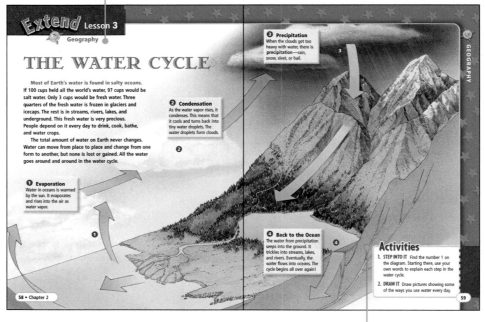

Write, talk, draw, and debate!

# ❸ Skills

## Skill Building  Learn map, graph, and study skills, as well as citizenship skills for life.

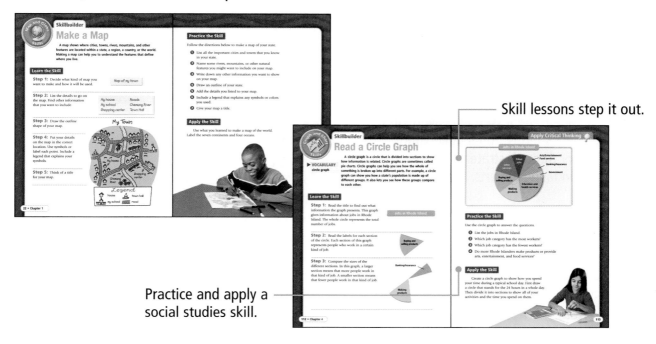

Skill lessons step it out.

Practice and apply a social studies skill.

# ❹ References

## Citizenship Handbook
The back of your book includes sections you'll refer to again and again.

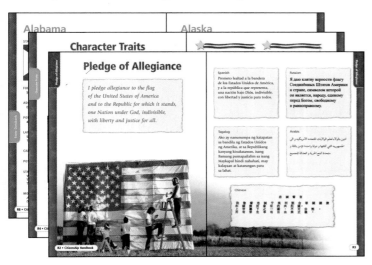

## Resources
Look for atlas maps, a glossary of social studies terms, and an index.

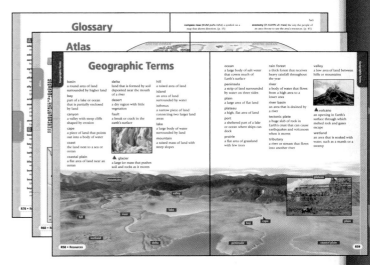

# Reading Social Studies

*Your book includes many features to help you be a successful reader. Here's what you will find:*

## VOCABULARY SUPPORT

Every chapter and lesson helps you with social studies terms. You'll build your vocabulary through strategies you're learning in language arts.

### Preview
Get a jump start on four important words from the chapter.

### Vocabulary Strategies
Focus on word roots, prefixes, suffixes, or compound words, for example.

### Vocabulary Practice
Reuse words in the reviews, skills, and extends. Show that you know your vocabulary.

## READING STRATEGIES

Look for the reading strategy and quick tip at the beginning of each chapter.

### Predict and Infer
Before you read, think about what you'll learn.

### Monitor and Clarify
Check your understanding. Could you explain what you just read to someone else.

### Question
Stop and ask yourself a questions. Did you understand what you read?

### Summarize
After you read, think about the most important ideas of the lesson.

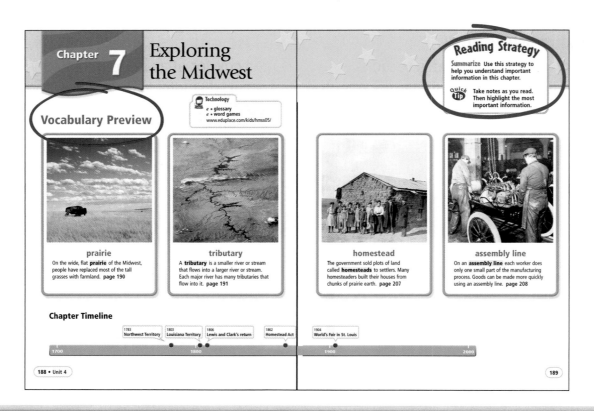

Chapter 7 — Exploring the Midwest

**Vocabulary Preview**

**Technology**
e • glossary
e • word games
www.eduplace.com/kids/hmss05/

**prairie**
On the wide, flat **prairie** of the Midwest, people have replaced most of the tall grasses with farmland. **page 190**

**tributary**
A **tributary** is a smaller river or stream that flows into a larger river or stream. Each major river has many tributaries that flow into it. **page 191**

**homestead**
The government sold plots of land called **homesteads** to settlers. Many homesteaders built their houses from chunks of prairie earth. **page 207**

**assembly line**
On an **assembly line** each worker does only one small part of the manufacturing process. Goods can be made more quickly using an assembly line. **page 208**

**Reading Strategy**
**Summarize** Use this strategy to help you understand important information in this chapter.

**Quick Tip** Take notes as you read. Then highlight the most important information.

**Chapter Timeline**

| 1783 Northwest Territory | 1803 Louisiana Territory | 1806 Lewis and Clark's return | 1862 Homestead Act | 1904 World's Fair in St. Louis |

1700     1800     1900     2000

188 • Unit 4

189

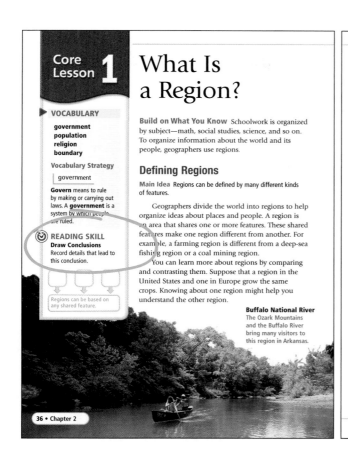

### Core Lesson 1

# What Is a Region?

**Build on What You Know** Schoolwork is organized by subject—math, social studies, science, and so on. To organize information about the world and its people, geographers use regions.

## Defining Regions

**Main Idea** Regions can be defined by many different kinds of features.

Geographers divide the world into regions to help organize ideas about places and people. A region is an area that shares one or more features. These shared features make one region different from another. For example, a farming region is different from a deep-sea fishing region or a coal mining region.

You can learn more about regions by comparing and contrasting them. Suppose that a region in the United States and one in Europe grow the same crops. Knowing about one region might help you understand the other region.

**Buffalo National River**
The Ozark Mountains and the Buffalo River bring many visitors to this region in Arkansas.

36 • Chapter 2

---

**One Place, Many Regions**

One place can belong to many regions. For example, Elizabeth, New Jersey, is part of New York City's metropolitan region. Trains, buses, and roads connect the city to New York. Elizabeth also belongs to the region called the East. This region is based on location within the United States.

Elizabeth is also part of New Jersey. As a state, New Jersey is a political region. As one of the 13 original colonies, it is part of a larger historical region. Depending on certain facts about its population, Elizabeth may belong to several other regions, too.

**REVIEW** In what ways do people use regions to make decisions?

**George Washington Bridge**
This bridge connects New York City to a wider metropolitan region.

**Lesson Summary**

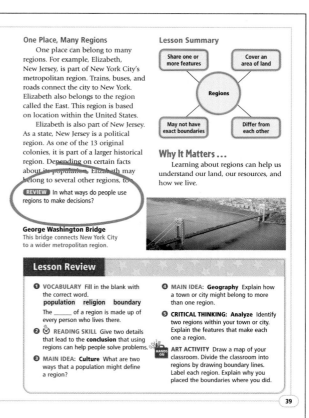

Share one or more features — Cover an area of land — Regions — May not have exact boundaries — Differ from each other

**Why It Matters . . .**

Learning about regions can help us understand our land, our resources, and how we live.

### Lesson Review

❶ **VOCABULARY** Fill in the blank with the correct word.
population   religion   boundary
The _____ of a region is made up of every person who lives there.

❷ **READING SKILL** Give two details that lead to the **conclusion** that using regions can help people solve problems.

❸ **MAIN IDEA: Culture** What are two ways that a population might define a region?

❹ **MAIN IDEA: Geography** Explain how a town or city might belong to more than one region.

❺ **CRITICAL THINKING: Analyze** Identify two regions within your town or city. Explain the features that make each one a region.

**ART ACTIVITY** Draw a map of your classroom. Divide the classroom into regions by drawing boundary lines. Label each region. Explain why you placed the boundaries where you did.

39

---

## READING SKILLS

As you read, organize the information. These reading skills will help you:

**Sequence**

**Cause and Effect**

**Compare and Contrast**

**Problem and Solution**

**Draw Conclusions**

**Predict Outcomes**

**Categorize (or) Classify**

**Main Idea and Details**

## COMPREHENSION SUPPORT

**Build on What You Know**
Check your prior knowledge. You may already know a lot!

**Review Questions**
Connect with the text. Did you understand what you just read?

**Summaries**
Look for three ways to summarize–a list, an organizer, or a paragraph.

# Constitution Day

★ ★ ★ ★ ★ ★ ★ ★ ★ ★ ★ ★ ★ ★ ★ ★ ★ ★ ★ ★ ★ ★ ★ ★ ★

What are all the things a government should do? That's a big question. Leaders of our new nation, over 200 years ago, had to decide the answer. Their goal was to create a plan for the United States government. They wanted a government that could protect the common good and serve the people. The plan they created was called the Constitution of the United States. They signed it on September 17, 1787. A special part of the Constitution, called the Bill of Rights, listed rights the Constitution would protect.

Today, the Constitution still organizes our government and protects our rights. We celebrate Constitution Day and Citizenship Day during the week of September 17.

Visitors can view the original Constitution at the National Archives Building in Washington, D.C.

The Constitution begins with the words "We the People," which shows that it was written by and for the people of the United States.

Today, the Constitution has 4,440 words. It is the oldest and shortest written constitution in the world.

Two of the people who worked on the Constitution, George Washington and James Madison, later became Presidents of the new country.

## Activity

**WHAT ARE YOUR RIGHTS?** The Bill of Rights protects many important rights including freedom of religion, freedom of speech, and freedom of the press. Choose one of these rights and create a display. Use images and captions to show how people enjoy this freedom.

# UNIT 1

## The Land of the United States

**The Big Idea**

**What do you like most about the place where you live?**

" *The thing that struck me most all over the United States was the physical beauty of the country, and the great beauty of the cities.* "

–Gertrude Stein, writer, 1937

**United States**

ARCTIC OCEAN

RUSSIA

AK

CANADA

km 0    300
mi 0    300

PACIFIC OCEAN

170°W
70°N
60°N
150°W
140°W

PACIFIC OCEAN

40°N

30°N

130°W

km 0   50 100
mi 0   50 100

HI

160°W

155°W

20°N

PACIFIC OCEAN

120°W

110°W

km 0   150   300
mi 0   150   300

C A N A D A

WA

OR

ID

MT

WY

ND

SD

MN

NE

IA

GREAT PLAINS

ROCKY MOUNTAINS

NV

Great Salt Lake

Great Basin

UT

CA

Central Valley

Mojave

Death Valley

Desert

AZ

Sonoran Desert

Colorado River

CO

Arkansas River

KS

OK

NM

TX

Rio Grande

Missouri River

MEXICO

**Unit Preview**

### Geography
Places influence how people live
**Chapter 1, page 6**

### Land and Water
People often settle near rivers
**Chapter 1, page 19**

### Natural Resources
Oil produces energy
**Chapter 1, page 26**

C A N A D A

L. Superior

WI

L. Michigan

MI

L. Huron

L. Erie

L. Ontario

N T R A L
A I N S

IL

IN

OH

Ohio River

Mississippi River

KY

TN

MS

AL

LA

GA

FL

Gulf of Mexico

APPALACHIAN MOUNTAINS

PA

WV

VA

NC

SC

NY

VT

NH

MA

RI

CT

NJ

MD

DE

ME

C O A S T A L   P L A I N

ATLANTIC OCEAN

50°N

60°W

40°N

30°N

70°W

80°W

90°W

N
NE
NW
E
W
SE
SW
S

**LEGEND**
— National border
— State border
— Regional border
☐ Evergreen forest
☐ Mixed forest
☐ Grassland
☐ Arid
☐ Tundra

## Connect to...
# The Nation

## U.S. Elevation

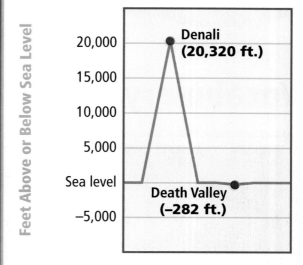

Feet Above or Below Sea Level

20,000 — Denali (20,320 ft.)
15,000
10,000
5,000
Sea level — Death Valley (−282 ft.)
−5,000

Denali (Mt. McKinley) in Alaska is the highest point in the United States. Death Valley in California is the lowest point.

What are the highest and lowest points in your state or community?

Current events on the web!

Read social studies articles about current events at:
**www.eduplace.com/kids/hmss/**

**Climate Regions**
Parts of Alaska have a cold, polar climate **Chapter 2, page 55**

## Vocabulary Preview

**Technology**

*e* • **glossary**
*e* • **word games**
www.eduplace.com/kids/hmss05/

### geography

**Geography** is the study of our world and our place in it. It describes the land, water, and living things that surround us.
**page 6**

### region

A **region** is an area that has certain features. It might have certain landforms, such as mountains and glaciers.
**page 11**

# Reading Strategy

**Predict and Infer** Use this strategy as you read the lessons in this chapter.

Look at the pictures in a lesson to make predictions. What do you think you will read about?

## erosion

**Erosion** is the wearing away of land by wind, water, or ice. It can happen very slowly and gradually. It can also happen quickly during a severe storm or flood. **page 17**

## natural resources

**Natural resources** supply people with food, fuel, shelter, and clothing. Examples of natural resources include water, trees, and soil. **page 24**

# The Geography of Our World

## VOCABULARY

**geography**
**environment**
**hemisphere**
**region**

**Vocabulary Strategy**

geography

The word part **geo-** means earth, and **-graphy** means writing. Writing about or describing the earth is **geography.**

## READING SKILL

**Main Idea and Details**
For the first main idea, write down details that support it.

Main Idea: Geographers describe places and people.

**Build on What You Know**  How would you describe your neighborhood? Perhaps you would talk about people, buildings, trees, rivers, or hills. These features are all part of the geography of your home.

## Welcome to Geography

Main Idea  Geographers describe places and people.

What is geography? **Geography** is the study of the people and places of Earth. It explains the forces that shape the land. It explores how living things are connected to the places where they live.

Geography helps us understand our environment. An **environment** includes all the surroundings and conditions that affect living things. Water, land, plants, animals, and weather are all part of an environment. People depend on their environment for food and fuel. People also change their environment.

You'll learn about these changes as you learn about geography. You'll also discover wonderful places and people. Geography shows you the world, and it also shows how you are a part of it.

**Earth** This photo shows what Earth looks like from space.

## Where, Why, and What

Geographers ask three questions about a place: Where is it? Why is it there? What is it like there? The answers to these questions let them describe and explain the place.

The answer to "Where is it?" tells the location of a place. How would you describe the location of your home? You could say what other places are close to it. For example, you could say that it's down the street from a park. You could also give your address. Geographers describe locations in both of these ways.

The answer to "Why is it there?" takes some careful detective work.

Geographers look for clues about the forces that created mountains, rivers, and other features. They search for information that explains why people settled in a specific place. They find reasons why some communities grew and some disappeared.

The answer to "What is it like there?" describes all the things and people in a place. Geographers know that every place has special features. These features make it different from every other place. Some are physical features. Others are human features.

**REVIEW** What are two ways to describe the location of a place?

## Physical and Human Features

Physical features are things we find in nature. They include landforms, such as mountains and valleys. They include bodies of water, such as lakes and rivers. Wind and rain are examples of physical features. Plants, animals, trees, and soil are physical features, too.

Human features describe the way people live in a place. Geographers look at the languages people speak in different places. They look at the kinds of food people eat. They study the jobs people have and the beliefs they hold. Geographers describe the buildings in an area and how people use them. All of these human features help make a place special.

# Where in the World Are You?

**Main Idea** Globes and maps can show the exact location of any place on Earth's surface.

If you could travel in space, you'd see that Earth is shaped like a ball. This shape is called a sphere. A globe is a model of Earth. It is shaped like a sphere, too.

A globe shows Earth's continents, or large masses of land. The seven continents are Africa, Antarctica, Asia, Australia, Europe, North America, and South America. North America is the third largest continent. Only Asia and Africa are bigger. The United States is part of North America.

**Beijing, China** Look closely at this photograph. Can you read the signs? What do the buildings look like? Such details are human features of Beijing, a city in China.

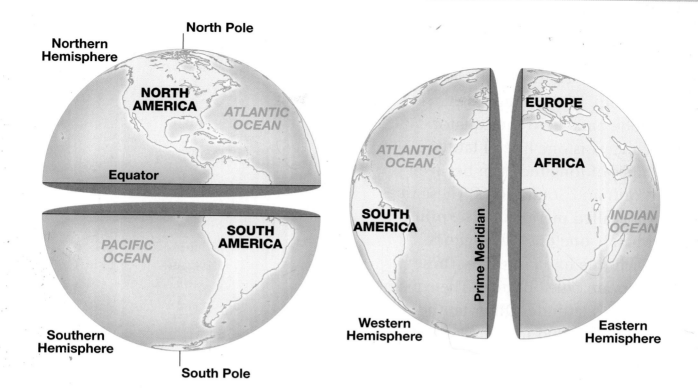

## Northern and Southern Hemispheres

The equator divides Earth in half. One half is the Northern Hemisphere, and the other half is the Southern Hemisphere.

**SKILL** **Reading Visuals** In which hemisphere is the North Pole?

## Western and Eastern Hemispheres

The prime meridian also divides Earth into two hemispheres. They are the Western Hemisphere and the Eastern Hemisphere.

## Earth's Oceans

A globe also shows Earth's oceans. There are four oceans: the Atlantic, Arctic, Indian, and Pacific. Each ocean is a huge body of salty water. The Atlantic Ocean is the saltiest.

The Pacific Ocean is the largest ocean on Earth. It covers about 64 million square miles. That is nearly 18 times the size of the United States. The Pacific Ocean contains the deepest point in the world, the Marianas Trench. It is almost 7 miles deep. The Pacific also has about 300 active volcanoes.

## Four Hemispheres

Geographers divide Earth's surface into hemispheres. A **hemisphere** is one half of Earth's surface. Two lines divide Earth into hemispheres. The equator divides Earth into the Northern and Southern hemispheres. The prime meridian divides Earth into Eastern and Western hemispheres. The United States is located in the Northern and Western hemispheres.

**REVIEW** What physical features does a globe show?

## Latitude, Longitude, and Maps

Geographers have a system for naming exact locations. It uses two sets of lines. Lines of latitude circle the globe parallel to the equator. The equator is one line of latitude.

Lines of longitude run between the North and South poles. These lines are also called meridians. The prime meridian is one line of longitude.

Each line has a number. These numbers are called degrees. The equator is 0 degrees latitude. Other latitude lines are measured in degrees north or south. The prime meridian is 0 degrees longitude. Other longitude lines are measured in degrees east or west.

To give the exact location of a place, find the degrees of the latitude line and the longitude line that cross there. For example, the city of New Orleans, Louisiana, is located at 30 degrees north, 90 degrees west. The location can be written like this: 30°N, 90°W. This is the "address" that geographers use for New Orleans.

You can use a map with latitude and longitude to find the exact location of any place on Earth's surface. A map is like a picture of Earth's surface. We use maps to show many things. Some maps show the shape of the land. Others show streets in a city. Maps can show how many people live in a place. They can show the weather. This book will help you read many kinds of maps.

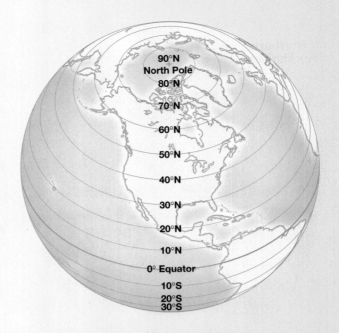

**Lines of Latitude** These lines are called parallels. Degrees of latitude measure how far north or south of the equator a place is.

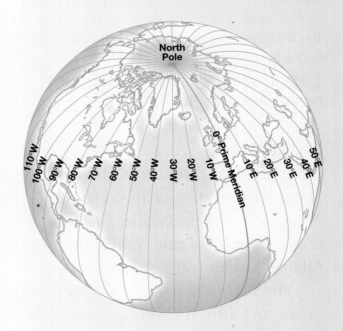

**Lines of Longitude** Meridians measure how far east or west of the prime meridian a place is. All meridians run through the North and South poles.

## What's Special About Your Region?

Do you live near mountains or a desert? Is your home located near an ocean or a lake? Is it warm or cold there? What kinds of work do people do? What plants and animals do you see? The answers to these questions describe the region in which you live. A **region** is an area that is defined by certain features. For example, a language region is an area in which most people speak the same language. A desert region has very dry weather.

Geographers use regions to show how places are alike and different. There are many kinds of regions. As you study geography, you will learn about the different regions of the United States. You will find out why people settled certain regions and how these places have changed over time.

**REVIEW** Why are maps useful?

**Using a Globe** You can use a globe to locate places anywhere on Earth.

### Lesson Summary

- Geography is the study of the people and places of Earth.
- Globes and maps can show the exact location of a place.
- Regions are areas that share features in common.

## Why It Matters ...

Geography helps us understand the world we live in.

---

## Lesson Review

**1 VOCABULARY** Fill in the blank with the correct word.

**environment**  **hemisphere**  **region**

A(n) _____ is one half of the earth.

**2 READING SKILL** Give two **details** that describe how geographers answer the question "Why is it there?"

**3 MAIN IDEA: Geography** What is the difference between physical features and human features of a place?

**4 MAIN IDEA: Geography** For what purpose do geographers use lines of latitude and longitude?

**5 CRITICAL THINKING: Analyze** What physical and human features describe the place where you live?

**WRITING ACTIVITY** Describe the location of your school. Write a paragraph that tells what your school is near. Think about landforms, buildings, streets, and bodies of water.

# Geography in Daily Life

"Where am I?" Geographers have many tools to help answer this question. Long ago, people used tools such as poles and chains to make maps. Today, satellites and computers can help describe locations on Earth. GPS receivers and GIS maps are two modern tools.

People create maps for many purposes. The map shown here is a bike map. It shows which roads have a bike lane and how steep the roads are. It even shows where to find the nearest bike shop, in case you get a flat tire!

Tamarack Lane

HAWTHORN HILL

**R**

Redwood Road

Cottonwood Road

**B**

## GPS Receiver

GPS stands for Global Positioning System. A GPS receiver uses signals from satellites to tell you exactly where you are.

## GIS Map

A GIS, or Geographic Information System, is a computer system that can create maps with layers of information. A bike map could have layers for roads, bike paths, and bike shops.

Bicycle data

Buildings

Roads

Reality

Oak Creek

**R**

Willow Way

ELMWOOD GOLF COURSE

Poplar Parkway

**B**

Cedar River

SYCAMORE PARK

**R**

Spruce Street

Shoreline Expressway

LAKE LINDEN

## BIKE MAP

Bike path

Road with bike lane

Bike route (Low-traffic street)

>> Uphill slope

Difficult intersection

**B** Bike shop

**R** Public restroom

## Activities

1. **TALK ABOUT IT** When would GPS be useful to you? In what types of jobs would GPS be useful?

2. **DRAW YOUR OWN** Make a map of your neighborhood that shows only the streets. Then use different colors to add layers to your map. Each layer should show a different kind of information. You might add homes, schools, trees, mailboxes, and so on.

## Skillbuilder

# Review Map Skills

► **VOCABULARY**

legend
compass rose
scale

A globe is a round model of our planet, Earth. A map is a flat drawing of Earth's surface. Because maps are flat, they can appear in books or on your computer. Maps show where places are located in relation to other places. They can also show different types of information, such as the land's physical features or the borders of states or countries.

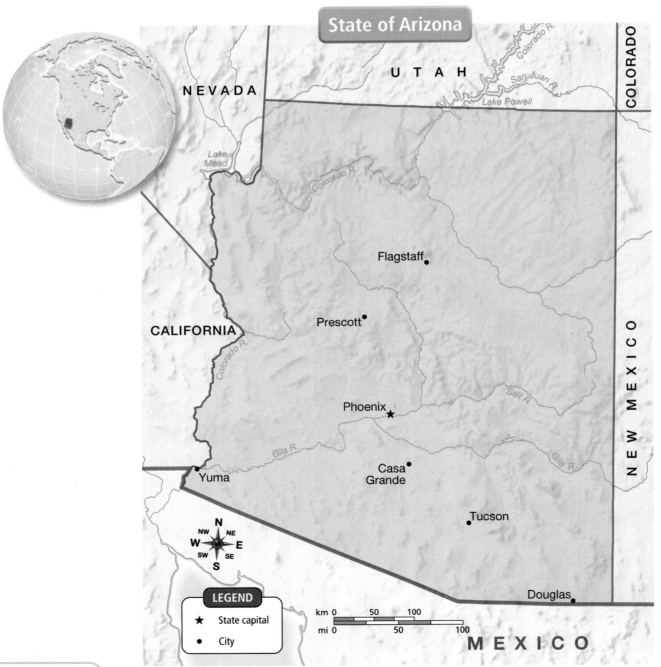

State of Arizona

LEGEND

★ State capital

• City

## Learn the Skill

**Step 1:** Read the map's title. A title tells you what the map's subject is. The map on page 14 is about the state of Arizona.

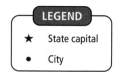
State of Arizona

**Step 2:** Look at the map's legend. A **legend** tells you what different symbols on the map mean.

LEGEND
★  State capital
•  City

**Step 3:** Check directions and distances. A **compass rose** shows direction. The map **scale** allows you to measure distances on a map. Different maps have different scales.

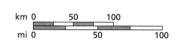

## Practice the Skill

Use the map on page 14 to answer the questions.

❶ What city is the capital of Arizona?

❷ In what direction would a person travel to get from Prescott to Flagstaff?

## Apply the Skill

Use the map on page 27 to answer the following questions.

❶ What is the title of the map?

❷ Using the scale of the map, what distance is represented by one inch on this map?

❸ What symbol is used to show a city?

# Land and Water

**Build on What You Know** What natural features are located near your community? These features affect the way people live in your area.

## VOCABULARY

**tectonic plate**
**erosion**
**glacier**
**basin**

### Vocabulary Strategy

glacier

**Glacier** comes from **glace,** the French word for ice. A glacier is a huge mass of ice.

### READING SKILL

**Cause and Effect** Chart the effects of forces that change Earth's surface.

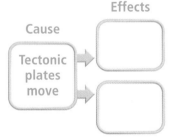

## Major Landforms

**Main Idea** Many forces shape the land.

Long before people arrived, natural forces shaped the land that became the United States. Some changes took place on Earth's surface. Some forces acted deep underground.

For example, beneath Earth's crust lie many tectonic plates. A **tectonic plate** is a huge slab of slowly moving rock. About 50 million years ago, tectonic plates pushed together. They caused rocks within Earth's crust to break and move. This created the Rocky Mountains that stretch from Canada to New Mexico. This process created the Appalachian Mountains, too. They run from Maine to Alabama.

Natural forces still change the land today. Moving tectonic plates can cause earthquakes and volcanoes. Melted rock from volcanoes can form mountains.

**Mount Jefferson** Volcanoes created the Cascade Mountains in the northwest United States.

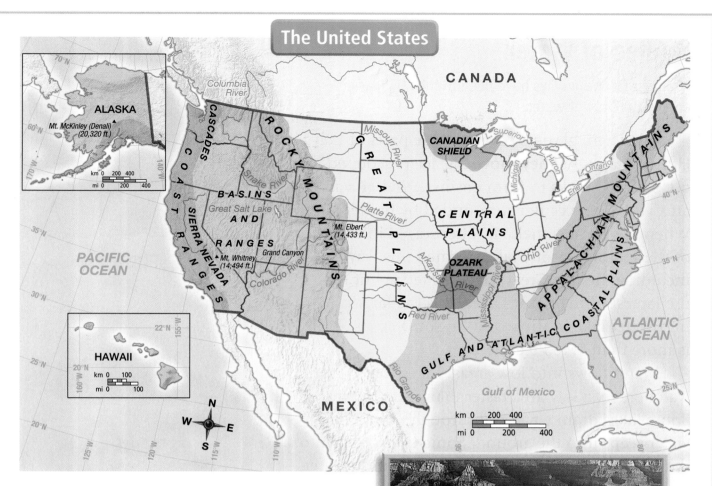

**ALASKA**
Mt. McKinley (Denali)
(20,320 ft.)
km 0   200   400
mi 0   200   400

Columbia River

CASCADES

COAST RANGES

SIERRA NEVADA

ROCKY MOUNTAINS

BASINS AND RANGES

Great Salt Lake

Snake River

Mt. Elbert
(14,433 ft.)

Grand Canyon

Mt. Whitney
(14,494 ft.)

Colorado River

PACIFIC OCEAN

CANADA

Missouri River

CANADIAN SHIELD

L. Superior

Platte River

GREAT PLAINS

CENTRAL PLAINS

L. Michigan

L. Huron

L. Ontario

L. Erie

Ohio River

Arkansas River

OZARK PLATEAU

Mississippi River

APPALACHIAN MOUNTAINS

ATLANTIC COASTAL PLAINS

Red River

GULF AND ATLANTIC COASTAL PLAINS

ATLANTIC OCEAN

HAWAII
km 0   100
mi 0   100

Rio Grande

MEXICO

Gulf of Mexico

km 0   200   400
mi 0   200   400

N W E S

**Landforms** The United States has landforms that include mountains and plains.

**SKILL** **Reading Maps** Which U.S. mountains are closest to the Atlantic Ocean?

## The Forces of Erosion

The Appalachian Mountains have been shaped by erosion. **Erosion** is a process of wearing away rock and soil. Rivers, streams, and oceans can cut into rock over time. Water erosion created our deepest valleys and canyons. The Colorado River carved deep into the Grand Canyon.

Wind erosion helped widen the Grand Canyon. Wind blows sand against rock and wears it away. Wind can also carry away soil. This can happen when the soil is dry and there are few plants to hold down the soil.

**Grand Canyon** Over time, wind erosion made the Grand Canyon wider.

Glaciers cause erosion, too. A **glacier** is a huge mass of slowly moving ice. Glaciers push soil and rocks as they move. They flatten some areas and leave piles of earth in others. Glaciers have shaped hills, valleys, and plains. Plains are large areas of flat land.

**REVIEW** What forces can shape the land?

17

# Bodies of Water

**Main Idea** Waterways have been formed by glaciers and by the flow of water.

Long ago, glaciers covered large parts of the United States. As they moved, glaciers scooped out soil and rocks to form basins. A **basin** is an area with a low center surrounded by higher land. When the glaciers melted, water stayed in some of these basins. Many lakes formed this way, including the five Great Lakes. Lake Superior is the largest of the Great Lakes. It is the largest freshwater lake in the world. In some spots, it is more than 1,300 feet deep.

Water flows into low areas. Lakes form when water enters a low area faster than it can leave. Some lakes drain water out through rivers. Some water seeps into the ground. Some evaporates into the air. Lakes are important sources of fresh water.

Utah's Great Salt Lake is the largest inland body of salt water in the Western Hemisphere. However, it is less than 15 feet deep in most places. The water that runs into the lake contains minerals. This water can escape only by evaporating, and it evaporates very quickly. The minerals remain. This makes the lake much saltier than the ocean.

Pacific Ocean on the coast of Maui, Hawaii

Lobster boat, Penobscot Bay, Maine

Lake Superior in Minnesota

Tide flat on Willapa Bay, Washington

## Flowing Rivers

Rivers form as water moves over land from a high area to a lower area. Water flows downhill in creeks and streams. Creeks and streams join to form rivers. Rivers flow down into oceans. That is why rivers west of the high Rocky Mountains flow west toward the Pacific Ocean.

The Mississippi River is the second longest river in North America. It flows from Minnesota all the way to the Gulf of Mexico in Louisiana. Many other streams and rivers flow into it. These include the Missouri and Ohio rivers.

Since the earliest times, people have settled along rivers. Rivers bring water for drinking and farming. They help people travel and move goods. Their steady flow creates power to run machines. Many major cities have grown up beside rivers.

**REVIEW** In what way did glaciers create the Great Lakes?

**Mississippi River** Water from 31 states enters the Mississippi. It is one of the world's busiest shipping routes.

## Lesson Summary

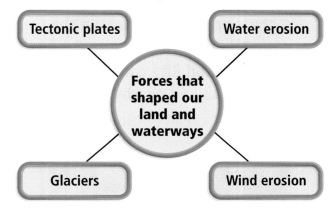

Tectonic plates

Water erosion

Forces that shaped our land and waterways

Glaciers

Wind erosion

## Why It Matters ...

Landforms and bodies of water influence how and where we live.

---

## Lesson Review

❶ **VOCABULARY** Write a paragraph that uses **basin, erosion,** and **glacier.**

❷ **READING SKILL** What **effects** did tectonic plates and erosion have on the land?

❸ **MAIN IDEA: Geography** What forces cause mountains to form?

❹ **MAIN IDEA: Geography** Why do rivers flow toward oceans?

❺ **CRITICAL THINKING: Draw Conclusions** What is one thing people could do to slow the process of wind erosion on a piece of land?

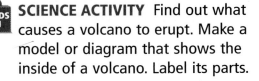

**SCIENCE ACTIVITY** Find out what causes a volcano to erupt. Make a model or diagram that shows the inside of a volcano. Label its parts.

# Gulf Coast Hurricanes

**Conditions need to be just right for hurricanes to form.** First, they need warm ocean water. The air above must be cooler than the water. The wind must be blowing in one direction and at a constant speed. These conditions occur in several places around the world. One place is in the Gulf of Mexico.

Two major hurricanes formed in this region in 2005. Hurricanes Katrina and Rita caused many billions of dollars of damage in Louisiana and nearby states. They changed the landscape and economy of the region, as well as the lives of people living there.

**Hurricane Katrina** This photograph was taken from space. It shows Hurricane Katrina heading towards the Gulf Coast. When it made landfall in Louisiana, wind speeds were as high as 145 miles an hour.

**Building Houses** About 250,000 homes were damaged or destroyed by Hurricane Katrina. Many people, like these students from New Orleans, worked together to build new homes on the Gulf Coast.

**Sending Supplies** Chris Duhon, a basketball player from Slidell, Louisiana, organized many boxes of supplies to be sent to Louisiana. After every big hurricane, citizens help out by donating money and supplies.

# Activities

1. **TALK ABOUT IT** In what ways can knowing how hurricanes form help people prepare for hurricanes in the future?

2. **CREATE IT** Find out more about how hurricanes form. Make a model or diagram showing what you learned.

**Map and Globe Skills**

## Skillbuilder

# Make a Map

A map shows where cities, towns, rivers, mountains, and other features are located within a state, a region, a country, or the world. Making a map can help you to understand the features that define where you live.

### Learn the Skill

**Step 1:** Decide what kind of map you want to make and how it will be used.

Map of my town

**Step 2:** List the details to go on the map. Find other information that you want to include.

| My house | Roads |
|---|---|
| My school | Chemung River |
| Shopping center | Town Hall |

**Step 3:** Draw the outline shape of your map.

**Step 4:** Put your details on the map in the correct location. Use symbols or label each point. Include a legend that explains your symbols.

**Step 5:** Think of a title for your map.

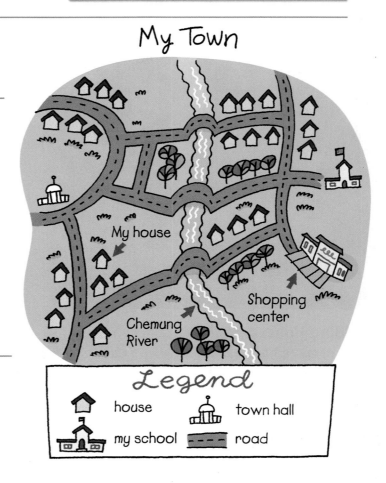

My Town

My house

Chemung River

Shopping center

Legend

house    town hall

my school    road

## Practice the Skill

Follow the directions below to make a map of your state.

**1** List all the important cities and towns that you know in your state.

**2** Name some rivers, mountains, or other natural features you might want to include on your map.

**3** Write down any other information you want to show on your map.

**4** Draw an outline of your state.

**5** Add the details you listed to your map.

**6** Include a legend that explains any symbols or colors you used.

**7** Give your map a title.

## Apply the Skill

Use what you learned to make a map of the world. Label the seven continents and four oceans.

# Resources of the United States

**VOCABULARY**

natural resources
renewable resources
nonrenewable
 resources
product
fossil fuel

**Vocabulary Strategy**

nonrenewable resources

The prefix **non–** means
not. **Nonrenewable**
means not able to be
renewed.

**READING SKILL**
**Categorize** List examples
of natural resources. Put
each example in one of
two categories.

Natural Resources

| Renewable | Nonrenewable |
|-----------|--------------|
|           |              |

**Build on What You Know** The paper in this book
was made from trees. Goods that you use every day
come from things we find in nature.

## A Land of Rich Resources

**Main Idea** People use the things they find in their
environment.

People depend on natural resources.
**Natural resources** are things from the natural
environment that people use. People use natural
resources for food, fuel, shelter, and clothing.

The United States has many natural resources.
The first people who lived here used resources in
many ways. They drank the clear water. They hunted
animals and fish for food. They built homes from
wood, from dried mud, and from animal skins.

Natural resources attracted Europeans to North
America. These resources helped our nation grow.
Now we must protect them and use them wisely.

**Natural Resources** Trees, soil, and
fresh water are some of the natural
resources of the United States.

**Renewable or Nonrenewable?** Nature can replace the trees we cut down. It cannot replace the coal we take from mines.

## Types of Resources

Many of Earth's resources are renewable. **Renewable resources** are things that the environment can replace after we use them. Trees and other living things are renewable resources. New trees grow to replace the ones people cut down. Baby fish grow to replace the fish that people catch for food.

We must be careful to use our renewable resources wisely. It takes a long time to replace many of them. Human activities can affect this process. For example, people can harm the soil in ways that make it useless for farming. They can destroy whole species of plants and animals.

Some of Earth's resources are nonrenewable. **Nonrenewable resources** are things that nature cannot replace after they are used. Earth has only a limited supply of them. Minerals like copper and iron are nonrenewable. Most fuels we use are nonrenewable, too. They were formed in Earth's crust over millions of years. Once we use up our supply, they will be gone forever.

Sunlight is another important resource. It is not renewable. However, the sun will give energy for billions of years. Sunlight is a flow resource. Wind and water are flow resources, too. We can use their energy as they flow, or move, through the environment.

**REVIEW** What is a natural resource?

# Using Natural Resources

**Main Idea**  Many natural resources are found across the United States.

People in the United States use natural resources in many ways. The land is an important resource. Rich soil covers large parts of the country. This soil is good for farming. We use almost half of the land in the United States to raise crops and livestock. Much of the food we produce feeds people in other parts of the world.

We also have large forests. Their trees give us a good supply of wood. Workers use trees to produce lumber for building. People also use trees to make paper and wood products, such as furniture. A **product** is something that is made from natural resources.

All plants and people need water. We need water to drink and to grow our crops. The ocean waters off our shores are an important source of seafood. Our many rivers provide good travel routes. Their flow also helps generate power.

Minerals are natural resources that lie deep in the ground. Miners dig up many minerals. Minerals like gold and silver once attracted many people to our western states. Today, copper and iron mining are major businesses. People also mine building materials like limestone and granite.

**Oil Rig**  Oil is a fossil fuel. Oil rigs drill oil from beneath the ocean floor.

## Energy Resources

Everyone depends on natural resources for energy. We use energy to light our homes and power our cars. We use it to keep warm in winter and cool in summer. It runs machines we use to do our work.

Most of the energy we use comes from fossil fuels. A **fossil fuel** is an energy source formed by the remains of things that lived long ago. Coal, natural gas, and oil are fossil fuels. The United States produces much of the world's fossil fuels. It also uses much more fuel than any other country. Fossil fuels are nonrenewable resources. One day the supply will run out. Before that happens, we will need to find new sources of energy.

**REVIEW**  Why are natural resources important to the people of the United States?

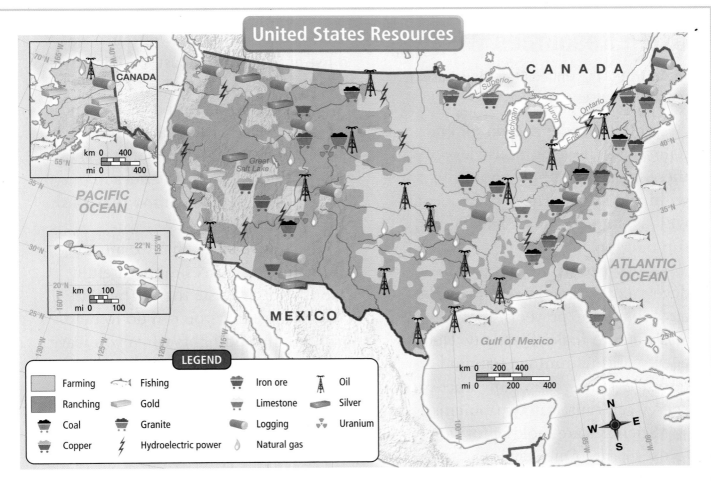

# United States Resources

**LEGEND**

| | | | | | |
|---|---|---|---|---|---|
| Farming | Fishing | Iron ore | Oil |
| Ranching | Gold | Limestone | Silver |
| Coal | Granite | Logging | Uranium |
| Copper | Hydroelectric power | Natural gas | |

**A Rich Nation** This map shows where some of our nation's many resources are located.

**SKILL** **Reading Maps** Which resources are found in your part of the country?

**Open Pit Copper Mine** Most copper ore comes from open pit mines. Miners remove layers of soil to find the ore.

**Propane Storage Tanks** Propane gas is a fossil fuel that people use to heat and cool their homes.

27

# Using Resources Wisely

**Main Idea** The United States must use its natural resources wisely.

Americans depend on oil and natural gas. If we don't use less of these fuels, our supply could run out within 100 years. The supply of coal will last longer, but someday it will run out, too.

Many people are working to develop other energy resources. We already use the power of moving wind and water to make electricity. Nuclear energy uses uranium, a natural resource. However, making nuclear energy can cause safety problems.

Scientists are looking for safer ways to use energy. One way is to use power from the sun. Another way is to draw power from heat deep within Earth's crust. Today, very little of our energy comes from these sources.

**Flow Resources** Solar panels (right) collect energy from the sun. Wind turbines (below) gather energy from moving air.

Fuel is not the only resource we must protect. In the past, people have not always used natural resources wisely. They have dumped waste into lakes and rivers. They have burned fuels that harm the atmosphere. They have cut down too many trees in our forests. They have taken too many fish from our oceans.

Today, we know that we must use our natural resources more carefully and try not to waste them. There are many things that you can do to help. You can turn off lights when you leave a room. You can use less water when you brush your teeth. You can recycle the bottles, cans, and paper you use. These are just a few of the ways that Americans can work together to protect our environment.

## Our Greatest Resource

Natural resources have helped the United States grow. Americans are lucky to live in a land that offers so many resources. However, a country needs more than natural resources. The growth of a nation depends on its people, too.

People provide the ideas, the inventions, and the labor that help turn natural resources into useful products. These products can make life better for everyone. In the United States, people are free to choose what products they make, sell, and buy.

Americans have worked hard to build the nation we have today. You will build the nation we'll have in the future. This book will help you learn about our land and the way we use it. You will also learn about our country's greatest resource—people just like you.

**REVIEW** How can you help protect natural resources?

**Recycling** Many products can be recycled, or made into new products, after people have used them.

## Lesson Summary

People need natural resources to live. The United States uses natural resources to produce food and energy and to make things we need and want.

## Why It Matters . . .

The way we use our natural resources today affects the way we'll live tomorrow.

## Lesson Review

❶ **VOCABULARY** Explain why a **fossil fuel** is a **natural resource.**

❷ **READING SKILL** What sources of energy would you place in the **category** of flow resources?

❸ **MAIN IDEA: Geography** Explain the difference between a renewable resource and a nonrenewable resource.

❹ **MAIN IDEA: Geography** What sources of energy can people use instead of fossil fuels?

❺ **CRITICAL THINKING: Synthesize** In what way does recycling help to protect natural resources?

**WRITING ACTIVITY** Think of a way to protect resources or save energy in your school or community. Write a speech to share your idea with others.

# Dr. Maria Telkes

## 1900–1995

Some people call Dr. Maria Telkes "the Sun Queen." She invented ways to use the sun for energy. Her inventions helped people use fewer nonrenewable resources. Telkes designed solar, or sun-powered, ovens. She also invented a solar-powered system to turn ocean water into drinking water.

In 1948, Telkes designed the heating system for the Dover House in Dover, Massachusetts. On the south wall of this house, solar collectors gathered heat from the sun. This heat was used to warm the rooms of the house.

Telkes worked with solar energy for 50 years. She designed new systems that provided both heat and electricity for homes. Today, people can use solar energy to heat and cool their houses and to generate electricity.

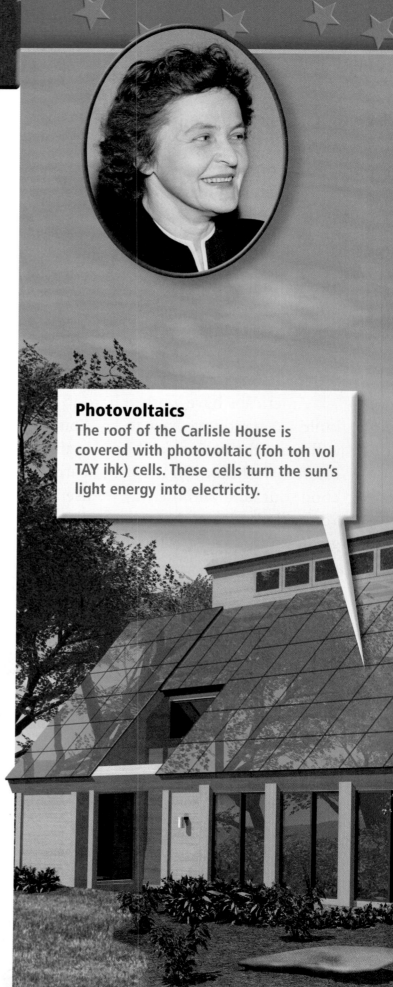

**Photovoltaics**
The roof of the Carlisle House is covered with photovoltaic (foh toh vol TAY ihk) cells. These cells turn the sun's light energy into electricity.

**Carlisle House in Massachusetts**
Dr. Telkes helped design this house in 1980. It needs no fossil fuels. Its heat and electricity come from the sun.

## Solar Oven

Reflector panels send the sun's rays into the oven. The solar heat is trapped, and the temperature can reach 350°F inside. This is hot enough to bake bread or roast a chicken.

# Activities

1. **THINK ABOUT IT** In what ways did Dr. Telkes show **responsibility** toward the use of natural resources?

2. **WRITE ABOUT IT** Write a story set in the future. Describe new ways that people use the sun's energy. For example, they might use it at home, in cars, and in new kinds of sports.

 **Technology** Read more biographies at Education Place. www.eduplace.com/kids/hmss05/

## Visual Summary

1. – 3. ✏️ Write a description of each item named below.

**Hemispheres**

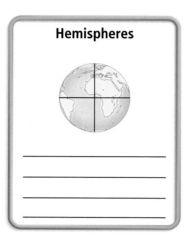

_____
_____
_____
_____

**Erosion**

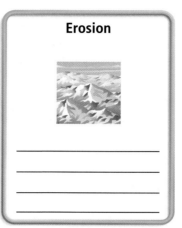

_____
_____
_____
_____

**Resources**

_____
_____
_____
_____

## Facts and Main Ideas

✔️ **TEST PREP** Answer each question below.

4. **Geography** What three questions about a place do geographers answer?

5. **Geography** Explain how glaciers shape landforms.

6. **Culture** Why did people in the past settle near rivers?

7. **Economics** What are some ways in which Americans use natural resources?

8. **Technology** Name two energy resources that have been developed to use instead of oil and gas.

## Vocabulary

✔️ **TEST PREP** Choose the correct word from the list below to complete each sentence.

**region,** p. 11
**glacier,** p. 17
**product,** p. 26

9. A _____ is something that is made from natural resources.

10. An area defined by certain features is a _____.

11. A _____ is a huge mass of slowly moving ice.

## TEST PREP  Review Map Skills

Study the Wisconsin map below. Then use your map skills to answer each question.

12. What is the capital of Wisconsin?

   A. Green Bay
   B. Milwaukee
   C. Madison
   D. La Crosse

13. In which direction should a person travel to go from Madison to Milwaukee?

   A. north
   B. south
   C. east
   D. west

## TEST PREP  Write a short paragraph to answer each question below.

14. **Summarize**  Why is geography useful to people?

15. **Cause and Effect**  Why should people protect both renewable and nonrenewable resources?

# Activities

**Art Activity**  Create a map that shows the landforms and bodies of water in your area.

**Writing Activity**  Find out more about new energy and fuel sources besides fossil fuels. Write a research report explaining what you discover.

**Technology**
**Writing Process Tips**
Get help with your research report at:
www.eduplace.com/kids/hmss05/

## Chapter 2

# Understanding Regions

**Technology**

*e* • **glossary**
*e* • **word games**
www.eduplace.com/kids/hmss05/

## Vocabulary Preview

### government

The **government** of the United States makes laws that affect its citizens in many ways. Each country has its own government. **page 37**

### agriculture

**Agriculture** is everything that has to do with farming. People who grow crops and raise livestock are involved in agriculture. **page 45**

# Reading Strategy

**Monitor and Clarify** As you read the lessons in this chapter, use this strategy to check your understanding.

**Quick Tip** Pause and ask yourself if you understand what you are reading. Reread, if you need to.

## precipitation

Rain, sleet, snow, and hail are all forms of **precipitation.** Some areas of the United States receive more precipitation than other areas. **page 53**

## elevation

The **elevation** of a place is measured against the height of the sea. A tall mountain has a high elevation, because it rises many feet above sea level. **page 53**

# Core Lesson 1

# What Is a Region?

## VOCABULARY

government
population
religion
boundary

**Vocabulary Strategy**

government

**Govern** means to rule by making or carrying out laws. A **government** is a system by which people are ruled.

## READING SKILL

**Draw Conclusions**
Record details that lead to this conclusion.

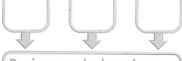

Regions can be based on any shared feature.

**Build on What You Know** Schoolwork is organized by subject—math, social studies, science, and so on. To organize information about the world and its people, geographers use regions.

## Defining Regions

**Main Idea** Regions can be defined by many different kinds of features.

Geographers divide the world into regions to help organize ideas about places and people. A region is an area that shares one or more features. These shared features make one region different from another. For example, a farming region is different from a deep-sea fishing region or a coal mining region.

You can learn more about regions by comparing and contrasting them. Suppose that a region in the United States and one in Europe grow the same crops. Knowing about one region might help you understand the other region.

**Buffalo National River**
The Ozark Mountains and the Buffalo River bring many visitors to this region in Arkansas.

**Iowa Corn Field** The Corn Belt is a U.S. region where corn is the main crop.

## Features in Common

Regions can be based on any shared feature. Countries, states, and cities are regions that have the same government. **Government** is a system of making and carrying out rules and laws. Other regions are based on landforms or plant life.

Regions can also be based on features of the population. **Population** means the people who live in an area. People in one region may share a language or a religion. **Religion** is a system of faith or worship.

Regions come in all shapes and sizes. A region can be as small as a neighborhood, or it can be as large as a hemisphere. The size and shape of a region can change over time. For example, a city can grow larger as more people move in and build new neighborhoods.

## Borders, Boundaries, and Belts

Regions occupy space or land. In some types of regions, people have created lines to show exactly where the regions begin and end. These lines are borders. Borders separate political regions, such as states or countries.

Most other regions do not have borders. They have boundaries. A **boundary** is the edge of a region. The boundary may be a natural one, such as a river. It may be an artificial one, such as a road. Boundaries are often less exact than borders. A change from one region to another may take place over many miles.

Belts are regions that have one feature stretching across a broad area. Some well-known belts in the United States include the Corn Belt, the Sun Belt, and the Frost Belt.

**REVIEW** What kind of region has borders?

# How Regions Are Used

**Main Idea** Thinking about regions helps government, business, and other organizations deal with problems.

Geographers are not the only ones who create and use regions. Creating regions is a way for people to think about and organize large spaces. Governments, businesses, and other kinds of organizations use regions to do their jobs better.

## Using Regions

Governments divide their countries or states into regions. This helps them keep track of resources and understand the needs of their people. The U.S. government collects facts on the people, environment, and natural resources in each region. It uses this information to plan the best way to use resources. This information also helps the government provide services to people who need them.

People use regions to help make decisions. For example, suppose a company that makes winter coats wants to open a new factory. The company would want to know which regions have plenty of workers to work in the factory. To decide where to try to sell its coats, the company would need to find out which regions have cold winters. To decide what styles to make, the company might find out what kinds of coats the people in each region like to wear.

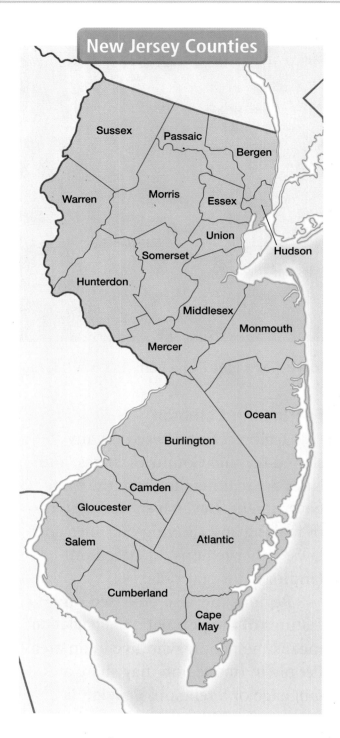

**New Jersey Counties**

**State Counties** Most states are divided into regions called counties. Each county government provides services to its people. These services include education, roads, and health care.

## One Place, Many Regions

One place can belong to many regions. For example, Elizabeth, New Jersey, is part of New York City's metropolitan region. Trains, buses, and roads connect the city to New York. Elizabeth also belongs to the region called the East. This region is based on location within the United States.

Elizabeth is also part of New Jersey. As a state, New Jersey is a political region. As one of the 13 original colonies, it is part of a larger historical region. Depending on certain facts about its population, Elizabeth may belong to several other regions, too.

**REVIEW** In what ways do people use regions to make decisions?

**George Washington Bridge**
This bridge connects New York City to a wider metropolitan region.

## Lesson Summary

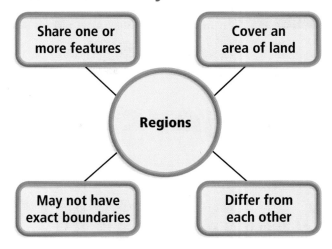

Share one or more features

Cover an area of land

Regions

May not have exact boundaries

Differ from each other

## Why It Matters ...

Learning about regions can help us understand our land, our resources, and how we live.

## Lesson Review

**① VOCABULARY** Fill in the blank with the correct word.
**population   religion   boundary**
The _____ of a region is made up of every person who lives there.

**② READING SKILL** Give two details that lead to the **conclusion** that using regions can help people solve problems.

**③ MAIN IDEA: Culture** What are two ways that a population might define a region?

**④ MAIN IDEA: Geography** Explain how a town or city might belong to more than one region.

**⑤ CRITICAL THINKING: Analyze** Identify two regions within your town or city. Explain the features that make each one a region.

**HANDS ON**

**ART ACTIVITY** Draw a map of your classroom. Divide the classroom into regions by drawing boundary lines. Label each region. Explain why you placed the boundaries where you did.

# Borders and Boundaries

Borders show where a political region begins and ends. You usually know when you cross a border. You might see a sign that says "Welcome to Wisconsin." You might need to show your passport to move between countries.

People often use natural boundaries as borders because these boundaries already divide the land into regions. For example, a river called the Rio Grande (REE-oh GRAHN-day) forms part of the border between the United States and Mexico. Islands like Hawaii are surrounded by ocean on all sides.

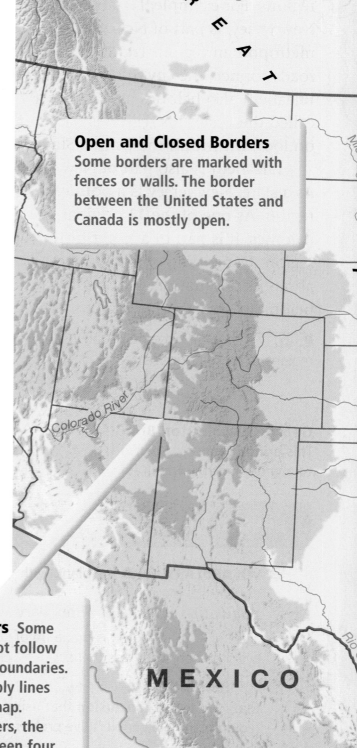

**Open and Closed Borders** Some borders are marked with fences or walls. The border between the United States and Canada is mostly open.

**Four Corners** Some borders do not follow any natural boundaries. They are simply lines drawn on a map. At Four Corners, the borders between four states meet in a +.

**Borders Across Water** The border between the United States and Canada crosses through several Great Lakes.

CANADA

Lake Superior

Lake Huron

Lake Michigan

Lake Ontario

Lake Erie

CENTRAL PLAINS

Ohio River

APPALACHIAN MTS.

Arkansas River

Mississippi River

Red River

**Wide Boundaries** A boundary can be a gradual change between regions. For example, the boundary between mountains and plains may be a wide area of rolling hills.

**Natural Boundaries as Borders** Many states have rivers as borders. The Mississippi River forms part of the border between Arkansas and Mississippi.

# Activities

1. **TALK ABOUT IT** What borders have you crossed? Discuss what it's like to cross a state border and to cross a national border.

2. **DRAW YOUR OWN** Draw a map of the land around your school. Note all the boundaries, including fences, roads, woods, and so on.

# Regions of the United States

**VOCABULARY**

**urban**
**suburban**
**rural**
**economy**
**agriculture**

**Vocabulary Strategy**

suburban

One meaning of the prefix **sub-** is "a part of something larger." A **suburban** area has smaller towns that are part of a larger area.

**READING SKILL**

**Classify** List some features of two kinds of regions in the United States.

Features

| Natural | Human |
|---------|-------|
|         |       |

**Build on What You Know** South, west, and east are directions on a compass. They are also regions of the United States.

## Types of Regions

**Main Idea** Natural regions are defined by physical features, such as landforms. Human regions are defined by groups of people who live in them.

To understand the United States, we divide it into regions. These regions are based on many different physical and human features.

### Natural Regions

One way to divide the United States into regions is to base the regions on physical features, such as land and water. The United States has mountain regions, valleys, plateaus, and plains. Plant life defines other regions, such as wetlands, grasslands, and forests.

Other natural regions are defined by the soil, animals, or minerals there. River basins are one kind of water system region. A river basin is the whole area that is drained by a river.

**Rocky Mountains**
This region can be defined by mountains and forests.

**Three Kinds of Human Regions** What features do you see in each region shown here? How are the regions different?

## Human Regions

People also define regions by human features, such as religion or language. Human regions may change. They can grow larger or smaller. A region may even lose the feature that first made it a region.

If you were to travel across the country, you would find many types of human regions. For example, the history shared by many Latino people in the southwestern states forms a region. The major religion in Utah and parts of some nearby states is Mormon. Other regions can be defined by the kinds of work people do. For example, parts of Kansas are in the Wheat Belt, a region where many people grow wheat. Silicon Valley is a region in California where people work in computer-related jobs.

We can also base regions on the types of communities people live in. Many people live in urban regions. **Urban** means in a city. Other people live in suburban areas. **Suburban** means in smaller towns near a city. The urban and suburban regions together form a metropolitan or greater city region.

Other people live in rural regions. **Rural** means country areas with fewer people. Rural areas have no large cities. They have small towns or villages and plenty of open land.

Another way to define a region is by who owns the land. The government owns regions of public land. Land owned by individuals is private.

**REVIEW** Over time, what might happen to regions that are based on human features?

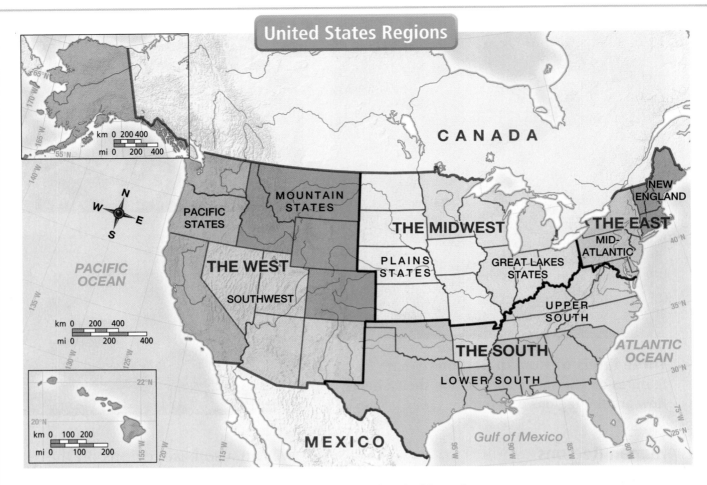

United States Regions

MOUNTAIN STATES

PACIFIC STATES

THE WEST

SOUTHWEST

PACIFIC OCEAN

CANADA

THE MIDWEST

PLAINS STATES

GREAT LAKES STATES

THE SOUTH

LOWER SOUTH

UPPER SOUTH

NEW ENGLAND

THE EAST

MID-ATLANTIC

ATLANTIC OCEAN

MEXICO

Gulf of Mexico

**Regions and Subregions** The United States can be divided into four major regions. Each region has smaller subregions.

**SKILL** **Reading Maps** Which major region includes the Pacific States?

# States and Regions

**Main Idea** The states in each major region share natural and human features.

In this book, you will learn about four major regions of the United States. They are the East, the South, the Midwest, and the West. Their names tell their geographic location.

States in the same region are located close together. They are divided by state borders, but they often share natural features. For example, they may have have similar landforms, plants, and animals.

States within a region may depend on the same natural resources. For example, several states in the West use the same rivers to water their farmland.

**Bald Eagle** The bald eagle lives in every state except Hawaii.

## Human Links Within Regions

Human features link the states in each region. For example, Spain and then Mexico once controlled much of the area now called the West. So, the states in the West share a common history. States within a region are also linked by their economy. The **economy** is the way the people of an area choose to use the area's resources. In the southern states, for example, both agriculture and factories are important to the economy. **Agriculture** is the business of farming.

Sometimes our experiences lead us to think about a region in a certain way. For some, the Midwest means basketball because the sport is very popular there. For the East, people may think of New York City or the New Jersey shore. These ideas are only a tiny part of a bigger picture.

In this book, you will learn about many important features of each region. This will help you better understand the land in which you live.

**REVIEW** Why does each state belong to a certain region?

### Lesson Summary

- People use physical and human features to define regions.
- The United States can be divided into four major regions: East, South, Midwest, and West.
- Each major region can be divided into two or more subregions.
- States within each region share physical and human features.

## Why It Matters ...

Each region in the United States has features that make it different.

---

## Lesson Review

**❶ VOCABULARY** Explain the difference between **rural** and **urban** regions.

**❷ READING SKILL** What kinds of regions can be **classified** as human regions? Explain.

**❸ MAIN IDEA: Geography** Name two natural features that can define a region.

**❹ MAIN IDEA: Geography** What features do states in a region share?

**❺ FACTS TO KNOW** Name the four major regions of the United States.

**❻ CRITICAL THINKING: Synthesize** "Regions shaped by human features can change over time." Give an example that supports this statement.

**WRITING ACTIVITY** Write a script for a radio program. Describe some physical and human features of your state to help listeners understand the region.

# Poems of America

THE WEST
THE MIDWEST
THE EAST
THE SOUTH

**Pictures show what a region looks like, but poems can tell what a region feels like.** Poets use words to share the sights, sounds, smells, and feel of places they love. Take a poetry tour of the nation's four major regions.

## *Watercolor Maine*

THE EAST
Maine

C. Drew Lamm

The buoy bell sings Bar Harbor
sings the coast of Maine
to the fog.

Lobsters clap in traps.
The great quartz rocks
twist waves into fireworks.

Red lobster boats bob above barnacled anchors.
Blueberries sprinkle the shore.
Mail boat chugs to the Cranberry Islands,
Captain's black coffee rocks on the floor.

Morning light wakens the edges of bells
whets the rock and
sea.

Just another Monday Maine day waking.
The poet lifts her brush and starts her painting.

# Some Rivers

Frank Asch

Some rivers rush to the sea.
They push and tumble and fall.
But the Everglades is a river
with no hurry in her at all.
Soaking the cypress
that grows so tall;
nursing a frog,
so quiet and small;
she flows but a mile
in the course of a day,
with plenty of time
to think on the way.

But how can she cope
with the acres of corn
and sorrowful cities that drain her?
With hunters and tourists and levees
that chain and stain and pain her?
Does the half of her that's left
think only of the past?
Or does she think of her future
and how long it will last?
Some rivers rush to the sea.
They push and tumble and fall.
But the Everglades is a river
with no hurry in her at all.

**Look Closely** Some cypress trees in Florida are about 700 years old.

47

# This Is Indiana

Rebecca Kai Dotlich

This is Indiana,
the place that I love—
with wide open spaces
and stars above.
It's a bountiful wheat,
sweet corn growing land;
home of James Whitcomb Riley
and his *Raggedy Man*.

This is Indiana,
where the Wabash flows;
where the steel mills stand,
and the tulip tree grows.
Where the limestone quarries
for buildings reside,
and the Indy 500
is known worldwide.

This is Indiana,
veined with fields and farms.
Scored with rivers and lakes,
paved with bridges and barns.
Embroidered with churches
on rich, fertile land—
in a homeland of Hoosiers,

and basketball fans!

# Gold

Pat Mora

When Sun paints the desert
with its gold,
I climb the hills.
Wind runs round boulders, ruffles
my hair. I sit on my favorite rock,
lizards for company, a rabbit,
ears stiff in the shade
of a saguaro.
In the wind, we're all
eye to eye.

Sparrow on saguaro watches
rabbit watch us in the gold
of sun setting.
Hawk sails on waves of light, sees
sparrow, rabbit, lizards, me,
our eyes shining,
watching red and purple
    sand rivers stream down the hills.

I stretch my arms wide as the sky
like hawk extends her wings
in all the gold light of this, home.

**Look Closely** The saguaro
cactus can grow up to
50 feet high.

# Activities

1. **DRAW IT** Choose one of the four poems.
   Make a poster that tells why people should
   visit the region the poem describes.

2. **WRITE ABOUT IT** Write a poem about the
   region you live in. Be sure to include
   important details and features of your region.

## Skillbuilder

# Use Latitude and Longitude

▶ **VOCABULARY**

latitude lines
parallels
longitude lines
meridian

Lines of latitude and longitude are imaginary lines drawn on a globe or map. Using these lines can help you give an exact location for any place in the world. **Latitude lines**, or **parallels**, run east and west and measure distances north and south of the equator. **Longitude lines**, or **meridians**, run north and south and measure distances east and west of the prime meridian.

## Learn the Skill

**Step 1:** Study the latitude lines circling this globe. The parallel in the middle of the globe is called the equator. The equator is located at 0° (zero degrees) latitude.

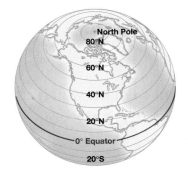

**Step 2:** Look at the longitude lines circling this globe. The prime meridian is located at 0° longitude.

**Step 3:** Look at the map. You can record the location of a place by identifying the parallel and the meridian on which it lies. For example, New Orleans, Louisiana, is found at 30°N, 90°W.

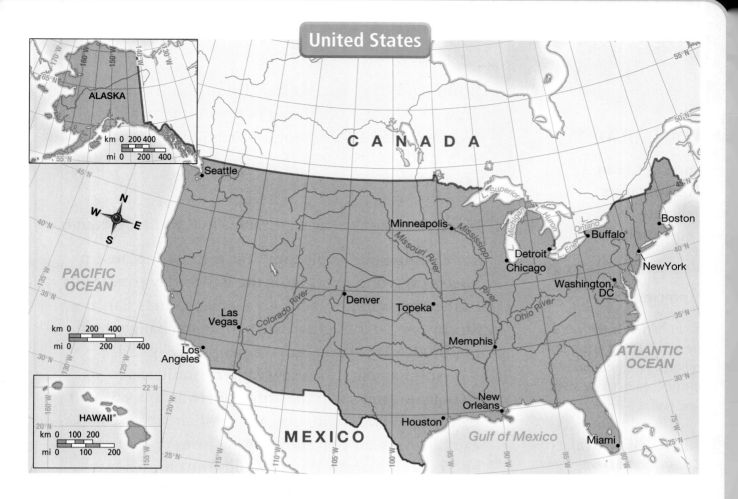

United States

ALASKA

CANADA

Seattle

Minneapolis
Missouri River
Mississippi
L. Superior
L. Michigan
L. Huron
L. Ontario
L. Erie
Boston
Buffalo
Detroit
Chicago
New York
Washington, DC

PACIFIC OCEAN

Denver
Topeka
Ohio River
Colorado River
Las Vegas

Memphis

Los Angeles

ATLANTIC OCEAN

HAWAII

MEXICO

New Orleans
Houston

Gulf of Mexico

Miami

## Practice the Skill

Use the map to answer the questions.

1. What city is located at 35°N, 90°W?

2. What is the location of Denver, Colorado?

## Apply the Skill

Use latitude and longitude to identify the locations of three other places in the United States.

# Climate Regions

**Build on What You Know** Think about what you do when the sun is shining or when it is raining. Weather often affects people's activities.

## Weather and Climate

**Main Idea** The air around the earth affects weather every day.

People like to talk about the weather because it affects everyone. Weather is the day-to-day conditions in the atmosphere, or the air that surrounds Earth. Stormy weather might cause people to change their plans. A sunny day can make people feel good.

Air movements cause weather conditions to change. Air moves in the atmosphere as it is warmed by the sun. Warm air rises, and cool air sinks. This explains why air that moves away from the equator and cools will sink. When a cold front moves over an area, it may cause thunderstorms or snow flurries. A cold front is the edge of a mass of cold air. Warm fronts bring steady rain or snow. During the year, changes in the seasons affect this pattern of air movement.

**Hurricane** This swirling air pattern causes a storm with high winds.

## VOCABULARY

precipitation
temperature
climate
elevation

**Vocabulary Strategy**

| precipitation

You often hear the word **precipitation** in weather reports. Precipitation includes rain, snow, sleet, and hail.

## READING SKILL

**Cause and Effect** Three major factors can affect climate. As you read, chart the effect that each factor has on climate.

| Cause | Effect |
|-------|--------|
|       |        |

## Conditions and Climate

When people talk about weather, they describe certain conditions. These conditions include wind speed and direction, amount of moisture in the air, and precipitation. **Precipitation** is water that falls to the earth as rain, snow, sleet, or hail. Another condition is temperature. **Temperature** is a measure of how hot or cold the air is.

Weather affects daily activities. Climate affects how people live and work all year long. **Climate** is the usual weather conditions in a place over a long period of time. Scientists must study a region for at least 30 years before they can understand its climate.

Three factors affect climate. The first is latitude, or distance from the equator. Places that are located farther from the equator get less heat from the sun. They also have less daylight in the winter. These factors result in colder temperatures.

**Haines, Alaska** At about 59°N latitude, Haines has long winter nights. However, its coastal location results in mild temperatures at sea level.

The second factor is distance from a major body of water. Places closer to an ocean have a smaller range of temperatures. For example, a city near an ocean might have temperatures around 40°F in the winter and 65°F in the summer. An area far from an ocean might range from –15°F in the winter to 85°F in the summer.

The third factor is elevation. **Elevation** is the height of the land. At higher elevations, temperatures are usually lower. Also, areas on one side of a mountain range may be drier than areas on the other side. This is because clouds drop their moisture before rising over mountains.

**REVIEW** What causes daily changes in the weather?

# A Land of Many Climates

**Main Idea** Climate regions have different patterns of temperature and precipitation.

Geographers divide the world into six main climate regions. The regions are based on temperature and amounts of precipitation. These six regions can be divided into subregions.

The tropical humid region has mild winters. Temperatures rarely fall below 65°F. Its subregions differ in the amounts of rain they get at different times of the year. Hawaii is in the tropical wet subregion. It has rain year-round. Florida's tropical wet and dry subregion has rainy and dry seasons.

The dry region has very little precipitation. The semiarid subregion near the Rocky Mountains is a little moister than the desert subregion. Areas in the dry region are often surrounded by mountains. The mountains prevent much rainfall from reaching the area.

Several states belong to the marine climate region. Areas in the subregion called humid subtropical have hot, sticky summers with thunderstorms and mild winters. The marine subregion has mild, wet winters and short, dry summers. California's Mediterranean subregion has long, dry summers and small amounts of rain in the winter.

**Climate Regions** The United States has 11 climate regions.

**SKILL** **Reading Maps** Which state has areas in the polar region?

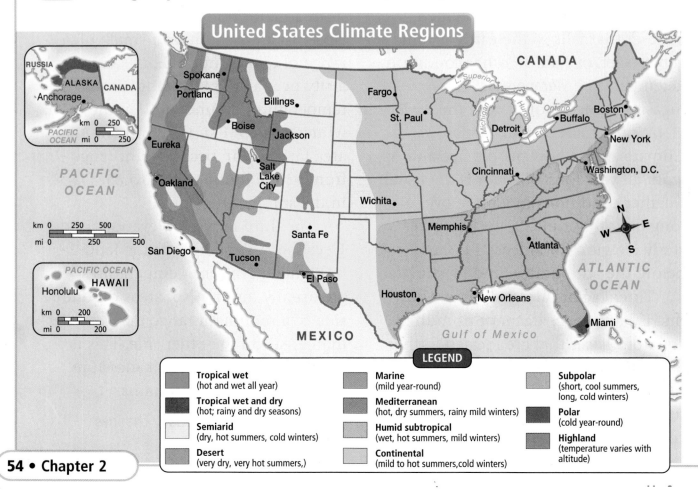

**United States Climate Regions**

**LEGEND**

- **Tropical wet** (hot and wet all year)
- **Tropical wet and dry** (hot; rainy and dry seasons)
- **Semiarid** (dry, hot summers, cold winters)
- **Desert** (very dry, very hot summers,)
- **Marine** (mild year-round)
- **Mediterranean** (hot, dry summers, rainy mild winters)
- **Humid subtropical** (wet, hot summers, mild winters)
- **Continental** (mild to hot summers, cold winters)
- **Subpolar** (short, cool summers, long, cold winters)
- **Polar** (cold year-round)
- **Highland** (temperature varies with altitude)

The continental climate region has cold winters. Arctic air brings snowstorms to this subregion. Summers range from hot to cool. The part of Alaska in the subpolar subregion has long winters and short, cool summers.

Northern Alaska is in the polar region. The average temperature of even the warmest month is below 50°F.

The highest mountains of the United States are in the highland climate region. The mountains are usually cooler and wetter than the lower land around them.

**REVIEW** What factors are used to divide the United States into climate regions and subregions?

## Major Climate Regions

Tropical wet region

Desert region

Polar region

Highland region

Marine region

Continental region

# Climate and People

**Main Idea** A region's climate may affect the behavior and economic activities of a region.

Climate affects every part of life in our world. Climate determines which plants will grow. For example, in northern Alaska, only mosses, shrubs, and tiny trees grow on the frozen tundra. In the dry region, most of the plants need little moisture or can send down deep roots to find water.

The plant life and climate affect the animals found in a region. For example, only animals that can live with scarce food supplies and cold temperatures in the winter can live in New England or the upper Midwest. People, too, must learn to deal with the climate and the plants and animals of their region.

The special features of each climate region affect how people live.

Today, people have found ways to lessen the effects of their environment. Houses in cold regions have furnaces for heat. Air conditioning makes people in hot areas more comfortable. People in dry regions have found ways to control water resources. This helps ensure they have enough for drinking and for watering crops.

However, climate still has a major impact on how people live. It can either help or limit economic activities. For example, California's Central Valley is a major farming area. Its climate provides two growing seasons. In contrast, the short growing seasons in Maine and Alaska limit farming.

## Dealing with Different Climates

Climate also affects people's way of life. In cold climates, people listen to weather reports to prepare for winter snow and ice. They wear heavy clothes and drive carefully on snowy roads. People in warmer climates may have to spray for bugs. On sunny days, they may need to wear sunglasses and protect their skin with sun block.

All regions can have severe weather. Southern and eastern coastal areas may have hurricanes. These are storms with strong and damaging winds. Blizzards and tornadoes occur frequently in the Midwest region. A blizzard is a heavy snowstorm with strong winds. A tornado is a twisting column of air. Both of these can destroy buildings and crops.

Over many years, natural and human processes can change climates. Some scientists believe that people's use of fossil fuels is affecting climate.

The earth's surface appears to be warming. This could cause changes in precipitation and more violent weather events.

**REVIEW** In what ways are people affected by extreme weather events?

### Lesson Summary

There are six major kinds of climate region in the world. Each region and its subregions are defined by temperature, precipitation, and other conditions. Scientists study these conditions over many years to draw conclusions about the climate. Latitude, distance from large bodies of water, and elevation all influence climate. In turn, climate affects plant, animal, and human life in each region.

## Why It Matters ...

Climate in a region affects the clothes people wear, the things they do for fun, and the work they do.

## Lesson Review

❶ **VOCABULARY** What is the difference between weather and **climate?**

❷ **READING SKILL** Explain one **effect** of climate on the economic activity of a region.

❸ **MAIN IDEA: Geography** What landforms affect climate?

❹ **MAIN IDEA: Technology** In what ways do people today deal with very hot or cold temperatures?

❺ **FACTS TO KNOW** What are the six major climate regions?

❻ **CRITICAL THINKING: Compare and Contrast** Describe your climate region. Then compare its features to a climate region next to it.

**WRITING ACTIVITY** Find out more about hurricanes, tornadoes, or blizzards. Use your information to write a short story about a severe weather event.

# THE WATER CYCLE

Most of Earth's water is found in salty oceans. If 100 cups held all the world's water, 97 cups would be salt water. Only 3 cups would be fresh water. Three quarters of the fresh water is frozen in glaciers and icecaps. The rest is in streams, rivers, lakes, and underground. This fresh water is very precious. People depend on it every day to drink, cook, bathe, and water crops.

The total amount of water on Earth never changes. Water can move from place to place and change from one form to another, but none is lost or gained. All the water goes around and around in the water cycle.

**❷ Condensation**
As the water vapor rises, it condenses. This means that it cools and turns back into tiny water droplets. The water droplets form clouds.

❷

**❶ Evaporation**
Water in oceans is warmed by the sun. It evaporates and rises into the air as water vapor.

❶

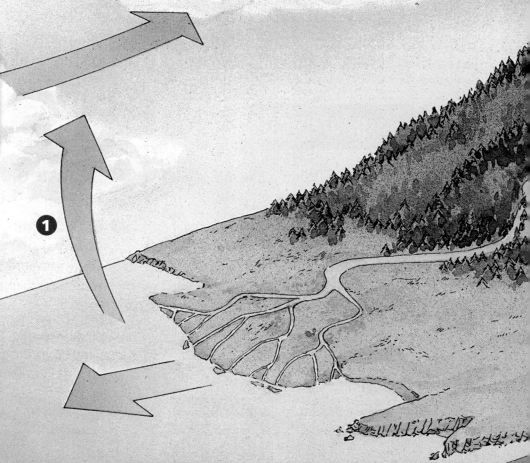

**3** **Precipitation**
When the clouds get too heavy with water, there is **precipitation**—rain, snow, sleet, or hail.

3

**4** **Back to the Ocean**
The water from precipitation seeps into the ground. It trickles into streams, lakes, and rivers. Eventually, the water flows into oceans. The cycle begins all over again!

4

# Activities

1. **STEP INTO IT** Find the number 1 on the diagram. Starting there, use your own words to explain each step in the water cycle.

2. **DRAW IT** Draw pictures showing some of the ways you use water every day.

**59**

## Visual Summary

**1. – 3.** ✏️ Write a description of each item named below.

| Regions | |
|---|---|
| Government | |
| Natural | |
| Climate | |

## Facts and Main Ideas

✔️ **TEST PREP** Answer each question below.

4. **Geography** What kinds of features can people use to divide places into regions?

5. **Government** In what ways do governments use regions?

6. **Geography** Explain the difference between urban, rural, and suburban regions.

7. **Geography** What is the difference between weather and climate?

8. **Culture** Describe three ways the climate of an area affects how people live.

## Vocabulary

✔️ **TEST PREP** Choose the correct word from the list below to complete each sentence.

**boundary,** p. 37
**economy,** p. 45
**precipitation,** p. 53

9. The _____ of a region is the way people use the region's resources.

10. Water that falls to the earth as rain, snow, sleet, or hail is called _____.

11. A _____ marks the edge of a region.

## Apply Skills

**✔ TEST PREP  Use Latitude and Longitude**  Study the Missouri map below. Then use what you have learned about latitude and longitude to answer each question.

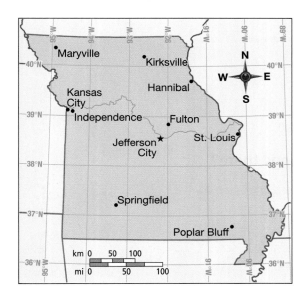

12. Which city on the map is closest to 37°N, 93°W?

    **A.** Jefferson City
    **B.** Maryville
    **C.** Hannibal
    **D.** Springfield

13. Which latitude and longitude lines are closest to the city of Fulton, Missouri?

    **A.** 37°N, 94°W
    **B.** 39°N, 92°W
    **C.** 40°N, 93°W
    **D.** 38°N, 92°W

## Critical Thinking

**✔ TEST PREP**  Write a short paragraph to answer each question below.

14. **Compare and Contrast**  What are some ways in which the four major regions of the United States may differ?

15. **Infer**  Why might a major change of climate in a region have a negative affect on the people and the economy of that region?

# Activities

**Research Activity**  Use library or Internet resources to find out more about how the processing of fossil fuels such as coal has affected air quality. Create a chart that shows the causes and effects on the environment.

**Writing Activity**  Write a personal narrative telling how the climate in your area affects your daily life. Give an example from your own experience.

**Technology**
**Writing Process Tips**
Get help with your narrative at:
**www.eduplace.com/kids/hmss05/**

# Geography Where You Live

You can explore the geography in your state. Start by thinking like a geographer. How might you describe where your state is? What is it like there? Why are different things there? The answers affect your everyday life.

**My State**

- **Where is it?**
- **What is it like there?**
- **Why are certain things there?**

To explore a state such as Wyoming, geographers might look at its landforms and resources as well as how people use the land.

## Find Out!

### Explore your state's geography.

✔ **Start with maps.**
Check out the United States Geographic Society on line. Or look at maps at the library to find landforms and bodies of water in your state.

✔ **Check the weather.**
Find out about the weather and climate in different parts of your state. The National Weather Service has a website.

✔ **Visit your state's department of natural resources website.**
Learn ways to protect your state's natural resources.

✔ **Talk to a geographer.**
Ask about the ways people affect the environment in your state.

Use your state handbook to keep track of the information you find.

# Review and Test Prep

## Vocabulary and Main Ideas

✓ **TEST PREP** Write a sentence to answer each question.

1. Why is it important to understand our **environment?**

2. What three things can cause **erosion?**

3. From what were **fossil fuels** formed?

4. In what way are **boundaries** and borders similar?

5. What is the difference between an **urban** area and a **rural** area?

6. What three factors affect **climate?**

## Critical Thinking

✓ **TEST PREP** Write a short paragraph to answer each question.

7. **Draw Conclusions** Why is it important for the United States to find new sources of energy?

8. **Summarize** What are several ways to define regions?

## Apply Skills

✓ **TEST PREP** Study the Eastern United States Resources map below. Then use your map skills to answer each question.

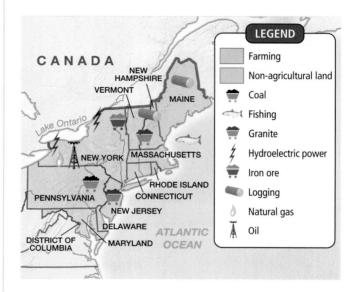

9. What energy resources are found in the East?

   **A.** gold, granite, and copper
   **B.** coal, natural gas, oil, and hydroelectric power
   **C.** fishing and logging
   **D.** no energy resources

10. Which resource is found in large amounts in Maine?

    **A.** coal
    **B.** fossil fuels
    **C.** uranium
    **D.** forests

## Unit Activity

### Make a Travel Brochure

- Choose a part of the country that you think has interesting features.

- Fold a sheet of paper in half. Write the name of the place on the front cover. Draw a picture or map of the region.

- Inside the brochure, research and list interesting facts about the region.

- Find or draw pictures of the region. Include captions.

- Post the brochure in your classroom.

## At the Library

**Look for this book at your school or public library.**

*Hottest Coldest Highest Deepest*
by Steve Jenkins

Illustrations and brief text highlight some of the most unique places on Earth.

## CURRENT EVENTS
## WEEKLY (WR) READER

### Current Events Project

**Learn about famous people from one of the 50 states.**

- Choose one state. Find information about famous Americans who came from that state.

- Draw an outline of the state.

- List some of the state's famous people in your drawing, and write one sentence about each person.

- Post your drawing in the classroom.

**Technology**
Weekly Reader online offers social studies articles. Go to:
**www.eduplace.com/kids/hmss/**

## Read About It

**Look in your classroom for these Social Studies Independent Books.**

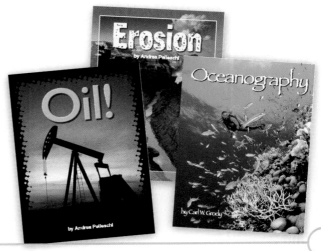

# UNIT 2

## The East

### The Big Idea

**What makes our country free?**

"We must trust the people. We must trust each other. . . . We must protect our own basic rights by protecting the rights of others."

—Faye Wattleton,
leader for women's rights, 1986

# Almanac

## United States Time Zones

5 o'clock
**Alaska Time Zone**

4 o'clock
**Hawaii-Aleutian Time Zone**

6 o'clock
**Pacific Time Zone**

7 o'clock
**Mountain Time Zone**

8 o'clock
**Central Time Zone**

ARCTIC OCEAN
170°W   130°W
70°N
km 0    300
mi 0    300
AK
Fairbanks
Anchorage
Juneau
CANADA
PACIFIC OCEAN
150°W

PACIFIC OCEAN

160°W   155°W
Honolulu · Kailua
HI
km 0  50 100
mi 0  50 100
20°N
PACIFIC OCEAN
Hilo
130°W

30°N

Seattle
Spokane
Olympia
WA
Portland
Salem
OR
Helena
MT
Billings
ND
Bismarck   Fargo
MN
St. Paul
Minneapolis
Boise
ID
Pocatello
WY
Casper
SD
Pierre
Sioux Falls
IA
Cedar Rapi
Cheyenne
NE
Omaha  Des Moin
Lincoln
Reno
Sacramento
Carson City
Salt Lake City
Provo
Denver
Topeka   Kansa City
San Francisco
NV
UT
CO
Colorado Springs
KS
Jefferson Cit
Wichita
MC
CA
Las Vegas
Los Angeles
Santa Fe
Albuquerque
OK
Tulsa
Oklahoma City
Fort Sm
San Diego
AZ
Phoenix
NM
Litt Roc
Tucson
El Paso
Dallas
TX
Austin
San Antonio   Houston
L

MEXICO

Tropic of Cancer

120°W   110°W

**Unit Preview**

**Mineral Resources**
Coal is mined in the East
**Chapter 3, page 78**

**Textile Mills**
Early factories used water-powered machines
**Chapter 3, page 94**

**Seafood**
Lobster is a popular New England food
**Chapter 4, page 109**

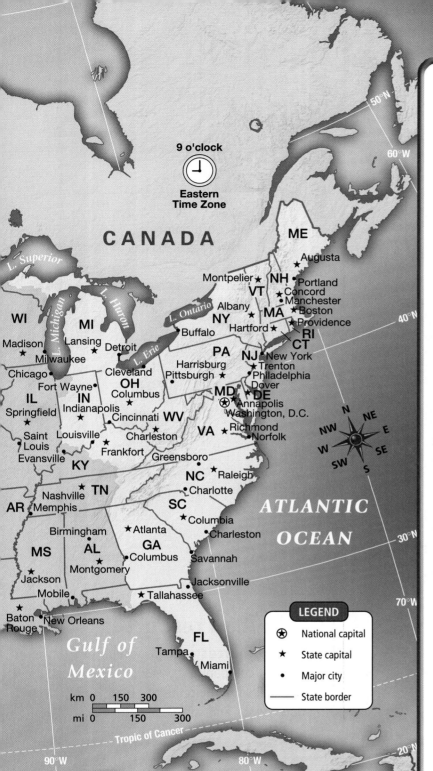

9 o'clock

Eastern
Time Zone

CANADA

ME
• Augusta

Montpelier ★ NH • Portland
VT • Concord
• Manchester
Albany MA ★ • Boston
NY ★ • Providence
• Buffalo Hartford ★ RI
CT

L. Superior

WI
L. Michigan
MI

Madison ★ Lansing ★ Detroit
• Milwaukee
Chicago • Cleveland • Harrisburg
Fort Wayne • OH Columbus
IL IN
Springfield ★ Indianapolis ★
• Cincinnati WV
Saint Louisville VA ★ Richmond
Louis ★ Frankfort Charleston ★ • Norfolk
Evansville KY
Greensboro
Nashville ★ TN NC ★ Raleigh
AR • Charlotte
• Memphis SC
Birmingham • Columbia
MS Atlanta ★ • Charleston
AL GA
• Columbus • Savannah
Jackson ★ Montgomery
Mobile • • Jacksonville
Baton • New Orleans ★ Tallahassee
Rouge
Gulf of FL
Mexico Tampa •
• Miami

L. Huron
L. Ontario
L. Erie

PA
Pittsburgh ★
NJ ★ New York
★ Trenton
• Philadelphia
MD ★ DE Dover
⊛ ★ Annapolis
Washington, D.C.

ATLANTIC

OCEAN

N
NW NE
W E
SW SE
S

**LEGEND**
⊛ National capital
★ State capital
• Major city
— State border

km 0   150   300
mi 0   150   300

Tropic of Cancer

50°N
60°W
40°N
30°N
70°W
20°N
90°W   80°W

**Grand Central Terminal**
Many people in New York City commute by train **Chapter 4, page 114**

# Connect to...
# The Nation

## U.S. Land Area

The area of the East is 174,045 square miles.

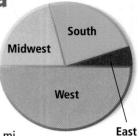

South
Midwest
West
East

| | | |
|---|---|---|
| East | 174,045 | sq. mi |
| West | 1,752,951 | sq. mi |
| Midwest | 751,426 | sq. mi |
| South | 859,016 | sq. mi |

## U.S. Population

The population of the East is 60,246,523 people.

East
Midwest
West
South

| | | |
|---|---|---|
| East | 60,246,523 | people |
| South | 93,584,675 | people |
| West | 63,197,932 | people |
| Midwest | 64,392,776 | people |

Compare the East with other regions. The East has a smaller land area, but about the same population. What might this mean for people and where they live in the East?

## Vocabulary Preview

**Technology**

*e* • **glossary**
*e* • **word games**
www.eduplace.com/kids/hmss05/

### coast

Many people enjoy beaches along the **coast.** The United States has a long east coast, a long west coast, and a southern coast along the Gulf of Mexico. **page 72**

### human resources

**Human resources** are a very important part of any company. Workers provide needed skills that help the company produce goods and services. **page 82**

## Chapter Timeline

1620
**Pilgrims in Massachusetts**

1776
**Declaration of Independence**

1500        1600        1700

# Reading Strategy

**Summarize** As you read, use the summarize strategy to focus on important ideas.

Review the main ideas to get started. Then look for important details that support the main idea.

## culture

Art, music, food, and customs are part of a **culture.** Everything about how a group of people thinks, works, and lives is part of their culture. **page 90**

## industry

A business that uses machines and people to make a large amount of goods is called an **industry.** There are many industries in the United States. **page 95**

1813
**Lowell's power loom**

**Many African Americans move north**

1800          1900          2000

# Land and Climate

## VOCABULARY

coast
coastal plain
cape
bay

## Vocabulary Strategy

coastal plain

A **coast** is land next to an ocean. A **coastal plain** is a plain next to an ocean.

## READING SKILL

**Main Idea and Details**
List details that describe the mountains of the East.

Mountains

**Build on What You Know** Think of a road that cuts through a mountain. You would see many layers of rock. Scientists can tell the age of mountains by looking at these layers. The Appalachian Mountains are hundreds of millions of years old.

## Land and Water of the East

**Main Idea** The East has many landforms and bodies of water.

The region between the Atlantic Ocean and the Great Lakes is known as the East. Canada borders the region to the north. Our nation's capital, Washington, D.C., is at the southern tip.

The East includes six states in New England and five Mid-Atlantic states. Some of our nation's oldest cities are in the New England region. The nation's largest city, New York, is in the Mid-Atlantic region.

Nine states in the East are on the coast. A **coast** is land that borders an ocean. Coastal areas form a landform region called the coastal plain. A **coastal plain** is flat, level land along a coast.

**Western New York** The Genesee River flows between steep cliffs and thick forests. The cliffs show layers of rock.

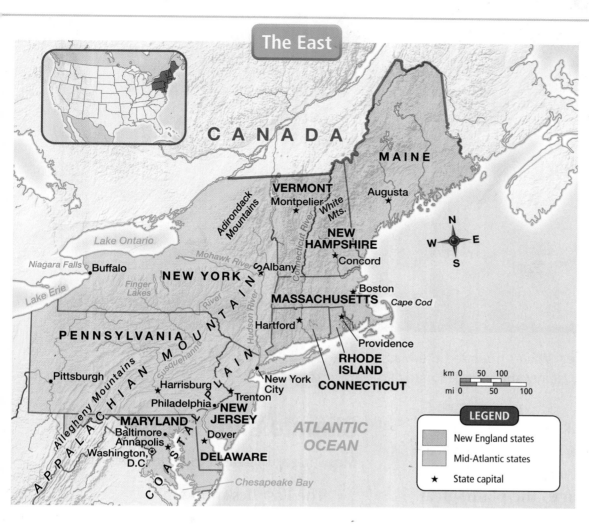

**The East** Two main landform regions are the Appalachian Mountains and the coastal plain.

## Mountains and Plains

The Appalachian Mountains were formed by the movement of the earth. Over millions of years, two moving continents came together. The land between them slowly buckled and rose up. These huge piles of rocks became the Appalachians.

Wind, weather, and the water flowing in rivers slowly wore the Appalachians down. Glaciers also changed the mountains' shape. They carved out valleys or leveled the land with the rocks and dirt they left behind.

East of the Appalachians is the coastal plain. In northern New England, this plain lies mostly underwater.

It is wider from Massachusetts to Florida. Here, the plain has major cities, farms, and factories. Rock and sand left from glaciers formed islands with sandy beaches, such as Long Island. They also formed capes, such as Cape Cod. A **cape** is a point of land that sticks out into the water.

More people live on the coastal plain than in the mountains. The land is less rugged and closer to water routes. In the mountains, some people mine coal or cut down trees for timber. People also farm on the mountainsides and in the mountain valleys.

**REVIEW** Why are more cities built on the coastal plain than in the mountains?

**Winter Nor'easter** Waves pounded the Massachusetts coast in this March 2001 storm. Heavy snow forced many schools to close.

## Bodies of Water

The East is a land of lakes, rivers, and ocean. As rivers flow from mountains down to the plain, great changes in elevation create waterfalls. Waterfalls made early travel on rivers difficult. However, people learned to use the water's force to power machines in mills and factories. The usefulness of water power led to the growth of major cities on these waterways.

People built settlements near the best harbors along the Atlantic coast. These settlements grew into cities. Ships carrying people and goods from other continents arrived in the harbors and bays. A **bay** is a body of water partly surrounded by land but open to the sea. The Chesapeake Bay, which reaches into Maryland, is important for shipping. It also supports thousands of plants and animals.

## Climate and Its Effects

**Main Idea** The East has a temperate climate.

The East lies in the middle latitudes, about halfway between the North Pole and the equator. This location gives it four seasons and a temperate climate. Temperate means without extremes, such as the very cold weather in the Arctic or the very hot weather near the equator. Cool breezes blow from the Atlantic Ocean on hot days, and warm breezes blow on cold days. Winters in the East are cold and snowy, though, and summers are warm and humid.

The East sometimes has storms called "nor'easters." These storms bring strong winds from the northeast. Nor'easters also bring high ocean waves and heavy snow or rain. People need warm clothing and snow shovels to help them cope with winter conditions.

## Plants and Animals

Climate affects the plants and animals that can live in a region. In the East, trees such as maple, birch, hickory, and oak drop their leaves before winter. This helps them survive the lack of water in the frozen soil.

Eastern animals must cope with both cold winters and changing food supplies. Squirrels bury nuts during the warmer months. In the winter, when food is hard to find, they can dig up the nuts and eat them. Other animals, such as black bears, hibernate during the winter. They use leaves and twigs to make a den in a cave or other shelter. Then they sleep for up to 100 days. Raccoons, skunks, and chipmunks also hibernate during the winter.

**REVIEW** In what ways does the climate of the East affect people, animals, and plants?

## Lesson Summary

- The landforms of the East include mountains and plains.
- Rivers, harbors, and bays are important for development.
- The climate of the East is temperate, but winters are cold and snowy.

## Why It Matters ...

Water power, travel routes, and a temperate climate helped the East develop.

**Black Bear** Bears sleep through the coldest part of eastern winters.

## Lesson Review

❶ **VOCABULARY** Write a paragraph about the eastern **coast.** Include **capes** and **bays** in your paragraph.

❷ ⏱ **READING SKILL** List two **details** that support this **main idea:** People learned to use bodies of water in the East.

❸ **MAIN IDEA: Geography** Describe two landforms and two waterways that a visitor to the East might see.

❹ **MAIN IDEA: Culture** Explain one effect of the climate on people's lives in the East.

❺ **CRITICAL THINKING: Fact and Opinion** Write one fact about New England. Then write an opinion based on that fact.

**HANDS ON** **SCIENCE ACTIVITY** Use a reference book, such as an encyclopedia, to find out why the leaves of certain trees change color in the fall. Draw a diagram to show the process.

# How Glaciers Shaped the Land

**A glacier is an awesome force.** It can lift a rock as large as a house and carry it across a continent. It can dig a hole big enough to become a large lake. During the last ice age, glaciers covered nearly a third of the world's land. As they moved across the land, these ice sheets crushed and scraped the earth. They carved out many new landforms. About 21,000 years ago, the ice sheets began to melt. This melting left behind new landforms, too.

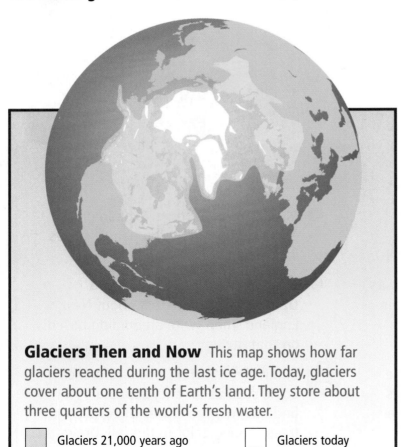

**Glaciers Then and Now** This map shows how far glaciers reached during the last ice age. Today, glaciers cover about one tenth of Earth's land. They store about three quarters of the world's fresh water.

☐ Glaciers 21,000 years ago          ☐ Glaciers today

**Cape Cod** As glaciers flow, they pick up rocks and dirt. They also push mounds of earth in front of them. When they melt, glaciers drop this material in huge piles. Cape Cod in Massachusetts was formed this way.

**Mountain glacier**

**Rocks and dirt**

**Ice Sheets** These glaciers form when snow piles up for many years without melting. It takes about 1,000 years for snow to become glacial ice. In some parts of Antarctica, the ice is over two and a half miles thick.

# Activities

1. **THINK ABOUT IT** In what ways is a mountain glacier like a river? In what ways is it different?

2. **WRITE ABOUT IT** What would it be like to live during an ice age? Write a creative story about life in a new ice age.

# Resources and Economy

## VOCABULARY

**market economy**
**profit**
**human resources**
**capital resources**

### Vocabulary Strategy

market economy

A **market** is a place where you can choose what to buy. A **market economy** lets people choose what they buy, make, and sell.

## READING SKILL

**Classify** Use a chart to list some natural resources of the East.

```
        Natural resources
    ┌─────────┬─────────┐
  ┌───┐     ┌───┐     ┌───┐
  └───┘     └───┘     └───┘
```

**Build on What You Know** Suppose you want to sell lemonade in your neighborhood. What price will you charge? Every business owner must choose what to sell, where to sell it, and for how much.

## Natural Resources of the East

**Main Idea** The natural resources of the East include forests, soil, and minerals.

The East has fewer of some natural resources than other regions. For example, western states have more minerals than eastern states. However, the East has rivers, forests, farmland, fish, and the ocean. People use these resources to make goods for themselves and to sell to other people.

The Appalachian Mountains contain coal. Workers mine coal in Pennsylvania. Power plants burn it to make electricity. In Maine and Vermont, workers dig out granite and marble. These kinds of stone are used in buildings and monuments.

**Coal Mine** Workers take coal from mine shafts dug deep into the ground.

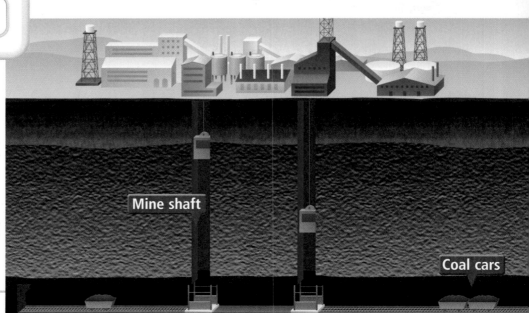

Mine shaft

Coal cars

## Natural Resources of the East

| Resource | Uses |
|---|---|
| Granite | Stones for building |
| Marble | Monuments, tombs, parts of buildings |
| Coal | Fuel to make electricity, steel, iron, glass, stone, paper |
| Forests/Wood | Building materials, furniture, paper, fuel, maple syrup |
| Soil | Fruits, vegetables, grain, dairy cows |
| Fish | Food, fertilizer |
| Rivers/Ocean | Moving goods or people, source of water and power, fish |

**SKILL** **Reading Charts** Which resources are used for fuel or power?

**Apple Picking in New York** In the fall, Easterners can pick their own apples.

## Using the East's Resources

In the East, many houses are made of wood. Forests provide wood for buildings, paper, furniture, and fuel. Wood can also be used to make chemicals for many other products, including plastics and textiles.

Do you like pancakes with syrup for breakfast? Maple syrup comes from sugar maple trees. Vermont produces more maple syrup than any other state. Maine, Massachusetts, New York, and New Hampshire also produce syrup.

The soil and climate of the East allow farmers to use their land in different ways. Blueberries grow well in the soil of Maine and New Hampshire. The soil of the Aroostook Valley in Maine is perfect for potatoes.

Massachusetts and New Jersey have sandy marshes where farmers can grow cranberries. The warm, rainy summers in New York and Vermont make grasses grow well. These conditions are good for dairy cows, which eat the grasses. Eastern farmers also grow vegetables such as tomatoes, corn, and beans. Some farmers raise fruit trees, including apple and peach trees.

The Atlantic Ocean is an important resource for the East. From Maine to Maryland, people catch lobsters, sardines, flounder, and bass. Maryland and Delaware produce many blue crabs.

**REVIEW** Why is the farmland of the East an important natural resource?

# Working in the East

**Main Idea** In a market economy, people decide what to make, buy, and sell.

A nation's economy is the system in which it uses resources to meet its needs and wants. The United States has a market economy. In a **market economy,** people are free to decide what to make, how to make it, and for whom to make it. If the law allows it, they can run any business they want.

A market economy is different from a command economy. In a command economy, the government decides what to make, who will make it, and who will get it. The government also sets the prices for goods.

Business owners keep their profits in a market economy. **Profit** is the money left over after a business pays its expenses. Some businesses make profits by selling natural resources. Others make goods from resources. Then they sell the goods. Paper, maple syrup, and furniture are goods.

Some businesses sell services that people want. A service is any kind of work that one person does for another person as a job. Lawyers, plumbers, and engineers all provide services. In recent years, more and more people have worked in service businesses. Many of these service jobs involve computers, or information technology.

**Market Economy** In a market economy, people have many choices.

## Trading Resources

Businesses use trade to get the resources they want. Trade begins when one person has what another wants. These people exchange resources or money for goods or services. In that way, both people get what they want. When people trade a lot, the economy grows.

Moving goods is important for trade. Imagine that a chemical factory in Delaware needs to buy raw materials from an owner in another region. The factory must pay a trucking company to bring the materials to the factory. Many businesses settle near big cities because the roads, waterways, and airports in these cities make trade easier.

Factories in the East make many kinds of goods. For example, New Jersey businesses make chemicals, medicines, machinery, and clothing. In Connecticut, factory workers make weapons, sewing machines, jet engines, and clocks.

Many eastern businesses provide services. For example, banks offer a safe place for people to keep their money. Banks also lend money to people. Many banks started in eastern cities. Today, Philadelphia and New York City are important banking centers. In banks, people can work as bank tellers, loan officers, and even computer programmers.

**REVIEW** How is making goods different from performing services?

### Service Businesses in the East

| | |
|---|---|
| Banking | Insurance |
| Communication | Legal services |
| Education | Recreation |
| Engineering | Repairs |
| Health care | Restaurants |
| Hotels | Tourism |

**Services** Restaurants perform a service. The chart shows other service businesses that provide jobs in the East.

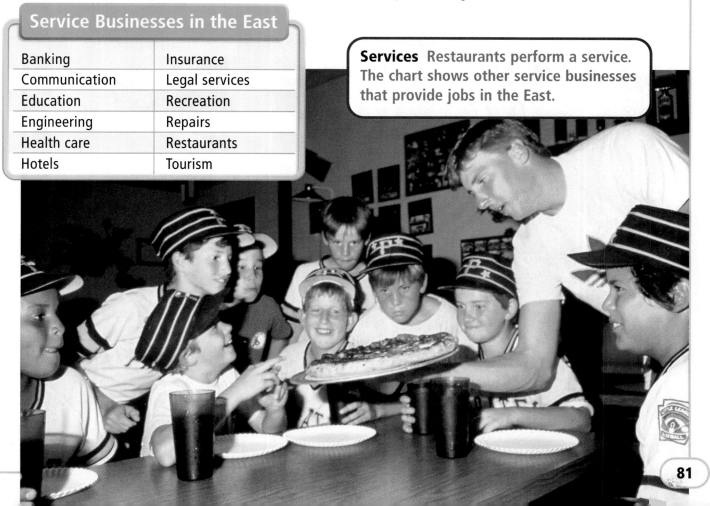

# Elements of Business

**Main Idea** In a system of private ownership, individuals own the factors of production.

A business needs equipment, workers, and often some raw materials. These things are the factors of production. Factors of production are the people and materials needed to make goods or provide services. The four factors are labor, capital, land, and entrepreneurship (ahn truh pruh NUHR ship). Entrepreneurs are people who are willing to take the risk of starting a new business.

**Factors of Production** Skilled workers are needed to make sap into maple syrup.

**SKILL** **Reading Visuals** What capital resources do you see in the pictures below?

Some businesses use natural resources. All businesses use human resources and capital resources. **Human resources** are the services, knowledge, skills, and intelligence that workers provide. **Capital resources** are the tools, machines, buildings, and other equipment that a business uses to make goods or provide services.

The East has a long tradition of successful businesses. Settlers near York, Maine, built the nation's first sawmill in 1623. Philadelphia had the nation's first bank and its first daily newspaper in the 1780s. Some of the nation's oldest companies still operate in the East today.

## Maple Syrup Production

  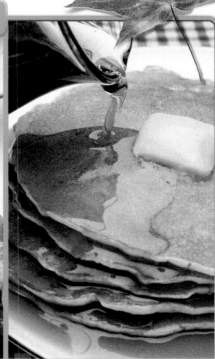

Natural and capital resources + Human resource = Product

## Entrepreneurs and Ownership

Entrepreneurs are people who use the factors of production to start new businesses. Entrepreneurs take risks when they start new businesses. They invest their time and money in their businesses. However, people might not want to buy their goods or services. Then, instead of making a profit, the entrepreneurs could lose money. Entrepreneurs must plan carefully and work hard to have the best chance of earning a profit.

Entrepreneurs own their own businesses. Private ownership is an important part of a market economy. Private ownership means that individual people, not the government, own the factors of production. Individuals also make their own business decisions, hoping to earn a profit.

**REVIEW** Why is private ownership important in a market economy?

**Entrepreneurship** A person who opens a new store is an entrepreneur.

### Lesson Summary

- People use the natural resources of the East to make products and trade with businesses in other areas.

- Businesses make profits by selling resources, goods, and services.

- Entrepreneurship and resources—natural, human, and capital—are necessary in any business.

## Why It Matters ...

A market economy can give people more freedom to choose how they work and live.

---

## Lesson Review

❶ **VOCABULARY** Explain how **human resources** and **capital resoures** are used to make goods.

❷ **READING SKILL** List two things that can be **classified** as human resources and two that can be classified as capital resources.

❸ **MAIN IDEA: Geography** What are two natural resources of the East, and how are they used?

❹ **MAIN IDEA: Economics** In what way is a market economy different from a command economy?

❺ **CRITICAL THINKING: Analyze** Why might someone start a business near a city?

**HANDS ON** **INTERVIEW ACTIVITY** Interview several adults who work in different jobs. Ask each person if his or her job involves making a product or providing a service. Make a chart of these products and services.

# Money AND Banks

How much do you know about banks and money? Mrs. Fuller's class is studying money. She and her students visit a bank to learn more.

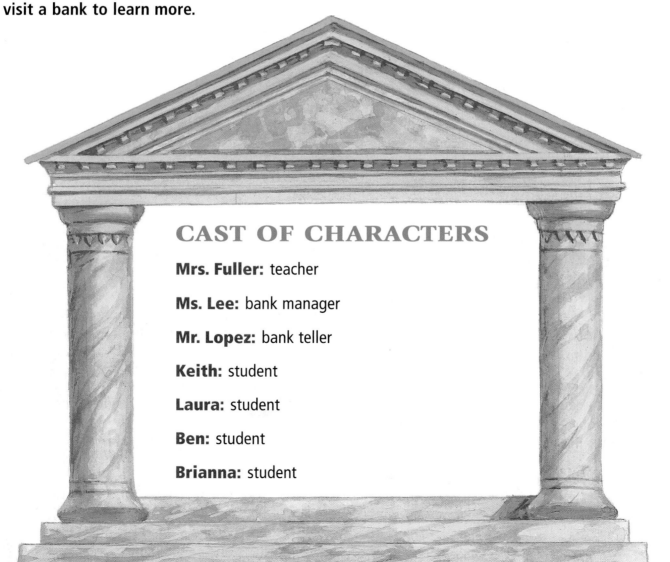

## CAST OF CHARACTERS

**Mrs. Fuller:** teacher

**Ms. Lee:** bank manager

**Mr. Lopez:** bank teller

**Keith:** student

**Laura:** student

**Ben:** student

**Brianna:** student

**Ms. Lee:** Welcome to our bank! Everything at a bank is related to money.

**Mrs. Fuller:** What exactly *is* money? Keith, can you tell us?

**Keith:** Money is coins and bills that have a certain value. We use money to buy the things we want.

**Mrs. Fuller:** Good! Coins and bills are one kind of money. The money people keep in their checking accounts is another kind.

**Laura:** Where do coins and bills come from? Do you make them at the bank?

**Ms. Lee:** No, the government does that. They print paper money, and they mint coins.

**Keith:** But aren't banks part of the government?

**Mrs. Fuller:** No, banks are privately owned businesses. The government has rules that guide the decisions banks make.

**Laura:** What exactly do banks do, then?

**Ms. Lee:** We help people to keep their money safe. Our big vault is a lot safer than a sock or a mattress! Also, when you put your money in the bank, it earns interest.

**Brianna:** What's interest?

**Mrs. Fuller:** Interest is an amount of money the bank pays to customers who keep their money here. But banks also receive interest when they make loans.

**Ben:** Banks make loans? I don't get it. I thought they kept money safe for people. Why do they loan it out?

**Ms. Lee:** Well, suppose a person wants to buy something expensive, like a house or a car. The person might not have enough money to pay for it all at once. So, the bank gives the person a loan for the whole amount. Then the person pays the money back slowly over time, with interest.

**Mrs. Fuller:** The person must pay back more than he or she borrowed. That's the interest. That's how the bank earns money.

**Ms. Lee:** All kinds of people in the community want loans, including farmers, business people, and factory owners.

**Mrs. Fuller:** That's one reason banks are so important in the community. They provide the funds for big projects that people and businesses couldn't afford on their own.

**Brianna:** Ms. Lee, when I put my money in the bank, how do I get it out again when I want it?

**Ms. Lee:** That's a great question. Let's go talk to Mr. Lopez. He'll tell you about deposits and withdrawals.

**Mr. Lopez:** Hello! I'm a bank teller. I work at the counter here and help people when they want to put money into their accounts or take it out.

**Keith:** Putting money in is called making a deposit, right? Taking money out is called making a withdrawal.

**Mr. Lopez:** That's right. When you make a deposit or a withdrawal, I update your account by entering all the information into the computer. Then I give you a receipt.

**Ben:** Is a checking account the same as a savings account?

**Laura:** No! When you have a checking account you can write checks. Right?

**Mr. Lopez:** Right. Checks are notes promising that your bank will pay money from your account in the amount written on the check. It's a good way to pay when you don't want to use cash.

**Mrs. Fuller:** Well, thank you so much for talking to us about banks. We all learned a lot.

**Keith, Laura, Ben, and Brianna:** Yes, thank you!

# Activities

1. **EXPLAIN IT** Ask an adult to explain the meanings of these phrases and terms: bounce a check, balance a checkbook, collateral (for a loan). Then explain them in your own words.

2. **THINK ABOUT IT** Make a list of businesses in your area. Then list the kinds of resources each business might buy with a bank loan.

## Skillbuilder

# Use Reference Materials

To find facts about a topic, you can use reference materials. Reference books include encyclopedias, atlases, almanacs, and dictionaries. Nonfiction books and the Internet are other sources of information.

► **VOCABULARY**
index
search engine

### Learn the Skill

**Step 1:** Decide on the topic you want to explore. Then list words or ideas that are related to your topic. These key words will help you find information.

Topic: The East

agriculture in the East
East's economy
Eastern farms
Eastern U.S. crops
New England farming
Mid-Atlantic agriculture

**Step 2:** Choose reference sources that might have the information you need. Encyclopedias have basic facts on many people, places, things, and events. Atlases have maps and geographical information. Almanacs give up-to-date facts. The Internet offers a wide variety of information. Ask a librarian to help you find Web sites you can trust.

**Step 3:** Use your key words or ideas to look up information in your sources. Many reference sources organize information alphabetically. Other sources have indexes. An **index** is an alphabetical listing of the topics in a book. To find information on the Internet, type key words into a computer **search engine.** A search engine is a Web site that finds other Web sites related to your key words.

temperature, 395
**United States**
  East
    agriculture, 692
    industry, 694
    minerals, 697
    population, 700
  Midwest
    agriculture, 840

New England farming    ↗ **Search**

**Search results for** *New England farming*

Showing 1–10 of 433,657

1. **New England Farming**
State and county yearly reports. Fruit, vegeta other crops, livestock, dairy. Total spending. Total income. Exports …

2. **New England Farms**
Complete list of farms in New England. Lists grown. Provides map of farm locations …

3. **New England Farmer's Association**
Support for farmers of New England. Non-pr organization …

**1** Which reference source do you think would be the most helpful in locating major cities in the East?

**2** Suppose you want to find the populations of the largest cities in the United States. Which reference source do you think would be the most helpful?

**3** Make a list of key words that would help you find information about the major industries of the East.

**4** Which reference source would you use to find basic facts about a topic?

## Apply the Skill

Write a short paragraph explaining the steps you would take to find information on mineral resources of the East.

# People of the East

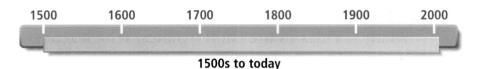

| 1500 | 1600 | 1700 | 1800 | 1900 | 2000 |

**1500s to today**

**Build on What You Know**  Suppose you want to build a fort. Your first step is to look around and see what materials are available. The first people to live in a region must also learn to use the available resources.

## First Peoples

**Main Idea**  Natural resources affected American Indian cultures in the East.

Many groups have helped shape the culture of the East. **Culture** is the way of life of a particular group of people. It includes the group's beliefs and values. Art, religion, language, customs, and history are all part of a group's culture.

American Indians have lived in the East for thousands of years. In the past, nations such as the Haudenosaunee (hoh deh noh SHAW nee) used the resources of the land to survive. They governed themselves and traded with other nations.

**VOCABULARY**

culture
constitution
slavery
industry
immigration

**Vocabulary Strategy**

immigration

**Im-** means into. The verb **migrate** means to move. **Immigration** is moving into another country.

**READING SKILL**
**Cause and Effect**  As you read, show the effects of the natural environment on American Indian cultures.

| Cause | Effect |
| --- | --- |
|  |  |

**Haudenosaunee Longhouse**  Longhouses were 200 to 300 feet long. Inside, each family had its own living area.

## Natural Resources and Culture

American Indian nations used natural resources differently. In the north, the growing season was short. So, nations such as the Micmac mostly hunted to get food. They moved often to follow the animals. In the winter, the Micmac hunted sea mammals and land animals. They also fished and collected plants and shellfish.

In the south, where the growing season was longer, the Lenni Lenape (LEHN-ee LEHN-uh-pee) grew both corn and tobacco. Families came together to fish and farm during the long summer growing season.

Families hunted separately in the winter. Large family groups lived together in longhouses. A chief and a council led each community. The rich natural resources of the region could support larger groups of people.

Today, American Indians in the East have a modern lifestyle. At the same time, they work to preserve their cultures. Some groups, such as the Wampanoag (wahm puh NOH ag) of Massachusetts, have their own governments.

**REVIEW** How did climate and natural resources affect American Indian cultures in the past?

**Two Language Groups**
Coastal nations in the East spoke Algonquian. Central woodland nations spoke the Iroquoian language.

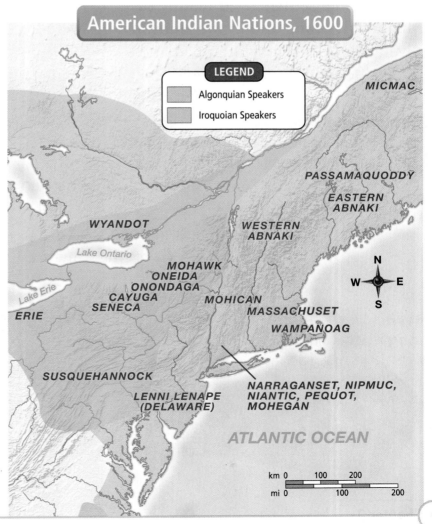

**American Indian Nations, 1600**

LEGEND
- Algonquian Speakers
- Iroquoian Speakers

MICMAC

PASSAMAQUODDY

EASTERN ABNAKI

WYANDOT

WESTERN ABNAKI

Lake Ontario

MOHAWK
ONEIDA
ONONDAGA
CAYUGA
SENECA

MOHICAN

Lake Erie

ERIE

MASSACHUSET

WAMPANOAG

N
W   E
S

SUSQUEHANNOCK

LENNI LENAPE (DELAWARE)

NARRAGANSET, NIPMUC, NIANTIC, PEQUOT, MOHEGAN

ATLANTIC OCEAN

km 0    100    200
mi 0        100        200

# Colonies and Traders

**Main Idea** European colonists settled the East and built a new nation.

By the 1500s, explorers from Europe reached North America. The first English colonists, or settlers, arrived in the East in the early 1600s. One group, the Pilgrims, came to Massachusetts in 1620. The Pilgrims were seeking a place to practice their religion freely. Another religious group, the Puritans, soon followed.

Around the same time, the Dutch and the French began to trade with American Indians. American Indians traded furs for pots, cloth, tools, and beads. Dutch settlers lived mainly on Manhattan Island and in the Hudson River valley. The French trapped and traded along the St. Lawrence River.

**Wampum Belt** Algonquian Indians made this belt from beads called wampum. Many Europeans traded wampum for furs.

## Conflict in the Colonies

The English colonies grew as more Europeans arrived. They built towns and started farms and businesses. Sometimes they fought with American Indians over land and resources. There were times of peace, but there were also some terrible wars. Finally, American Indians in the East were forced from most of their land.

By the mid-1700s, many colonists disliked English rule. War between the Americans and the English broke out in Massachusetts. It spread to the other colonies. In 1776, American leaders met in Philadelphia. They declared that the colonies should rule themselves. When the Revolutionary War ended, Americans were free to govern themselves.

**The Thirteen Colonies**

CANADA

Claimed by New York and New Hampshire

NEW HAMPSHIRE
NEW YORK
MASSACHUSETTS
PENNSYLVANIA
RHODE ISLAND
CONNECTICUT
NEW JERSEY
DELAWARE
VIRGINIA
MARYLAND
NORTH CAROLINA
SOUTH CAROLINA
GEORGIA

APPALACHIAN MOUNTAINS

L. Superior
L. Michigan
L. Huron
L. Ontario
L. Erie

ATLANTIC OCEAN

40°N
35°N

km 0   200   400
mi 0   200   400

80°W   75°W   70°W   65°W

**English Colonies** After the Revolutionary War, these colonies formed the new nation of the United States.

## A New Nation

As a new nation, the United States of America needed a new government. Leaders from all the states met to write a constitution. A **constitution** is a plan for creating and running a government. The new constitution was designed to keep Americans free from unfair rule. However, it did not secure freedom for everyone. For example, it left out women and American Indians.

The new constitution also left out hundreds of thousands of Africans who had been forced into slavery. **Slavery** is an unjust system in which one person owns another. Since the 1500s, Europeans had brought captives from Africa to North and South America.

Most enslaved Africans worked in the South. Until the late 1700s, slavery was legal in much of the East, too. Eastern ships traded goods for slaves. Some easterners grew rich from this trade.

Other easterners grew wealthy from the shipbuilding business. People used the tall, straight trees of the north to build whalers and sailing ships. Hunting whales also became a huge business. People wanted whale oil to use as lamp fuel.

**REVIEW** In what ways did the East change after Europeans arrived?

**Signing the Constitution** In 1787, American leaders met in Philadelphia to sign the new United States Constitution.

# Factories and Workers

**Main Idea** People from Europe and from rural areas came to cities to work in factories.

By the end of the 1700s, new inventions began to change life in the East. Before then, most people worked on farms or made things by hand. To get goods such as textiles, or woven cloth, Americans traded with England. This cloth was made in factories with large machines.

Then, in 1790, **Samuel Slater** built the first water-powered spinning machine in the United States. This machine made yarn from cotton. Other entrepreneurs soon built textile mills alongside rivers in the East.

Rhode Island and Pennsylvania had dozens of these mills. Machines could make yarn much faster and more cheaply than people working by hand.

In 1813, **Francis Cabot Lowell** brought the power loom to the East. A loom is a machine that weaves cloth. Lowell first saw the loom in an English textile mill. When he returned to Massachusetts, he built a loom with the same design. Now cotton could be spun into yarn and then woven into cloth in one big factory. Lowell hired young, unmarried women to work in his factories. Many of these women moved from farms to the growing mill towns to take these jobs.

**Water-powered Mill** Early textile factories used water power to run the machines.

Looms for weaving

Machines for spinning

Water wheel

River water

## The Growth of Industries

The growth of the textile industry led to more industries. An **industry** is a business that makes goods in factories. People built factories to make textile machines and other tools. These new industries needed even more labor. Workers moved from farms to cities. Eastern cities grew quickly.

By the late 1800s, millions of people had immigrated from Europe to the United States looking for factory jobs. **Immigration** is the movement of people from one nation to another. Many immigrants settled in the East. Immigrants from southern and eastern Europe wanted to escape war and poverty. They hoped to find better lives in America.

African Americans also worked in factories in the East. In 1865, slavery had become illegal in the United States.

Large numbers of African Americans left the South. Many moved to northern cities in the early 1900s. Like the European immigrants, they were looking for a better life.

**REVIEW** What caused many immigrants to come to the United States in the late 1800s?

## Lesson Summary

> 1500s—American Indians in the East hunted, farmed, and fished.

> 1600s–1700s—Europeans arrived in the East. English colonies grew into a new nation.

> 1800s—Growth in industries brought people to cities to work in factories.

## Why It Matters ...

England's colonies in the East grew into the United States of today.

## Lesson Review

1620 **Pilgrims settle in Massachusetts**

1776 **Colonies declare independence**

1813 **Lowell builds power loom**

1600　1700　1800　1900

① **VOCABULARY** Explain one way that **immigration** helped the growth of **industry** in the East.

② **READING SKILL** Name one **effect** Europeans had on American Indians.

③ **MAIN IDEA: Culture** Name two ways that American Indians used resources.

④ **MAIN IDEA: Technology** What led to the growth of big factories in the East?

⑤ **TIMELINE SKILL** In what year did the Pilgrims settle in Massachusetts?

⑥ **CRITICAL THINKING: Synthesize** What are two main reasons that people choose to move from one region to another?

**WRITING ACTIVITY** Find a folktale, myth, or legend from a culture in this lesson. Tell the story with your own words and pictures.

# An Algonquian Year

BY Michael McCurdy

**Long before white settlers arrived in North America, Algonquian Indians used the moon to mark the months of each year.** Each month's full moon had a special name that reflected the Algonquians' activities for that month. In March, they gathered sap from sugar maple trees. In September, they harvested food for the winter.

## Sap Moon • MARCH

Life seems to stir again in the northeastern lands. With great anticipation, the Algonquians wait for the sap to rise in the trees. While there is still snow on the ground, the women and children gather in their sugar camps to collect sap from several different kinds of trees, including box elder, walnut, hickory, birch, and black cherry. The sweetest sap of all, though, comes from the sugar maple.

There is a carnival-like atmosphere as the women use tomahawks to cut deep slashes in the bark of the maple trees. They then attach a twig or flat stick to each tree at the bottom of the slash, allowing the sap to drip slowly down the twig and into tightly made buckets of birch bark, which are carefully folded in such a way as to not lose a single drop of the sap. The prized liquid is then poured into hollowed-out logs, into which red-hot stones are dropped in order to bring the sap to a boil. More stones are added until most of the sap's water has turned into steam and disappeared, leaving behind a thick, sweet syrup. Indian children pour a little of the syrup on the snow, creating a kind of sugar candy.

According to legend, Algonquians learned to gather maple sap by watching gray squirrels gnaw the bark of maple trees and lick the juice that oozed from the tree. The Algonquian tribes will one day show the white settlers how to make maple syrup.

# Harvest Moon • SEPTEMBER

It is now harvest time for most of the northeastern Algonquian tribes. Any surplus of dried corn is stored snugly in baskets, to be placed within well-covered underground cellars lined with birch bark. The last of the ripened vegetables are hung up to dry, and meat is cut into thin strips and smoked. Fish is hung on racks over slow-burning, smoky fires.

The difficult and uncertain winter months lie ahead, and a return to winter quarters will come soon. Algonquians hold a celebration to give thanks to the spirits and to the Creator for a good harvest. But there is never enough stored food to meet the tribe's needs until spring. Hunters must prepare to track game during the coming winter. They spend time making arrowheads, sharpening stone spear blades, and repairing canoes and bows. Though times may become difficult, Algonquian families are always generous, sharing their food with anyone who comes by. They know that they, too, might someday be hungry and in need of another's generosity.

# Activities

1. **STEP INTO IT** Look closely at the picture on page 98. What Harvest Moon activities does the picture show?

2. **WRITE ABOUT IT** What are some similarities between how the Algonquians once lived and how we live today? Make a list of these things and share it with your classmates.

## Skillbuilder

# Make a Timeline

People often look at a timeline to find out when important events took place. A timeline shows events in the order in which they happened. Timelines are usually divided by years, decades, or centuries. A **decade** is a period of 10 years. A **century** is a period of 100 years. You can use a timeline to find out the amount of time between events.

▶ **VOCABULARY**
decade
century

## Learn the Skill

**Step 1:** Some timelines have titles. If there is a title, read it to find out the subject of the timeline.

**Step 2:** Look at the beginning date and the ending date to find out how much time the timeline covers.

**Step 3:** Look at the events described in the timeline. Read the dates on the timeline to find out when the events happened. Figure out how the events are related to each other.

### Major Events in the American Revolution

1775
**First shots of the war fired at Lexington and Concord**

1776
**Colonies declare independence**

1778
**France enters war on side of Americans**

1781
**Final battle of the war at Yorktown**

1774    1776    1778    1780    1782

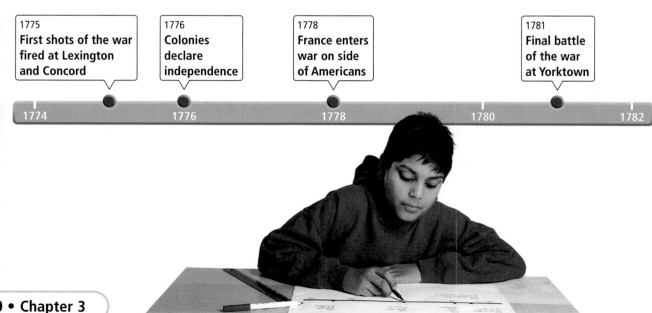

## Practice the Skill

Use the timeline on page 100 to answer the questions.

**1** What does the title tell you about the events in the timeline?

**2** How many years does the timeline cover?

**3** When did the fighting begin?

**4** How long after the start of the war did the colonies declare independence?

**5** Where did the final battle of the war take place, and when?

## Apply the Skill

Read the paragraph below. List the events and their dates in the order in which they happened. Then use your list to create a timeline.

> George Washington, the commander-in-chief of the Continental Army, was born in Virginia in 1732. He had his first military experience in 1754, during the French and Indian War. In 1775, he returned to the military to command the Continental Army. After the American victory at Yorktown, the Constitutional Convention elected Washington as first President of the republic in 1789. In 1792, six decades after his birth, Washington won reelection for a second term as President.

1700    1710    1720    1730    1740    1750    1760    1770    1780    1790    1800

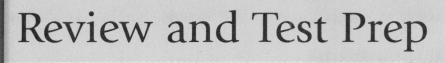

## Visual Summary

**1. – 3.** ✏️ Write a description of each item named below.

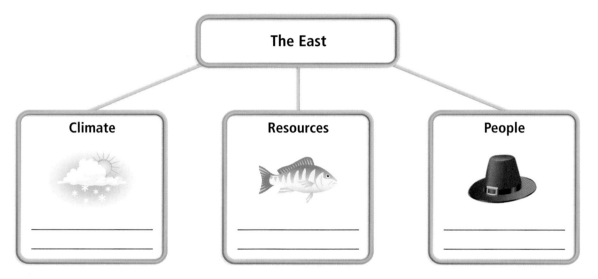

The East

Climate

Resources

People

_____
_____

_____
_____

_____
_____

## Facts and Main Ideas

✔️ **TEST PREP** Answer each question below.

4. **Geography** In what ways have glaciers affected landforms in the East?

5. **Economics** In a market economy, what decisions must a business owner make?

6. **Economics** In what ways do businesses get resources?

7. **Culture** Why did northern American Indian groups develop a different culture from groups that lived farther south?

8. **Technology** In the 1800s and early 1900s, why did many people move to cities in the East?

## Vocabulary

✔️ **TEST PREP** Choose the correct word from the list below to complete each sentence.

**bay,** p. 74
**profit,** p. 80
**culture,** p. 90

9. _____ is the money left over after a business pays its expenses.

10. A body of water protected by land but open to the sea is a _____.

11. The way of life of a group of people is their _____.

| 1620 **Pilgrims arrive in Massachusetts** | 1776 **Declaration of Independence** | 1790 **Samuel Slater's water-powered spinning machine** | 1813 **Francis Cabot Lowell's power loom** |

1600        1700                1800                1900

## Apply Skills

☑ **TEST PREP  Use Reference Materials** Use what you have learned about reference materials to answer each question.

12. Which source would be the most helpful in locating major rivers in the East?

   **A.** an atlas
   **B.** an encyclopedia
   **C.** an almanac
   **D.** the Internet

13. What would be the best way to find out whether a book titled *Indians of the Northeast* has information about the Lenni Lenape?

   **A.** Look up "Lenni Lenape" in the index.
   **B.** Read the book cover.
   **C.** Skim all of the pages.
   **D.** Look at all the pictures.

14. Which key word would be most helpful in finding information about early settlers in the East?

   **A.** East
   **B.** settlers
   **C.** Europe
   **D.** Pilgrims

## Critical Thinking

☑ **TEST PREP** Write a short paragraph to answer each question below.

15. **Cause and Effect** Why did many people in the East settle on the coast or near rivers?

16. **Infer** What might be a reason that Lowell hired young women to work in his factories?

## Timeline

Use the Chapter Summary Timeline above to answer each question.

17. In what year did the Pilgrims arrive in Massachusetts?

18. Was the power loom used before or after Slater's spinning machine?

# Activities

**Art Activity** Draw pictures of some of the natural resources of the East that show how people have used them.

**Writing Activity** Write a description of what a northern city in the early 1900s might have been like. Include what people came to cities for and from where they came. Tell what kind of work they might find.

**Technology**
**Writing Process Tips**
Get help with your writing at:
www.eduplace.com/kids/hmss/

## Chapter 4

# Living in the East

**Technology**

*e* • **glossary**
*e* • **word games**
www.eduplace.com/kids/hmss05/

## Vocabulary Preview

### manufacturing

**Manufacturing** is the process of making products, often with machines. Computer chips, tools, toys, and many kinds of food are manufactured in factories. **page 108**

### commuter

Most **commuters** travel to work by car, subway, bus, or train. Some travel by ferry, by bicycle, or even by plane. Commuting to work can take a long time each day. **page 108**

# Reading Strategy

**Question** As you read the lessons in this chapter, ask yourself questions to check your understanding.

Ask yourself what you want to know more about. After you read, go back to find the answer.

## judicial branch

The **judicial branch** is the part of government relating to the law and the courts. Lawyers and judges are part of the judicial branch. **page 116**

## governor

Each state in the United States has a **governor.** The governor has the power to put laws into action. **page 116**

## What's Special About
# New England

### VOCABULARY

**suburb**
**university**
**manufacturing**
**commuter**

**Vocabulary Strategy**

university

Find the word **universe** in **university.** The universe includes all things. A **university** is a school that teaches all or many subjects.

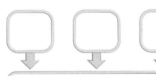
### READING SKILL
**Draw Conclusions**
Chart facts that lead to the conclusion below.

Conclusion: New England is a region of diversity.

**Build on What You Know** Think about the region in which you live. What would a visitor notice? Your region has things that make it unique or special. New England also has many unique features.

## Where People Live

**Main Idea** The Puritans helped make Boston an important economic center. They also built many schools and churches.

Six states in the East form the region called New England. These states are Connecticut, Maine, Massachusetts, New Hampshire, Rhode Island, and Vermont. Captain **John Smith** mapped this region in 1614. He gave New England its name.

Boston is the capital of Massachusetts. It is the largest city in New England. Boston's first settlers helped make the city an important shipping center.

Shipping is no longer a major industry in Boston. Today, the city is the financial and trading center of New England. Banking, insurance, and other business services support the economy.

**Boston** Many businesses today are located along Boston Harbor.

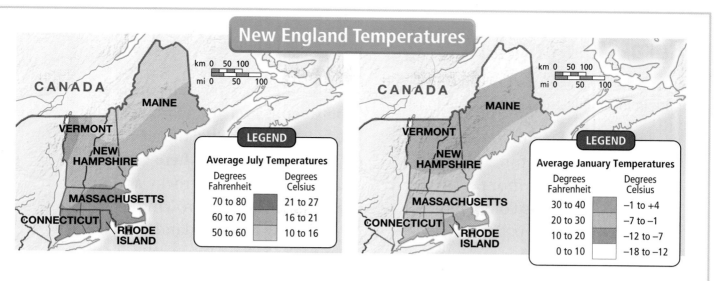

**New England Temperatures**

LEGEND

**Average July Temperatures**

| Degrees Fahrenheit | Degrees Celsius |
|---|---|
| 70 to 80 | 21 to 27 |
| 60 to 70 | 16 to 21 |
| 50 to 60 | 10 to 16 |

LEGEND

**Average January Temperatures**

| Degrees Fahrenheit | | Degrees Celsius |
|---|---|---|
| 30 to 40 | | −1 to +4 |
| 20 to 30 | | −7 to −1 |
| 10 to 20 | | −12 to −7 |
| 0 to 10 | | −18 to −12 |

**New England Climate** New England has warm summers and cool winters.

**SKILL** **Reading Maps** Which New England state has the coldest winters?

## Boston and Beyond

Boston's people have come from many places, including Europe, Africa, Asia, and Latin America. Many immigrants from Ireland started coming to Boston in the mid-1800s. In the late 1800s, many people from Italy settled in Boston. African Americans have lived in Boston since colonial times, but many more moved there from the South after World War I.

Beginning in the 1950s, thousands of people moved from Boston to its suburbs. A **suburb** is a community that grows up outside of a city. Many businesses also moved to the suburbs. Today, factories around Boston make many goods, including high technology products. Publishing and printing are important industries, too. Some people in the suburbs take cars, buses, and trains to work in Boston. Many ride the subway, or underground train.

## Schools and Churches

The Puritans who settled Boston developed strong social institutions, including schools and churches. A social institution is an organization that helps the public. In 1635, Puritans built the first free school in America. A year later, they built Harvard, the first American college. Harvard later became a university. A **university** is a school with several colleges that each focus on one area of study.

Religion was the most important subject in Puritan schools and colleges. Young children studied a book called the *New England Primer*. It taught the alphabet with rhymes and religious sayings. Today, New England has hundreds of colleges and universities. It also has many churches, synagogues, mosques, and other places of worship.

**REVIEW** What kinds of social institutions did the Puritans build?

# Rural New England

**Main Idea** Many rural New Englanders farm, work in local industries, or commute to cities.

Rural New England includes areas north or west of Boston, mostly in New Hampshire, Vermont, and Maine. This rugged land has cold winters. Rural New Englanders live mostly in valleys and lowlands.

## Life in Rural New England

Rural life often means farming. However, most people in rural New England are not farmers. Instead, many work in service industries, such as tourism. Some work in manufacturing.

**Manufacturing** is making goods from other materials. Many workers are commuters. A **commuter** travels between home and work each day.

Rural New England does have farms, but farming there can be difficult. The soil is rocky and not always fertile. The growing season is short. Few New Englanders make a living on farms. Those who do often produce one crop, such as blueberries or potatoes, or raise dairy cows.

Life on a dairy farm takes hard work. A typical day begins at 5:00 A.M. and does not end until 8:00 P.M. Farmers must milk and feed the cows each day and clean the stalls. In the summer, they must also tend their crops.

**Cost of Living** Living in a city usually costs more than living in a rural area, like the Vermont farm shown below.

**SKILL** **Reading Graphs** What costs about the same in both rural and urban New England?

### Average Prices in New England

| Urban Areas | Rural Areas |
|---|---|
| ADMIT ONE Movie Ticket $9 | ADMIT ONE Movie Ticket $8 |
| $20 | $10 |
| $240,000 | $57,500 |

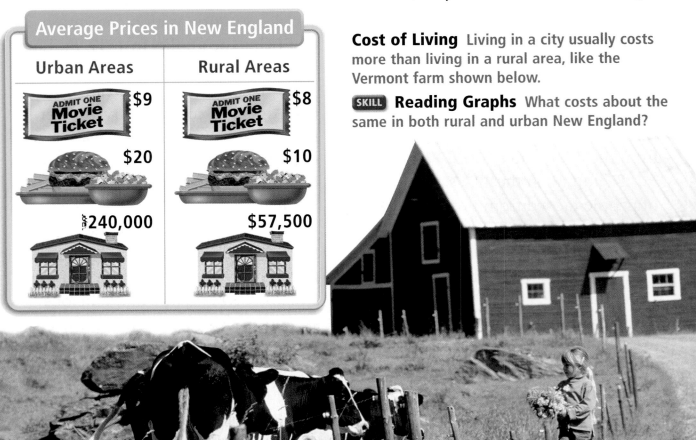

## Vacationing in New England

New England has much to offer visitors. History lovers can walk Boston's Freedom Trail or visit colonial villages. People can ski on mountains in the winter and relax on sandy beaches in the summer. New England is also popular in the fall, when trees blaze with color.

Many festivals celebrate New England culture. New Hampshire holds a Dog Sled Derby in winter. Vermont has a Maple Festival in April. Maine offers a Lobster Festival in August. In New England, you can find a festival during every season.

**REVIEW** In what ways do rural New Englanders make a living?

Seafood dishes, such as lobster and clam chowder, are New England specialties.

## Lesson Summary

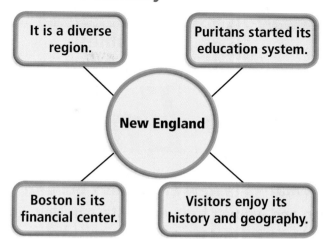

It is a diverse region.

Puritans started its education system.

**New England**

Boston is its financial center.

Visitors enjoy its history and geography.

## Why It Matters ...

New England's history and social institutions helped shape its culture.

## Lesson Review

❶ **VOCABULARY** Choose the word that best completes the sentence.
**suburb    manufacturing    university**

People who work in a city and live in a _____ must commute to work.

❷ 🕑 **READING SKILL** Name two facts about New England and tell how they help you **draw the conclusion** that the region offers a variety of things to do.

❸ **MAIN IDEA: Culture** Name two contributions the Puritans made to New England life.

❹ **MAIN IDEA: Geography** In what ways has New England's geography affected farming in the region?

❺ **FACTS TO KNOW** What are the six New England states?

❻ **CRITICAL THINKING: Compare and Contrast** In what ways is rural life different from city life in New England?

✏️ **WRITING ACTIVITY** Write a letter to a friend describing what you might see on a trip to New England. Include a picture with your letter.

# New Englanders

**What have New Englanders done for our country?**
Men and women from every state in New England have
worked hard and made a difference.

## Noah **Webster** 1758–1843

After the American Revolution, children in the
United States still learned to read and spell
using books from England. Noah Webster
believed that the new country should have its
own textbooks written in American English.
He decided to write spelling, grammar,
and reading books for American schools.
Webster also wrote the first American
dictionary. It took him 27 years to finish
*An American Dictionary of the English
Language.* The book had 70,000 entries.
Webster included American words
that had never been in a dictionary
before, such as *skunk* and *chowder*.

While working on his dictionary,
Webster learned 26 languages so he
could explain where the words in our
language came from.

# Madeleine **Kunin**

Throughout her life, Madeleine Kunin (KYOO nin) has served the people of the United States. She started as a state representative in Vermont. In 1985, she became the first woman governor of Vermont. She worked hard to improve schools and protect the environment. In 1993, Kunin was chosen by President Clinton to be Deputy Secretary of Education. From 1996 to 1999, she served as U.S. Ambassador to Switzerland.

# An **Wang** 1920–1990

An Wang was an inventor. He was born in China and came to the United States when he was 25 years old. He studied at Harvard **University**. In 1951, he set up his own company, Wang Laboratories. Because he was a creative inventor and a good businessman, Wang Laboratories was very successful. By the late 1970s, the company was a leader in desktop computers. An Wang became a wealthy man. He used his money to help others. Wang donated large sums to support education and other causes.

## Activities

1. **TALK ABOUT IT** Discuss how each of these three people showed **patriotism** in his or her work.

2. **LOOK IT UP** Use a dictionary to find five English words that come from other languages. Challenge your friends to guess where they came from.

**Technology** Read more biographies at Education Place. www.eduplace.com/kids/hmss05/

## Skillbuilder

# Read a Circle Graph

▶ **VOCABULARY**
circle graph

A **circle graph** is a circle that is divided into sections to show how information is related. Circle graphs are sometimes called pie charts. Circle graphs can help you see how the whole of something is broken up into different parts. For example, a circle graph can show you how a state's population is made up of different groups. It also lets you see how these groups compare to each other.

## Learn the Skill

**Step 1:** Read the title to find out what information the graph presents. This graph gives information about jobs in Rhode Island. The whole circle represents the total number of jobs.

Jobs in Rhode Island

**Step 2:** Read the labels for each section of the circle. Each section of this graph represents people who work in a certain kind of job.

Buying and selling products

**Step 3:** Compare the sizes of the different sections. In this graph, a larger section means that more people work in that kind of job. A smaller section means that fewer people work in that kind of job.

Banking/Insurance

Making products

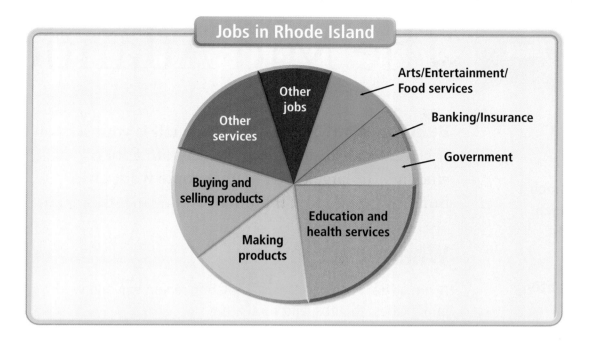

Jobs in Rhode Island

- Other jobs
- Other services
- Buying and selling products
- Making products
- Education and health services
- Arts/Entertainment/Food services
- Banking/Insurance
- Government

## Practice the Skill

Use the circle graph to answer the questions.

1. List the jobs in Rhode Island.
2. Which job category has the most workers?
3. Which job category has the fewest workers?
4. Do more Rhode Islanders make products or provide arts, entertainment, and food services?

## Apply the Skill

Create a circle graph to show how you spend your time during a typical school day. First draw a circle that stands for the 24 hours in a whole day. Then divide it into sections to show all of your activities and the time you spend on them.

**Grand Central Terminal**
More than 150,000 commuters use this train station in New York each day.

# What's Special About
# The Mid-Atlantic

**Build on What You Know** How tall is your school? If it were 100 stories tall, it would hold a lot of students! In large cities, many people work in buildings even taller than that.

## Where People Live

**Main Idea** People in the Mid-Atlantic region live and work in big cities, suburbs, and rural areas.

The Mid-Atlantic region contains Delaware, Maryland, New Jersey, New York, Pennsylvania, and the nation's capital, Washington, D.C. It is the most thickly settled region in the nation. Many major cities are found in the Mid-Atlantic. One is New York City, the largest city in the United States.

New York's location at the mouth of the Hudson River led to its growth. European settlers used the river and New York's harbor to move goods from inland North America to Europe. Shipping led to the growth of trade. Today, New York is a world center for banking, publishing, advertising, and technology.

## Living in New York City

New York City started on an island called Manhattan. As the city grew, people settled in four new neighborhoods—Queens, Staten Island, the Bronx, and Brooklyn. Today, skyscrapers fill Manhattan. A **skyscraper** is a very tall building.

New York is filled with people from around the world. More than eight million people live in the city. Millions of others visit each year. They come to shop, to go to museums, and to attend plays. Most people rely on subways, buses, or taxis to move around this crowded city.

## Suburbs of the Mid-Atlantic

Suburbs surround the major cities of the Mid-Atlantic region. People began to move from cities to the suburbs in the 1800s. They wanted to find less crowded places to live.

Some people commute from their homes in the suburbs to jobs in the city. Others work in businesses near their homes. People in suburbs often drive their cars to work, to schools, and to shopping malls.

**REVIEW** Why was New York's location important to its growth?

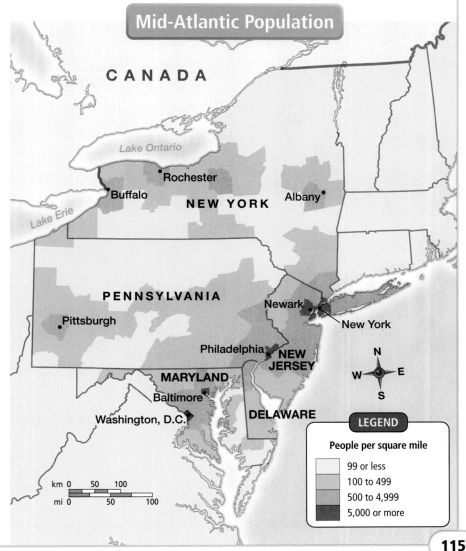

**Mid-Atlantic Population**

**Mid-Atlantic Population**
The coastal plain of the Mid-Atlantic region is the most populated.

LEGEND

People per square mile

99 or less
100 to 499
500 to 4,999
5,000 or more

## Rural Areas

Although urban and suburban areas cover much of the Mid-Atlantic, forest and farmland fill large areas, too. The soil here is much easier to farm than it is in New England. Mid-Atlantic farms produce flowers, chickens, and many dairy products. Mines in Pennsylvania rank fourth in producing the most coal in the United States.

The natural environment and historic landmarks draw millions of visitors to the Mid-Atlantic states. They enjoy winter sports in the mountains of New York and Pennsylvania. They sunbathe on Delaware and New Jersey beaches. They boat and fish in the Chesapeake Bay. Many visitors also tour our nation's capital.

# State Governments

**Main Idea** State government is divided into three branches.

Each state has a capital city where the state government is located. Within the state capital is a state house or a building called the capitol. This is where lawmakers, or legislators, meet.

Each state has a constitution. The constitution divides state government into three parts, or branches. These are the legislative, executive, and judicial branches. The **legislative branch** makes laws. The **executive branch** puts the laws into action. The **judicial branch** interprets, or explains, the laws in the courts.

Suppose the legislative branch of the New Jersey government made a law that provided money for new parks. The governor would sign the law to put it into action. The **governor** is the official who leads the executive branch. If people disagreed about the law, the judicial branch would have to decide exactly what the law meant.

**Annapolis, Maryland** Maryland's capitol is the oldest still in use. It was built in 1772.

**SKILL** **Reading Charts** Which people in Maryland's government are not elected?

## Maryland State Government

| Executive | Legislative | Judicial |
|---|---|---|
| **Governor** <br> • Elected by the voters <br> • Serves a 4-year term | **Senators, Delegates** <br> • Elected by the voters <br> • Serve 4-year terms | **Judges** <br> • Some elected by voters <br> • Some appointed to 10-year terms |

## Public and Private Services

State governments are public institutions. That means they serve the state's people and communities. State services for the public include education, fire and police protection, and highways. States pay for public services by collecting taxes. A tax is a fee paid to the government. States may tax the money people earn, the property they own, and the things they buy.

State services are public. Services provided by a group or individual are private. For example, New Jersey builds public roads for everyone to use. However, private companies sell the cars and trucks that travel on the roads.

**REVIEW** What are the three branches of state government, and what do they do?

## Lesson Summary

- The Mid-Atlantic has many large cities surrounded by suburbs.
- New York City, a financial and industrial center, is the biggest city in this region.
- Rural regions of the Mid-Atlantic support farming, mining, and tourism.
- State governments divide power among three branches.

## Why It Matters ...

Millions of people live and work in the Mid-Atlantic region. Workers in this region provide goods and services to the entire nation and the world.

## Lesson Review

**1 VOCABULARY** Match each vocabulary term with its description.

**executive branch**
**legislative branch**     **judicial branch**

(a) makes laws; (b) explains laws in court; (c) puts laws into action

**2 ☝ READING SKILL Compare and contrast** public and private services.

**3 MAIN IDEA: Culture** In what ways is living in a city different from living in a rural area?

**4 MAIN IDEA: Geography** What is one difference between a capital city and other cities?

**5 FACTS TO KNOW** Which branch of government does the governor lead?

**6 CRITICAL THINKING: Infer** Why do you think people from so many countries live in New York City?

**HANDS ON** **CURRENT EVENTS ACTIVITY** Read about what is happening in one Mid-Atlantic state. What is one major issue the state's government is dealing with?

# Washington, D.C.

Just as each state has a capital, our nation has one, too. Washington, D.C., is the capital of the United States. It was built in the 1790s and named after President George Washington.

Like state governments, the national government has three branches. Each branch has a specific job to do. Each branch also has the power to check, or limit, the work of the other branches. This is to help prevent any person or group from having too much power.

The top officials in each branch work in special buildings. Locate these buildings on the map.

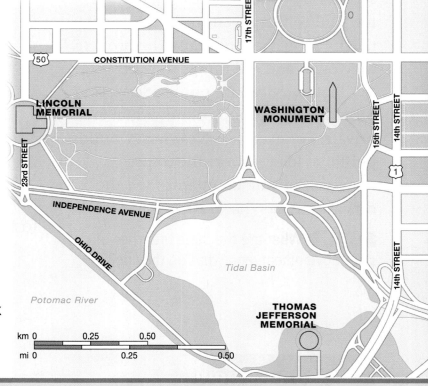

## ❶ White House

The President of the United States lives and works in the White House. The President heads the **executive branch,** which puts laws into action.

## ❷ United States Capitol

U.S. Representatives and Senators do their work in the Capitol. The House of Representatives and the Senate are the **legislative branch,** which writes and passes laws.

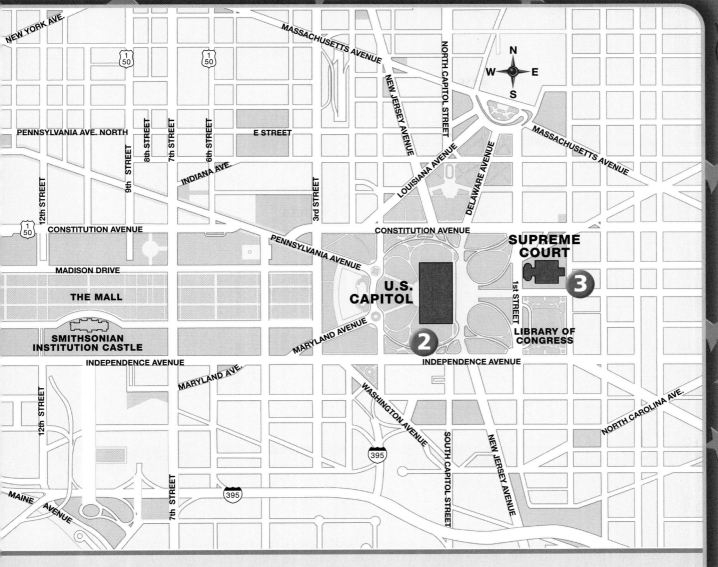

**③ Supreme Court**

The Supreme Court heads the **judicial branch** and meets in the Supreme Court building. The Supreme Court makes sure that laws agree with the U.S. Constitution.

# Activities

1. **TALK ABOUT IT** If you went to Washington, D.C., which place would you visit first? Discuss why you would like to go to this place.

2. **ACT IT OUT** Create a skit about lawmaking. One or two students can play each branch of government. Show how the branches work together to make a law and decide whether it is fair.

## Visual Summary

1. – 4.  Write a description of each item named below.

Boston

_____
_____
_____

New York City

_____
_____
_____

Suburbs

_____
_____
_____

Three branches of
state government

_____
_____
_____

## Facts and Main Ideas

✔ **TEST PREP** Answer each question below.

5. **Geography** Which six states make up New England?

6. **Culture** What social institutions did the Puritans develop?

7. **Economics** Which industries have replaced shipping in Boston's economy?

8. **Government** What happens if someone challenges or disagrees with a state law?

9. **Economics** What are taxes paid to the government used for?

## Vocabulary

✔ **TEST PREP** Choose the correct word from the list below to complete each sentence.

**manufacturing,** p. 108
**commuter,** p. 108
**governor,** p. 116

10. When the _____ of a state signs a law, the law is put into action.

11. People who work in _____ make goods from other materials.

12. A _____ travels between home and work each day.

## Apply Skills

✔️ **TEST PREP  Read a Circle Graph**
Study the circle graph below. Then use your graph skills to answer each question.

**Mid-Atlantic State Populations**

Total Population: 45,751,947

13. In which Mid-Atlantic state do the most people live?

   A. Pennsylvania
   B. Maryland
   C. New Jersey
   D. New York

14. Which two Mid-Atlantic states have the lowest population?

   A. Maryland and Delaware
   B. Pennsylvania and Maryland
   C. Delaware and New Jersey
   D. New York and Pennsylvania

## Critical Thinking

✔️ **TEST PREP**  Write a short paragraph to answer each question below. Use details to support your response.

15. **Compare and Contrast**  Compare farming in New England with farming in the Mid-Atlantic states.

16. **Draw Conclusions**  In what way did the growth of eastern suburbs affect the big cities?

# Activities

**Research Activity**  Use library or Internet resources to find out more about the *New England Primer* used in Puritan schools. Write a paragraph contrasting the primer with a textbook you use today.

HANDS ON

**Writing Activity**  Write a personal essay telling whether you prefer living in the city or the suburbs. Give reasons to support your opinion.

**Technology**
**Writing Process Tips**
Get help with your essay at:
www.eduplace.com/kids/hmss05/

# My State Handbook
## GOVERNMENT

## Government Where You Live

In the United States, government is meant to protect people's rights. Leaders in your state's government help make the rules and laws for your state. Who are your state leaders? What does your state do to help citizens and protect the environment? Your state's government affects your life every day.

**My State's Government**

| Executive branch | Legislative branch | Judicial branch |

Most states have a capitol building. This is the capitol building in Sacramento, California.

**Find Out!**

## Explore your state's government.

✅ **Start with your state government website.**
Who is the governor? Which officials are elected or appointed?

✅ **Read your local newspaper.**
Use the index on the first page to find articles or editorials telling about state laws or special state projects.

✅ **Visit or call a local representative.**
Find out what his or her responsibilities are.

✅ **Check the phone book.**
Look up the listings for your state government to find out what kind of services the state provides.

Use your state handbook to keep track of the information you find.

# Review and Test Prep

## Vocabulary and Main Ideas

✓ **TEST PREP** Write a sentence to answer each question.

1. What are some of the features of a **coastal plain?**

2. Why did people build settlements near harbors and **bays?**

3. What is the difference between a **market economy** and a command economy?

4. Name one effect that **slavery** had on the East.

5. Why do more people in rural New England work in **manufacturing** than in farming?

6. What branch of government includes the **governor?**

## Critical Thinking

✓ **TEST PREP** Write a short paragraph to answer each question.

7. **Cause and Effect** What are some natural resources of the East? How do they help determine the jobs that people do?

8. **Compare** In what ways are New York City and Boston similar?

## Apply Skills

✓ **TEST PREP** Use the timeline below and what you have learned about timelines to answer each question.

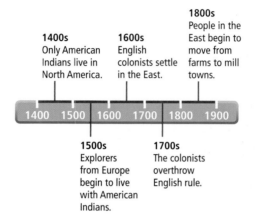

**1400s** Only American Indians live in North America.

**1600s** English colonists settle in the East.

**1800s** People in the East begin to move from farms to mill towns.

**1500s** Explorers from Europe begin to live with American Indians.

**1700s** The colonists overthrow English rule.

9. When did life in America begin to change for American Indians?

   **A.** in the 1800s
   **B.** in the 1700s
   **C.** in the 1600s
   **D.** in the 1500s

10. About how long after English colonists settled in the East did people begin to move to mill towns?

   **A.** 400 years
   **B.** 300 years
   **C.** 200 years
   **D.** 100 years

## Unit Activity

### Make a State Government Poster

- Make a chart of the three branches of your state government. List the name of the governor and other top officials.

- Find out when and where the state legislature meets and what law they are planning to vote on. Add the information to your poster.

- Write a sentence stating how you think they should vote on the issue.

- Present your poster to the class.

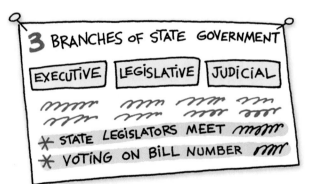

## At the Library

**You may find this book at your school or public library.**

*Capital*

by Lynn Curlee

This history of Washington, D.C., provides information on the National Mall.

## CURRENT EVENTS
## WEEKLY (WR) READER

### Current Events Project

**Create a bulletin board about the freedoms that people in the United States have.**

- Find information about the Constitution and the Bill of Rights.

- Pick one of the ten amendments. Think about how it keeps Americans free today.

- Write a paragraph about your amendment. Include drawings of people using their freedom.

- Post your paragraph on a bulletin board.

 **Technology**
Weekly Reader online offers social studies articles. Go to:
**www.eduplace.com/kids/hmss/**

## Read About It

**Look in your classroom for these Social Studies Independent Books.**

# UNIT 3

# The South

**The Big Idea**

## What makes our American culture special?

"*America is not anything if it consists of each of us. It is something only if it consists of all of us.*"

—Woodrow Wilson, 1916
28th President of the United States

# Almanac

## Land Use in the United States

ARCTIC OCEAN

170°W
70°N

RUSSIA

km 0    300
mi 0    300

AK    CANADA

60°N

PACIFIC OCEAN

150°W    140°W

40°N

PACIFIC OCEAN

30°N

130°W

km 0   50   100
mi 0   50   100

160°W

HI    155°W

20°N

PACIFIC OCEAN   Hawaii

120°W

WA

OR

MT

ID

WY

ND

MN

SD

NE

Great Salt Lake

UT

NV

CA

Colorado River

CO

Arkansas River

KS

AZ

NM

OK

TX

Rio Grande

110°W

km 0   150   300
mi 0   150   300

MEXICO

Missouri River

## Unit Preview

### Mangrove Tree

Plants and animals have adapted to Florida's swamps
**Chapter 5, page 135**

### TVA Dam

Many southerners get their electricity from dams
**Chapter 5, page 142**

### Sit-In

African Americans gained civil rights
**Chapter 5, page 152**

## LEGEND

| | | | |
|---|---|---|---|
| 🐟 | Fishing | | Farming |
| ⚒ | Mining | | Forestry |
| — | Regional boundary | | Hunting |
| ■ | Manufacturing and trade | | Raising livestock |
| | | | Little activity |

CANADA

L. Superior
L. Michigan
L. Huron
L. Ontario
L. Erie

WI
MI
NY
VT
ME
NH
MA
RI
CT
NJ
DE
MD
PA
OH
IN
IL
WV
VA
KY
NC
TN
SC
AR
MS
AL
GA
LA
FL

Ohio River
Mississippi River

50°N
60°W
40°N
30°N
70°W
80°W
90°W

N NE
NW E
W SE
SW S

ATLANTIC OCEAN

Gulf of Mexico

**Texas Cattle**
Ranching is a major industry in Texas
**Chapter 6, page 172**

**Connect to**

# The Nation

## Southern Agriculture

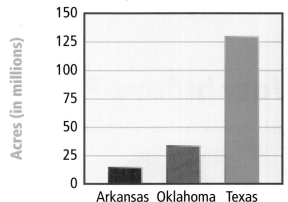

Acres (in millions)

150
125
100
75
50
25
0

Arkansas  Oklahoma  Texas

These three states have the most farmland in the South.

## U.S. Agriculture

There are more than 940 million acres of farmland in the United States. How many acres of farmland are there in your state?

CURRENT EVENTS

**WEEKLY (WR) READER**

Current events on the web!

Read social studies articles about current events at:
**www.eduplace.com/kids/hmss/**

## Vocabulary Preview

**Technology**

e • glossary
e • word games
www.eduplace.com/kids/hmss05/

### producer

A **producer** uses workers, resources, and equipment to make products. For example, a farmer uses seeds, soil, and tractors to raise corn. **page 143**

### consumer

A **consumer** buys and uses products made by a producer. If the product is peanut butter, the consumer will probably eat it! **page 143**

## Chapter Timeline

1607
**English colony at Jamestown**

1500          1600                    1700

# Reading Strategy

**Monitor and Clarify** Use this strategy to check your understanding of the events in this chapter.

**Quick Tip** Stop to check that you understand what you are reading. Reread, if you have to.

## opportunity cost

The **opportunity cost** of any choice is the item you did not choose. For example, if you choose to spend your money on a game, the opportunity cost is the book or toy you did not buy. **page 145**

## civil rights

During the **civil rights** protests of the 1950s and 1960s, African Americans demanded their legal rights as U.S. citizens. Other groups such as women and Latinos also worked to gain equality. **page 152**

1865
**End of Civil War**

1955
**Montgomery bus boycott**

1800        1900        2000

# Land and Climate

## VOCABULARY

peninsula
interior
delta
adapt

**Vocabulary Strategy**

interior

**Interior** is a synonym for inland. Both words describe a place that is away from a coast or border.

## READING SKILL
**Compare and Contrast**
As you read, use a chart to show how the Upper South and the Lower South are alike and different.

Upper South    Lower South

**Build on What You Know** What does the land look like where you live? Does it have many different landforms? The South has a little bit of everything, from rugged mountains to low, swampy wetlands.

## Land and Water of the South

**Main Idea** The South has many different landforms and waterways, including mountains, plains, rivers, and wetlands.

Fourteen states make up the South. This region can be divided into two smaller regions—the Upper South and the Lower South.

The South has many kinds of landforms. For example, the Upper South has many plateaus, hills, and valleys. Plateaus are high, flat areas. They can be found in Arkansas, Virginia, and West Virginia. Kentucky, Virginia, and Tennessee have rolling hills and rich river valleys.

Both the Upper South and the Lower South have low coastal plains and wetlands. Parts of Florida, Alabama, Mississippi, and Louisiana are at sea level. These lowland states have beaches, swamps, and marshes. Many rivers also flow through the South.

Wetlands in the South support wildlife, including alligators.

**The South** Waterways are a central feature of this region.

**SKILL** **Reading Maps** Which rivers form state borders?

## Coastal Plains and Highlands

The South's coastline is formed by the Gulf and Atlantic coastal plains. These coastal plains are lowlands. The Gulf coastal plain stretches from the mouth of the Rio Grande in Texas to the tip of the Florida peninsula in the Gulf of Mexico. A **peninsula** is a piece of land surrounded by water on three sides. The Atlantic coastal plain extends from Florida along the Atlantic Ocean to Virginia.

The Appalachians and the Ozark Plateau are the highest landforms in the South. These highlands are in the interior. An **interior** place is away from a coast or border.

## Wetlands and Water

The South's largest river—the Mississippi—fans out into a huge delta at the Gulf of Mexico. A **delta** is a triangle-shaped area at the mouth of a river. The river brings rich soil to the delta. Swamps and marshes are other wetlands. Wetlands, like the Everglades in Florida, have water on or near the surface of the soil.

Water affects where people live. Big cities have grown near coasts and rivers because people use water to travel and to move goods.

**REVIEW** In what ways is the Gulf coastal plain different from the Ozark Plateau?

# Climate and Wildlife

**Main Idea** The climate of the South is warm, but it varies across the region.

The South tends to be warmer and moister than northern regions. In winter, many people visit the South to avoid cold northern temperatures.

The South has more than one climate. Factors that control climate are latitude, elevation, and closeness to water. Because the South is quite close to the equator, its climate is warmer than regions farther away from the equator. The southern latitude also results in a longer growing season than regions farther north. Farmers in coastal regions of the South can grow crops for most of the year.

## Seasons and Severe Weather

Coastal areas of the South are usually warm. The ocean helps keep the air temperature steady. Winter is mild in the lowlands of the Mississippi Delta. Summer, however, is hot and humid. Humid means moist, or having a lot of water vapor in the air.

At higher elevations, winter is not as warm as in the coastal plains. The Ozark highlands can have severe weather. Frequent tornadoes strike in Texas, Oklahoma, and Florida.

The South has many tropical storms that can cause heavy flooding and other damage. Most start in the Atlantic Ocean. Some grow into hurricanes. Between 1900 and 1996, Texas had 36 hurricanes. Florida had 57.

**Hurricane Damage** Hurricanes bring strong winds, heavy rain, and large ocean waves. When these tropical storms hit land, they can cause damage to buildings, trees, and anything else in their path.

## Plants and Animals

Plants and animals have adapted to the climate in the South. To **adapt** means to change in order to better fit the environment. For example, mangrove trees have adapted over the centuries to survive in salty Florida swamps. They've developed broad roots that arch above the muddy soil. These roots work like snorkels. They help provide oxygen to the tree as water levels rise and fall.

Animals adapt to life in their environment, too. Some sea turtles have adapted and survived since the time of the dinosaurs. These turtles nest on beaches. The females bury their eggs in the sand. The turtles have learned to dig nests above the reach of high tides to protect their eggs.

**REVIEW** Why does the South have such a variety of climates?

**Mangrove Tree** Several root systems can support one mangrove tree.

## Lesson Summary

The South has a long coastline and many rivers. Most people live on the coastal plains. The warm climate gives the South a long growing season. Plants and animals have adapted to the environment and the climate.

## Why It Matters . . .

The warm climate and rich natural resources have allowed people to build a successful economy in the South.

---

## Lesson Review

❶ **VOCABULARY** Choose the best word to fill in the blank:
**delta   interior   peninsula**

Florida is a(n) _____.

❷ **READING SKILL** In what ways does the climate of the South **contrast** with the climate of northern regions?

❸ **MAIN IDEA: Geography** Describe one major landform and one kind of waterway found in the South.

❹ **MAIN IDEA: Geography** In what ways can the climate of the South make life difficult at times?

❺ **CRITICAL THINKING: Analyze** What might people do to adapt to the climate of the South?

**HANDS ON** **MAP MAKING** Draw a map of the South. Outline all the states. Then use a color to show where the coastal plain is.

# Storm Warriors

**by Elisa Carbone**

**Hurricanes have caused many shipwrecks along the Atlantic coast.** In the 1890s, brave surfmen worked on the islands of North Carolina's Outer Banks. They kept watch along the beach. They used heavy surfboats to rescue sailors in trouble. The crew of the Pea Island Life-Saving Station were known as "storm warriors." They were led by Keeper Richard Etheridge. In this story, young Nathan learns first-hand what a hurricane is like.

The storm threw sand and rain against the shutters like handfuls of pebbles. With each gust the station shivered and swayed, and the surf, already crashing over the boat ramp, rumbled in my ears like thunder.

Mr. Etheridge canceled the evening and night patrols. There was no beach left to patrol, only rolling ocean from sea side to sound side. The lookout deck patrol would have to be enough, he said.

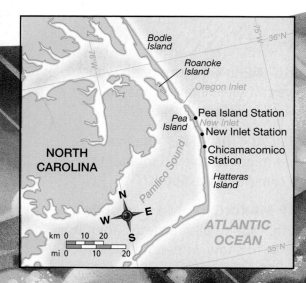

We opened cans of peaches for supper. No one wanted to venture through the waves to the cookhouse. As we sat eating, a loud pounding sounded on the double doors at the end of the station. I looked up. Who would be out in this raging storm?

There was a frozen moment as the surfmen looked at each other and waited. The pounding came again, water splashed in between the doors, and in an instant everyone was on their feet. "Take life preservers!" Mr. Etheridge shouted.

"Hoist the chairs!" someone else cried, and "Get those doors *open*!"

Men threw chairs onto the table, Mr. Bowser strapped a cork life jacket onto my chest, and the ocean exploded into the room. Waves of seawater rushed past my legs. A stray chair slammed against my shin, knocked me down, and I swallowed a huge gulp of salt water.

"Take the boy upstairs!" Mr. Bowser yelled.

Daddy yanked my arm and dragged me to my feet. I was coughing and spitting out salt. As he pushed me up the steps, I looked back. Another wave rolled in through the open back doors of the station house and out the open front doors. The men scurried to gather floating debris: firewood, the bellows, a footstool. They threw it all onto the "higher ground" of the table, Beaver stove, and bookshelves.

Upstairs in the dormer, Daddy slapped me on the back to help me stop choking. "You going to be all right up here?" he asked.

I nodded. He left to go help the surfmen, and I plopped down on a wooden trunk. Even though the night was warm, I shivered in my clammy clothes. I looked out the tiny porthole window at the dark, tangled sea. Lines of foam crisscrossed it in a confused jumble. And downstairs, high tide rumbled through the dining hall as if the station had been built not on dry land but in the belly of the sea itself.

The tide receded, and when the last wave had rolled through the station house, the front and back doors were finally shut against the buffeting wind and rain. I ventured back downstairs. Sand, seaweed, and shells littered the floor, and the table and other high surfaces were cluttered with everything from dishes and chairs to a white ceramic spittoon.

"I'm not sweeping until I'm sure the last of those waves has hit that door," said Mr. Wescott.

As if summoned, a rogue wave gave a rap against the back doors, squirting in more salt water. "You see?" he said, raising both eyebrows. He leaned against the table to wait.

Dorman Pugh came down from his patrol on the lookout deck and surveyed the mess. His face was drenched, and water dripped off his rain suit onto the floor. He pulled a chair off the table and sat down with a thud. "This is no northeaster," he said, wiping his face with one hand. "As sure as I'm alive, we're in the jaws of a hurricane."

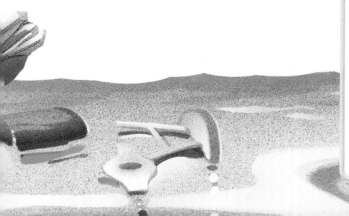

## Activities

1. **WRITE ABOUT IT** Make a list of words in the excerpt that tell what a hurricane is like. Then use the words to write your own description of a hurricane.

2. **RESEARCH IT** Find out about the Gold Life-Saving Medal awarded to the crew of the Pea Island Life-Saving Station. When was it awarded? Why?

Citizenship Skills

## Skillbuilder

# Understand Point of View

▶ **VOCABULARY**

**point of view**

**Point of view** is the way someone looks at a topic or situation. For example, people often have different points of view about how to use the land in their region. The statements below are two different points of view about a place called Riverside Park.

### Andrea's Point of View

"Our community is growing fast. We need more homes, schools, stores, and roads for all the people who want to move here. I think the best solution is to build at Riverside Park. It's a vast area, so there's plenty of room. Plants, birds, and other animals could still live in areas that are not cleared. The new homes and stores will boost the economy of our community."

### Carlos's Point of View

"Many people want to move to our beautiful region. Riverside Park is one feature that makes it special. Building on this precious land would be a huge mistake. The area provides a home for many plants and animals. Covering the land with roads and buildings will harm our environment. Worse, our grandchildren will not be able to enjoy the natural beauty of the park."

## Learn the Skill

**Step 1:** Read the statements carefully. Figure out what their subject is.

**Step 2:** Look for phrases like "I think," "in my opinion," or "I believe." These phrases signal the author's opinion. Also look for positive or negative words that give you more clues about the author's feelings.

**Step 3:** Describe the author's opinion about the subject.

**Step 4:** Look for facts that support the author's point of view.

## Practice the Skill

Use the statements on page 140 to answer the questions.

1. What is the subject of both passages?
2. Describe each person's point of view on the subject.
3. What facts do Andrea and Carlos present? Do those facts support their points of view?

## Apply the Skill

What is your point of view about Riverside Park? Write a paragraph that states your point of view. Be sure to provide good reasons for your opinion.

# Resources and Economy

**VOCABULARY**

dam
producer
consumer
scarcity
opportunity cost

**Vocabulary Strategy**

producer, consumer

**Producer** and **consumer** end with **-er.** This ending can mean a person who does something.

**READING SKILL**

**Categorize** As you read, sort the resources of the South into three groups.

| Natural resources | Goods | Services |
|---|---|---|
| | | |

**Build on What You Know** What snacks do you like? Some people enjoy chicken wings. Others like peanut butter or orange juice. The raw materials for these products are grown in the South.

## Production in the South

**Main Idea** People use the natural resources of the South to fuel a strong economy.

Like people everywhere, southerners use resources to produce goods and services. For example, they use water moving through dams to make electricity. A **dam** is a barrier built across a waterway to control the flow and level of water. Dams show how natural, human, and capital resources work together. In this case, water, people, and machines work together to produce electricity. The Tennessee Valley Authority, or TVA, has 29 dams that make power.

**Fort Loudoun Dam** This TVA dam is in Knoxville, Tennessee. The TVA is the largest power company in the United States.

Capital resource: dam

Natural resource: water

## Goods and Services from Natural Resources

| Natural Resource | Goods and Services |
|---|---|
| Rich soil | Cotton fabric, orange juice, peaches, pecans, peanuts |
| Waterways | Fish sticks, sea salt, boating, water power |
| Warm climate | Amusement parks, golf, vacation hotels |
| Oil and gas | Gasoline, plastics |
| Coal deposits | Coal, electricity |
| Forests | Paper, lumber |

**Georgia Peanuts** Southerners use natural resources to create many goods and services. For example, farmers grow peanuts. Factory workers turn them into peanut butter.

## Producers and Consumers

In manufacturing, producers turn raw materials into goods. A **producer** is someone who makes or sells goods or services for consumers. A **consumer** is someone who buys or uses goods and services.

People can be both producers and consumers. Suppose a manufacturer in North Carolina produces chairs. Before making a chair, the manufacturer will consume, or buy, wood, glue, and labor. That manufacturer is both a consumer and a producer.

The South has many resources that producers can use to make products.

People grow more peanuts, cotton, rice, and sugar cane here than in any other region. Coal and oil lie below the ground. Fish and shellfish live in the waters. Producers use all of these resources. Every year, for example, Texas produces nearly five million bales of raw cotton. In other southern states, workers in textile mills spin the cotton. They produce cotton yarn. Then other manufacturers use the yarn to produce cloth, t-shirts, towels, and other cotton products.

**REVIEW** What factors of production are needed to create cotton t-shirts?

# A Diverse Economy

**Main Idea** Producers and consumers make choices about how to use resources.

The South's economy once relied mainly on farming. Farming is still very important. Texas, North Carolina, Georgia, and Florida rank in the top ten states for farm income. Leading products include rice, cotton, tobacco, sugar cane, oranges, chickens, hogs, and cattle. In today's economy, many other industries also thrive in a region rich with natural and human resources.

Many southerners work in manufacturing and service industries. In the Piedmont region, many people work in textile mills. In North Carolina alone, the cotton industry employs nearly 75,000 people. These workers make yarn, cloth, carpets, and rugs.

Millions of acres of forests in Alabama, Arkansas, and Georgia provide jobs in the lumber and paper industries.

Top coal mining states include West Virginia, Kentucky, and Texas. Coal and other resources help create power and energy. Thousands of southerners work in the oil industry. Texas and Florida rank in the top four states for aerospace employment.

Tourism and service industries also play a vital role. One of the leading service industries in the South is ground and air transportation.

Hundreds of thousands of southerners work for the government. The U.S. government, including the military, is one of the largest employers in the South. Most government employees in the South live in Texas, Virginia, and Florida.

**The Cotton Industry** Cotton creates many jobs in the South.
**SKILL** **Reading Graphs** Which state has the most jobs from cotton?

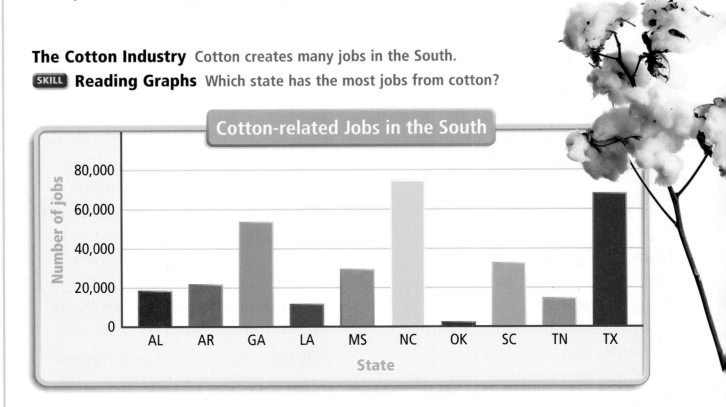

Cotton-related Jobs in the South

## Making Economic Choices

Consumers decide whether or not to buy something. Producers try to provide goods and services that consumers will want to buy. Producers decide what resources to use. They also set prices for their goods and services.

Scarcity affects prices. **Scarcity** means there are not enough resources to provide a product or service that people want. For example, suppose a winter frost hurt orange groves in Florida. With a scarcity of oranges, the price of orange juice would go up.

As a consumer, you could decide to buy a cheaper kind of juice. If you buy expensive orange juice, you will have less money to spend on something else. This is an example of opportunity cost. An **opportunity cost** is what someone gives up to get something else.

Every economic choice has an opportunity cost. Like consumers, businesses also face opportunity cost.

Suppose an orange juice company buys new equipment. The company would have less money to spend on other things, such as a new building.

**REVIEW** What choices do producers and consumers make?

### Lesson Summary

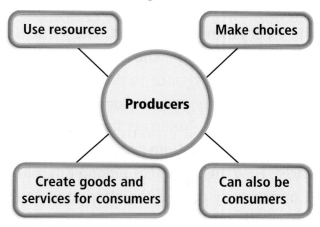

### Why It Matters...

The choices that producers and consumers make determine how resources are used in the nation's economy.

---

## Lesson Review

❶ **VOCABULARY** Write a short paragraph using **producer** and **consumer.**

❷ **READING SKILL** How would you **categorize** orange juice? Is it a natural resource, a manufactured good, or a service?

❸ **MAIN IDEA: Economics** Give two examples of how producers and consumers use natural resources.

❹ **MAIN IDEA: Economics** What factors affect producers' decisions about what goods and services to provide?

❺ **CRITICAL THINKING: Evaluate** Why should people consider the opportunity cost when they make a choice?

✏️ **WRITING ACTIVITY** Write a paragraph describing some goods and services that you consume.

# Making Choices

People never have enough time or money to do everything they want. They must make choices. When people choose one thing, they often give up the chance to do something else.

Both producers and consumers make economic choices. Producers try to plan the best way to earn income from producing goods and services. They make choices among alternatives. The opportunity cost of the alternative they choose is the income they could have earned from the alternative they did not choose.

Consumers have opportunity costs, too. Let's look at Pedro. He has been helping his mom take care of his younger brother and has earned $12. The first choice he makes is whether to save his money or spend it now.

Pedro likes these action figures. However, he is saving for a robot construction kit, which costs almost $50. If he buys the action figures now, it will take him longer to save for the kit. In other words, the opportunity cost of buying the action figures now would be the chance to get a robot kit in the future.

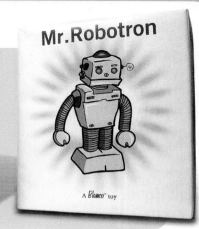

Pedro decides to save more money. He walks pets for neighbors and earns $10. When he has saved enough to buy a kit, he goes to several stores to find the best price. The kit he likes best costs $5 more than all the others.

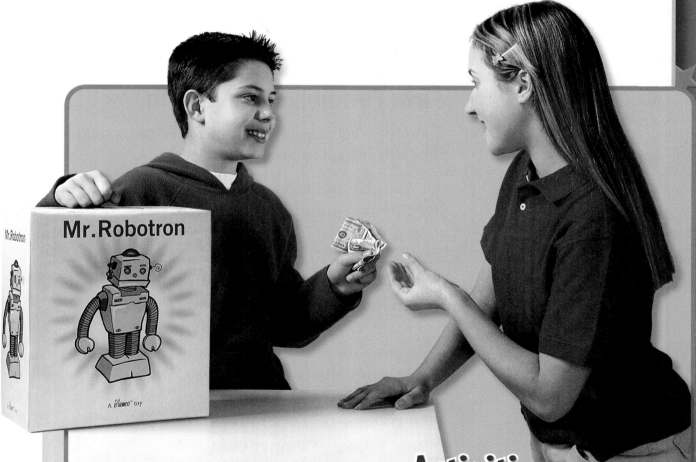

Pedro decides to get a less expensive kit that is almost as good. He saves the extra $5 to spend or save for something else. He can't have everything, but he's happy about the choices he made with his money!

# Activities

1. **TALK ABOUT IT** Explain why Pedro didn't buy the action figures when he had $12.

2. **WRITE ABOUT IT** Write about a time when you chose between two things. Explain the opportunity cost of the choice you made.

ECONOMICS

147

# People of the South

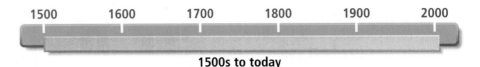

| 1500 | 1600 | 1700 | 1800 | 1900 | 2000 |

**1500s to today**

## VOCABULARY

**export**
**civil rights**
**boycott**

**Vocabulary Strategy**

> export

The **ex-** in **export** means outside. Exports are goods that exit, or are sent out of, a country.

## READING SKILL

**Sequence** Write the order in which groups settled in the South.

**Build on What You Know** When did your ancestors or relatives come to America? Where did they live? American Indians were the first people to settle in the South.

## First Peoples in the South

**Main Idea** Both American Indians and European settlers depended on local resources to survive.

Before Europeans arrived, American Indians had lived in the South for thousands of years. The early Eastern Woodlands people collected wild plants and seeds. They saved the best seeds for planting in the rich soil. Other American Indian groups learned how to farm from the Eastern Woodlands Indians.

Many groups, or nations, of American Indians in the South became skilled farmers. The largest nations included the Choctaw, Cherokee, Creek, and Seminole. Most planted three important crops: corn, beans, and squash. After Europeans arrived, the Choctaw, Chickasaw, and Seminole traded fur and deerskins for cloth, weapons, and iron tools.

American Indians planted corn, beans, and squash. The beans climbed the corn stalks. The low squash plants kept the soil moist.

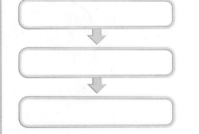

**Jamestown, Virginia** Today, visitors can tour a rebuilt Jamestown settlement and Powhatan village. People who lived in the Jamestown colony left behind this coin.

## Early Colonies

In the 1500s, people from Europe began to settle in the South. Spain built a permanent settlement in Florida in 1565. In 1607, the English established their first permanent colony at Jamestown, Virginia. In 1619, a Dutch ship brought the first enslaved Africans to Jamestown. These people had been captured in Africa. They were forced to work in the colony.

The South's warm weather and rich soil helped the people in Jamestown and other colonies survive. American Indians taught the Europeans how to raise corn. The Europeans planted their first crop of tobacco in 1612.

The next year, they sent some tobacco to England. Tobacco soon became a major export. An **export** is a product that is sent out of a country to be sold or traded.

Tobacco became the colony's most important crop. In Virginia, people used it for money instead of silver and gold. Within 20 years, thousands of pounds were being exported to England each year. The colonists also grew rice and other crops. Within 100 years, tobacco and rice made up almost two fifths of all exports from the colonies.

**REVIEW** Why did farmers in the South grow tobacco and rice?

# A Plantation Economy

**Main Idea** Planters used new inventions and the work of enslaved people to make profits.

The population of the South grew as more European settlers and enslaved Africans arrived. Plantations began to replace some small farms. Plantations are large farms that grow mostly one crop. The main crops on southern plantations were rice, cotton, hemp, tobacco, indigo, and sugar.

New inventions and ideas helped many plantations become successful. **Eli Whitney** invented the cotton gin, which made it easy to remove the seeds from cotton. **Eliza Lucas Pinckney** encouraged people to raise indigo. The seeds from this plant are used to make blue dye for cloth. **Norbert Rillieux** (ril YEU) invented a tool to make sugar production cheaper and faster.

## The System of Slavery

Big plantations were like small villages. They had houses, barns, fields, and warehouses. Wealthy plantation owners had fine houses, clothing, jewels, and art.

A successful plantation needed many workers. To get these workers, many plantation owners chose to buy enslaved Africans. In some southern states, the population of enslaved Africans was greater than the population of whites.

Life on a plantation was very different for slaves than it was for the plantation owners. Slaves lived in rough cabins. They owned little clothing or furniture. Owners could beat them or sell them at any time.

Many enslaved people ran away. Others broke tools, worked slowly, or pretended to be sick. A few attacked plantation owners.

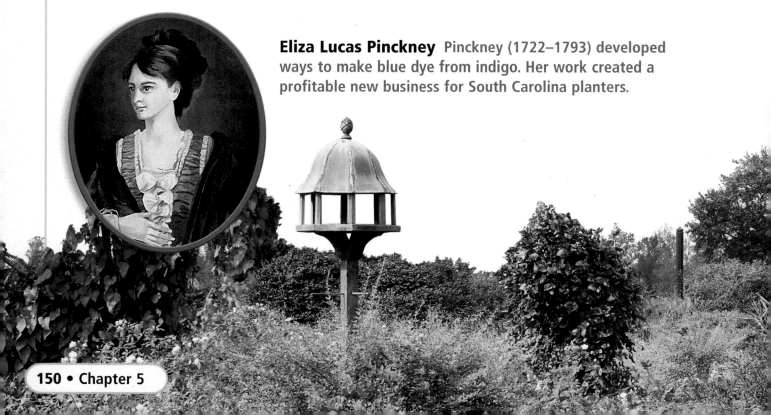

**Eliza Lucas Pinckney** Pinckney (1722–1793) developed ways to make blue dye from indigo. Her work created a profitable new business for South Carolina planters.

## The Civil War

Most southerners did not enslave people. Some thought that slavery was wrong. People in both the North and the South argued about whether or not slavery should be ended.

Northern states passed laws against slavery. Other laws made slavery illegal in parts of the West. Many southerners fought the laws outlawing slavery. They believed that the laws were unfair and would hurt their economy.

People in the North and South could not agree about slavery. By the spring of 1861, eleven southern states had voted to leave the United States. They formed a separate country, the Confederate States of America.

At that time, **Abraham Lincoln** was President of the United States. He believed that the country could not be "half slave and half free." He wanted to unify the country. The North and South went to war. For four terrible years, Americans fought each other in the Civil War. In 1865, the South lost. Slavery was outlawed. More than 4 million African Americans were freed.

**REVIEW** In what ways were the lives of plantation owners and enslaved workers different?

**Norbert Rillieux** Rillieux (1806–1894) was born in New Orleans and studied engineering in France. His evaporating pan made sugar production much safer for workers.

A South Carolina Cotton Plantation

# Civil Rights and Progress

**Main Idea**  African Americans worked hard to gain equal rights.

One hundred years after the Civil War, African Americans still struggled for their rights. The Civil War had ended slavery, but African Americans did not receive equal treatment. Most of them had no money, land, or education. As a result, they had trouble starting farms or businesses. They often had to eat, shop, and go to school in places separate from whites. African Americans were also denied the same civil rights that others had. **Civil rights** are the rights that every citizen has by law. Some states prevented African Americans from voting.

**Sit-in Protest**  Four students sat at a lunch counter in Greensboro, North Carolina. In 1960, only white people were allowed to sit at this counter.

**SKILL** **Reading Visuals**  Why is this kind of protest called "non-violent protest"?

## The Struggle for Civil Rights

Many Americans worked to win equality for everyone. In 1920, women won the right to vote. In 1954, the Supreme Court outlawed separate schools for white and black children.

In 1955, a courageous woman named **Rosa Parks** refused to give up her bus seat to a white passenger. This simple act sparked a protest in Alabama. **Dr. Martin Luther King, Jr.,** helped organize a bus boycott. In a **boycott,** people refuse to do business with a person or company. African Americans refused to ride buses in Montgomery, Alabama, until they could sit wherever they wanted. The boycott worked. The bus company agreed to treat all passengers equally.

Soon boycotts and protests were taking place all over the South. These protests inspired other groups. Women, American Indians, Latinos, and others began to demand their civil rights.

## The South Today

Today, African Americans hold important positions in every area of American life. **Dr. Condoleezza Rice** was the first African American woman to serve as Secretary of State. In 1996, businessman **John H. Johnson** received the Presidential Medal of Freedom.

The South today also has a diverse economy. Modern businesses and industries exist in every southern state. For example, workers in Alabama produce cotton, steel, and electronics. They also develop products for missiles and space flight.

**REVIEW** Why did African Americans boycott and protest in the 1950s and 1960s?

## Lesson Summary

American Indians and European settlers both thrived on the rich resources of the South. The southern economy was built partly through slave labor. Europeans enslaved people from Africa to work on plantations. Slavery ended with the Civil War, but it was many years before African Americans and others gained full civil rights.

## Why It Matters ...

The battle for civil rights won freedoms and greater equality for all Americans.

**Condoleezza Rice** Dr. Rice served as National Security Advisor before becoming Secretary of State.

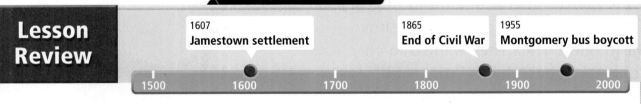

## Lesson Review

| | 1607 Jamestown settlement | | 1865 End of Civil War | 1955 Montgomery bus boycott |
|---|---|---|---|---|
| 1500 | 1600 | 1700 | 1800 | 1900 | 2000 |

❶ **VOCABULARY** Explain how people have used **boycotts** to win their **civil rights.**

❷ **READING SKILL** In what **sequence** did people settle in the South?

❸ **MAIN IDEA: Geography** What was one way American Indians and early colonists used the South's resources?

❹ **MAIN IDEA: Citizenship** What did people do to win their civil rights in the 1950s and 1960s?

❺ **TIMELINE SKILL** What event happened 90 years before the Montgomery bus boycott?

❻ **CRITICAL THINKING: Infer** President Lincoln did not want the country to be "half slave and half free." What do you think he meant by this?

**WRITING ACTIVITY** Use library resources to learn more about a civil rights leader. Write a one-page report on how this person helped others gain equal rights.

# Civil Rights Leaders

Television and newspapers brought news of the civil rights struggle in the South to the nation. These three people were all part of major events that helped shape the civil rights movement.

## Dr. Martin Luther King, Jr. (1929–1968)

Martin Luther King, Jr., was one of many speakers at the March on Washington in August 1963. A crowd of 250,000 people had gathered in Washington, D.C. They wanted to encourage Congress to pass the civil rights bill. King gave a speech that made people excited. He imagined a future when everyone in America could work together for freedom and democracy. The Civil Rights Act was passed in 1964. Dr. King won the Nobel Peace Prize the same year.

" And as we walk, we must make the pledge that we shall always march ahead. We cannot turn back. "
— from Dr. Martin Luther King's "I Have a Dream" speech in 1963

## James Meredith

James Meredith had good grades and a career in the Air Force, but the University of Mississippi would not admit him. There were no African American students at the school. In 1962, a court ordered the school to accept him. Federal marshals were sent to protect him from angry crowds. In spite of people who didn't want him to attend the school, Meredith graduated in 1963. After graduation, he continued to work for civil rights.

## Ruby Bridges Hall

Until 1960, William Frantz Public School in New Orleans, Louisiana, was for white children only. A court decided the school must teach children of all races. On November 14, six-year-old Ruby Bridges became the first African American child to go to the school. Every day, Ruby went to an empty classroom. Her teacher taught her all alone. Ruby's courage helped change the school system. The next year, she went to class with other children, both white and black.

This painting by Norman Rockwell refers to Ruby Bridges's first day at school.

# Activities

1. **TALK ABOUT IT** How did each leader show **patriotism** by supporting the American ideals of freedom and justice?

2. **WRITE A LETTER** Write a letter to one of these people. Tell the person what you think about his or her actions in the civil rights movement.

 **Technology** Read more biographies at Education Place. www.eduplace.com/kids/hmss05/

Reading and Thinking Skills

## Skillbuilder

# Interpret Historical Images

A photograph captures a moment in time. It can also give valuable information about a period in history. Learn more about the civil rights movement by studying the photograph below.

**March on Washington** On August 28, 1963, about 250,000 people gathered in Washington, D.C., to protest unfair treatment of African Americans in the South. They also pushed Congress to pass new civil rights laws.

## Learn the Skill

**Step 1:** Look at the photograph carefully. Then read the title and caption to learn more about it. Add that information to what you already know about the event or time period.

**Step 2:** Ask yourself what you have learned from the photograph. How does the picture make you feel? What do you think is the photographer's point of view on the subject?

## Practice the Skill

Use the photograph on page 156 to answer the questions.

1. What does the caption tell you about the event in the photograph?

2. What do the signs of the marchers say? What does this tell you about the South in the early 1960s?

3. Do you think the photographer supported the march or disapproved of it? Why?

## Apply the Skill

Choose one photograph from the first five chapters of this textbook. Explain what information you can get from the photograph. Also explain how it helps you understand ideas in the text.

## Visual Summary

**1. – 3.** ✏️ Write a description of each item named below.

| Landforms of the South | Southern Industries | Civil War, 1861–1865 |
|---|---|---|
| 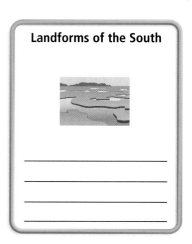 |  | 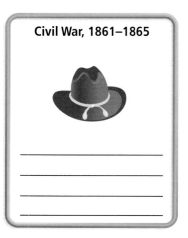 |

## Facts and Main Ideas

✔️ **TEST PREP** Answer each question below.

4. **Geography** Explain how climate has affected the way people live in the South.

5. **Economics** In what ways do the choices of producers and consumers affect the economy?

6. **Culture** What did many American Indian groups learn from the Eastern Woodland Indians?

7. **Technology** What inventions changed farming in the South?

8. **History** What rights did African Americans fight for in the 1950s and 1960s?

## Vocabulary

✔️ **TEST PREP** Choose the correct word from the list below to complete each sentence.

**peninsula,** p. 133
**scarcity,** p. 145
**export,** p. 149

9. A(n) _____ is sent out of the country to be sold or traded.

10. A(n) _____ is surrounded on three sides by water.

11. A shortage of resources is called _____.

1607 English settle Jamestown

1865 Slavery ends

1920 Women gain the right to vote

1955 Montgomery bus boycott

1600    1700    1800    1900    2000

## Apply Skills

✔ TEST PREP **Understand Point of View** Use the passage below and what you have learned about point of view to answer each question.

Every year, more and more people visit our region's beaches. These shores were once a place to relax and enjoy the natural landscape and wildlife. Today the beaches are lined with hotels and restaurants. It is difficult to escape the noise of jet-skis and motor boats. The growth of the tourism industry has ruined what's special about where we live.

**12.** What is the subject of the passage?

   **A.** the benefit of tourism on the economy
   **B.** the effect of tourism on the region
   **C.** the beauty of the natural landscape
   **D.** the number of people who travel

**13.** Which statement best describes the author's point of view?

   **A.** Jet-skis and motor boats are noisy.
   **B.** Most hotels are too far from the beach.
   **C.** People should not be allowed to eat at the beach.
   **D.** Tourism has hurt the natural beauty of the region.

## Critical Thinking

✔ TEST PREP Write a short paragraph to answer each question below.

**14. Generalize** In what way would you describe the economy of the South? Why?

**15. Compare and Contrast** What are some advantages and disadvantages of the South's climate?

## Timeline

Use the Chapter Summary Timeline to answer the question.

**16.** How many years passed between the end of slavery and the Montgomery bus boycott?

# Activities

HANDS ON **Speaking Activity** Find out more about one of the inventors mentioned in the chapter. Prepare a speech explaining what that person did and how it affected the South's economy.

**Writing Activity** Do you think that protests are an effective way for people to fight for their rights? Write a personal essay explaining your point of view. Give reasons to support your opinion.

**Technology**
**Writing Process Tips**
Get help with your essay at:
**www.eduplace.com/kids/hmss05/**

## Vocabulary Preview

**Technology**

*e* • **glossary**
*e* • **word games**
www.eduplace.com/kids/hmss05/

### transportation

Many kinds of **transportation** are used to carry people and goods. Boats, barges, trucks, and trains often carry heavy goods. **page 162**

### communication

Letters and newspapers are forms of **communication** that have been used for a long time. New communication tools, such as cell phones, are used today. **page 165**

# Reading Strategy

**Question** As you read the lessons in this chapter, ask yourself questions about important ideas.

**Quick Tip** List questions you have. When you finish reading, go back to find the answers.

## planned community

Some communities grow slowly over many years. A **planned community** is built all at once. Many planned communities are in the suburbs of small and large cities.
**page 171**

## pollution

**Pollution** is harmful to the environment. People are finding new ways to keep the water, air, and soil clean.
**page 173**

## What's Special About
# The Upper South

**Build on What You Know** Think about the last time a package was delivered to your home. The company that delivered it might be from the Upper South. Many big shipping companies have their main offices there.

## Where People Live

**Main Idea** The Upper South is a region of sharp contrasts, from rural and forested areas to many large cities and suburbs.

The Upper South is made up of six states. Most are rural and forested. Arkansas, for example, is known as "The Natural State" because almost all of its land area is covered with mountains, valleys, forests, and farm fields. Many people live in these lush rural areas, but most people live in cities and towns. In both Arkansas and Tennessee, for example, more than half of the people live in urban areas.

Many of these cities are important business centers. Memphis, Tennessee, is a bustling transportation center. **Transportation** is the business of carrying people or goods from one place to another.

**Water Transportation** The Mississippi River provides transportation through Memphis, Tennessee.

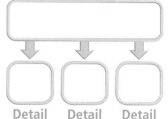

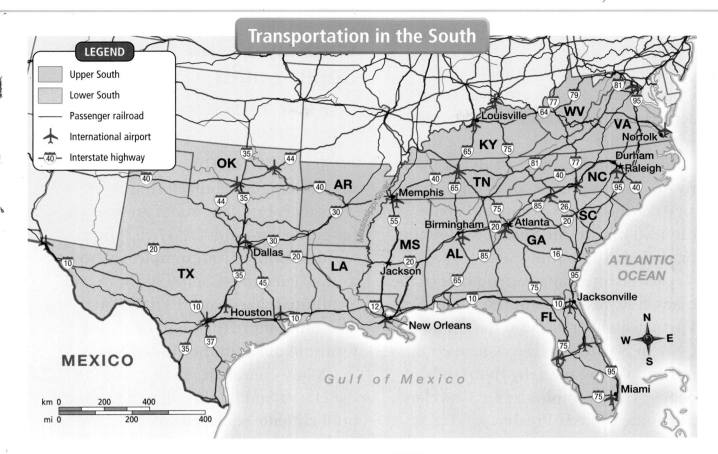

**Transportation in the South**

LEGEND
- ⬜ Upper South
- ⬜ Lower South
- —— Passenger railroad
- ✈ International airport
- —40— Interstate highway

**Distribution** Packages from all over the world pass through Memphis.

SKILL **Reading Maps** In what ways can people ship goods from Memphis?

## Memphis, Tennessee

Memphis has been called "America's Distribution Center." It is a distribution hub. A **hub** is a major center of activity. Many people in Memphis work to distribute, or ship, goods throughout the world. Memphis International Airport ships more air cargo than any other airport in the world.

Many other people in Memphis work in health care and tourism. Tourists enjoy visiting the National Civil Rights Museum and many other sites. Since Memphis is near the state border, many workers commute there from Arkansas and Mississippi.

## Rural Life in the Upper South

Farmers in the Upper South grow cotton, tobacco, and rice. They also raise chickens, cattle, and horses. In Kentucky, champion racehorses graze on the area's lush grass. Many horse farms also dot the countryside in Tennessee and Virginia.

Mining plays an important role in rural areas of the region. Vast mineral deposits make West Virginia a leading producer of coal.

Folk culture in the Appalachians includes storytelling, quilting, and music played on the fiddle and banjo. The songs tell about life in the hills.

REVIEW What makes Memphis an important business center?

## Things to Do

The natural environment of the Upper South offers a great variety of activities for tourists and the people who live there. People who love the outdoors can fish and raft in the many rivers. They can hunt for diamonds in an Arkansas diamond mine. People can also hike in the Smoky Mountains or explore Mammoth Cave.

Music lovers may attend one of the many festivals in North Carolina, West Virginia, and Kentucky. At the Grand Ole Opry in Nashville, visitors hear country music. Every year, many thousands of people visit Memphis to see Graceland, the home of **Elvis Presley.**

History lovers may head for Virginia, where they can experience Colonial Williamsburg. They can also tour Mount Vernon, the home of **George Washington,** or Monticello, the home of **Thomas Jefferson.**

# Working in the Upper South

**Main Idea** The Upper South is home to a large amount of manufacturing and industry.

People in the Upper South work in a variety of manufacturing and industry jobs. Many states are known for particular products. High Point, North Carolina, for example, is known as the "Furniture Capital of the World." Furniture makers in the High Point area build more than half of all the furniture made in the United States.

Many companies have moved to the Upper South. They like the region's mild climate, educated workers, and industry-friendly laws. Textiles have long been an important industry in the Piedmont region of the Upper South. Today, the region's skilled textile workers help attract new or foreign textile companies to the Piedmont.

**Mammoth Cave** This place in Kentucky has more than 350 miles of connected underground caves.

## The Communications Industry

People's need to exchange ideas and information led to the growth of Research Triangle Park in North Carolina. When people do **research,** they study something carefully to learn more about it. Research Triangle Park links three research universities in Durham, Raleigh, and Chapel Hill. Researchers there explore new ideas in medicine, computers, and communications. **Communication** is the exchange of information.

Newspapers, mail, and magazines are older forms of communication. Newer forms use technology to send messages more quickly over long distances. The Internet is a huge communications network connecting one computer to other computers around the world.

**REVIEW** Describe two of the major industries of the Upper South.

**The Internet** These students use the Internet to find information, play games, and stay in touch with classmates.

## Lesson Summary

- The Upper South has large cities as well as rural areas.
- Farming, mining, transportation, and communications are major industries in the region.

## Why It Matters...

Businesses in the Upper South serve people throughout the world.

---

## Lesson Review

**1 VOCABULARY** Use **research** and **hub** in a paragraph about the Upper South.

**2 READING SKILL** List two **details** that prove the Upper South offers a variety of things to do.

**3 MAIN IDEA: Geography** In what ways do people use the natural resources of the Upper South?

**4 MAIN IDEA: Economics** In what ways do industries in the Upper South link the region to other parts of the world?

**5 PEOPLE TO KNOW** Which U.S. President lived in Mount Vernon?

**6 CRITICAL THINKING: Infer** In what way might Memphis's location have helped it become a transportation and distribution center?

**WRITING ACTIVITY** Write a letter to Thomas Jefferson. Describe a form of transportation or communication you think he would enjoy using if he were alive today.

# The Ocoee River

Natural resources are great for a region's economy, but they can also be fun! Many people enjoy outdoor activities in the Upper South each year. These three children and their parents are going rafting on the Ocoee (oh KOH ee) River in Tennessee.

## Cast of Characters

**Rachel Fulton:** guide

**Rico Hirayama:** guide

**Kara Smith:** 12 years old

**Diane Smith:** Kara's mother

**Dylan Sharp:** 12 years old

**Matthew Sharp:** 14 years old

**Brad Sharp:** Matthew and Dylan's father

**Lynette Sharp:** Matthew and Dylan's mother

**Rachel:** OK, everyone, gather around. I'm Rachel, and this is Rico. We are your guides today. We're going to be rafting on the middle section of the Ocoee River.

**Rico:** The Middle Ocoee is one of the most popular whitewater rafting spots in the whole country. It has a five-mile stretch of whitewater rapids.

**Dylan:** Is the water really white?

**Kara:** No, it's just regular water. It looks white and frothy because it's flowing really fast through a steep part of the river.

**Rachel:** That's right. Now, let's make sure we're prepared for the trip. I see that everyone has a life jacket and a helmet. Is everyone here at least 12 years old?

**Kara, Dylan, and Matthew:** Yes!

**Rachel:** Good. You must be at least 12 to raft on the river.

**Matthew:** Is this where they held the whitewater rafting races in the 1996 Olympics?

**Brad:** No, I think that was on the Upper Ocoee, right?

**Rico:** Right. On certain days each summer, water is released into the Upper Ocoee. That's when we offer trips on that section of the river.

**Kara:** Wait, what do you mean the water is released? Isn't it flowing all the time?

**Lynette:** I've done some research about this. The Ocoee has three dams that block water flow. The TVA—the Tennessee Valley Authority—uses most of the water to make electricity. However, some water is released into the river. They have special release days every year just for whitewater rafting.

**Rachel:** That's right. The dams also control floods and provide water for cities and industries in the area.

**Diane:** How do the dams affect people who like to fish?

**Brad:** All three of the dams have reservoirs, which are lakes created by the dams. We've gone boating and fishing there. There are camping, hiking, and picnic areas, too.

**Dylan:** What about the fish and plants in the river? How do the dams affect them?

**Rico:** Well, dams are pretty hard on things that live in the water. For one thing, they make it hard for fish and other creatures to migrate.

**Lynette:** Also, by stopping the flow of the water, dams can cause riverbeds to dry up. Then the fish have nowhere to live.

**Matthew:** Power companies hold the water back until they need to make more electricity. Then they release the water, making the river's water level go way up.

**Rico:** Right. River creatures can deal with changes in water level that come from natural things, like the seasons. However, they have no way to cope with the whole river being turned on and off like a faucet.

**Brad:** Even when the dams release water, it's often much colder than the river would normally be. Native fishes can't survive in this cold water. So, the government puts in fish that can live in cold water, such as trout.

**Look Closely** Rafters wear helmets and life jackets to protect themselves.

**Diane:** OK, but the rafting on the river must bring a lot of jobs to the area. That's a benefit.

**Matthew:** When they release the water, it makes some of the coolest rafting anywhere!

**Dylan:** True. The rafters and tour guides benefit. All the people who use the electricity and drink the water benefit. I'm still worried about the fish, though!

**Rachel:** It's hard to balance what everyone needs and wants. Of course, the fish can't speak for themselves. Environmental groups try to protect fish and other river life from harm.

**Diane:** I guess dams have both benefits and drawbacks.

**Kara:** Well, I'm ready to go whitewater rafting!

**Dylan and Matthew:** Me, too! Me, too!

## Activities

1. **ACT IT OUT** Act out a skit about the importance of showing **respect** for river life.

2. **WRITE ABOUT IT** Diane and Kara Smith decide to write letters to friends about their trip. What would each say about the Ocoee River?

## What's Special About
# The Lower South

**VOCABULARY**

ethnic group
planned community
pollution

**Vocabulary Strategy**

| planned community

When you **plan,** you decide ahead of time how to do something. Builders follow a plan to create a **planned community.**

**READING SKILL**
**Cause and Effect** Fill in a chart to show what caused Houston to grow in the 20th century.

| Cause | Effect |
|-------|--------|
|       |        |

**French Quarter Festival** This festival celebrates the culture of New Orleans, Louisiana.

**Build on What You Know** What would be a fun trip for you? Would you go to a beach, a big city, or an amusement park? The Lower South has all these things.

## Where People Live

**Main Idea** People who live in the Lower South come from a variety of cultures with their own traditions and celebrations.

The Lower South covers one corner of the United States. The climate of the Lower South is mostly warm and damp. Texas and Oklahoma, however, are mostly dry.

Many ethnic groups live in the Lower South. An **ethnic group** includes people who share the same culture. Languages, music, food, and art show this great variety of ethnic groups. For example, more than 90 languages are spoken in the Houston area. Hundreds of thousands of Cuban Americans live in Florida. African Americans, Puerto Ricans, and Seminole Indians live there, too. Creoles, descendants of early French and Spanish settlers, live in Louisiana. Another ethnic group in Louisiana is the Cajuns, descendants of early French Canadians.

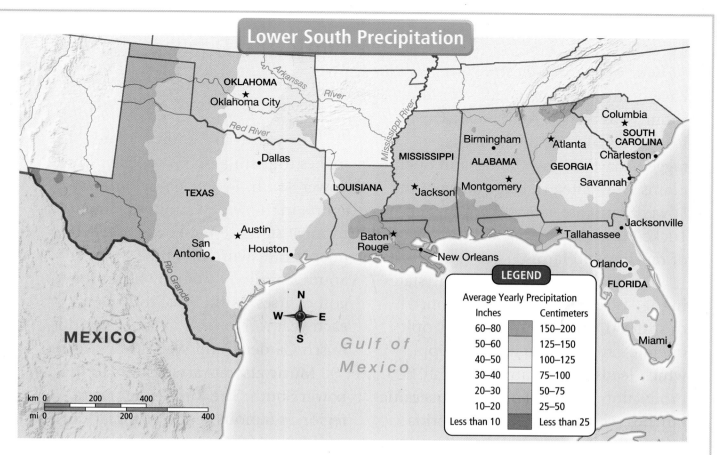

## Lower South Precipitation

OKLAHOMA
★
Oklahoma City

Red River

Arkansas River

Mississippi River

TEXAS

Dallas

MISSISSIPPI

Birmingham
•

ALABAMA

Columbia
★
SOUTH
CAROLINA

★Atlanta

GEORGIA

Charleston •

Austin
★

San
Antonio •

Houston •

LOUISIANA

★Jackson

Montgomery
★

Savannah •

★Tallahassee

Jacksonville •

Baton
Rouge ★

New Orleans

Orlando •

FLORIDA

Rio Grande

MEXICO

N
W — E
S

Gulf of
Mexico

Miami •

**LEGEND**

Average Yearly Precipitation

| Inches | | Centimeters |
|---|---|---|
| 60–80 | | 150–200 |
| 50–60 | | 125–150 |
| 40–50 | | 100–125 |
| 30–40 | | 75–100 |
| 20–30 | | 50–75 |
| 10–20 | | 25–50 |
| Less than 10 | | Less than 25 |

km 0    200    400
mi 0    200    400

**Lower South Precipitation** From east to west, the climate in the Lower South becomes drier.

**SKILL** **Reading Maps** Which city receives more rain each year—Austin or Tallahassee?

## Houston, Texas

Houston is the largest city in the South. In 1901, a large deposit of oil was discovered near Houston. Soon, oil companies and workers poured into the area. Then, in 1914, the Houston Ship Channel was built. This waterway connects Houston to Galveston Bay. It lets big ships from the Gulf of Mexico travel to Houston. Today, Houston is one of the three largest U.S. ports.

Oil is just one of many industries in Houston. The city is also home to the Texas Medical Center, which is the world's largest medical center.

The suburbs are home to the Johnson Space Center. Here, Mission Control Center directs activities on space shuttle and other space missions.

Outside Houston, many people live in suburbs or in nearby planned communities. A **planned community** is a place to live that is mapped out ahead of time. Unlike most other communities, it usually limits the number of people who can live there. Each planned community contains homes, roads, parks, and pools. Some have shopping centers and schools, too.

**REVIEW** How did natural resources affect the growth of Houston?

171

## Rural Life

The eight states of the Lower South have many large and small cities and suburbs, as well as rural areas. The rural areas include thick forests, ragged coastlines, wetlands, and open plains and plateaus. Large areas of the Lower South are sparsely populated. Tucked into this setting are many kinds of ranches and farms.

Except for Oklahoma, all the states in the Lower South are major sources of seafood, especially shrimp. People operate catfish farms in Mississippi, which leads the country in catfish production. Texas is famous for its cattle ranches. The citrus groves of Florida top the state's agricultural economy.

**Texas Cattle** The first Santa Gertrudis cattle were bred on a ranch in southern Texas. These cattle can thrive in the hot, dry climate of the Lower South.

# Work and Recreation

**Main Idea** The tourism and space industries are important to the Lower South's economy.

The year-round mild climate makes tourism a major industry in the Lower South. People enjoy outdoor sports in the warm southern climate. In most states of the Lower South, people can swim, raft, hike, or fish. South Carolina has many beautiful golf courses. Millions of tourists travel each year to Florida to visit SeaWorld, Busch Gardens, and Walt Disney World.

Music also attracts visitors to the Lower South. The Mississippi Delta region is famous as the birthplace of the blues. African American musicians in New Orleans, Louisiana, developed jazz in the early 1900s. Cajun and zydeco music are also popular in Louisiana. Zydeco blends the music of French, Caribbean, and African American cultures.

## Research in the Lower South

The Lower South has many research centers. Space research is done in many states. Texas has the Johnson Space Center. The Kennedy Space Center is in Florida. The Marshall Space Center is in Alabama. In Mississippi, scientists at the Stennis Space Center test rocket systems.

Other research is done as well. Scientists in Louisiana research water pollution. **Pollution** is anything that makes something impure or dirty. Scientists are learning how to keep chemicals and germs out of the Mississippi River.

All these research centers provide thousands of jobs.

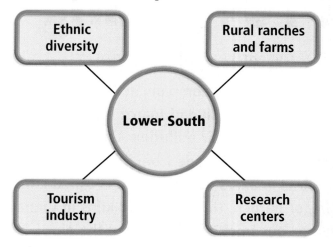

**Space Shuttle** Space shuttle missions launch from the Kennedy Space Center.

Some workers are scientists. Others work in offices or around the buildings.

**REVIEW** What are two kinds of work people do in the Lower South?

### Lesson Summary

```
        Ethnic                    Rural ranches
       diversity                   and farms
                  \            /
                  Lower South
                  /            \
       Tourism                    Research
       industry                   centers
```

### Why It Matters...
The Lower South is one of the fastest growing regions in the United States.

---

## Lesson Review

① **VOCABULARY** Use the terms **ethnic group** and **planned community** to describe the Lower South.

② **READING SKILL** What **effect** does climate have on the tourism industry?

③ **MAIN IDEA: Culture** In what way is life in Houston different from life in a rural area?

④ **MAIN IDEA: Technology** Why is technology important to the economy of the Lower South?

⑤ **PLACES TO KNOW** In what city did musicians develop jazz?

⑥ **CRITICAL THINKING: Evaluate** Why would water pollution harm the seafood industry? Give reasons for your answer.

 **SPEAKING ACTIVITY** Find a recording of jazz, cajun, or zydeco music at the library. Listen to the music and discuss why you like it or don't like it.

HANDS ON

# Preventing Pollution

**Preventing pollution costs a lot less than cleaning it up.** An electric company in El Paso, Texas, is helping brick makers in Ciudad Juárez (see-eu-DAHD WAHR-ehz), Mexico, control air pollution. Ciudad Juárez is just across the Rio Grande from El Paso.

Brick makers use large ovens called kilns to fire, or harden, the bricks. Old kilns in Ciudad Juárez put smoke and dust into the air. El Paso Electric is replacing 60 old kilns with new kilns that cycle smoke to help remove pollution.

The new system is better for the environment and for people. It cuts the amount of toxic gases put into the air by four fifths. The brick makers are healthier and safer.

Chimney

Bricks being fired

❶ Fuel is burned here. The heat fires the bricks loaded above.

Air pollution from traditional kilns can cause serious health problems for people living nearby.

Cleaner smoke

**❸** These raw bricks filter air pollution created by the burning fuels. They will be fired later.

Bricks filtering out pollution

**❷** An underground tunnel sends gases and heat to the second kiln.

# Activities

1. **DRAW IT** Suppose a fire is lit in the kiln on the right. Show where the heat and gases would travel to reach the bricks in the other kiln.

2. **TALK ABOUT IT** Why would a company from the United States want to help brick makers in Mexico? Discuss why the new kilns are good for people on both sides of the border.

# Write a Report

You have heard about the importance of the Everglades, but you want to learn more. What is this region? What makes it special? You can answer these questions by writing a report. A **report** presents information that you have researched. Writing a report is a way to share what you have learned with others.

► **VOCABULARY**
report

## Learn the Skill

**Step 1:** Choose a topic. Then brainstorm key words and ideas about your topic.

**Step 2:** Use your key words and ideas to find information in reference materials.

**Step 3:** Take notes. Be sure to write down the name of the source. Then organize your notes according to main points and details. The details in these notes support the main point that the Everglades is a marshy region in southern Florida.

Source: Encyclopedia Britannica
What is the Everglades?
marshy region in southern Florida
water overflows Lake Okeechobee
water travels over saw grass
  in broad river
river ends in swamps on southwestern
  tip of Florida

**Step 4:** Write your report. Start with an opening paragraph that introduces your topic and main points. Then, write a separate body paragraph for each main point. Support the main points with details. Finally, write a closing paragraph that summarizes what you have written.

The Everglades is a marshy region in southern Florida. During the rainy season, water spills over from Lake Okeechobee. Then the water flows south over high saw grass in a broad river. The river ends in swamps on the Gulf of Mexico and the Florida Bay.

Use the notes to write a sample body paragraph of a report on the Everglades.

What makes the Everglades special?
  an important wetland
  has wading birds, alligators, snakes
      and turtles
  tropical trees and bushes on small islands
  deer, bears, and wildcats on the islands

Use what you have learned to find information about Poverty Point State Historic Site in Louisiana or the Grand Village of the Natchez Indians in Mississippi. Write a report about the topic.

# Review and Test Prep

## Visual Summary

1. – 2. ✏ → Write a description of each item named below.

Life in the South

The Upper South

_____

_____

The Lower South

_____

_____

## Facts and Main Ideas

✔ **TEST PREP** Answer each question below.

3. **Geography** In what ways are the natural resources of the Upper South used?

4. **Culture** What attracts tourists to both the Upper and Lower South?

5. **Economics** Why do many industries move to the Upper South?

6. **Culture** Name two groups who have influenced the culture of the Lower South.

7. **Geography** What would a visitor see in the rural areas of the Lower South?

## Vocabulary

✔ **TEST PREP** Choose the correct word from the list below to complete each sentence.

**research,** p. 165
**planned community,** p. 171
**pollution,** p. 173

8. Anything that makes something impure or dirty is _____.

9. When people study something carefully in order to learn more about it, they are doing _____.

10. A _____ has homes, roads, and sometimes schools and places to shop.

✔️ **TEST PREP Write a Report** Use what you have learned about writing a report to answer each question.

**11.** What is the main purpose of a report?

   **A.** to persuade

   **B.** to present information

   **C.** to describe a point of view

   **D.** to entertain

**12.** The Everglades is home to a wide variety of animals. Which detail supports this main point?

   **A.** The Everglades is located in southern Florida.

   **B.** The Everglades is an important wetland.

   **C.** Alligators, snakes, and turtles live in the marshes.

   **D.** Many birds fly south in the winter.

**13.** What is the main purpose of a closing paragraph?

   **A.** to introduce the topic and main points

   **B.** to summarize what has been written

   **C.** to support main points with details

   **D.** to identify sources of information

✔️ **TEST PREP** Write a short paragraph to answer each question below.

**14. Fact and Opinion** Is it a fact or an opinion that Memphis, Tennessee, deserves its nickname as America's Distribution Center? Why?

**15. Draw Conclusions** What do you think might happen to the South's economy if the climate suddenly became much colder? Use details to support your conclusion.

# Activities

**Music Activity** Use library or Internet resources to find out more about the Grand Ole Opry in Nashville, Tennessee. Tell the names of some famous musicians who have performed there.

**Writing Activity** Find out more about ways that scientists are learning to prevent pollution of the Mississippi River. Write a research report explaining what you discover.

**Technology**
**Writing Process Tips**
Get help with your report at:
**www.eduplace.com/kids/hmss05/**

## Culture Where You Live

Your state has a culture. Where does it come from? People past and present help create this culture. The ideas people have, the clothes they wear, their religions, languages, and traditions, are part of it.

My State's Culture

| Languages | Religions and traditions | Food and recreation |

Eating turkey is a Thanksgiving tradition.

## Find Out!

### Explore your state's culture.

✓ **Start with the phone book.**
Look in the restaurant section. Find out the different kinds of foods people eat and the countries that are represented.

✓ **Visit your state museum.**
Go with an adult or look at its website. Find out which groups of people have settled in your state and what traditions people follow.

✓ **Check out your local library or bookstore.**
These probably have special sections that tell about your state's culture.

✓ **Use the website for your state tourist board or cultural council.**
They may have maps and brochures that tell about special events, fairs, festivals, and more.

Use your state handbook to keep track of the information you find.

# Review and Test Prep

## Vocabulary and Main Ideas

✓ **TEST PREP** Write a sentence to answer each question.

1. Why might a **delta** be a good place for farming?

2. What is one reason that people build **dams?**

3. Explain how people can be both **producers** and **consumers.**

4. What were two effects of the bus **boycott** in Montgomery, Alabama?

5. Name two older forms of **communication** and one newer form.

6. What is one difference between **planned communities** and other kinds of communities?

## Critical Thinking

✓ **TEST PREP** Write a short paragraph to answer each question.

7. **Compare and Contrast** Does the southern economy offer more or fewer opportunities for workers today than in the past? Give examples.

8. **Summarize** What are some tourist attractions and activities in the Upper South and in the Lower South?

## Apply Skills

✓ **TEST PREP** Use the photo below and what you have learned about interpreting historical images to answer the questions that follow.

Greensboro Sit-In Protest, 1960

9. Why do you think this form of protest was effective?

   **A.** It was a nonviolent form of protest.
   **B.** The protest was in a restaurant.
   **C.** The people protesting were angry with the restaurant's customers.
   **D.** The photographer agreed with the protesters.

10. What does this photograph tell you about the time period?

    **A.** Protests were happening only in the South.
    **B.** African Americans wished to gain equal rights.
    **C.** All southerners wanted peace.
    **D.** It was a time of prosperity.

## Unit Activity

**The Big Idea**

### Make a Unity and Diversity Stamp

- Review the pictures in this unit. Think about how they show the unity and diversity of American culture.

- Draw a picture that you think represents both unity and diversity.

- Use the ideas from this picture to make a large postage stamp that shows the unity and diversity of American culture.

- Display the stamp in your classroom.

## At the Library

**Look for this book at your school or public library.**

*I Have a Dream*
by Dr. Martin Luther King, Jr.
Paintings accompany the author's historic speech on equality and brotherhood.

**CURRENT EVENTS**

# WEEKLY (WR) READER

### Current Events Project

**Plan a celebration of a region's culture.**

- Find information about the culture of one region of the country.

- Think of ways to celebrate the culture of the region.

- Write a plan for a one-day celebration with several events.

- Post your plan on a bulletin board and explain it to a classmate.

**Technology**
Weekly Reader online offers social studies articles. Go to:
**www.eduplace.com/kids/hmss/**

## Read About It

**Look in your classroom for these Social Studies Independent Books.**

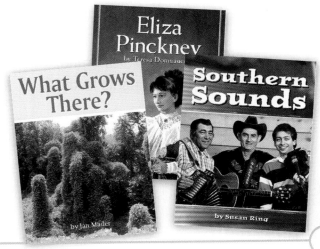

# UNIT 4

## The Midwest

**The Big Idea**

### What will you do to earn a living?

*"Money is necessary — both to support a family and to advance causes one believes in."*

—Coretta Scott King, civil rights leader

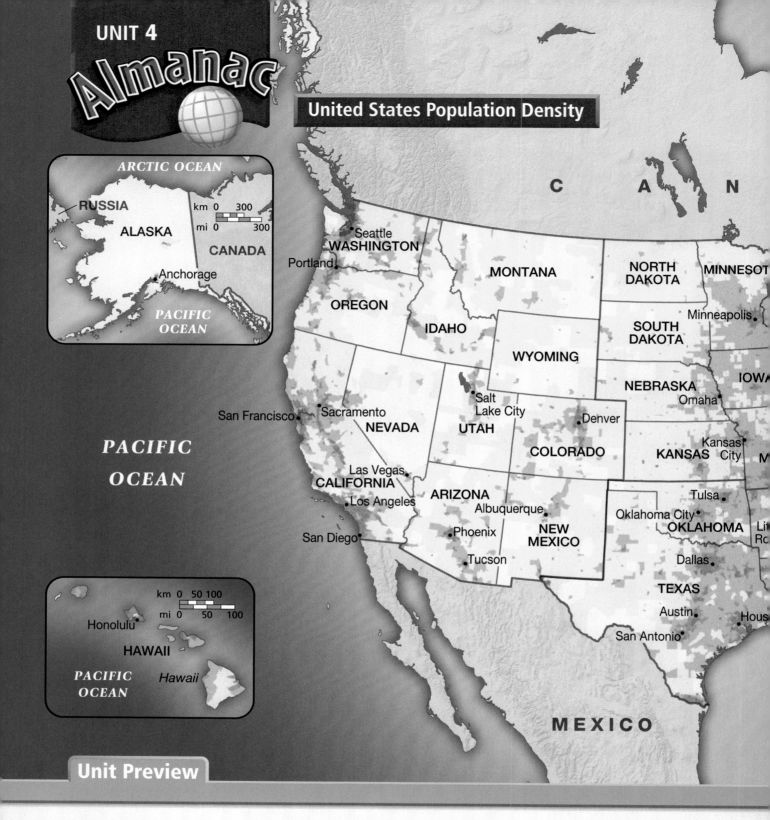

# UNIT 4

## Almanac

## United States Population Density

**ARCTIC OCEAN**

RUSSIA

ALASKA

CANADA

Anchorage

km 0    300
mi 0    300

*PACIFIC OCEAN*

*PACIFIC OCEAN*

C A N A N

Seattle
**WASHINGTON**
Portland

MONTANA

NORTH DAKOTA

MINNESOT

**OREGON**

IDAHO

SOUTH DAKOTA

Minneapolis

WYOMING

NEBRASKA

IOW

Omaha

Salt Lake City

Denver

San Francisco
Sacramento
**NEVADA**
UTAH
COLORADO
KANSAS
Kansas City
M

Las Vegas
**CALIFORNIA**
Los Angeles
ARIZONA
Albuquerque
Tulsa
Oklahoma City
**OKLAHOMA**
Li
Ro

San Diego
Phoenix
**NEW MEXICO**
Dallas

Tucson
**TEXAS**

Austin
Hous

San Antonio

km 0  50 100
mi 0  50  100

Honolulu

**HAWAII**

*PACIFIC OCEAN*

*Hawaii*

M E X I C O

## Unit Preview

**Farmland**
Much of the country's farmland is in the Midwest
**Chapter 7, page 190**

**Automobile Factory**
Henry Ford changed the way cars were made
**Chapter 7, page 208**

**Wrigley Field**
One of the country's oldest ballparks is in Chicago
**Chapter 8, page 220**

## MAP

**A          D          A**

NEW HAMPSHIRE
VERMONT
MAINE

*L. Superior*

WI

*L. Michigan*          *L. Huron*

MICHIGAN

*L. Ontario*

NEW YORK
Buffalo    Hartford
MASSACHUSETTS
• Boston

Detroit •          *L. Erie*
Cleveland •          New York •
RHODE ISLAND
Providence
CONNECTICUT

Chicago •          PENNSYLVANIA
Pittsburgh •          Philadelphia
NEW JERSEY

ILLINOIS          OHIO
Columbus •          Baltimore •
Indianapolis •          Cincinnati •          Washington,          DELAWARE
INDIANA          WEST          D.C.          MARYLAND
VIRGINIA          Virginia Beach
St. Louis •          Louisville •          VIRGINIA

KENTUCKY          Raleigh •
NORTH
CAROLINA

ATLANTIC
OCEAN

Nashville •          Charlotte •
TENNESSEE

AK          Memphis •          Columbia •
SOUTH
CAROLINA

N
NW    NE
W          E
SW    SE
S

Birmingham •          Atlanta •

MISSISSIPPI          GEORGIA

Jackson •
ALABAMA

Baton
Rouge •          Jacksonville •

LA
New Orleans •

Orlando •
Tampa •
FLORIDA
Miami •

*Gulf of
Mexico*

km  0    150   300
mi  0    150   300

### LEGEND
— Regional border
**People per square mile**
Less than 1
1 to 9
10 to 49
50 to 99
100 to 249
250 or More

---

## Connect to ... The Nation

### Midwest Population Growth

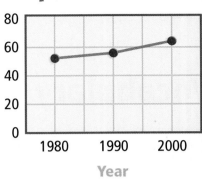

Population (in millions): 80, 60, 40, 20, 0
Year: 1980, 1990, 2000

By about how much did the Midwest's population grow from 1980 to 2000?

### U.S. Population Growth

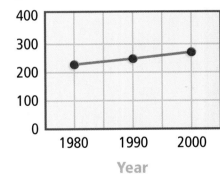

Population (in millions): 400, 300, 200, 100, 0
Year: 1980, 1990, 2000

How is the Midwest's population growth different from growth in the United States?

**CURRENT     EVENTS
WEEKLY (WR) READER**

**Current events on the web!**

Read social studies articles about current events at:
**www.eduplace.com/kids/hmss/**

---

### Tornadoes
The Plains States often have severe weather
**Chapter 8, page 229**

## Vocabulary Preview

**Technology**

*e •* **glossary**
*e •* **word games**
www.eduplace.com/kids/hmss05/

### prairie

On the wide, flat **prairie** of the Midwest, people have replaced most of the tall grasses with farmland. **page 190**

### tributary

A **tributary** is a smaller river or stream that flows into a larger river or stream. Each major river has many tributaries that flow into it. **page 191**

## Chapter Timeline

| 1783 Northwest Territory | 1803 Louisiana Territory | 1806 Lewis and Clark's return | 1862 Homestead Act |

1700

1800

# Reading Strategy

**Summarize** Use this strategy to help you understand important information in this chapter.

**Quick Tip** Take notes as you read. Then highlight the most important information.

## homestead

The government sold plots of land called **homesteads** to settlers. Many homesteaders built their houses from chunks of prairie earth. **page 207**

## assembly line

On an **assembly line** each worker does only one small part of the manufacturing process. Goods can be made more quickly using an assembly line. **page 208**

1904
**World's Fair in St. Louis**

1900          2000

# Land and Climate

## VOCABULARY

prairie
tributary
levee
lock

**Vocabulary Strategy**

tributary

**Tributary** and **contribute** have the same root. **Contribute** means to give or add to something. A **tributary** adds water to a larger stream or river.

## READING SKILL

**Cause and Effect**
How did waterways affect settlement in the Midwest? List causes on the chart.

| Cause | Effect |
| --- | --- |
|  |  |

**Build on What You Know** Does wind seem harsher out in the open than in a forest? The Midwest has lots of flat, open plains. What might the wind feel like there?

## Land and Water of the Midwest

**Main Idea** The Midwest is a central region of wide open plains, thick woods, and huge waterways.

The Midwest lies in the middle of the country. Canada lies to the north. The Rocky Mountains and the Appalachian Mountains lie on either side of it.

The eastern part of this region features the Great Lakes. The land is mostly flat, with some hilly areas. The rainfall here supports deep forests. Pine forests in the north can withstand the harsh climate. The south has a mix of trees.

West of the Great Lakes are the Great Plains. The climate is drier here. Prairie grasses cover much of the land. A **prairie** is a dry, mostly flat grassland with few trees. People have turned prairies into farmland. Much of the country's wheat and corn is grown here.

**Iowa Farmland** Midwestern farmers have turned grasslands into farms.

The Midwest

CANADA

LEGEND
Great Lakes States
Plains States
★ State capital

NORTH DAKOTA
★ Bismarck

Mesabi Range

Lake Superior

MINNESOTA

M I C H I G A N

Lake Huron

Lake Ontario

SOUTH DAKOTA
★ Pierre

St. Paul
Minneapolis ★

WISCONSIN

Lake Michigan

Lansing ★

Lake Erie

Black Hills

Missouri River

Madison ★
Milwaukee

Detroit

Mississippi River

IOWA
Des Moines ★

Chicago

Cleveland

OHIO

NEBRASKA
Omaha
Lincoln ★

Platte River

Illinois River

Wabash River

Indianapolis ★

Columbus ★

ILLINOIS

INDIANA

N
W    E
S

Topeka ★

Kansas City

Springfield ★

Arkansas River

KANSAS

St. Louis
Jefferson City ★
MISSOURI

Ohio River

km 0   100  200
mi 0   100  200

**Midwest Regions** The Midwest includes the Plains States and the Great Lakes States.

## Water Resources

The Midwest has two main waterways. The Great Lakes are one of them. Glaciers created these five lakes. They form the world's largest body of fresh water. Rivers and canals connect the lakes to the Atlantic Ocean and the Gulf of Mexico. Ships reach the lakes through these waterways.

The Mississippi River is the second main waterway. With its major tributaries, the Missouri and Ohio rivers, it forms the nation's largest river system. A **tributary** is a river or stream that flows into another river. Dams and levees help limit floods on these rivers. A **levee** is a high river bank that stops the river from overflowing.

Before the invention of railroads, travel on waterways was faster and less expensive than land travel. Towns along water routes became trading centers. Some, such as Chicago and Milwaukee, became large cities.

Waterfalls can make river travel difficult. Locks can help ships get past waterfalls. A **lock** is a part of a waterway that is closed off by gates. Ships enter a lock. Then, people let water into or out of it. As the water level goes up or down, so does the ship. The lock at St. Anthony Falls in Minneapolis raises and lowers ships by 50 feet.

**REVIEW** What are the major regions and waterways of the Midwest?

# Climate, Plants, Animals

**Main Idea** The Midwest can have severe weather.

The location of the Midwest affects its climate. There is no ocean nearby to warm the land in winter and cool it in summer. As a result, the climate varies more than in coastal regions. In parts of the Midwest, the temperature can change as much as 100°F between winter and summer.

The Great Lakes are not as big as an ocean, but they affect the climate by adding moisture to the air. In winter, this moisture causes lake effect snow.

Fierce snowstorms called blizzards often strike the region. People have adapted, though. They wear layers of clothing. They use covered walkways to get from one building to another.

People also find ways to enjoy winter. They go skiing, skating, and icefishing. They hold winter festivals.

Tornadoes often hit the Midwest in warmer weather. Tornadoes are strong, spinning storms with high winds.

**SKILL Reading Charts** Which two states have had the highest temperatures?

## Extreme Temperatures in the Midwest

| State | Highest | Lowest |
|-------|---------|--------|
| Illinois | 117°F | −36°F |
| Indiana | 116°F | −36°F |
| Iowa | 118°F | −47°F |
| Kansas | 121°F | −40°F |
| Michigan | 112°F | −51°F |
| Minnesota | 114°F | −60°F |
| Missouri | 118°F | −40°F |
| Nebraska | 118°F | −47°F |
| North Dakota | 121°F | −60°F |
| Ohio | 113°F | −39°F |
| South Dakota | 120°F | −58°F |
| Wisconsin | 114°F | −55°F |

## Lake Effect Snow

❶ Warm, moist air rises from the lake and meets cold, dry air.

❷ The cold air freezes the moisture and drops it as snow over the land.

## Midwestern Plants and Animals

Plants and animals have adapted to the region's climate extremes. For example, some prairie grasses have deep roots. They help the plants find moisture. Pine trees keep their needles for years. This saves energy and helps the trees survive harsh weather.

Animals have also adapted. Some birds migrate to warmer places. Prairie dogs dig underground dens that protect them from severe weather. A prairie dog is a rodent that belongs to the squirrel family.

Millions of bison, or buffalo, once roamed the Great Plains. Thick coats of fur kept them warm. Hunters wanted this fur. By 1885, they had killed all but a few hundred bison. Then people started protecting bison. Today, about 150,000 bison live in the United States.

**REVIEW** How have people and wildlife adapted to the climate of the Midwest?

## Lesson Summary

- Landforms of the Midwest include prairies, hills, and forests.
- The two main waterways are the Great Lakes and the Mississippi River system.
- The Midwest is very hot in summer and very cold in winter.

## Why It Matters . . .

People, plants, and animals have adapted to the Midwest's climate and made it their home.

**Prairie Dog** The prairie dog, found in the Midwest, is not really a dog. It is a rodent.

## Lesson Review

❶ **VOCABULARY** Write a paragraph showing that you know what **levee** and **lock** mean.

❷ 🔄 **READING SKILL** Explain one **cause** of the growth of Chicago.

❸ **MAIN IDEA: Geography** Name the major midwestern landforms.

❹ **MAIN IDEA: Geography** How does location affect climate in the Midwest?

❺ **CRITICAL THINKING: Evaluate** In what ways might the Midwest be different without its large rivers and tributaries?

✏️ **WRITING ACTIVITY** Suppose a student from Florida was moving to the Midwest. What clothes should the student bring? Write a letter explaining what the student should pack.

# The **Mighty** Mississippi

**The Mississippi River flows through ten of the fifty states.** It starts in Minnesota and ends in Louisiana at the Gulf of Mexico. People use the river for many purposes. Its water is used for drinking, for making electricity, and for transporting people and goods. Barges on the Mississippi carry grain, coal, gravel, petroleum products, chemicals, paper, wood, coffee, iron, and steel. This powerful river provides many benefits, but people can never completely tame it.

**Water**
The Mississippi is a source of fresh water for millions of people who live in nearby towns and cities.

**Agriculture**
Farmers use water from the Mississippi to grow cotton, corn, soybeans, and rice. Others use the water to raise catfish.

**Transportation**
For hundreds of years, the river has been like a highway. Today, there is more traffic than ever. Each year, people ship about 500 million tons of cargo on the river.

## Recreation

Every year, more than 12 million people visit the upper Mississippi to boat, fish, and enjoy the scenery. These visitors create jobs for people who live near the river.

## Floods and Levees

The U.S. government has built **levees** and other structures to try to control the river's yearly floods. However, levees prevent natural wetlands from soaking up extra water. This may make flooding worse downstream.

## Towns

Many towns are along the river. When people built levees, they thought it was safe to build near the river's edge. However, flooding still takes place sometimes. Some people think that homes should be built on higher ground.

# Activities

1. **DRAW YOUR OWN** Draw a picture of life on the Mississippi. Show people using the river in at least three ways.

2. **RESEARCH IT** Find out about dams and locks. How do they work? Why are they used? How many are there on the Mississippi? Write about your findings.

# Resources and Economy

**Build on What You Know** How often do you go to the market? Do they have many kinds of cereal, cheese, and bread? These foods come from the Midwest.

## Using Midwestern Resources

**Main Idea** Resources provide products and jobs.

The Midwest has many natural resources. Water, rich soil, and minerals helped the region become a major farming and manufacturing center.

People use the Midwest's water resources in many ways. Farmers water their crops. More than 26 million people drink water from the Great Lakes. Rivers and lakes provide transportation. Barges and ships carry resources, such as coal. Large manufacturing centers have grown along waterways.

In parts of the Midwest, the soil and climate support dense forests. Forests provide lumber and wood products, such as plywood and paper.

**Wakeboarding** Midwesterners enjoy many activities on the region's lakes and rivers.

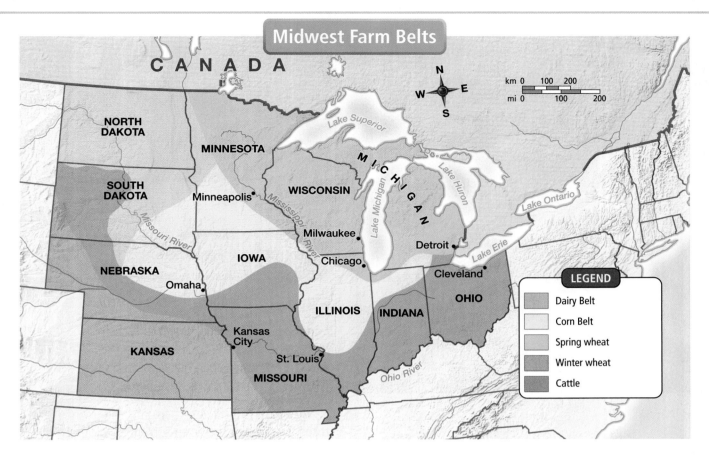

**Midwest Farm Belts** The Midwest has rich soil, hot summers, and plenty of rain.

**SKILL** Reading Maps Where is spring wheat the most important crop?

## A Farming Region

In the early 1800s, the Midwest's rich soil attracted many farmers. Today, fields of wheat, corn, and soybeans stretch for miles. Iowa, Illinois, and Nebraska produce more corn than any other states.

Midwestern farmers also grow hay, fruits, and vegetables. They raise hogs and dairy cows. Wisconsin is called America's Dairyland. Minnesota is called the Bread and Butter State. Many people work in farm-related industries. Some workers make food products such as jam or cereal. Some build tractors. Others ship food around the world.

## Mining and Other Industries

Valuable minerals lie below the Midwest's soil. These include stone and minerals used for making cement. Lead is another valuable mineral. People use it to make batteries and computers. Illinois is important in the coal industry. Much of the nation's iron ore comes from Minnesota and Michigan. Workers use iron ore to make steel.

Steel is used to make products that range from tools to planes, boats, bridges, and cars. Detroit, Michigan, is famous for its automobile industry. Its nickname is "Motor City."

**REVIEW** Name two midwestern industries.

| Some Goods and Services from the Midwest | |
| --- | --- |
| **Region** | **Goods and Services** |
| **Plains States** | banking, health care, chemical products, insurance, houses, telephone services, auto sales, real estate, tires, hotels |
| **Great Lakes States** | health care, banking, airlines, electronic equipment, medicines, engineering, business services, cars and trucks |

# The Midwest's Economy

**Main Idea** The Midwest's economy was built around its natural resources and the laws of supply and demand.

If you were a manufacturer, you might want to build your factory in the Midwest. The region has many natural resources. It has many skilled workers. It also has waterways for moving goods. Many manufacturers built factories in the Midwest to make products such as cars and musical instruments.

Service industries have also grown in the Midwest. A service is an activity a person or company does for someone else. For example, the transportation industry provides a service. Factories decide to bring raw materials in and ship finished goods out to consumers.

**Service Industries in the Midwest**
Services such as banking do not come directly from natural resources.

**SKILL** **Reading Charts** Which goods and services might a traveler use?

Many midwestern cities have good railroads, streets, and waterways to serve consumers. Indianapolis, Chicago, Kansas City, and other cities in the region serve as transportation hubs.

People and businesses also want banking, health, and communication services. If someone wants to buy or sell a home, the person can talk to a real estate agent. These services and others have become major industries in the Midwest.

## Supply and Demand

The laws of supply and demand can help you understand the Midwest's economy—and the economy of all regions. **Supply** is how much of a product producers will make at different prices. **Demand** is how much of a product consumers will buy at different prices.

Supply and demand affect each other. Suppose a company makes a delicious new cereal. Many people want to buy it. When demand for the cereal rises, the price also rises. That is because people are willing to pay a higher price for what they want. At the higher price, the cereal maker will make more of its new cereal. Over time, the higher price will attract more suppliers. As more suppliers enter the market, the supply increases. Prices begin to go down.

Midwestern farmers supply many products, including milk, corn, and meat. When there is an increase in demand, prices rise. Farmers earn more income, but consumers pay higher prices. When there is an increase in supply, prices fall. Farmers earn less income, but consumers pay lower prices.

**REVIEW** Why have certain businesses grown in the Midwest?

### Lesson Summary

The Midwest has many natural and human resources. As a result, farming and manufacturing industries have grown there. Like industries everywhere, they are affected by supply and demand.

## Why It Matters ...

Midwestern businesses grow when there is demand for their products.

## Lesson Review

❶ **VOCABULARY** Explain what happens to the **supply** of a product when **demand** for it increases.

❷ **READING SKILL** Which industries did you **classify** as services?

❸ **MAIN IDEA: Geography** Name three farm industries of the Midwest.

❹ **MAIN IDEA: Economics** How does high demand affect producers?

❺ **CRITICAL THINKING: Draw Conclusions** What makes iron ore such an important mineral?

**HANDS ON**

**DRAMA ACTIVITY** Write a skit about a person selling two trading cards. Few people want to buy one of the cards. Many people want the other card. Show how demand affects the price of the cards. Perform the skit with your classmates.

# Supply and Demand

**Most of the world's popcorn is grown in the Midwest.** Selling popcorn is a good way for movie theaters to earn money. Theater owners must decide how much popcorn to make each day and what to charge for each box.

## Supply

The **supply** of popcorn is how much theater owners are willing and able to sell at different prices. Look at the chart and think about how the price affects the supply.

### Supply of Popcorn

| Price of one box of popcorn | Amount owners will produce at each price |
|---|---|
| 50 cents | 10 boxes |
| $1 | 50 boxes |
| $4 | 300 boxes |
| $7 | 600 boxes |
| $10 | 800 boxes |

## Demand

The **demand** for popcorn is how much people are willing and able to buy at different prices. If the popcorn's price is low, many people will buy it. However, when the price goes up, people will buy less. The chart shows how price affects demand.

### Demand of Popcorn

| Price of one box of popcorn | Amount people will buy at each price |
|---|---|
| 50 cents | 800 boxes |
| $1 | 600 boxes |
| $4 | 300 boxes |
| $7 | 50 boxes |
| $10 | 10 boxes |

| Supply Greater Than Demand | Demand Greater Than Supply | Supply Equals Demand |
|---|---|---|

## Too Much Popcorn

The seller has set a high price. He planned to sell 600 boxes of popcorn. But at this high price, people demanded only a few boxes.

## Not Enough Popcorn

The seller has set a low price. He planned to sell only a few boxes of popcorn. But at this low price, people demanded a lot of boxes.

## Just Enough Popcorn

The seller has the right amount of popcorn and customers. According to the charts on page 200, the seller is making 300 boxes of popcorn and charging $4 per box.

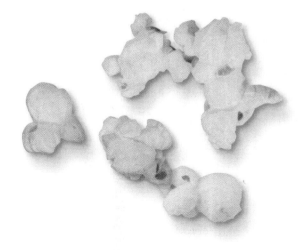

# Activities

1. **TALK ABOUT IT** Why will the theater owners sell less popcorn if the price rises above $4 per box?

2. **CHART IT** Make your own supply and demand charts for a product.

# Skillbuilder

# Use a Special Purpose Map

Some maps have a special purpose. They use different symbols to tell about the special features of a place. The map below tells you about resources in the Midwest.

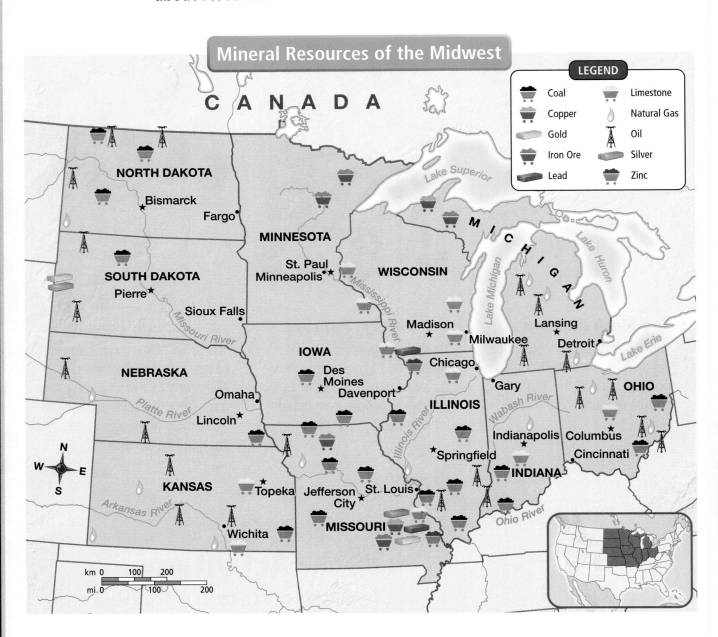

Mineral Resources of the Midwest

LEGEND

| | |
|---|---|
| Coal | Limestone |
| Copper | Natural Gas |
| Gold | Oil |
| Iron Ore | Silver |
| Lead | Zinc |

CANADA

NORTH DAKOTA
Bismarck
Fargo

MINNESOTA
Lake Superior

SOUTH DAKOTA
Pierre
Sioux Falls
Missouri River

St. Paul
Minneapolis
WISCONSIN
Mississippi River

MICHIGAN
Lake Michigan
Lake Huron
Lansing
Detroit
Lake Erie

NEBRASKA
Omaha
Lincoln
Platte River

IOWA
Des Moines
Davenport

Madison
Milwaukee
Chicago
Gary

OHIO
Columbus
Cincinnati

KANSAS
Topeka
Arkansas River
Wichita

Jefferson City
St. Louis
MISSOURI

ILLINOIS
Springfield
Illinois River
Wabash River
INDIANA
Indianapolis
Ohio River

N
W E
S

km 0    100    200
mi 0    100    200

## Learn the Skill

**Step 1:** Read the map title to find out what kind of information is shown on the map.

Mineral Resources of the Midwest

**Step 2:** Study the map's legend. Notice that each symbol represents one of the different mineral resources found in the Midwest.

LEGEND

Coal     Limestone

Copper     Natural gas

Gold     Oil

Iron ore     Silver

Lead     Zinc

**Step 3:** Note where the symbols from the legend appear on the map. For example, the coal symbol appears in North Dakota. This shows that coal is mined in that state.

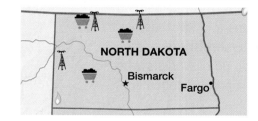

NORTH DAKOTA

Bismarck

Fargo

## Practice the Skill

Use the map on page 202 to answer the questions.

**1** Look at the legend. Name seven mineral resources that are found in the Midwest region.

**2** According to the map, which mineral resources are found in the state of Wisconsin?

**3** Based on this map, which mineral resource is found most widely in the Midwest?

## Apply the Skill

Study the special purpose map on page 197. Then write a paragraph that summarizes the information shown on the map.

# People of the Midwest

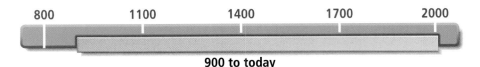

800 1100 1400 1700 2000

**900 to today**

## VOCABULARY

homestead
reservation
assembly line

**Vocabulary Strategy**

assembly line

To **assemble** something means to put it together. An **assembly line** is made up of workers who put a product together.

## READING SKILL

**Sequence** Who first lived in the Midwest? Chart the order in which people came to the region.

| 1 | |
| 2 | |
| 3 | |
| 4 | |

**Build on What You Know** What would happen if your family moved to a new town? You would need to make some changes in your life. The first people in the Midwest had to change their lives in many ways.

## The Midwest's First People

**Main Idea** Many American Indian groups lived in the Midwest region.

People have lived in the Midwest for centuries. Early American Indian groups lived in the Great Lakes region. Some of these groups farmed and made tools from stone and bone. Some built huge earth mounds that served as temples or burial mounds.

The mound-building Indians disappeared before Europeans arrived in the 1600s. Other groups took their place, including the Wyandot (WHY uhn dot), Haudenosaunee, Shawnee, Miami, and Ottawa. These Woodland Indians built houses with wood frames.

**Cahokia Mounds**
This mound was built by American Indians who lived in present-day Illinois from about 900 to 1500.

## The Plains Indians

Other American Indian groups lived on the Great Plains. Some built homes and farmed. Others were nomadic. This means they traveled from place to place.

Nomadic Plains Indians followed and hunted the buffalo. In the 1500s, Spanish explorers brought horses to North America. Plains hunters quickly learned to use these animals. Horses made it much easier to hunt buffalo.

When they traveled, Plains Indians carried their homes with them. These homes, called tepees, were easy to take apart and move. They were made of poles covered with animal skins.

## Struggles for Control

American Indians traded with the arriving Europeans. The American Indians wanted knives and tools. The Europeans wanted furs and land. Some were willing to take the land by force.

In the mid-1700s, England and France went to war for control of the Ohio region. The British won in 1763, when the two countries signed the Treaty of Paris. **Pontiac,** an Ottawa chief, had fought with the French. After the war, he kept fighting the British until 1765. Today, about 4,700 midwesterners describe themselves as Ottawa.

**REVIEW** How did horses change the lives of the Plains Indians long ago?

**Tepee** Nomadic Plains Indians carried their homes with them when they moved.

# Early Settlers

**Main Idea** The Midwest attracted a large population.

In 1783, the United States gained control of the Northwest Territory from the British. This area included most of the present-day Great Lakes region.

Then, in 1803, President **Thomas Jefferson** bought the Louisiana Territory from France. This doubled the size of the United States. Jefferson sent **Meriwether Lewis** and **William Clark** to explore the region. They returned from their 8,000-mile journey in 1806. They brought back information about the region, its plants and animals, and American Indian cultures.

Settlers moved into these new areas. They came for many reasons. Eastern farmers came looking for new land. Soldiers came to claim land promised to them by the government. Many Germans and Scandinavians immigrated to the Midwest. They wanted religious freedom and better lives. By 1880, more than 70 percent of Minnesota's non–American Indian population was made up of immigrants and their children.

**A Growing Nation** The United States greatly increased in size between 1787 and 1803.

**SKILL** **Reading Maps** In which direction did the Louisiana Territory expand the United States?

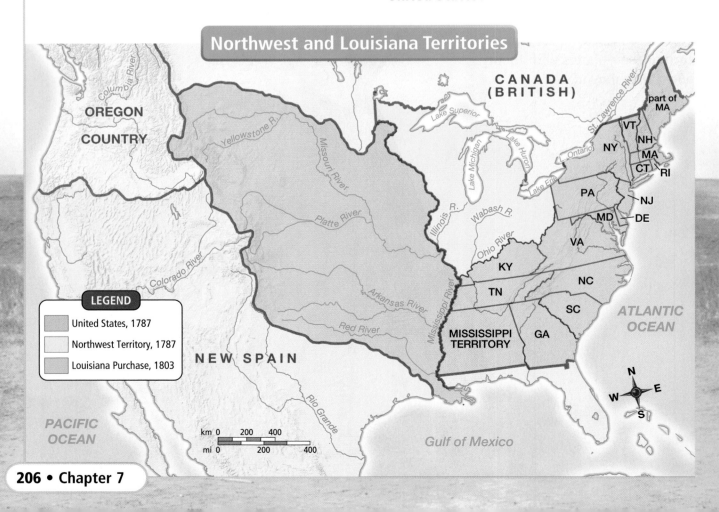

**Northwest and Louisiana Territories**

Columbia River

CANADA
(BRITISH)

OREGON
COUNTRY

Yellowstone R.

Missouri River

Lake Superior

part of MA

St. Lawrence River

VT
NH

Lake Michigan

Lake Huron

Ontario
NY

MA

CT
RI

Lake Erie

Platte River

Illinois R.

Wabash R.

PA

NJ

MD
DE

Colorado River

Ohio River

VA

KY

NC

LEGEND

United States, 1787

Arkansas River

TN

Northwest Territory, 1787

Mississippi River

SC

ATLANTIC
OCEAN

Red River

Louisiana Purchase, 1803

NEW SPAIN

MISSISSIPPI
TERRITORY

GA

N
W — E
S

PACIFIC
OCEAN

Rio Grande

km 0    200    400
mi 0    200    400

Gulf of Mexico

## Homesteaders on the Great Plains

Settlers did not rush to the Great Plains at first. However, in 1862, Congress passed the Homestead Act. A **homestead** is a piece of land given to someone to settle and farm there. The Homestead Act offered Great Plains land for a small fee to people who would live there for five years. People learned to farm this treeless land.

Life was hard for homesteaders. They often had to deal with harsh weather, prairie fires, and clouds of grasshoppers. Because there were too few trees to build wooden houses, people built houses of sod. Sod is large chunks of soil held together by plant roots.

In spite of the hardships, many homesteaders continued to arrive. They pushed American Indians off the land. Hunters had killed nearly all of the buffalo, the American Indians' main food supply. Some American Indians fought, but most were forced to move to reservations. A **reservation** is land that is set aside by the government for American Indians.

**REVIEW** What were two reasons that the United States grew?

**Sod School House** Sod houses could be small and dirty. Snakes and mice often lived in the walls.

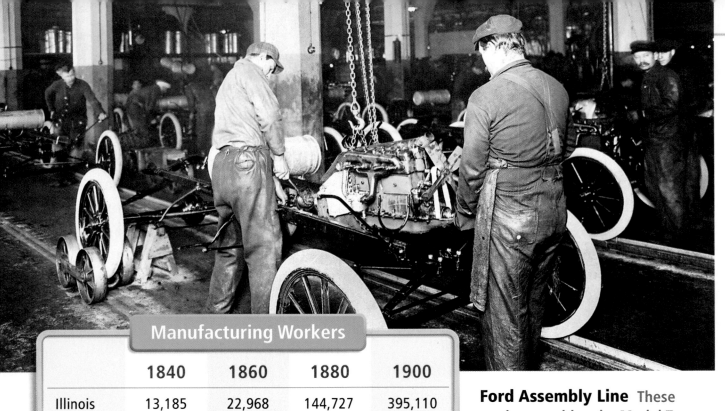

| Manufacturing Workers | | | |
|---|---|---|---|
| | 1840 | 1860 | 1880 | 1900 |
| Illinois | 13,185 | 22,968 | 144,727 | 395,110 |
| Iowa | 1,629 | 6,307 | 28,372 | 58,553 |
| Michigan | 6,890 | 23,190 | 77,591 | 162,355 |
| Missouri | 11,100 | 19,681 | 63,995 | 134,975 |

**Ford Assembly Line** These workers could make Model T automobiles quickly and cheaply.

**SKILL** **Reading Charts** What happened to the number of manufacturing workers in the Midwest between 1840 and 1900?

# Midwestern Cities

**Main Idea** Midwestern cities grew because of industry and good transportation routes.

In the late 1800s, many Americans moved from farms to cities. City factories needed workers. In Detroit, **Henry Ford** improved the assembly line for his automobile factory. On an assembly line, each worker does one small part of the job as a product moves along the line.

New settlers helped midwestern cities grow. After World War I, for example, many African Americans moved from the South to the Midwest. They hoped to get good factory jobs.

## St. Louis, Missouri

St. Louis lies just south of where the Missouri River flows into the Mississippi. It began as a French fur-trading post in 1764. Later, many western settlers stopped there for supplies. Today, the Gateway Arch stands as a monument to the pioneers who passed through St. Louis.

Transportation helped St. Louis become an important city. Steamboats and trains brought goods and people from all over the country. By the 1890s, skyscrapers rose above busy downtown streets. St. Louis remains a transportation hub and an industrial center today.

## Minneapolis, Minnesota

Minneapolis grew along the Mississippi River during the mid-1800s. Waterfalls provided power for mills that turned wheat into flour and timber into lumber. By the 1880s, the city was producing millions of barrels of flour each year. During the 20th century, manufacturing, food processing, computers, and health services became major industries.

Today, more than 380,000 people live in Minneapolis. In bad weather, people can walk in the city's enclosed skyway system. Visitors to the Mill City Museum learn how flour mills helped the city grow.

**REVIEW** Why did midwestern cities grow?

**Minneapolis** The Mississippi River flows through Minneapolis.

## Lesson Summary

American Indians lived in Midwest

United States gained Northwest and Louisiana territories

Homesteaders and immigrants came to region

Big cities and industry grew

## Why It Matters...

Many people have moved to midwestern cities for better jobs.

## Lesson Review

| 1783 Northwest Territory | 1803 Louisiana Territory | | 1862 Homestead Act |

1780   1795   1810   1825   1840   1855   1870

❶ **VOCABULARY** Write a paragraph contrasting a **homestead** and a **reservation.**

❷ **READING SKILL** Show the **sequence** of events that led to St. Louis's growth.

❸ **MAIN IDEA: Government** What government actions brought people to the Great Plains?

❹ **MAIN IDEA: Economics** What factors help explain why Minneapolis grew?

❺ **TIMELINE SKILL** Which territory did the nation gain first, Northwest or Louisiana?

❻ **CRITICAL THINKING: Evaluate** Would you rather work on an assembly line or make something all by yourself? Why?

**WRITING ACTIVITY** Many homesteaders kept journals. Write a journal entry that one of the children might write. Describe a funny or scary event.

209

# Lewis AND Clark

President Thomas Jefferson bought the Louisiana Territory in 1803. At the time, he knew little about the huge piece of land he had bought. He sent Meriwether Lewis and William Clark to explore and map the land west of the Mississippi River.

The journey of Lewis and Clark was a major event in U.S. history. Their explorations led others to journey to the West. Trace their journey on the map, starting in St. Louis.

**⑤ Fort Clatsop**
Columbia River

**④** Missouri River
Traveler's Rest
**Great Falls**
**Three Forks**
**Lemhi Pass**

Meriwether Lewis

William Clark

*"Ocean in view! O! the joy!"*

— William Clark,
November 7, 1805

**❶ May 1804:**
## The Journey Begins!
Lewis, Clark, and their team of more than 40 men headed up the Missouri River into land unexplored by Europeans. It would be a two year trip.

**❷ September 1804:**
## Across the Plains
In the grasslands of what is now South Dakota, the group saw "new" animals such as prairie dogs, pronghorn antelope, coyotes, and jackrabbits. They also saw herds of thousands of buffalo.

**❸ October 1804–April 1805:**
## The First Winter
The group built a winter fort near the villages of the Mandan and Hidatsa people. Here, a Shoshone Indian woman named Sacagawea (sak uh guh WEE uh) helped the men find food.

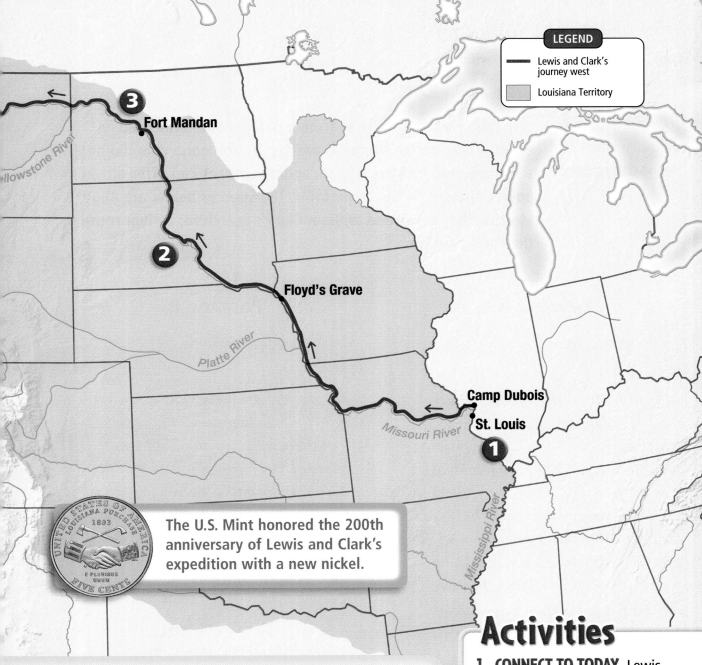

LEGEND
— Lewis and Clark's journey west
  Louisiana Territory

**3** Fort Mandan

Yellowstone River

**2**

Floyd's Grave

Platte River

Camp Dubois

St. Louis

**1**

Missouri River

Mississippi River

The U.S. Mint honored the 200th anniversary of Lewis and Clark's expedition with a new nickel.

**4** June 1805:
# The Great Falls
Five huge waterfalls blocked the group's travel. It took a month to carry boats and supplies 18 miles to a safe spot up the river.

**5** December 1805–March 1806:
# The Pacific!
The group spent the winter at Fort Clatsop, waiting for the right time to head home. By the time they completed their journey in September 1806, they had traveled about 8,000 miles.

# Activities

1. **CONNECT TO TODAY** Lewis and Clark showed **courage** by going on their journey. Talk about someone you know who has done something courageous.

2. **RESEARCH IT** Read more about Lewis and Clark's journey. Write a series of journal entries about why Sacagawea helped the expedition.

## Skillbuilder

# Identify Primary and Secondary Sources

▶ **VOCABULARY**

primary source
secondary source

A primary source comes from a person who witnessed an event. A secondary source is written by someone who did not see the event. Primary and secondary sources can offer different points of view on the same topic. The sources below are about Merriwether Lewis and William Clark's search for a river route to the Pacific Ocean.

### Passage A

*After traveling up the Missouri River through Montana, Lewis and Clark had to make a decision. The Missouri became two rivers. Only one would take them to the Pacific Ocean. Before deciding, Lewis and some men explored the river to the right. Clark and a group followed the left. When they returned to their camp, both Lewis and Clark felt the left river was the Missouri. The others in their group disagreed. Lewis named the river on the right after his cousin, Maria.*

### Passage B

*The whole of my party to a man except myself was fully persuaded [convinced] that this river [the right river] was the Missouri, but being fully of opinion that it was neither the main stream nor that which it would be advisable [wise] for us to take, I determined [decided] to give it a name and in honor of Miss Maria Wood called it Maria's River.*

—The Lewis and Clark Journals, June 8, 1805

## Learn the Skill

**Step 1:** Read the sources carefully. What is their subject?

**Step 2:** Identify the primary source. Look for words such as **I, my, we,** and **our.** Also look for personal details. These hint that the writer was actually at the event being described.

**Step 3:** Find the secondary source. Secondary sources do not include personal information about the event. Often, secondary sources summarize or analyze an event.

## Practice the Skill

Use the passages on page 212 to answer the questions.

1. Which is the primary source, and which is the secondary source? How do you know?

2. Which facts are the same in both sources?

3. What details do you learn from the secondary source that are not included in the primary source?

## Apply the Skill

Using a newspaper, find one example of a primary source and one example of a secondary source. Write a paragraph explaining how the two sources are similar and how they are different.

## Visual Summary

**1. – 3.** ✏️ Write a description of each item named below.

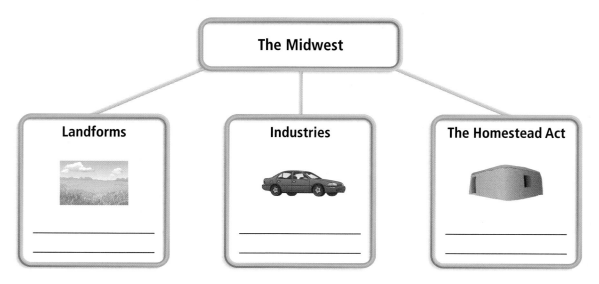

The Midwest

Landforms

Industries

The Homestead Act

## Facts and Main Ideas

☑️ **TEST PREP** Answer each question below.

4. **Geography** Why are the Great Lakes and the Mississippi River important?

5. **Geography** Why do so many food products come from the Midwest?

6. **Economics** What usually happens to prices when there is great demand for a product?

7. **Culture** What did early European settlers to the Midwest want from the American Indians who lived there?

8. **History** What did gaining control of the Northwest Territory mean to the United States?

## Vocabulary

☑️ **TEST PREP** Choose the correct word from the list below to complete each sentence.

**tributary,** p. 191
**supply,** p. 199
**assembly line,** p. 208

9. A _____ is a river or stream that flows into another river.

10. In an _____, each worker does a small part of the whole job.

11. _____ is how much of a product producers will make at different prices.

| 1763 England and France sign the Treaty of Paris | 1783 U.S. gains Northwest Territory from the British | 1803 U.S. buys Louisiana Territory from France | 1862 Congress passes the Homestead Act |

1700     1800     1900

## Apply Skills

✓ **TEST PREP** **Read a Special Purpose Map** Study the Crystal Lake Beach map below. Then use your map skills to answer each question.

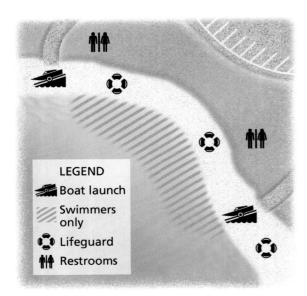

LEGEND
🚤 Boat launch
⫻ Swimmers only
🛟 Lifeguard
🚻 Restrooms

**12.** What is the purpose of the map?

   **A.** to sell boats
   **B.** to provide a guide for visitors
   **C.** to keep people out of the lake
   **D.** to identify wildlife

**13.** How many places for people to put their boats into the water does the map show?

   **A.** two
   **B.** three
   **C.** four
   **D.** none

## Critical Thinking

✓ **TEST PREP** Write a short paragraph to answer each question below.

**14.** **Cause and Effect** Describe effects of the Homestead Act on the Midwest.

**15.** **Compare and Contrast** Describe differences between the Plains Indians and the Woodland Indians of the Great Lakes.

## Timeline

Use the Chapter Summary Timeline to answer the question.

**16.** In what year did the United States gain control of the Northwest Territory?

# Activities

**HANDS ON**

**Drama Activity** Write a script for a dialogue between two homesteaders. Tell why they have come to the Great Plains and what they hope for.

**Writing Activity** Write a personal essay telling what you think about what happened to American Indians when settlers started arriving in their homeland. Give reasons for your opinion.

**Technology**
**Writing Process Tips**
Get help with your paragraph at:
www.eduplace.com/kids/hmss/

# Living in the Midwest

**Technology**

*e* • **glossary**
*e* • **word games**
www.eduplace.com/kids/hmss05/

## Vocabulary Preview

### elevated train

Both subways and **elevated trains** help people travel quickly without getting in the way of city traffic. Elevated trains travel above the ground. **page 219**

### wages

Many workers receive hourly, daily, or weekly **wages** for their jobs. Others are paid a certain amount of money for a specific task. **page 219**

# Reading Strategy

**Question** Use this strategy as you read the lessons in this chapter.

Quick Tip Stop and ask yourself questions. Do you need to go back and reread for the answers?

## population density

In the Midwest, there are many areas with a low **population density.** People live far apart in these rural areas. The Midwest also has big cities where the population density is high. **page 230**

## grain elevator

**Grain elevators** are found throughout the Plains States, especially near railway lines. Farmers store grain there before transporting it to other parts of the country. **page 230**

**What's Special About**

# The Great Lakes States

## VOCABULARY

**elevated train**
**wages**

**Vocabulary Strategy**

elevated train

The word **elevate** means to raise. An **elevated train** runs on a track that is raised above the ground.

 **READING SKILL**
**Compare and Contrast**
Use a Venn diagram to compare and contrast the rural and urban areas of the Great Lakes States.

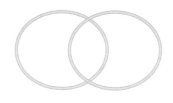

**Chicago, Illinois** This city of nearly three million people lies on the shore of Lake Michigan.

**Build on What You Know** Do you enjoy camping and fishing, or would you rather watch a baseball game? Would you like to explore a submarine or tour a cheese factory? You can do all of these things in the Great Lakes States.

## Where People Live

**Main Idea** People in the Great Lakes States live near large lakes, in vast rural areas, and in busy cities and suburbs.

The Great Lakes States include Ohio, Indiana, Illinois, Michigan, Wisconsin, and Minnesota. Each state borders one of the Great Lakes. The northern states, Michigan, Wisconsin, and Minnesota, have thick forests. The southern states have fertile land.

The map on the next page shows some major cities in the Great Lakes States. Most people in the region live in cities or their surrounding suburbs. Beyond the suburbs lies mostly rural land, where people who live on farms produce much of the nation's food.

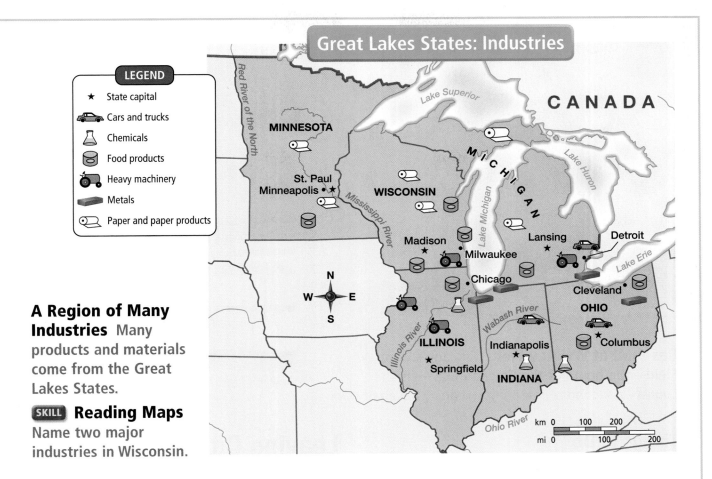

**LEGEND**

- ★ State capital
- Cars and trucks
- Chemicals
- Food products
- Heavy machinery
- Metals
- Paper and paper products

**A Region of Many Industries** Many products and materials come from the Great Lakes States.

**SKILL** Reading Maps Name two major industries in Wisconsin.

## Living in Chicago

Chicago, Illinois, has more people than any other city in the Great Lakes States. Chicago's location near important waterways, especially Lake Michigan, helped it become a trading center. Today, Chicago is a transportation hub and a leading manufacturing and business center.

People have been moving to Chicago in search of good jobs since the mid-1800s. As the city grew, public transportation became necessary to take workers to and from downtown Chicago. The "L," or elevated train, was built to carry many people without getting in the way of busy city traffic. An **elevated train** is a railway that runs above the ground on raised tracks.

## Rural Life

Although most people live in urban areas, the Great Lakes States are mostly rural. The region has more than 400,000 farms. In recent years, these farms have become more productive. However, fewer people work on farms. Today, many people work in manufacturing, as well as in health care, tourism, and other service industries.

In general, people in rural areas earn lower wages than urban workers. **Wages** are the payments for work. At the same time, the cost of living is often lower in rural areas. A rural home can cost less than half as much as a similar home in an urban area.

**REVIEW** What is an advantage of Chicago's elevated train?

219

**Baseball at Wrigley Field** Chicago's Wrigley Field—the home of the Chicago Cubs—is the country's second oldest Major League Baseball park.

### Things to Do

There are many things to do in the Great Lakes States. People who love the outdoors can go camping, fishing, boating, or swimming. Visitors can tour a lighthouse on the Great Lakes or a cheese factory in Wisconsin. Ice fishing, snowmobiling, and cross-country skiing are popular activities in the winter months.

Cities in the Great Lakes region offer a wide variety of activities. Sports fans can watch events at stadiums or speedways. People can enjoy art museums, theaters, and concerts. Many cities have special museums, such as Detroit's Museum of African American History. Visitors to Chicago can tour a submarine and a coal mine at the Museum of Science and Industry.

## Leaving Cities

**Main Idea** In recent years, many people have left cities to live in suburbs.

For many years, people viewed cities as places where they could earn higher wages and live a better life. People moved to Great Lakes cities from rural areas, other parts of the United States, and different countries. As a result, the cities grew rapidly.

Today, many people live outside of cities. Improvements in transportation allow people to live in suburbs. They travel to cities to work and shop. Improvements in technology allow some people to work at home. As more people moved out of cities, many businesses also moved. As a result, some suburbs have become business and industrial centers.

## Facing Challenges

Some Great Lakes cities, such as Detroit, have had many people move away over the past few decades. Cities develop problems when people leave. Businesses and schools close because not enough people use them. Buildings and homes may be abandoned, and crime may increase.

Growth in the suburbs can create environmental problems. If building is poorly planned, it may leave few natural areas for people to enjoy. Suburban life can increase air pollution because so many people drive cars instead of walking.

Many people are finding ways to face these challenges. Cities such as Detroit are rebuilding downtown areas to attract residents. Communities are working together to improve public transportation and reduce car use.

Governments are passing laws to save open space. These actions may help to improve life in some of the cities of the Great Lakes States.

**REVIEW** How can the growth of suburbs affect the environment?

### Lesson Summary

The Great Lakes States have busy urban areas and large rural areas. Many suburbs are growing as city populations decline. People are working together to face the challenges caused by the changes in population.

## Why It Matters . . .

Shifts in population are happening not only in the Great Lakes States, but also in other regions of the country. People everywhere are working to adjust to these changes.

---

## Lesson Review

**1** **VOCABULARY** Use **elevated train** in a paragraph that tells what you might see while riding this kind of train.

**2** **READING SKILL** **Compare and contrast** activities that take place in urban and in suburban areas.

**3** **MAIN IDEA: Geography** What feature do many major cities of the Great Lakes States share in common?

**4** **MAIN IDEA: Culture** In what ways can a declining population affect a city?

**5** **PLACES TO KNOW** Which Great Lakes city has the largest population?

**6** **CRITICAL THINKING: Fact and Opinion** Write one fact and one opinion about the Great Lakes States.

**HANDS ON** **DRAMA ACTIVITY** Plan a scene about a city council meeting. Play the roles of people who are brainstorming ways to rebuild a downtown area.

# Trouble at Fort La Pointe

**by Kathleen Ernst**

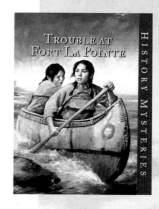

**For the Ojibwe people in 1732, La Pointe Island is a place to gather with friends and family during the warm summer months.** Suzette Choudoir is the daughter of an Ojibwe woman and a French *voyageur*, or fur trader. She is eager to paddle over to the island. As the story begins, she gazes at it across the sparkling water of Lake Superior.

She took a deep breath, enjoying the damp smell of earth, the lapping of the waves, and the sun warming her shoulders like a trader's wool blanket. Still smiling, Suzette glanced back at the camp. Smoke from morning fires twisted toward the sky, and the first shouts of children at play mixed with the mournful yipping of hungry dogs. It was good to be among more *wiigwams* again!

Ojibwe people moved with the seasons. During the cold winter months, when food was scarce, they scattered into the deep forest in small family camps. At the end of the long winter, it felt wonderful to move on to the sugaring camp, where perhaps a dozen families gathered to tap maple trees for sap to boil into syrup and sugar. And then Ojibwe people all over the mainland began making their way to the great summer village on La Pointe Island, just like Suzette's family. Each day now, more families arrived at the campground along the lakeshore and pitched *wiigwams* among the trees, waiting for good weather so they could cross to the island. Every passing day brought happy reunions with friends and relatives Suzette hadn't seen since last summer. . . .

**La Pointe Island in 1732**

Mainland

Lake Superior

Big Bay

La Pointe Island

Ojibwe camp

Fort La Pointe

And this year, because of the trappers' competition, her family would have even more to celebrate. This year—

"Suzette!"

Suzette grinned and waved when she saw Gabrielle Broussard emerge from the trees, carrying a copper kettle. Gabrielle was her best friend. They had both been born in the moon of blooming flowers, twelve years earlier. And they both had French fathers.

"*Aaniin*," Gabrielle greeted her. "What are you doing?"

"I'm going to find Papa. He walked out to the point, to get the best view of the lake. Want to come with me?"

Gabrielle splashed into the water to fill the kettle.

"Mama's waiting for me. What's your papa doing there?"

"Can't you guess? He's watching for the *voyageurs!*" Suzette's feet scuffed the earth in a little dance. Any day now, the songs of the French *voyageurs* would ring across the water from the east. They were paddling huge canoes filled with trade goods from a far-off place called Montréal. The trip took many weeks, down mighty rivers and across two great lakes. Their arrival on La Pointe Island would spark the wildly joyous gathering called *rendez-vous* by the French and *maawanji'iwin* by the Ojibwe. By the end of the short summer visit, the *voyageurs'* canoes would be loaded with the furs the Ojibwe trappers had been collecting all year. Then the *voyageurs* would say their good-byes and paddle back to Montréal before snowstorms and iced-over rivers made travel impossible.

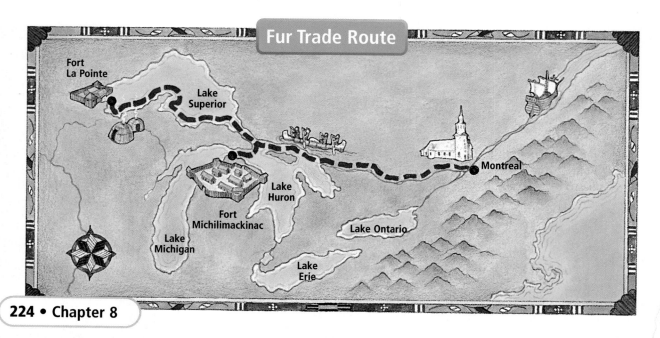

Fur Trade Route

"Papa can't wait to see his old friends again," Suzette added. Her own papa had been a *voyageur* for many years.

Gabrielle glanced to the east, her face wistful. "I'm waiting too."

Suzette stopped dancing. For a moment she had forgotten that Gabrielle's father would be among the paddlers. Gabrielle hadn't seen her father since the moon of shining leaves, when the woods blazed with red and yellow and the air held a promise of coming snow. Suzette chewed her lip. "I'm sure your papa will arrive soon, Gabrielle. I'm sure his journeys have been safe."

*Voyageurs* paddle a canoe along the fur trade route.

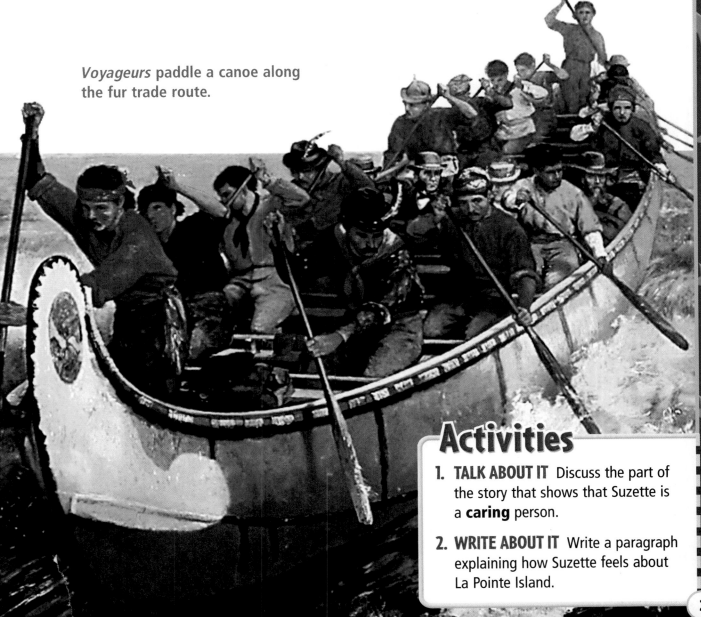

# Activities

1. **TALK ABOUT IT** Discuss the part of the story that shows that Suzette is a **caring** person.

2. **WRITE ABOUT IT** Write a paragraph explaining how Suzette feels about La Pointe Island.

## Skillbuilder

# Summarize

▶ **VOCABULARY**
summarize

To **summarize** means to tell the most important points of a piece of writing in your own words. Knowing how to write a summary can help you organize information and understand what you read.

> The Great Lakes became popular for recreation in the 1800s. People traveled by railroad to the clear, crystal waters of the lakes. There they soaked up the peace and quiet. In the 1900s, people sailed boats, canoed, and fished. Today, they still do! People visit parks such as Isle Royale or enjoy the sun on the beaches. The Great Lakes have long been a major source of recreation in the Midwest, and they continue to be.

## Learn the Skill

**Step 1:** Find the subject of the passage. It is what the passage is about.

**Step 2:** Identify the main points. These are ideas or examples that help explain the subject.

**Step 3:** Write a brief statement that describes the subject and one or two main points of the passage. Use your own words.

> Since the late 1800s, the Great Lakes have been a popular site for recreational activities such as boating, canoeing, fishing, and relaxing on the beaches.

If you are a sports fan, the Great Lakes States are the place to be. The Great Lakes States are home to seven Major League Baseball teams, six National Basketball Association teams, and seven National Football League teams. In Indianapolis, you can watch one of the country's most famous automobile races. In Chicago, you can visit America's second-oldest baseball park. All of these things make the Great Lakes States an exciting place for sports fans to live.

## Practice the Skill

Read the passage above. Then answer the questions that follow.

**1** What is the main point of the passage?

**2** Identify one detail that supports the main point.

**3** Summarize the passage in your own words.

## Apply the Skill

Use the steps you learned to help you summarize the effects of changing populations, as described on page 221 of your textbook.

**What's Special About**

# The Plains States

**population density**
**grain elevator**

**Vocabulary Strategy**

population density

The word **density** comes from **dense**. Dense means "packed closely together." **Population density** is how close together people live in a certain region.

 **READING SKILL**

**Main Idea and Details**
As you read, keep track of details that support the first main idea.

**Build on What You Know** How tall would the grass in a park grow if no one mowed it? Perhaps it would tickle your knees or come up to your chest. Now picture miles and miles of this grass and nothing else. That is what the Plains States once looked like.

## Where People Live

**Main Idea** The Plains States have a large amount of land and a small number of people.

The Plains States include North Dakota, South Dakota, Nebraska, Kansas, Iowa, and Missouri. Iowa and Missouri are actually part of the Central Lowlands physical region. The other states are part of the Great Plains. However, all six states are grouped because they are alike in some ways. In addition to cities, the Plains States have many rural areas where few people live.

The Central Lowlands have deep, fertile soil. The Great Plains are higher, drier, and rockier. The Great Plains contain sand hills and badlands. In the badlands, wind and water have carved the land into unusual shapes.

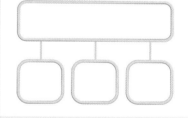

**South Dakota Wheatfield** The Plains region has vast areas of rural land.

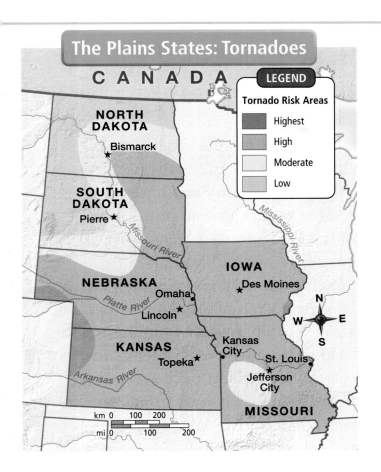

## The Plains States: Tornadoes

CANADA

**LEGEND**

**Tornado Risk Areas**
- Highest
- High
- Moderate
- Low

NORTH DAKOTA
Bismarck ★

SOUTH DAKOTA
Pierre ★

NEBRASKA
Omaha
Lincoln ★

KANSAS
Topeka ★

IOWA
★ Des Moines

Kansas City
St. Louis
Jefferson City ★

MISSOURI

Missouri River
Mississippi River
Platte River
Arkansas River

km 0    100   200
mi 0    100   200

N W E S

**Tornado in Kansas** The Plains States have many tornadoes.

**SKILL Reading Maps** Which three states have areas of highest risk for tornadoes?

## Cities of the Plains

The major cities of the Plains States grew up alongside rivers. In the past, water travel was easier than land travel. People and goods could reach places on rivers easily.

Omaha, Nebraska, is a good example. In 1854, settlers built a community of log buildings on the Missouri River. Their community became an important stop for other settlers traveling west. In 1863, work began on a railroad connecting Omaha and California. Workers also built a telegraph system between Omaha and California. It let people in the east and west communicate quickly.

By the 1870s, Omaha was a hub for river and railroad transportation.

Farmers shipped their crops and livestock to Omaha, where workers turned them into food products. Food processing is still important to Omaha's economy, as are the communications, health, and insurance industries. A modern transportation system has helped the city remain a regional hub.

Almost 400,000 people live in Omaha. The city has many colleges, theaters, and museums. Many tourists come to visit its excellent zoo. About 200,000 people attend the River City Roundup each year. This festival has parades, rodeo events, and activities that celebrate Omaha's history.

**REVIEW** Where are most major cities of the Plains States located?

**4H Fair, Nebraska** At rural fairs, children show the animals they have raised.

## Small Towns in the Plains States

While most people live in big cities, most of the Plains States are rural. These rural areas have a very low population density. **Population density** is a measure of how many people live in an area. For example, St. Louis has a population density of about 5,000 people per square mile. Rural areas may have a population density of just one person for every two square miles.

People living in small towns face certain challenges. Towns have fewer people to pay taxes for schools and other services. A town may have only a few stores. People may need to travel miles to see a movie or eat in a restaurant.

However, small towns have much to offer. Some Plains towns have big fairs each year. At the fairs, people enter farm animals, such as sheep, horses, and cattle, in competitions. Many towns have community bands or orchestras. Other activities include horseback riding, hunting, and fishing.

# Rural Lands on the Plains

**Main Idea** Fewer people live in the region's rural areas, but the land has many uses.

Miles of rural land separate many cities and towns in the Plains States. Much of the region was once a vast prairie. People plowed under most of the land, which they now use for growing crops and grazing cattle. Water towers and grain elevators may be the only tall buildings seen in rural areas. A **grain elevator** is a building used to store wheat or other grains.

Millions of visitors come to the Plains States each year. Some come to see Mount Rushmore, a huge sculpture of U.S. presidents in South Dakota. Others prefer the natural wonders, such as Chimney Rock in Nebraska.

**Grain Elevator** Water towers and grain elevators are common sights in the Plains States.

## Reservations Today

American Indians once lived throughout the Plains States. They depended on the large herds of buffalo that roamed the prairies. The buffalo provided food and clothing for the people who hunted them. Today, many Plains Indians live on reservations.

The U.S. government created the reservations. The army forced American Indian groups from their land after years of fighting. The government broke many of the promises it made to the American Indians, who kept only a small part of their former lands in the Plains. South Dakota is the Plains state with the most Indian reservation land. Two of its largest reservations are Cheyenne River and Pine Ridge. The Lakota people, sometimes known as the Sioux (soo), own these reservations.

**REVIEW** In what ways do people use the rural areas of the Plains States?

**Pine Ridge** Lakota children learn about their people's history from their elders.

## Lesson Summary

- The Plains States have fertile lands as well as dry, rocky areas.

- Most people in the region live in cities, but others live in small towns in rural farming areas.

- Many American Indians live on reservations in South Dakota and other Plains States.

## Why It Matters ...

For centuries, people have made a living in the Plains States.

---

## Lesson Review

**①** **VOCABULARY** Write a paragraph about the Plains States. Use **population density** and **grain elevator.**

**②** **READING SKILL** What **details** support the **main idea** that many people visit the Plains States?

**③** **MAIN IDEA: Geography** Why were large cities of the Plains States built along rivers?

**④** **MAIN IDEA: Geography** What is much of the land used for in rural areas of the Plains States?

**⑤** **CRITICAL THINKING: Draw Conclusions** Why do the Plains States have a low population density?

**WRITING ACTIVITY** Suppose you are helping to plan this year's River City Roundup in Omaha. Write your ideas for several activities that celebrate the city's history.

# The Sioux Today

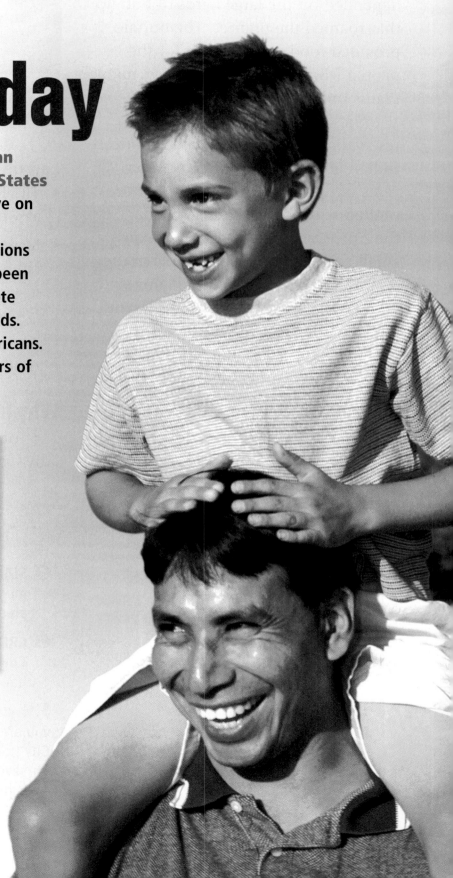

More than 300 American Indian reservations exist in the United States today. Well over 500,000 people live on these reservations.

The Sioux have lived on reservations since the 1880s. Life there has not been easy. Many reservations are in remote areas. The Sioux belong to two worlds. On one hand, they are modern Americans. On the other hand, they are members of the tribe and follow tribal laws.

**The News**
This newspaper is published by the Lakota Sioux Pine Ridge Reservation.

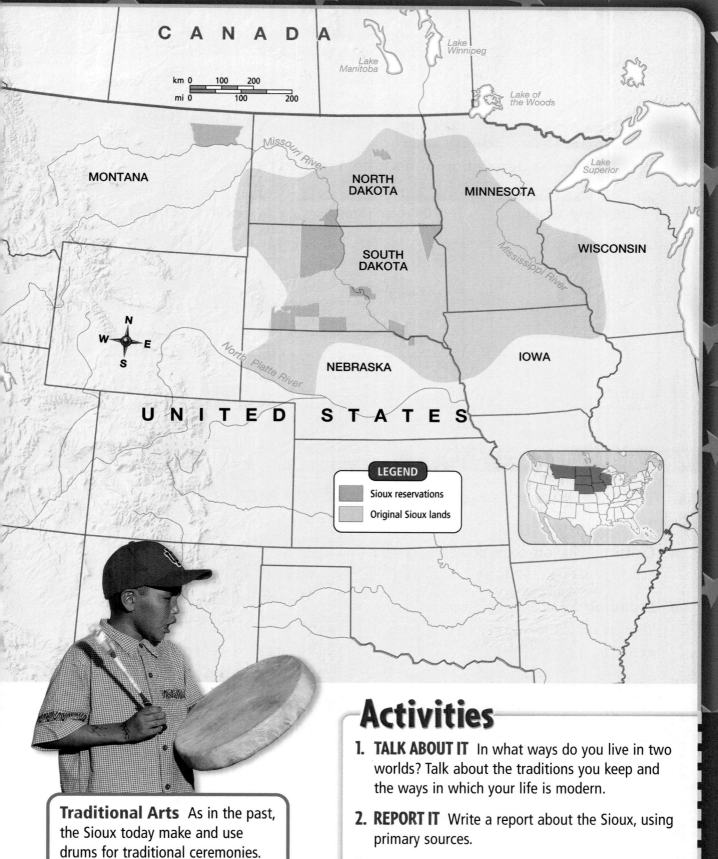

C A N A D A

Lake Winnipeg

Lake Manitoba

km 0    100    200
mi 0    100    200

Missouri River

Lake of the Woods

MONTANA

NORTH DAKOTA

MINNESOTA

Lake Superior

SOUTH DAKOTA

WISCONSIN

Mississippi River

N
W   E
S

North Platte River

NEBRASKA

IOWA

U N I T E D   S T A T E S

**LEGEND**

Sioux reservations

Original Sioux lands

**Traditional Arts** As in the past, the Sioux today make and use drums for traditional ceremonies.

# Activities

1. **TALK ABOUT IT** In what ways do you live in two worlds? Talk about the traditions you keep and the ways in which your life is modern.

2. **REPORT IT** Write a report about the Sioux, using primary sources.

**Technology** Visit Education Place for more primary sources. www.eduplace.com/kids/hmss05/

## Visual Summary

1. – 3. ✏️ Write a description of each item named below.

**Growth of Suburbs**

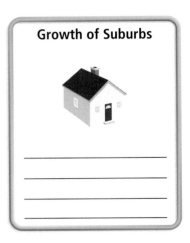

_____
_____
_____
_____

**Omaha, Nebraska**

_____
_____
_____
_____

**Indian Reservations**

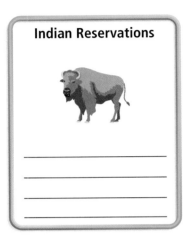

_____
_____
_____
_____

## Facts and Main Ideas

✔️ **TEST PREP** Answer each question below.

4. **Culture** What are some popular activities in the Great Lakes States?

5. **Economics** Is the cost of living usually lower in rural or urban areas? Give an example.

6. **Technology** Why would a city like Chicago need an elevated train?

7. **Geography** Why are most major cities of the Plains States located near rivers?

8. **Economics** In what way can a city's population affect the services that it is able to provide?

## Vocabulary

✔️ **TEST PREP** Choose the correct word from the list below to complete each sentence.

**elevated train,** p. 219
**population density,** p. 230
**grain elevator,** p. 230

9. The measurement of how many people live in an area is its _____.

10. A tall building used to store wheat or other crops is a _____.

11. An _____ is a railway that runs above the ground.

## Apply Skills

European settlers traveled to the Great Plains by covered wagons. There they found that the soil of the prairie was very fertile. Deep roots of the grasses made plowing difficult, though. In 1837, John Deere invented the steel-bladed plow. Soon, much of the prairie became farmland. Today, most of the land is used to raise crops and livestock.

12. What is the main point of this passage?

   **A.** John Deere invented the plow.

   **B.** Many people live on the prairie.

   **C.** The fertile soil of the prairie led to widespread farming.

   **D.** Rainfall affects prairie grass.

13. Which supports the main point of this passage?

   **A.** The steel-bladed plow was invented in 1837.

   **B.** Most of the prairie is used to raise crops and livestock.

   **C.** European settlers traveled to the Great Plains by covered wagons.

   **D.** The deep roots of the grasses were difficult to plow.

## Critical Thinking

✔ **TEST PREP** Write a short paragraph to answer each question below.

14. **Draw Conclusions** Why do you think farming is such an important part of the economy of the Great Lakes States? Give details to support your conclusion.

15. **Compare and Contrast** In what ways have the Plains States changed over the past 200 years?

# Activities

**Speaking Activity** Find out about life on an Indian reservation. How does the group that lives there carry on its language and traditions? Prepare a short talk to share what you learn. Use pictures or other visual aids.

**Writing Activity** Write a persuasive essay to convince others to move to the Great Lakes area. Give reasons to support your argument.

**Technology**
**Writing Process Tips**
Get help with your essay at:
www.eduplace.com/kids/hmss05/

# My State Handbook
## ECONOMICS

## The Economy Where You Live

Do you earn an allowance? Then you are part of your state's economy. People produce, sell, distribute, and buy goods and services as part of a system called the economy. How do people earn and spend money in your state? What are its major industries? Your state's economy affects your life every day.

### My State's Economy

- What industries does my state have?

- What jobs do people in these industries do?

SERVICE STATION

Human resource

Capital resources

Producers use natural, human, and capital resources to make products, such as snowboards.

## Find Out!

### Explore your state's economy.

✔ **Start by finding out the major industries of your state.**
Find an encyclopedia entry about your state. Or read the business sections of your state's newspapers.

✔ **Visit or call the Chamber of Commerce.**
Ask what businesses in your city or state employ the most people. What are the highest paying jobs in your state?

✔ **Visit your state government website.**
State government makes laws about business and also hires many people. Find out about any new laws that affect businesses.

✔ **Look at the want ads.**
What jobs are available in your state?

Use your state handbook to keep track of the information you find.

# Review and Test Prep

## Vocabulary and Main Ideas

✓ **TEST PREP** Write a sentence to answer each question.

1. Why might people who live near a river build a **levee?**

2. What are two things that can cause **demand** for a product to rise?

3. Why might the **supply** of a product rise if demand is high and the prices are high?

4. How does an **assembly line** work?

5. Why is Chicago's **elevated train** important to workers?

6. How does the **population density** of rural areas compare with that of urban areas?

## Critical Thinking

✓ **TEST PREP** Write a short paragraph to answer each question.

7. **Draw Conclusions** Why do you think so many people moved to the midwestern prairie to grow wheat and corn?

8. **Fact and Opinion** Is the following statement a fact or an opinion? "In the Midwest, the population is shifting from the cities to the suburbs." Why?

## Apply Skills

✓ **TEST PREP** Use the Great Lakes States Industries map below and what you have learned about special purpose maps to answer the questions that follow.

9. Which states are major producers of paper and paper products?

    A. Michigan, Indiana, and Ohio
    B. Minnesota, Wisconsin, and Michigan
    C. Illinois and Indiana
    D. Minnesota and Illinois

10. Which state produces heavy machinery, cars and trucks, and paper products?

    A. Indiana
    B. Ohio
    C. Minnesota
    D. Michigan

## Unit Activity

### Create a "Dream Job" Comic Strip

- Think about a job you would like to have in the future.

- Write the answers to these questions: Where will you work? What will you do in your job? What skills will you need? What will you like most about your job?

- Write a comic strip called "My Dream Job" in which you tell a friend all about your job. However, don't name the job!

- Have the class guess your dream job.

## At the Library

**This book can be found at your school or public library.**

*Lewis and Clark and Me: A Dog's Tale*
by Laurie Myers
Meriwether Lewis's dog Seaman tells the story of Lewis and Clark's expedition.

### Current Events Project

**Create a job bulletin board.**

- Find information about a job that you don't know much about.

- Read about what it is like to do the job. Learn what skills and education are needed for it.

- Write a description of the job.

- Post your description on a job bulletin board.

**Technology**
Weekly Reader online offers social studies articles. Go to:
**www.eduplace.com/kids/hmss/**

## Read About It

**Look in your classroom for these Social Studies Independent Books.**

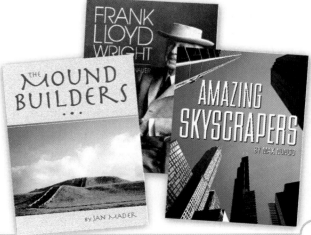

# UNIT 5

## The West

**The Big Idea**

### What is the story of your past?

"*The history of every country begins in the heart of a man or a woman.*"

—Willa Cather,
from *O Pioneers,* 1913

## United States Resources

ARCTIC OCEAN
170°W
70°N
RUSSIA
AK
km 0   300
mi 0   300
CANADA
60°N
PACIFIC OCEAN
Juneau
150°W   140°W

PACIFIC OCEAN

130°W
km 0  50 100
mi 0   50  100
Honolulu
HI
160°W
155°W
20°N
PACIFIC OCEAN
120°W

C A N

Olympia
WA
Salem
OR
Helena
MT
ND
Bismarck
MN
St. Paul
Boise
ID
SD
Pierre
Missouri River
Des Moines
IA
Great Salt Lake
Salt Lake City
WY
Cheyenne
NE
Lincoln
Sacramento
Carson City
NV
UT
Denver
CO
Arkansas River
Topeka
KS
Jefferson City
MO
CA
Colorado River
AZ
Phoenix
Santa Fe
NM
Oklahoma City
OK
Little Rock
TX
Austin
Rio Grande
MEXICO

km 0   150   300
mi 0   150   300
110°W

## Unit Preview

**Death Valley**
A desert below sea level
**Chapter 9, page 248**

**Pueblo Village**
Pueblo peoples built towns in the Southwest
**Chapter 9, page 263**

**Drip Irrigation**
Southwesterners must use water wisely
**Chapter 10, page 277**

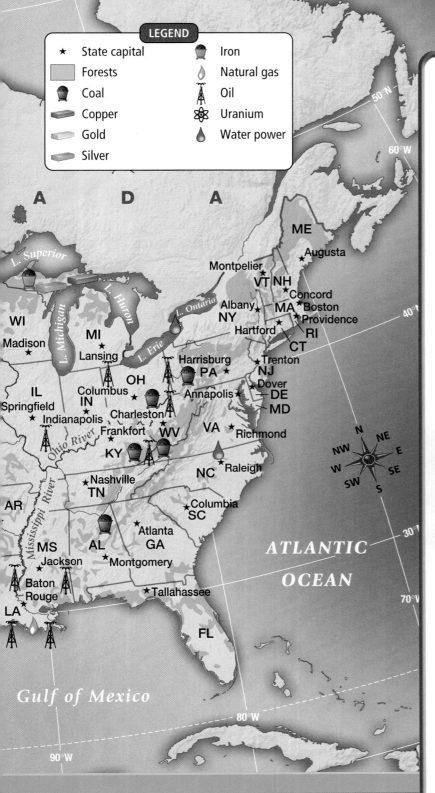

## LEGEND

★ State capital
▮ Forests
🪣 Coal
▭ Copper
▬ Gold
▭ Silver
🏮 Iron
🜊 Natural gas
🗼 Oil
☢ Uranium
💧 Water power

CANADA

L. Superior
L. Michigan
L. Huron
L. Ontario
L. Erie

ME
★ Augusta
Montpelier ★
VT NH
★ Concord
Albany ★ MA ★ Boston
NY ★ Providence
Hartford ★ RI
CT

WI
Madison ★
MI
Lansing ★
Harrisburg ★
PA ★ Trenton
NJ
OH
Columbus ★ Annapolis ★ Dover
IL
Springfield ★
IN
Indianapolis ★ Charleston DE
Frankfort ★ WV MD
KY VA ★ Richmond

Ohio River

Nashville ★
TN
NC ★ Raleigh

AR
Columbia ★
SC

Mississippi River

MS
Jackson ★
AL Atlanta
Montgomery ★ GA

Baton Rouge ★
LA
★ Tallahassee

FL

Gulf of Mexico

ATLANTIC
OCEAN

N NE
NW E
W SE
SW S

50°N
60°W
40°N
30°N
70°W
80°W
90°W

**Seattle**
Technology companies
employ many workers
**Chapter 10,
page 288**

Chapter 10, page 288

## Connect to
# The Nation

## U.S. Coal Production

Almost as much coal is mined in the West as in all other regions combined.

| The West | All Other Regions |
| --- | --- |
| 520 million tons | 575 million tons |

## U.S. Forest Lands

The West has almost as much forest land as all other regions combined.

| The West | All Other Regions |
| --- | --- |
| 362 million acres | 384 million acres |

Look at the two graphs. What can you tell about the natural resources of the West?

**CURRENT EVENTS**
**WEEKLY WR READER**

**Current events on the web!**

Read social studies articles about current events at:
**www.eduplace.com/kids/hmss/**

**Technology**
*e* • **glossary**
*e* • **word games**
www.eduplace.com/kids/hmss05/

# Vocabulary Preview

## geothermal

When a volcano erupts, it sends out **geothermal** energy in the form of lava and gas. Volcanic eruptions can cause a great deal of damage. **page 247**

## irrigation

In areas that don't get enough rainfall, farmers depend on **irrigation** to water their crops. The irrigation process often requires huge amounts of water. **page 248**

## Chapter Timeline

1610
**Spanish settlement in Santa Fe**

1500       1600       1700

# Reading Strategy

**Predict and Infer** Use this strategy before you read.

**Quick Tip** Look at titles and pictures. What can you tell about the places you will read about?

## specialization

**Specialization** means learning to do one thing well. A company might specialize in making one part of a computer. It would work with other companies to create the whole computer. **page 258**

## mission

The Spanish built **missions** in the areas that they conquered. Priests came to work in the missions. Some of the original mission buildings can still be seen today. **page 264**

1848
**California gold rush**

1869
**Transcontinental railroad**

1800        1900        2000

# Land and Climate

**VOCABULARY**

geothermal
irrigation
hydroelectric power
arid

**Vocabulary Strategy**

geothermal

The prefix **geo-** means earth. Thermal means heat. **Geothermal** is heat that comes from the earth.

**READING SKILL**

**Cause and Effect** Chart the forces that caused natural landforms in the West.

| Causes | Effects |
|--------|---------|
| Tectonic plates | The Rocky Mountains |

**Build on What You Know** Many movies show the West as hot and dusty. This is true for parts of the West. Other parts are cool and rainy.

## Land and Water of the West

**Main Idea** The West is divided by mountain ranges and rivers.

The West is a huge region of 13 states. Land and water separate two of these states from the others. The other 11 states lie east of the Pacific Ocean and between Canada and Mexico. The map shows how we divide these states into three regions. These are the Southwest, Mountain, and Pacific states.

Because the West is so big, its land and climate vary greatly. The region has towering mountains and deep valleys. It has dry deserts and tropical forests. It has frozen glaciers and smoking volcanoes. It has the country's warmest and coldest temperatures. The western states are each very different. Yet they are all rich in natural beauty and natural resources.

**Western Coastline** Much of the western coastline is rugged and rocky. Sea otters live in these areas.

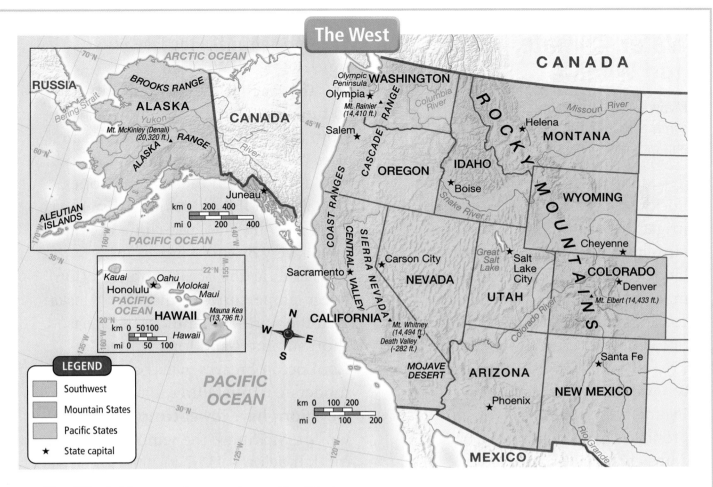

The West Three regions make up the West.

SKILL **Reading Maps** What separates Alaska from other western states?

## Mountains in the West

Four mountain systems run north and south in the West. The Rocky Mountains formed as tectonic plates pushed against each other, causing the earth's crust to fold. Today, movement along faults, or breaks in the crust, causes many earthquakes in the West.

Other mountains, like the volcanoes in the Cascades Range, formed when melted rock, or lava, bubbled up from openings in the earth's crust and hardened. Volcanoes release geothermal energy in the form of lava and gas. **Geothermal** refers to heat from beneath Earth's crust.

Between the mountains lie valleys, basins, and raised, flat areas called plateaus. Glaciers created some valleys, such as Yosemite Valley. Rivers carved out deep, steep-sided valleys called canyons. One example is the Grand Canyon in Arizona.

The landscape between the Rockies and the western ranges is rugged yet beautiful. It has ranching and mining businesses. Many tourists visit the area to ski and hike. Much of the land is set aside for people to enjoy nature.

**REVIEW** What are three major landforms found in the West?

# Water, Climate, and Wildlife

**Main Idea** Water affects the western climate. It supports the life of people, plants, and animals.

Many rivers flow west from the Rocky Mountains. Their water provides irrigation for millions of acres of farmland. **Irrigation** means supplying land with water. The need for water led many people in the West to settle in coastal areas that get the most rain.

People in the West use water carefully. For example, they use dams to produce hydroelectric power. **Hydroelectric power** is electricity produced from flowing water. Some dams create lakes, such as Lake Mead in the Mojave (moh HAH vee) Desert.

Other lakes in the West formed naturally. The Great Salt Lake has no outlet to the sea. Its water carries many minerals. As the water evaporates, it leaves these minerals behind. The minerals make the lake water much saltier than ocean water.

The Pacific Ocean affects climates in the West. Cool, moist air flows east from the northwest Pacific. As the air rises over the western ranges, it drops rain and snow on the western slopes. Dry air then flows down the eastern slopes, giving it an arid climate. **Arid** means very dry.

Latitude, the ocean, and elevation affect temperatures in the West. Alaska is in the northern latitudes, so it has short summers and long winters. Cool ocean breezes give coastal areas moderate temperatures. Places at high elevations have lower temperatures. On Mt. McKinley, the temperature can fall below −95°F.

**Elevation Extremes** Mount McKinley (small photo) is the highest spot in North America. Death Valley is the lowest. Summer temperatures there can reach 120°F.

## Plants and Animals of the West

Plant life varies with the climate. In Hawaii, orchids and other tropical plants thrive. Plants that need little water, such as cactus and mesquite (meh SKEET), grow in arid areas. Mesquite's deep roots can reach underground water. Giant redwood trees grow in wet coastal areas. In the mountains are some of Earth's oldest living things—bristlecone pine trees.

A variety of animals live in the West. The huge Alaskan brown bear can weigh 1,700 pounds. The moose is another large animal of the West. The California condor is the largest flying bird in North America. Elk, bighorn sheep, and cougars roam the mountains. Lizards, scorpions, tarantulas, and snakes have adapted to the dry heat of the Southwest.

**REVIEW** What factors influence temperature in the West?

## Lesson Summary

- Landforms in the West include mountains, valleys, plateaus, canyons, and basins.
- Westerners use rivers for power and for irrigation.
- The West has many climates.
- Plants and animals have adapted to the different climates.

## Why It Matters ...

Almost half the land in our country lies in the vast spaces of the West.

**Cougar** The cougar is an animal found in the West.

## Lesson Review

❶ **VOCABULARY** Write a paragraph that shows you know what **arid** and **irrigation** mean. Describe how westerners use rivers.

❷ **READING SKILL** What **caused** the plants and animals to adapt in the West?

❸ **MAIN IDEA: Technology** Why have people built dams on western rivers?

❹ **MAIN IDEA: Geography** Why is the land so varied in the West?

❺ **CRITICAL THINKING: Fact and Opinion** "The West is a moist, tropical region." Is this statement a fact or an opinion? Explain your answer.

**HANDS ON** **SCIENCE ACTIVITY** Find out what causes an earthquake. Use clay or blocks to demonstrate what happens during an earthquake.

# Which Way West?

Where should the geography group go on a field trip? After doing some research, they decided to go to the West. Then they had a meeting. They invited guests to help them decide which parts of the West to visit.

## Cast of Ten Characters

**Katia:** group president

**Daniel:** group club vice president

**Mrs. Oliver:** classroom teacher

**Ms. Malu:** geography advisor

**Paul:** group member

**Sherman:** group member

**Kelly:** group member

**Ms. Arthur:** invited guest

**Mr. Hall:** invited guest

**Mr. Valdez:** school librarian

**Katia:** Thanks for coming to our geography meeting. We have two guests today to help us figure out where to take our field trip. What do you think, Ms. Arthur?

**Ms. Arthur:** If you'd like to see wonderful desert animals and plants and also natural formations, think about Lake Mead in Nevada. It's on the edge of the Mojave Desert, right next to some tall mountains.

**Kelly:** Isn't that the lake formed by the Hoover Dam?

**Ms. Arthur:** Yes. It's a human-made lake. Bighorn sheep live in the hills, and so do all kinds of mice and ground squirrels. Because of the **arid** desert climate, most of the plants are cacti or shrubs. Some trees grow near the lake, though.

**Daniel:** Thanks. Lake Mead sounds great! Mr. Hall, could you tell us about your suggestion?

**Mr. Hall:** I like canyons myself. Here are some pictures I have of Canyon de Chelly (duh SHAY) in Arizona. It's full of caves and overhanging cliffs. The Anasazi built cliff dwellings there hundreds of years ago. There are many old petroglyphs, or rock pictures, to see.

**Paul:** Does anyone live there now?

**Mr. Hall:** Yes. Navajo Indians ranch and live in the canyon, and they mine nearby. The Navajo and the National Park Service manage the land together.

**Ms. Malu:** Does anyone else have other suggestions?

**Sherman:** I'd like to go to Alaska. Look at the picture I found. Where else could we see a glacier and a whale?

**Mr. Valdez:** Those glaciers are from the Little Ice Age, which began 4,000 years ago.

**Katia:** OK, we have three suggestions. What does everyone think about these places?

**Daniel:** I have a question about Lake Mead. Will the desert be too hot in June?

**Ms. Arthur:** That's a great question. The temperature there can reach above 100 degrees in June. It's good weather for lizards.

**Mrs. Oliver:** I went to school in southeast Alaska. I remember old-growth forests and very tall mountains. The days can be up to 18 hours long in late spring.

**Kelly:** That would give us more time to explore.

**Paul:** I don't think of Alaska as being in the West. It's so far north, and very cold.

**Ms. Malu:** The ocean keeps southern Alaska warmer in the winter and cooler in the summer. It's no colder than other northern states.

**Daniel:** Canyon de Chelly interests me. We could learn how the Anasazi used local plants for food.

**Mr. Hall:** Some of the plants and animals there arrived quite recently. The cottonwood trees were planted by the National Park Service in 1931 to stop erosion.

**Mr. Valdez:** Wild turkeys and beavers that once lived there died out. But both animals were brought back to the area in the late 1900s.

**Sherman:** If we went to Alaska, what could we learn about American Indian cultures?

**Mrs. Oliver:** The Tlingit and the Haida are two American Indian nations in that area. Remember that display of Tlingit carvings we saw at the local library?

**Katia:** Alaska seems pretty popular. Let's invite someone who knows about it to our next meeting.

**Mrs. Oliver:** I could bring my photos from when I was in school.

**Ms. Malu:** That would be wonderful. Thank you very much, Ms. Arthur and Mr. Hall, for joining us today. Goodbye, everyone, until the next meeting.

**Everyone:** Goodbye! Thank you!

## Activities

1. **TALK ABOUT IT** Talk about western places you would like to see. Tell why.

2. **RESEARCH IT** Research a place you would like to go. Write a paragraph describing it.

## Skillbuilder

# Distinguish Fact from Opinion

▶ **VOCABULARY**
fact
opinion

In an old TV program, a police officer often reminded witnesses to provide "just the facts" to describe a crime. He knew that opinions can often affect a person's judgment of the facts. A **fact** is a statement that can be proven true. An **opinion** is an idea or a belief. It is important to know the difference between facts and opinions when you read.

## Learn the Skill

**Step 1:** Identify opinions. Opinions often give a person's own feelings or judgments. Opinions may include terms such as **best, worst, should, I think,** or **I believe.**

**Step 2:** Identify facts. These often include details that can be proven to be true or false. They do not express feelings or beliefs.

**Step 3:** Understand the difference between facts and opinions. Remember that opinions can sometimes be supported by facts, but they cannot be proven.

**Passage A**

I think that California will break off from the rest of the country. During a big earthquake, the San Andreas fault will probably open up and cause California to drift out to sea. People should leave the state as soon as possible.

**Passage B**

The San Andreas fault is the boundary line between the Pacific Plate and the North American Plate. The Pacific Plate is moving northwest very slowly. The friction created as it moves against the North American Plate causes earthquakes.

**Passage C**

One of the worst earthquakes in California's history occurred in San Francisco in 1906. The earthquake and the fire that followed killed 700 people. Over 250,000 people were left homeless.

## Practice the Skill

Read the three passages. Then answer the questions.

**1** Which passage, A or B, includes opinions? How do you know? How do you know the statements in the other passage are facts?

**2** Look at passage C. Which sentence includes an opinion? Is the opinion supported by facts? Explain.

## Apply the Skill

Use facts from Lesson 1 of this chapter to form an opinion about the land and climate of the West. Support your opinion with at least two facts.

# Resources and Economy

**VOCABULARY**

**national park**
**specialization**

**Vocabulary Strategy**

specialization

Something that's **special** has one particular use. **Specialization** means a business makes only a few goods or provides one service.

**READING SKILL**
**Draw Conclusions** Chart facts that lead you to the conclusion below.

Natural resources help support many industries.

**Build on What You Know** If you were going to make a movie, where would you do it? What conditions would you look for? Many filmmakers choose the West.

## Using Resources

**Main Idea** Westerners have found ways to use their land, climate, water, and minerals.

The West has many natural resources. Farmers use the fertile soil and warm climate to raise many crops. Some crops, such as pineapples, avocados, and peas, are in great demand in other regions. Agriculture creates many jobs, and not just on farms. People work in processing, selling, and shipping food. People sell and repair farm equipment and conduct research on agriculture.

Huge forests in the West create jobs. People use trees for wood and paper. Thousands of workers cut lumber in sawmills. Other workers use this wood to make buildings and other products.

Oceans, rivers, and lakes are another important part of western life. Workers in the fishing industry bring seafood from coastal waters. Many more people fish, swim, and sail for fun.

**Orange Harvest** People in many other regions eat food grown in the West.

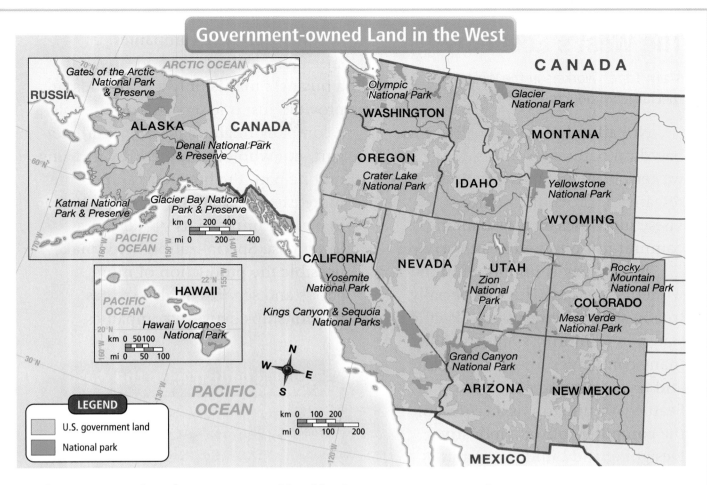

## Government-owned Land in the West

Gates of the Arctic National Park & Preserve
ARCTIC OCEAN
RUSSIA
ALASKA
CANADA
Denali National Park & Preserve
Katmai National Park & Preserve
Glacier Bay National Park & Preserve
km 0 200 400
mi 0 200 400
PACIFIC OCEAN

PACIFIC OCEAN
HAWAII
Hawaii Volcanoes National Park
km 0 50 100
mi 0 50 100

CANADA
Olympic National Park
WASHINGTON
Glacier National Park
MONTANA
OREGON
Crater Lake National Park
IDAHO
Yellowstone National Park
WYOMING
CALIFORNIA
Yosemite National Park
NEVADA
UTAH
Zion National Park
Rocky Mountain National Park
COLORADO
Kings Canyon & Sequoia National Parks
Mesa Verde National Park
Grand Canyon National Park
ARIZONA
NEW MEXICO
PACIFIC OCEAN
km 0 100 200
mi 0 100 200
MEXICO

**LEGEND**
U.S. government land
National park

**Government Land** Large areas of land in the West are protected by the federal government.

## Movies and Mines

Other industries depend on the West's climate. Aircraft companies came west because of the fine flying conditions. The movie industry came to Los Angeles because of the pleasant climate. Many tourists visit the West to enjoy the scenery and outdoor activities.

The West contains many mineral resources. Arizona and Utah supply much of the nation's copper. Western mines also produce gold, uranium, and coal. People work in mines to dig these minerals from the ground. Others work in industries that make products from minerals.

The U.S. government owns more than 600 million acres of land in the West. It has created national parks to preserve some areas. A **national park** is an area set aside by the federal government. Examples include Glacier, Yellowstone, and Grand Canyon.

Mining, logging, and livestock companies lease, or rent, some public land. The government lets them use the land's resources. They set rules for the use of public lands. People who own land privately can use it as they choose, as long as they obey the law.

**REVIEW** What are two ways that people use resources in the West?

# The West's Economy

**Main Idea** Workers in the West make specialized products.

Not all industries in the West are based on natural resources. Many western businesses involve doing research or providing services. These industries include banking, communications, and health services.

Technology is important in the western economy. This is especially true in some Southwest and Pacific states. In California's Silicon Valley, many companies research, develop, and make computer products. Seattle, Washington, is a center for the computer software industry. Designing and building aircraft is another leading industry.

**Software Development** Computer software designed in the West is used all over the world.

Many of these companies specialize. **Specialization** means that a business makes only a few goods or provides just one service. For example, a company might make one computer part, not whole computers. By focusing on one part, the business can become more expert at making that part. It can make and improve its product at a lower cost. Specialization helps make possible the production of more goods and services. It also creates relationships between companies.

## Service Industries in the West

Banking

Communications

Computer software

Health services

Transportation

## Skilled and Unskilled Workers

Many industries hire skilled workers. A skilled worker is someone who has received special training or education. For example, many people in the computer industry have advanced computer training. Skilled workers usually receive higher pay than unskilled workers. An unskilled worker is someone who does not need special training or education to do a job. An example is a laborer.

The Mountain States contain fewer urban areas and less industry than the Pacific and Southwest states. However, there are some technology jobs in the Mountain States. For example, Colorado has an active industry making medical equipment. Many people throughout the West work in service jobs, such as health care or construction. In Alaska and Hawaii, many people work for the government.

**REVIEW** Which parts of the West have the most technology companies?

**Phoenix Aerospace Workers** Many industries in the West depend on skilled workers.

## Lesson Summary

Farming, logging, and mining industries depend on the West's natural resources. Natural resources help the tourism industry, too. Most of the West's technology industries depend on skilled workers, not natural resources.

## Why It Matters...

Industries and consumers across the country depend on the West's natural resources.

---

## Lesson Review

❶ **VOCABULARY** Use **national park** and **specialization** in a paragraph about the West.

❷ **READING SKILL** What **conclusions** can you **draw** about the economy in the West?

❸ **MAIN IDEA: Government** How do private businesses use public land?

❹ **MAIN IDEA: Economics** Explain how companies specialize.

❺ **CRITICAL THINKING: Infer** Why do you think skilled workers usually get higher pay than unskilled workers?

**WRITING ACTIVITY** Write a news report. Tell how people use a natural resource in your area.

# Harmful or Useful?

**Are dams worth arguing over?** Some people think dams are useful. Others think they do more harm than good.

The O'Shaughnessy Dam in Yosemite National Park supplies electricity and water to San Francisco. It needs repairs. Some people say it should be removed. Both sides have written letters and articles to support their cause.

**O'Shaughnessy Dam** This dam was completed in 1923.

## Hetch Hetchy Valley, 1911

**Before the Dam** This photo shows how the Hetch Hetchy Valley looked before people built the O'Shaughnessy Dam.

## Hetch Hetchy Valley, Today

**After the Dam** Today, the Hetch Hetchy Valley is filled with water. The dam created this large reservoir.

## Why Remove the O'Shaughnessy Dam

- Dams can break and cause damage.

- It would be expensive to fix the dam.

- San Francisco can get water and power without the dam.

- The area around the dam should be restored to its natural state.

## Why Fix the O'Shaughnessy Dam

- Dams create lakes that people use for recreation.

- Dams provide almost half the renewable energy in the United States.

- San Francisco needs the power and the water.

- It is less expensive to keep the dam than to remove it.

## Activities

1. **STEP INTO IT** Describe what the valley looked like before the O'Shaughnessy Dam was built.

2. **WRITE ABOUT IT** Suppose you live near the Hetch Hetchy Valley in 1911. Write a letter explaining why you think a dam should or should not be built.

261

# People of the West

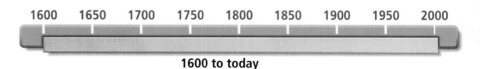

| 1600 | 1650 | 1700 | 1750 | 1800 | 1850 | 1900 | 1950 | 2000 |

**1600 to today**

## VOCABULARY

mission
wagon train
transcontinental
  railroad

**Vocabulary Strategy**

transcontinental railroad

The prefix **trans–** means across. The **transcontinental railroad** ran across North America.

## READING SKILL
**Sequence** Chart the order in which the groups arrived in the West.

| 1 | |
|---|---|
| 2 | |
| 3 | |
| 4 | |

**Build on What You Know** Suppose you moved to a land you knew nothing about. What would you need to survive? How would you spend your free time?

## Early Peoples of the West

**Main Idea** American Indians of the West, such as the Pueblo (PWEHB loh) and the Tlingit (TLING giht), have rich traditions.

Many scientists think that people first came to the West 15,000 years ago. Some scientists believe they crossed over a land bridge that once connected present-day Asia and Alaska. Over the centuries, people spread through the continent. In the West region, these people included the Aleut (al YOOT) and Inuit (IHN oo iht) in the north and the Hopi and Navajo in the south.

The first settlers of Hawaii were Polynesians. They came by a different route. They crossed thousands of miles of Pacific Ocean in canoes. Unlike the many groups on mainland North America, they shared a common culture. However, they too adapted to their new home.

**Pueblo Village** Buildings in Pueblo villages often stood several stories tall.

## A Closer Look at Pueblo Villages

About 700 years ago, people we now call the Pueblo lived in the Rio Grande area of present-day New Mexico. This area is arid. Yet the Pueblo were skilled farmers. They built irrigation ditches and dams to control water. They grew corn, beans, squash, and cotton. They also gathered wild plants and hunted animals.

Pueblo homes looked like huge apartment buildings. People built them using adobe (uh DOH bee), a type of clay. Some buildings had hundreds of rooms. The Pueblo were skilled at weaving baskets. They also made bowls, serving dishes, and jars from pottery. They painted them with colors made from plants and minerals. People traded these items for salt, food, and animal hides.

## A Closer Look at Tlingit Life

On the northwest coast, the Tlingit lived in large wooden houses. Unlike the Pueblo, the Tlingit did not raise crops. They got food by gathering wild plants, hunting, and fishing. The Tlingit used spears, bows, harpoons, and traps to catch animals. They also traded seal oil for furs from inland groups.

The Tlingit were fine artists. They wove baskets, hats, and blankets. Tlingit blankets showed a figure that had special meaning to the weaver's family or village group. Their blankets and their religious stories helped the Tlingit pass on their traditions to their children. Their traditions remain alive today.

Pueblo, Tlingit, and other American Indian groups still live in the West. Many still practice the skills of their ancestors. At the same time, they live and work in the modern world.

**REVIEW** What did different groups who settled the West have in common?

Rear wall of cave

Multi-story tower

Kiva for religious activities

# Spanish Settlements

**Main Idea** Spain influenced the architecture, customs, and food of the West.

In 1521, Spanish soldiers conquered the American Indians in present-day Mexico. They named the area New Spain. Then they traveled north. They reached present-day Kansas and followed the Pacific coast to present-day Canada. Many hoped to find gold. Others wanted to claim more land for Spain. Spanish priests traveled north, too. They wanted to teach Christianity to the American Indians.

**New Spain** Today, the culture in many places still shows Spain's influence.

**SKILL** **Reading Maps** Which mission was farthest north?

The Spanish made a settlement at Santa Fe in 1610. They spread into Arizona and California. New Spain grew to include land that today makes up the Southwest states, Texas, and Florida.

As the Spanish moved into an area, they came into conflict with the American Indians who lived there. The Spanish wanted to control both the land and its people. They used force to achieve these goals. Many American Indians died.

The Spanish wanted American Indians to accept Christianity. To do this, they set up missions. A **mission** is a settlement for teaching religion to local people. Many missions grew into cities. San Diego and San Francisco started as missions.

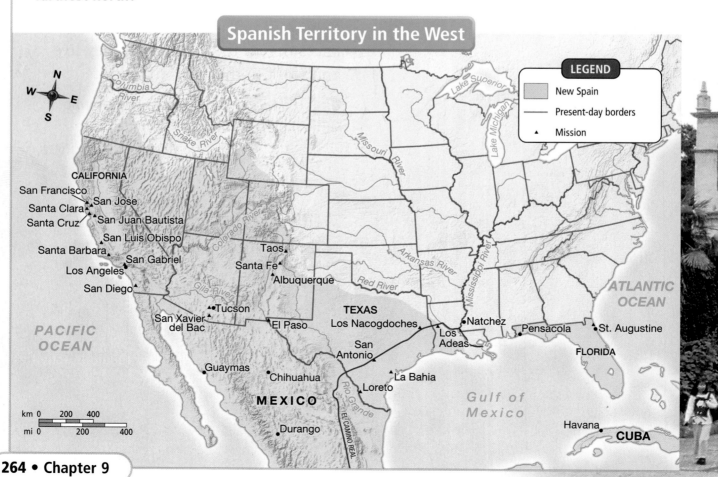

**Spanish Territory in the West**

LEGEND

New Spain

Present-day borders

▲ Mission

CALIFORNIA
San Francisco
San Jose
Santa Clara
Santa Cruz
San Juan Bautista
San Luis Obispo
Santa Barbara
San Gabriel
Los Angeles
San Diego
Tucson
San Xavier del Bac
Taos
Santa Fe
Albuquerque
El Paso
TEXAS
Los Nacogdoches
Natchez
Pensacola
St. Augustine
FLORIDA
San Antonio
Los Adeas
La Bahia
Loreto
Guaymas
Chihuahua
MEXICO
Durango

Columbia River
Snake River
Colorado River
Gila River
Missouri River
Arkansas River
Red River
Mississippi River
Rio Grande
EL CAMINO REAL

Lake Superior
Lake Michigan

PACIFIC OCEAN
ATLANTIC OCEAN
Gulf of Mexico
Havana
CUBA

km 0    200    400
mi 0    200    400

## Cultural Influences

The priests who ran the missions often taught more than religion. Some insisted that American Indians give up their cultures and live like Europeans. They taught them to speak Spanish. They taught them trades and crafts. The Pueblo raised Spanish crops, such as grapes and wheat. They raised Spanish animals, such as sheep, horses, and cattle.

The Spanish also learned from the American Indians. For example, they learned to build with adobe and to make tortillas and other foods.

Spain lost control of its American colonies in the 1800s. In 1821, Mexico won independence from Spain. Mexico at that time included land in the West.

**Carmel Mission** The Spanish built 21 missions in California.

Fifteen years later, Texas gained independence from Mexico. In 1845, Texas became part of the United States. The following year, the United States went to war with Mexico. The United States won. In 1848, it forced Mexico to give the Southwest region and California to the United States. In return, Mexico received $15 million.

The influence of the mission days is still strong in the West. Many places have Spanish names. A lot of towns are built around an open square, just as they are in Spain. Many people speak Spanish. Some foods and festivals in the region came from Spain and Mexico. Many people from Mexico and other Latin American countries still move to the West.

**REVIEW** Why did the Spanish build missions in New Spain?

## The Oregon Trail

**Oregon Trail** People met at the start of the trail in Missouri. They joined wagon trains, elected captains, and hired guides for the journey.

# More People Go West

**Main Idea** People traveled west to find gold, get land, or work on the railroads.

Small groups of trappers and traders had roamed the West since the early 1800s. After the United States took control of the region, many more people moved there.

### A Rush of Settlers

The West attracted new settlers for many reasons. In 1848, gold was discovered in California. Thousands of Americans, Chinese, and Europeans went to look for gold. Others came west to buy cheap land. They made a difficult six-month trip on the Oregon Trail in wagon trains. A **wagon train** was a line of wagons that carried settlers and everything they owned. Some came west for religious freedom. One group, the Mormons, set up their own government in Utah.

This rush of settlers affected American Indians. Settlers overran their hunting grounds. The new settlers wanted to own the land. Most American Indians believed that people could use land but could not own it.

Fighting soon broke out between American Indians and settlers. The U.S. Army drove the American Indians off their land. The government forced them to live on reservations, where many still live today.

**Gold Nuggets** During the Gold Rush, over 80,000 people went to California hoping to find gold.

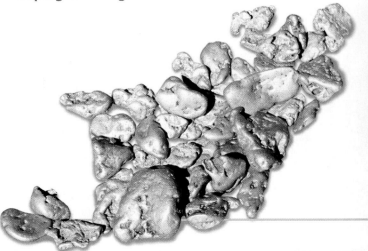

## The Fifty States

As the West grew, the United States government helped two companies build a transcontinental railroad. The **transcontinental railroad** was the first train system to link the East and West. Many Chinese immigrants helped build the railroad. Their hard work helped finish the job in 1869.

Good transportation helped the West's population grow faster. When a territory's population grew to a certain point, its people could ask Congress to make it a state. In 1959, the territories of Alaska and Hawaii became the last of our 50 states.

People from many cultures shaped the history of the West. Today, it is a region of great diversity.

**REVIEW** How did the transcontinental railroad affect population in the West?

## Lesson Summary

> The resources of the West influenced the life and culture of the people who lived there.

> The Spanish controlled the region as part of New Spain.

> A growing population forced American Indians from their land and formed new states.

> Today, the West has a very diverse culture.

## Why It Matters ...

Settling the West helped make the United States a large, powerful nation. It also brought many cultures together to create a unique American culture.

---

## Lesson Review

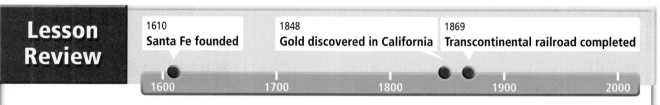

1610
Santa Fe founded

1848
Gold discovered in California

1869
Transcontinental railroad completed

1600    1700    1800    1900    2000

❶ **VOCABULARY** Compare a **wagon train** with the **transcontinental railroad.**

❷ **READING SKILL** List the people who came to the West after the Spanish in the correct **sequence.**

❸ **MAIN IDEA: Geography** Compare the ways in which the Pueblo and Tlingit got their food.

❹ **MAIN IDEA: Economics** What brought many Chinese people to the West during the 1800s?

❺ **TIMELINE SKILL** How many years after the discovery of gold in California was the railroad completed?

❻ **CRITICAL THINKING: Cause and Effect** What led to conflict between American Indians and settlers?

**HANDS ON**

**CITIZENSHIP ACTIVITY** Town squares can help people connect to a community. People gather in squares for many reasons. Draw a picture of a busy town square.

# Western Heroes

**What does a hero of the West look like?** She might be a woman driving her mule through a blizzard to deliver the mail on time. Or, he might be a sheriff, county clerk, or mayor.

## Mary Fields 1832–1914

Mary Fields was born into slavery in Tennessee. Unlike most enslaved African Americans, she learned to read and write. After the Civil War, Fields found work in Toledo, Ohio. She was six feet tall and very strong. She chopped wood and helped fix buildings.

Fields later moved west to a **mission** near Cascade, Montana. She hauled supplies through cold winters on the Montana frontier. People told many stories about her bravery, trustworthiness, and temper. She became a legend in Montana.

In 1895, Fields took a job delivering the U.S. mail. People called her "Stagecoach Mary." She delivered the mail in all kinds of bad weather, and she never missed a day. Fields's service helped people settle the new state of Montana.

# Elfego Baca 1865–1945

In the Southwest, Elfego Baca was a legend at age 19. As a young deputy sheriff, he was in a shootout with a large gang of cowboys. Baca held out alone against them for more than a day. The cowboys fired as many as 4,000 shots at Baca, but he was not injured.

Baca was born in New Mexico in the days of lawless frontier living. His early fame and bold personality helped him succeed in the many jobs he pursued. He worked as a lawyer, private detective, sheriff, real estate developer, county clerk, school superintendent, newspaper publisher, mayor, district attorney, and politician.

# Activities

1. **DRAW IT** Draw a picture of Mary Fields delivering mail in bad weather in Montana.

2. **WRITE ABOUT IT** Play the role of Elfego Baca. Write a short essay in which you apply for one of the jobs he had. Explain why your personality and experience make you the right person for the job.

**Technology** Read more biographies at Education Place. www.eduplace.com/kids/hmss05/

## Visual Summary

1. – 3. ✏ Write a description of each item named below.

**Mountains of the West**

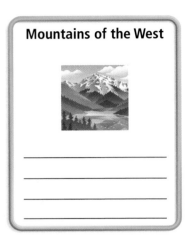

_____
_____
_____
_____

**Mineral Resources**

_____
_____
_____
_____

**Transcontinental Railroad**

_____
_____
_____
_____

## Facts and Main Ideas

✔ **TEST PREP** Answer each question below.

4. **Geography** Why is the plant and animal life in the West so varied?

5. **Geography** What are two factors that affected where people chose to settle in the West?

6. **Economics** What are three job opportunities that exist in the West?

7. **History** Who were the first people to live in the West, and where do scientists think they came from?

8. **Culture** In what ways did Spanish settlers and Pueblo Indians influence each other?

## Vocabulary

✔ **TEST PREP** Choose the correct word from the list below to complete each sentence.

**arid,** p. 248
**geothermal,** p. 247
**national park,** p. 257
**mission,** p. 264

9. A _____ is an area set aside by the federal government.

10. Heat that comes from beneath Earth's crust is _____.

11. A _____ is a settlement for teaching religion to local people.

12. _____ means very dry.

## CHAPTER SUMMARY TIMELINE

| 1519 Spanish conquer the Indians in Mexico | 1610 Spanish settle Santa Fe | | 1848 California gold rush begins | 1869 Transcontinental railroad is completed |

1500  1600  1700  1800  1900

## Apply Skills

✔ **TEST PREP  Distinguish Fact from Opinion** Use what you have learned about fact and opinion to answer each question.

13. Which of the following statements is a fact?

   **A.** The country's most beautiful landscape lies in the Pacific States.

   **B.** The West has the country's warmest and coldest temperatures.

   **C.** The western states are all pretty much the same.

   **D.** Alaska is by far the worst place to live.

14. Which of the following statements is an opinion?

   **A.** The Colorado River runs west from the Rocky Mountains.

   **B.** Mt. Elbert is the highest peak in the Rocky Mountains.

   **C.** The Rocky Mountains offer the best hiking and skiing in the country.

   **D.** Thousands of tourists visit the Rocky Mountains each year.

15. People should not go near an active volcano. What clue tells you that this statement is an opinion?

   **A.** It includes the word *should.*

   **B.** It gives the exact name of a place.

   **C.** It is supported by facts.

   **D.** It can be proven true.

## Critical Thinking

✔ **TEST PREP** Write a short paragraph to answer each question below.

16. **Summarize** Why did people move to the West between the 1600s and 1900s?

17. **Infer** What do you think might have happened if the United States had not won the Mexican-American War?

## Timeline

Use the Chapter Summary Timeline above to answer the question.

18. How many years after the California gold rush began was the transcontinental railroad completed?

# Activities

**Art Activity** Create a poster that highlights features of the West. You might include landforms, plants, animals, industries, and contributions from different cultures.

**Writing Activity** Write a short story about a family of settlers and the experiences they might have had traveling west in a wagon train. Do some research on wagon trains if necessary.

**Technology**
**Writing Process Tips**
Get help with your story at:
**www.eduplace.com/kids/hmss05/**

## Vocabulary Preview

**Technology**
e • glossary
e • word games
www.eduplace.com/kids/hmss05/

### conservation

The **conservation** of water and other resources is important in many communities. Using drip irrigation to slowly soak the soil is a way for farmers to conserve water.
**page 277**

### habitat

Forests, grasslands, deserts, mountains, marshes, and swamps are all different kinds of **habitat.** Each habitat has certain plants and animals that live in it.
**page 285**

# Reading Strategy

**Monitor and Clarify** As you read, use this strategy to check your understanding of the text.

 **Quick Tip** If you are confused about what is in a lesson, reread or read ahead.

## extinct

When an animal dies and there are no more of its kind anywhere on Earth, that animal has become **extinct.** The last known passenger pigeon died in 1914. **page 285**

## seasonal

A **seasonal** job lasts only for a certain season. For example, farmers might need workers to pick their strawberries only in the early summer. **page 290**

**What's Special About**

# The Southwest

## VOCABULARY

**weathering**
**conservation**

**Vocabulary Strategy**

conservation

When you **conserve** something, you try not to waste it. **Conservation** is saving and not wasting resources.

 **READING SKILL**
**Problem and Solution**
Chart ways in which people in the past worked to bring water to Phoenix.

| Problem | Solution |
|---------|----------|
| Water in Phoenix was scarce. | |

**Build on What You Know** Do you use air conditioning to stay cool? Air conditioning has made life in the Southwest more comfortable.

## Where People Live

**Main Idea** The Southwest has large cities as well as vast areas of open land.

Arizona, Nevada, New Mexico, and Utah are interior states, east of California and north of Mexico. They share a clear, dry climate. The landscape includes mountains, deserts, plateaus, and other dramatic landforms. The Southwest has large cities in the middle of deserts. It also has vast rural areas.

Phoenix, Arizona, is the region's largest city. The Hohokam were the first to live in this area. They built irrigation canals for their crops. Centuries later, settlers found the canals and rebuilt the settlement.

**Sante Fe, New Mexico** The Southwest has a wide variety of landscapes.

## Living in Phoenix

In the early 1900s, people built dams on nearby rivers to provide water for Phoenix. A stable water supply and the warm, dry climate attracted people and industries. Even more people moved to Phoenix in the 1950s, when air conditioning became available. Today, the city has more than one million people. Most people must drive to places because there are few buses and no subways.

Phoenix mixes new and old building styles. Tall office buildings are made of glass and steel. Other buildings are made of adobe. Homes and shopping centers reflect Spanish, Mexican, and American Indian styles.

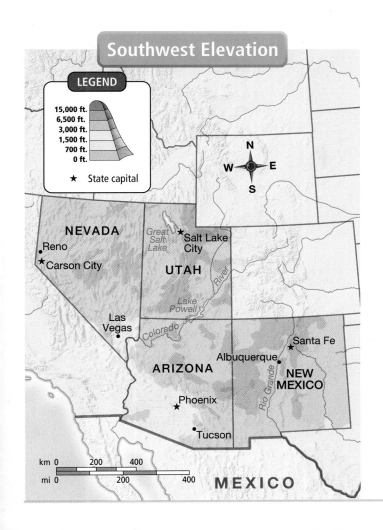

Southwest Elevation

LEGEND

15,000 ft.
6,500 ft.
3,000 ft.
1,500 ft.
700 ft.
0 ft.

★ State capital

NEVADA
Reno
★ Carson City
UTAH
Great Salt Lake
★ Salt Lake City
Lake Powell
Las Vegas
Colorado
ARIZONA
Phoenix
Tucson
Santa Fe ★
Albuquerque
NEW MEXICO
Rio Grande

km 0    200    400
mi 0    200    400

MEXICO

## Rural Life

Thousands of American Indians live in the Southwest. They live in rural areas and in cities. The largest American Indian reservation in the United States belongs to the Navajo. It covers about 16 million acres in rural Arizona, New Mexico, and Utah.

Some American Indians in the Southwest live in pueblos. A pueblo is a town made up of stone or adobe buildings. Today, most pueblos are in New Mexico along the Rio Grande. Modern Pueblo Indian groups include Pueblo, Hopi, Zuni, Acoma, and Laguna people. Many farm and raise livestock. Others teach school, run businesses, or hold other jobs.

The rural Southwest also has some of the oldest ranches in North America. People raise cattle, sheep, or horses on ranches. Some children who live on ranches ride buses over 20 miles to get to school. Many also have daily chores.

**REVIEW** Describe how the Spanish, Mexicans, and American Indians have influenced life in the Southwest.

**Southwest Elevation** Elevations in the Southwest vary widely.

**SKILL** **Reading Maps** Which city on the map has the lowest elevation?

# The Southwest Today

**Main Idea** Water in the Southwest has shaped both the land and people's lives.

The Southwest is known for wild rivers, high mountains, and beautiful canyons. Over millions of years, erosion, rivers, and weathering have shaped this desert land. **Weathering** is the breakdown of rock caused by wind, water, and weather. In Arizona, the Colorado River helped carve the mile-deep Grand Canyon. Erosion also shaped many natural arches in Utah.

Each year, millions of tourists visit the region to view the scenery. Many of them hike or bike in the mountains and canyons. Others paddle the rivers and swim in the lakes.

## Using Water

Water is scarce in the Southwest. Some areas, such as Las Vegas, Nevada, receive only about four inches of rain each year. Rivers are few and often overused. Many have been dammed to create reservoirs. Reservoirs are lakes used to store water.

The Colorado River and its reservoirs supply water to about 25 million people in the United States. It provides water for nearly four million acres of farmland. Because people use every drop the river holds, it actually dries up before reaching the sea.

**Roosevelt Dam** Water from the Roosevelt Dam irrigates thousands of acres of desert in Arizona.

**Monument Valley** Erosion created tall mesas and other landforms in Monument Valley. They rise up 1,000 feet from the desert in Arizona and Utah.

## Conserving Water

Southwesterners work hard at water conservation. **Conservation** means using something carefully and not wasting it. Cities such as Phoenix and Salt Lake City, Utah, often use local plants in their parks and public spaces. These plants have adapted to the dry region and do not need extra watering. Farmers conserve water by using drip irrigation. Instead of flooding the fields, water slowly soaks the soil.

**Drip Irrigation System** Southwestern farmers use drip irrigation, which drips water slowly at the roots of plants.

## Things to Do and See

Southwesterners value their land, culture, and history. Many people speak Spanish or American Indian languages as well as English. People attend rodeos and American Indian festivals and eat at Mexican restaurants. They visit national parks and ghost towns. At the Arizona-Sonoran Desert Museum, people view the region's animals and plants.

**REVIEW** How do people conserve water?

## Lesson Summary

- The Spanish, Mexicans, and American Indians have influenced the culture of the Southwest.

- Water in the Southwest has shaped both the land and its people.

## Why It Matters ...

People continue to move to the Southwest, one of the country's most diverse and fastest-growing regions.

## Lesson Review

❶ **VOCABULARY** Write a paragraph about the Southwest using **weathering** and **conservation.**

❷ **READING SKILL** In what ways have southwesterners helped to **solve the problem** of having little water?

❸ **MAIN IDEA: Culture** Explain one effect of the Southwest climate on people's lives.

❹ **MAIN IDEA: Geography** Explain how water has affected the landforms in the Southwest.

❺ **CRITICAL THINKING: Cause and Effect** Explain two causes of Phoenix's growth.

**HANDS ON** **DRAMA ACTIVITY** Write a skit to act out ways that people can conserve water.

# Conserving Water

**Water is a limited resource.** City and state governments in the Southwest encourage water **conservation.** New and improved technologies can help. For example, the Utah Division of Water Resources recommends front-loading washing machines and low-flush toilets.

People can save water in their yards and gardens, too. In Albuquerque, New Mexico, people can get money back from the city government for xeriscaping (ZIR ih skayp ing) their land. Xeriscaping is a kind of landscaping, or arranging plants to make an area look nice. To xeriscape a garden, people choose plants that need little water. They also water the plants in ways that conserve water.

**Water-conserving Machines** Front-loading washers save water as they clean people's laundry.

**Xeriscaping** Xeriscaped gardens can be as pretty as gardens that use three times as much water.

**Yarrow**
Yarrow can often be seen in meadows and along roadsides.

## Xeriscaping Plan

- ✔ Choose plants that don't need much water.

- ✔ Put water only where plants can use it. Don't spray water all over the garden.

- ✔ Cover soil with mulch or wood chips. This keeps water from evaporating.

- ✔ Add organic soil. Plants can get more nutrients and get water more easily.

**Look Closely**
Catmint's purple-blue flowers bloom in the spring and then again in the summer.

**Red Valerian**
Red Valerian, also known as Jupiter's Beard, grows well in poor soil.

# Activities

1. **TALK ABOUT IT** Discuss five ways that you could save water in your home.

2. **PRESENT IT** Create a water conservation plan for your school. Share it with your class.

279

Skills

# Make Decisions

You make decisions every day. A decision involves choosing what to do or what to say in a situation. Some decisions can be easy—like choosing what to wear or what to eat. Other decisions may require more thought. In this case, you must carefully consider the consequence of each choice.

## Learn the Skill

**Step 1:** Identify the decision you must make.

**Step 2:** List all of your choices.

**Step 3:** Consider the consequence of each choice, both good and bad.

**Step 4:** Make your decision. Choose the option with the best possible outcome.

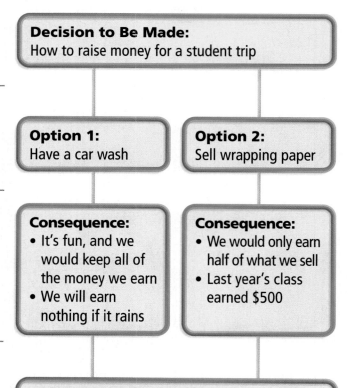

**Decision to Be Made:**
How to raise money for a student trip

**Option 1:**
Have a car wash

**Option 2:**
Sell wrapping paper

**Consequence:**
• It's fun, and we would keep all of the money we earn
• We will earn nothing if it rains

**Consequence:**
• We would only earn half of what we sell
• Last year's class earned $500

**Final Decision:** Sell wrapping paper

## Practice the Skill

Water is an important issue in the Southwest. Review Lesson 1 of this chapter. What decisions did people make about water? What choices did they have? What were the positive and negative consequences of each choice? Explain how the decisions people made about water have affected life in the Southwest.

## Apply the Skill

In a group or on your own, find out more about the water issue in the Southwest and other choices that the people and government have faced. Follow the step-by-step process to make your own decision about what more should be done.

**What's Special About**

# The Mountain States

**Build on What You Know** Imagine driving 100 miles to go to the dentist. In parts of the Mountain States, some people do just that.

## Cities and Rural Areas

**Main Idea** Most people in the Mountain States live in large cities and towns, but some prefer the rural areas.

Why are Colorado, Idaho, Montana, and Wyoming called the Mountain States? The Rocky Mountains run through them. There are also hills, plateaus, plains, and valleys. Few people live in rural areas because of the rugged land and harsh winters. Most live in cities or towns.

Denver is Colorado's capital. It is on a mile-high plain east of the Rockies. The mountains block moisture, keeping Denver's climate arid. Denver is an industrial and cultural center.

**Flight Simulator** In Denver, astronaut Anna Fisher trains for space missions.

## Rural Life

Most people in the Mountain States live in cities along the major rivers or in the valleys. Fewer people live in the rural communities and mining towns in the vast grassland and mountain areas.

The natural beauty of prairies, mountains, and sky surrounds the people who live in these rural areas. Montana is nicknamed "Big Sky Country." The population density of Montana is only about six people per square mile.

People in the rural communities of the Mountain States often have strong ties with one another. At the same time, these communities may have few basic services. There may be few doctors, dentists, hospitals, lawyers, or even schools. Some rural schools have only one teacher. Children may go to school with just a few other students.

People in rural areas of the Mountain States typically travel to cities to get much of what they need. These cities provide goods and services to a larger region. They are centers for industry, entertainment, and services such as health care. Many have colleges. People enjoy art exhibits, sporting events, plays, operas, and museums. Jackson, Wyoming, has a ski area in the middle of the town. In Durango, Colorado, people paddle their kayaks and rafts on the river that runs through town.

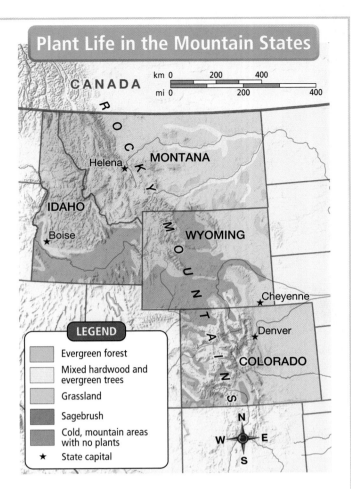

**Plant Life in the Mountain States**

LEGEND
- Evergreen forest
- Mixed hardwood and evergreen trees
- Grassland
- Sagebrush
- Cold, mountain areas with no plants
- ★ State capital

**Plant Life** Many kinds of plants grow in the Mountain States.

**SKILL Reading Maps** Which state has the largest evergreen forest areas?

In the Mountain States, the focus of rural life is the outdoors. Millions of cattle and sheep graze on ranches. National parks, forests, wildlife refuges, and undeveloped areas cover much of the region. One example is the Kootenai National Wildlife Refuge in northern Idaho. Visitors can see more than 220 kinds of birds in this refuge.

**REVIEW** Name two things the four Mountain States have in common.

283

**National Park Visitors in 1960 and 2000**

Number of visitors

- ■ 1960
- ■ 2000

3,500,000
3,000,000
2,500,000
2,000,000
1,500,000
1,000,000
500,000
0

Glacier   Rocky Mountain   Yellowstone

**Visiting the Mountain States** Tourism helps the economy of the Mountain States.

**SKILL** **Reading Graphs** Which national park had the most visitors in 2000?

# Recreation and Tourism

**Main Idea** Many people visit national parks, mountain resorts, and undeveloped areas in the Mountain States.

Many people work in the farming, mining, and forestry industries in the Mountain States. In recent years, the tourism industry has become very important to the economy. Each year, millions of visitors come to see the national parks, ski resorts, and vast undeveloped areas. These tourists spend money at businesses such as hotels and restaurants. This creates jobs.

## Touring the Mountain States

The Mountain States have many national parks, including Yellowstone, Rocky Mountain, and Glacier. National and state parks preserve the natural environment for people to enjoy. Some parks protect historic places.

The high elevations of the Mountain States provide a perfect location for winter sports. Aspen, Colorado, was an old mining town that is now a popular ski resort. Undeveloped areas attract people who enjoy hiking or fishing.

## Yellowstone National Park

Yellowstone is our nation's oldest national park. It is also one of the largest. The park's 3,472 square miles extend from Wyoming into southern Montana and eastern Idaho.

Yellowstone is one of the world's largest complete ecosystems in a temperate climate. An **ecosystem** is an environment and all its living things, working together as a unit. The vast area of Yellowstone supports many habitats. A **habitat** is the natural home of a plant or animal. For example, elk, bears, and wolves roam the meadows and forests. This is their habitat.

Yellowstone also provides a habitat for bison. Bison were once almost extinct. **Extinct** means no longer existing. Today, bison are a common sight in the park.

Yellowstone is famous for its geothermal activity. Geothermal refers to the heat of the earth's interior.

This heat causes eruptions. Geysers (GUY zerz), such as Old Faithful, shoot out towers of hot water. Visitors can also see brightly colored hot springs, bubbling mud pots, and hot steam vents, called fumaroles (FYOO muh rohlz).

**REVIEW** What attracts visitors to the Mountain States?

### Lesson Summary

Idaho, Montana, Colorado, and Wyoming have vast undeveloped areas, mountains, and national parks. Both urban and rural residents as well as tourists enjoy the many outdoor activities. Tourism boosts the economy and creates jobs.

## Why It Matters . . .

One way to see the vast beauty of the Mountain States is to visit its national parks.

## Lesson Review

❶ **VOCABULARY** Fill in the blank with the correct word.
habitat   elevation   extinct

Some animals have become _____ because of too much hunting.

❷ **READING SKILL Compare and contrast** the places that people visit in the Mountain States.

❸ **MAIN IDEA: Geography** Explain how Denver's location affects its climate.

❹ **MAIN IDEA: History** Why are national parks a valuable resource?

❺ **FACTS TO KNOW** Name four geothermal features in Yellowstone.

❻ **CRITICAL THINKING: Analyze** What can people do to help protect a national park?

**WRITING ACTIVITY** Write a speech about a national park in the Mountain States. Convince tourists to visit.

# Climate and Elevation

If you plan to climb a mountain, pack some clothes to keep you warm and dry. The climate is often colder and wetter in the mountains. Why? As you can see from this diagram, the answer is in the air.

Elevation affects weather, climate, and living things in all regions. Mountains across the United States have some things in common.

At higher elevations, there is less air pressure, so air cools. The trees are smaller because of the cooler air.

The bottom of a mountain is generally warmer and sunnier than the top.

# MOUNTAIN EXTREMES

## Wettest

Mount Wai'ale'ale (why ah lay ah lay) in Hawaii is one of the wettest spots in the world. Average rainfall is 444 inches per year at the top. The elevation there is 5,148 feet.

## Coldest

The lowest temperature recorded in the United States is −79.8° F. It was recorded in the Endicott Mountains of northern Alaska in 1971.

As the air goes over the mountain, it drops its moisture. The other side of the mountain can be very dry.

Cool air holds less water than warm air. As a result, water vapor in the air forms clouds, rain, fog, and snow.

# Activities

1. **MAKE YOUR OWN** Build a model of a mountain or draw a picture of one. Show which way the air travels and which sides are wet and dry.

2. **RESEARCH IT** Read about some of the animals that live on mountains. Explain how they have adapted to mountain life.

VOCABULARY

seasonal
migrant worker

Vocabulary Strategy

| migrant worker

Find the word **migrant** in **immigrant.** An immigrant moves from one country to another. A **migrant worker** moves from one place to another to find work.

READING SKILL

**Main Idea and Details**
Find details that support the first main idea of this lesson.

# What's Special About
# The Pacific States

**Build on What You Know** Do you like apples, oranges, grapes, and lettuce? The fruits and vegetables you eat may have been grown in the Pacific States.

## Cities of the Pacific States

**Main Idea** Major coastal cities in the Pacific States are ports and centers of industry.

The Pacific States are Alaska, California, Hawaii, Oregon, and Washington. Hawaii is a series of islands in the middle of the Pacific. The ocean affects the climate and how people live in this region.

### Seattle, Washington

Seattle is the largest city in Washington. It is a center for business, trade, and industry. Technology companies in the area employ tens of thousands of workers. Winters in Seattle are generally cloudy. Moist ocean air flows over the mountains of the Olympic Peninsula and drops rain on the city. Summers are generally sunny.

**Seattle** The Space Needle and Mount Rainier are two features of the Seattle skyline.

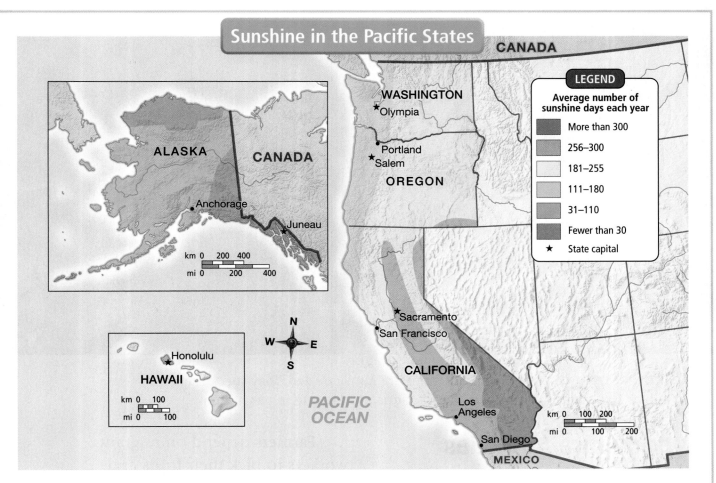

## Sunshine in the Pacific States

**LEGEND**

**Average number of sunshine days each year**

| | |
|---|---|
| | More than 300 |
| | 256–300 |
| | 181–255 |
| | 111–180 |
| | 31–110 |
| | Fewer than 30 |
| ★ | State capital |

**Pacific Sunshine** Some parts of the Pacific States receive sunshine nearly every day. Other parts receive little sunshine.

**SKILL** **Reading Maps** Which cities get the least sunshine?

## Port Cities

Seattle and other Pacific coastal cities are major seaports. Since the 1800s, many Asian immigrants have entered the United States through these cities. As a result, many Asian Americans live in the region today.

Port cities in the Pacific States carry on trade with many countries. Portland, Oregon, ships wheat to Asia and blueberries to Europe. Together, the busy ports of Los Angeles and Long Beach, California, move more cargo than the Port of New York. They form the world's third busiest port complex.

At Honolulu Harbor in Hawaii, ships carry goods to and from places all over the world.

Shipping is not these cities' only industry. San Francisco is a major international banking center. Los Angeles is home to the movie and television industries. Portland has software and high-technology businesses. Honolulu and many other places in Hawaii are important to the state's tourism industry.

**REVIEW** What is the importance of the seaports on the Pacific coast?

**California Lettuce** Most California farms are family owned. They specialize in one or two crops. California is the top agricultural state in our nation.

## Agriculture Activities

**Main Idea** The region's climate and open space allow for agriculture and outdoor activities.

The different climates of the Pacific region let farmers grow many different crops. In cool, wet coastal regions, farmers grow peas, broccoli, pears, apples, and strawberries. Farmers east of the Cascade Mountains raise wheat and sugar beets. During California's long growing season, farmers grow citrus fruits, almonds, figs, and kiwi. Tropical Hawaii produces more than 650,000 tons of pineapple each year.

Harvesting, or gathering, these crops is seasonal work. **Seasonal** means happening at certain times of the year. Each crop is ready to be picked at a certain time or season.

Farmers depend on migrant workers to pick their fruits and vegetables. A **migrant worker** moves from place to place doing seasonal work. In early summer, a migrant worker might pick strawberries in California. By fall, the same worker might be in Washington picking grapes. Migrant workers earn very little money. They often live in poor conditions. Some states, such as California, are trying to improve the lives of migrant workers.

The cities of the Pacific States support the rural agriculture industry. They have canning factories and other businesses that process raw foods into products. Ports and other transportation hubs in the Pacific States deliver these products to customers around the country and the world.

## Things to Do and See

People in the Pacific States enjoy activities such as skiing and riding bikes. Surfing is popular on many beaches. Surfing began in Hawaii. That state has over 1,600 surf spots.

The Pacific States have areas of rare natural beauty. Alaska's Arctic Wildlife Refuge preserves undeveloped areas. Hawaii Volcanoes National Park has Mauna Loa, a huge active volcano. Washington's Olympic National Park is known for its beautiful forests and coastline and its many glaciers.

**REVIEW** What industries support farming in the Pacific States?

**Surfing on the Pacific**
Surfing is a favorite water sport in Hawaii and California.

## Lesson Summary

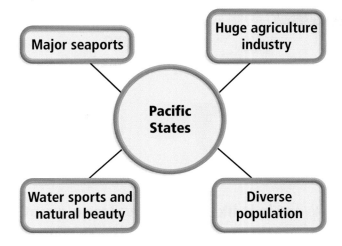

```
                Pacific
                States
```
- Major seaports
- Huge agriculture industry
- Water sports and natural beauty
- Diverse population

## Why It Matters...

The farmers of the Pacific States provide food for the nation and the world.

## Lesson Review

❶ **VOCABULARY** Write a paragraph explaining why farmers need **migrant workers** to do **seasonal** work for them.

❷ **READING SKILL** Use **details** to describe what crops people produce in the Pacific States.

❸ **MAIN IDEA: History** What effect has Asian immigration had on the Pacific coastal cities?

❹ **MAIN IDEA: Economy** What role do migrant workers play in the economy of the Pacific States?

❺ **CRITICAL THINKING: Evaluate** Name two natural areas in the Pacific States. Explain why each is important.

**HANDS ON** **MAP ACTIVITY** Research the crops grown in the Pacific States. Draw a map of the five states. Use symbols to show where each crop is grown.

# Rage of Fire

by Gloria Skurzynski and Alane Ferguson

**What is it like to see a volcano erupt?** Jack Landon, his sister Ashley, and their friend Danny Tran are about to find out. The three children have already had an exciting day. While hiking on Devastation Trail in Hawaii Volcanoes National Park, they talked about the legend of Pele, the volcano goddess. Then they became lost and took a path through Thurston Lava Tube, a dark, cave-like tunnel. A park ranger named Tricia Milewski helped them find Jack and Ashley's parents, Steven and Olivia. The story continues as the Landons and Danny finish a pleasant dinner at their hotel, Volcano House.

"Folks," the waiter said, setting hot cups of cappuccino in front of Steven and Olivia, "have you heard that a volcano is erupting?"

"See, Jack, what did I tell you?" Danny exclaimed. "I knew one would go off!"

"Where?" Steven asked.

"At Puu Oo. You won't want to miss it. Just drive about four miles down Chain of Craters Road to the Mauna Ulu parking area, then hike the trail about a mile to Puu Huluhulu. The eruption will still be five miles away from you, but don't worry, you'll see plenty. Oh, and don't forget your flashlights."

"Gotta run and grab my camera," Steven said, jumping up from the table. "I'll pick up some flashlights at the gift shop."

"Finish your cappuccino. It'll get cold," Olivia warned him.

"Hot lava's more important than hot java," he answered. "Be right back."

Olivia laughed. "He's absolutely right. You kids hurry and eat your dessert. We're in for a much bigger treat than chocolate pie."

What a wild ending to a wild day!

All the way over in the car, as daylight faded, they watched an orange glow tint the bottom of the clouds that hung in the sky above Puu Oo crater cone.

It was dark when they reached the parking area, but judging from the many jiggling flashlight beams they saw, dozens of people were hurrying down the trail.

Even before they rounded the last bend in the trail they heard a dull roar, like a jet plane taking off, followed by *ooohs* and *ahhhs* that rose from the watching crowd.

Then they saw it, too—a bright orange fountain of fire shooting up from Puu Oo crater cone, east of them.

Jack couldn't tear his eyes from the spectacle.

He'd seen lots of videotapes of volcanoes in action, but pictures could never begin to reveal the eeriness of that glow against the night sky. He was so caught up in it that he jumped when he felt a hand on his shoulder.

For a couple of seconds he didn't recognize the woman behind him, but then he realized it was Tricia Milewski, the park ranger from Thurston Lava Tube. She looked different out of uniform, her copper hair tied back in a scrunchie, a green zipper jacket replacing her uniform shirt.

"Hi," she said. "How do you like our fireworks?"

"Better than Fourth of July," Jack answered. And it was. These were nature's fireworks.

Compared with a pyrotechnic display like this one, anything humans could make was kindergarten stuff.

"There's better yet to come," Tricia told them as she peered through her binoculars. "Just wait. The crater's starting to overflow right now. Want to take a look?" she asked, handing Jack the binoculars.

Jack, Ashley, Danny, and Olivia took turns staring through the binoculars at the superheated lava rolling down the flanks of the cinder cone.

Steven was busy with his camera, so he got a magnified view, through his zoom lens, of the orange and black rivers of lava that began to descend the west slopes of Puu Oo like creeping fingers, moving slowly, but glowing brightly.

"Look at that!" Ashley exclaimed. "It's like melted chocolate on fire."

They watched for an hour, feeling a sense of closeness to the dozens of awestruck, appreciative people surrounding them, as everyone marveled at the majestic sight of a volcano in action.

"Incredible!" some of them would cry out. Or, "Isn't that beautiful? Pele's really cooking tonight!"

Then Olivia noticed Ashley's teeth chattering. "Hey, you guys are getting cold," she said. "I think we better get you to bed."

After saying goodnight to Tricia and the other friendly watchers whose names they didn't even know, the Landons returned reluctantly to their car and to their rooms in Volcano House.

## Activities

1. **STEP INTO IT**  Look at the pictures of this story. Then pretend you are Ashley, Danny, or Jack. Tell what it was like to see the erupting volcano.

2. **DRAW YOUR OWN**  Draw a comic strip that shows the events in this story. Use your drawings to tell the story to someone who hasn't read it.

## Visual Summary

1. – 3. ✏️➤ Write a description of each item named below.

**Life in the West**

| | |
|---|---|
| **The Southwest** | |
| **The Mountain States** | |
| **The Pacific States** | |

## Facts and Main Ideas

✔️ **TEST PREP** Answer each question below.

4. **Culture** What groups have influenced the culture of the Southwest?

5. **Geography** In what ways have people adapted to the Southwest's dry climate?

6. **Geography** What prevents many people from living in the rural areas of the Mountain States?

7. **Culture** What attracts people to the Mountain States?

8. **Economics** What factors help agriculture in the Pacific States?

## Vocabulary

✔️ **TEST PREP** Choose the correct word from the list below to complete each sentence.

**conservation,** p. 277
**ecosystem,** p. 285
**seasonal,** p. 290

9. The environment and the living things within it make up an _____.

10. Using something carefully to avoid wasting it is _____.

11. Activities that occur at certain times of the year are _____.

## Apply Skills

✔ **TEST PREP** **Make Decisions** Read the passage below. Then use the passage and what you have learned about making decisions to answer each question.

Carlos is looking for a place to live. He works in Phoenix, Arizona. His family lives outside of the city. If he moves near his family, he would have to drive many miles to work every day. If he lives in the city, he would be far from his family. Carlos decides he will live in the city and visit his family on the weekends.

**12.** What decision did Carlos face?

   **A.** where to live

   **B.** where to work

   **C.** if he should buy a car

   **D.** if he should quit his job

**13.** What will be a consequence of his decision?

   **A.** He will have to drive many miles to see his family.

   **B.** He will have to drive many miles to work.

   **C.** He will have to find a job outside of the city.

   **D.** He will not be able to see his family.

## Critical Thinking

✔ **TEST PREP** Write a short paragraph to answer each question below. Use details to support your response.

**14.** **Infer** Why do you think California's Los Angeles and Long Beach ports have become one of the world's busiest port complexes?

**15.** **Fact and Opinion** Is the statement that most southwesterners are careful about their water use a fact or an opinion? Give reasons for your answer.

# Activities

**Music Activity** Think about what you have learned in this chapter. Then write at least three lines for a song describing one of these areas.

**Writing Activity** Write a personal essay telling what you like most about the climate and natural features of your state.

**Technology**
**Writing Process Tips**
Get help with your story at:
www.eduplace.com/kids/hmss05/

# My State Handbook
## HISTORY

## History Where You Live

What do you know about the your state's past? People study state history to better understand the present and to think about the future. Who lived in your state before you and your family did? When did they build the first public school? Find out how the history of your state affects your life every day.

### My State's History

- Who were the first people in my state?
- What other people have settled here?
- Why did they choose to live here?
- When did my state become a state?

Outdoor market

Horse and wagon

Immigrants from around the world moved to New York City in the early 1900s.

**Find Out!**

## Explore your state's history.

✓ **Start with books.**
Your library has history books about your state. Encyclopedias may have timelines of events or tell about important people.

✓ **Talk to friends or family members.**
People you know may have lived in your state for many years. They can give you good ideas about what it was like.

✓ **Visit or call your state historical society.**
They may have a website for you to investigate.

✓ **Visit a museum.**
You can visit one of your state's museums or their websites. Find out more about who lived in your state in the past and who lives there today.

Use your state handbook to keep track of the information you find.

# Review and Test Prep

## Vocabulary and Main Ideas

✔ **TEST PREP** Write a sentence to answer each question.

1. What natural feature produces **geothermal** energy?

2. In what ways can **specialization** help a business?

3. What reasons did people have for traveling to the West in **wagon trains?**

4. What are two ways southwesterners practice water **conservation?**

5. Explain why Yellowstone National Park is an **ecosystem.**

6. Why do people who do **seasonal** work often need to move from place to place?

## Critical Thinking

✔ **TEST PREP** Write a short paragraph to answer each question.

7. **Draw Conclusions** In what way might water affect population growth in the Southwest in the future?

8. **Synthesize** In what ways do the land and climate of the West allow for a wide variety of wildlife? Give examples.

## Apply Skills

✔ **TEST PREP** Use the chart below and your decision-making skills to answer each question.

Colonists wanted more freedom from Britain.

Colonists wrote the declaration of Independence.

Colonists and Britain went to war.

The United States was established.

9. Why did the colonists decide to declare independence from Britain?

   A. They wanted to be ruled by Britain.
   B. They wanted Britain to be part of the United States.
   C. They wanted to be free from British rule.
   D. They wanted to move to Britain.

10. What did Britain decide to do after the colonies declared independence?

   A. It went to war with the colonists.
   B. It declared independence from the colonists.
   C. It helped the colonists fight.
   D. It wrote the Declaration of Independence.

## Unit Activity

### Make a Personal Timeline

- List important events in the history of your family or in your own life. Include dates, cultural celebrations, and events.

- Organize the events on a timeline.

- Draw pictures to illustrate the events.

- Share and compare timelines. Discuss how people's experiences connect them to their community.

## At the Library

**Find this book at your school or public library.**

*Dog of the Sea-Waves*
by James Rumford

Manu, one of the first people to settle Hawaii, becomes friends with a strange creature.

## CURRENT EVENTS
# WEEKLY (WR) READER

### Current Events Project

**Describe the history of a holiday that Americans celebrate today.**

- Find information about the holidays Americans celebrate.

- Learn about the history of one holiday.

- Write a paragraph telling why the holiday was created. Describe how people celebrate it today.

- Post your paragraph in a display about American holidays.

### Technology

Weekly Reader online offers social studies articles. Go to:

**www.eduplace.com/kids/hmss/**

## Read About It

**Look in your classroom for these Social Studies Independent Books.**

# Connections to Our World

**The Big Idea**

Why do you think the United States works with nations around the world?

*"We have learned to be citizens of the world, members of the human community."*

—Franklin D. Roosevelt, 1945
32nd President of the United States

**The United Nations**

303

# Almanac

## World Land Use

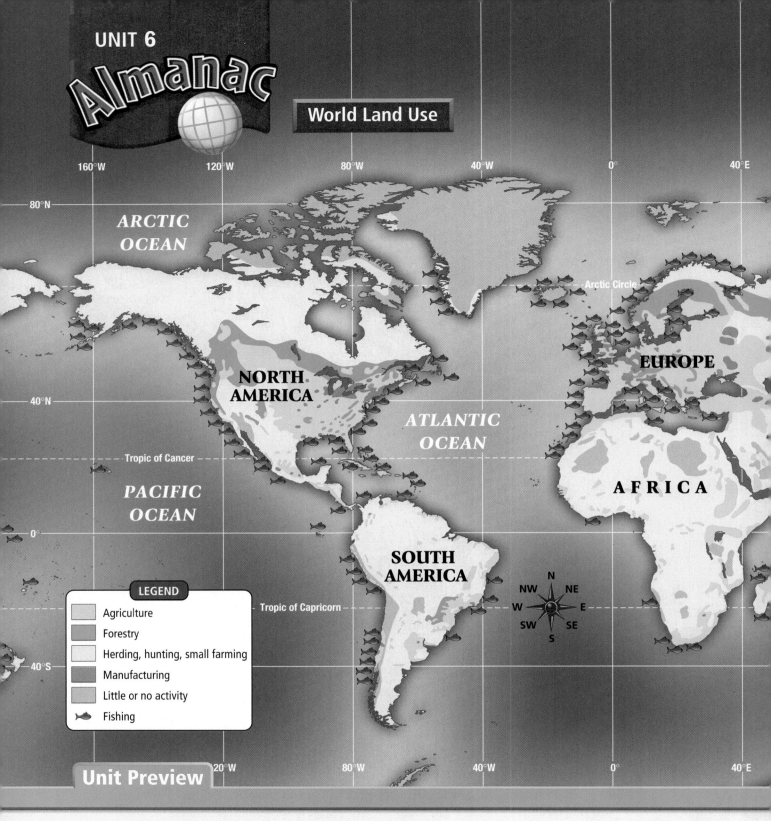

160°W    120°W    80°W    40°W    0°    40°E

80°N

**ARCTIC OCEAN**

Arctic Circle

**NORTH AMERICA**

**EUROPE**

40°N

**ATLANTIC OCEAN**

**AFRICA**

Tropic of Cancer

**PACIFIC OCEAN**

0°

**SOUTH AMERICA**

N
NW   NE
W   E
SW   SE
S

Tropic of Capricorn

### LEGEND

- Agriculture
- Forestry
- Herding, hunting, small farming
- Manufacturing
- Little or no activity
- Fishing

40°S

120°W    80°W    40°W    0°    40°E

## Unit Preview

### Democratic System
Voters elect representatives **Chapter 11, page 309**

### American Culture
Americans share many traditions **Chapter 11, page 317**

### Trade Partners
Countries in North America trade goods **Chapter 12, page 349**

# The World

## Top U.S. Trading Partners

| Country | Total Amount Traded, 2002 |
|---------|---------------------------|
| 1. Canada | $371 billion |
| 2. Mexico | $232 billion |
| 3. Japan | $173 billion |
| 4. China | $147 billion |
| 5. Germany | $ 89 billion |

Trade among the United States, Canada, and Mexico increased to a high level between 1992 and 2002. Look at the table. What was the total amount of U.S. trade with Canada and Mexico in 2002?

CURRENT    EVENTS

WEEKLY (WR) READER

**Current events on the web!**

Read social studies articles about current events at:
**www.eduplace.com/kids/hmss/**

80°E    120°E    160°E

80

ASIA

PACIFIC
OCEAN

40

- - - Tropic of Cancer - - - -

INDIAN
OCEAN

- - Tropic of Capricorn -

AUSTRALIA

40°S

km 0    1500    3000

mi 0    1500    3000

80°E    120°E    160°E

**United Nations**
The UN works for peace
**Chapter 12, page 354**

**Technology**
*e* • glossary
*e* • word games
www.eduplace.com/kids/hmss05/

# Vocabulary Preview

## citizen

A **citizen** of a country has special rights as well as special responsibilities. Immigrants often want to apply for citizenship in their new country.
**page 308**

## democracy

**Democracy** is government by the people. The United States government is a form of democracy in which citizens elect representatives to speak and vote for them.
**page 309**

# Reading Strategy

**Summarize** Use this strategy to help you understand important information in this chapter.

 **Quick Tip** Note the most important information and then put it into your own words.

## volunteer

Schools, hospitals, museums, and relief organizations depend on **volunteers.** These people work without pay. **page 317**

## province

The United States is divided into 50 states. Canada is divided into ten **provinces** and three large territories. Quebec is a Canadian province in which many people speak French. **page 321**

# United States Government

**Build on What You Know** An American flag probably hangs in your classroom. Schools in all fifty states have the same national flag. We are all part of the same nation, even when we live many miles apart.

## Government by the People

**Main Idea** Our government is made by the people, of the people, and for the people of the United States.

The United States has many regions. The land and the ways people live can differ from place to place. Yet all these people and places are part of the same nation.

Our government is "by the people." This means that the people hold the power to govern. We create the government. Our government is also "of the people" because each American citizen has a say in what the government does. A **citizen** is someone who is born in a country or who promises to be loyal to the country. The United States government is supposed to protect our rights and serve the "common good." This means the good of the whole population. That is why we say our government is "for the people."

**American Citizenship** People take an oath to become American citizens.

**Vice President**  **Speaker of the House**

**U.S. Senators and Representatives**

**United States Congress** American voters elect people to represent them in the government. Congress is made up of U.S. Senators and Representatives.

## How the People Rule

The United States is a democracy. A **democracy** is a system in which the people hold the power of government. The people decide who will lead them and what the government will do.

Democracy can take several forms. In many small towns, every person votes on every rule and decision. This does not work well, however, for a huge nation. Imagine if millions of citizens had to vote on every law. It would take far too long to make a decision.

Instead, the government of the United States is a representative democracy. A **representative** is a person who acts for a group of people. Citizens choose representatives to vote for them.

Our representatives make day-to-day decisions for the government. They represent the voters. That is what makes us a democracy.

Citizens decide who will represent them in elections. An **election** is the way voters choose people to serve in government. On election day, voters have the chance to cast their votes for the people they want to represent them. Whoever gets the most votes usually wins the election. Voting is the responsibility of citizens in a democratic system.

**REVIEW** What is the job of representatives in our democratic system?

## Liberty, Equality, and Justice for All

United States citizens generally agree on some basic ideas. We agree on the value of liberty. This is the freedom from control by others. We agree on the idea of justice and the rule of law. This means that laws should apply to everyone in the same way.

Before 1776, the states were colonies controlled by Great Britain. Many colonists wanted more liberty. They wrote the Declaration of Independence. It said that "all [people] are created equal" and that the people have a right to "life, liberty, and the pursuit of happiness." Colonists fought the British to win these rights. They established the United States.

# The Constitution

**Main Idea** Our constitution limits the power of the government and divides the government into three branches.

The leaders of the United States wrote a constitution in 1787. Our Constitution tries to ensure liberty, equality, and justice for all. It includes the Bill of Rights, which protects our rights and liberties. It sets firm limits on the power of government.

**Bill of Rights** The Bill of Rights says that all Americans have certain rights and freedoms.

**SKILL** **Reading Charts** What does the freedom of assembly allow Americans to do?

## Some Liberties Protected by the Bill of Rights

Freedom to Practice Your Religious Beliefs

Freedom of Speech

Freedom of the Press

Freedom of Assembly

## The Three Branches of Government

The Constitution sets up three branches, or sections, for our national government. This helps prevent any one part of the government from getting too powerful.

The legislative branch is the U.S. Congress. It makes the nation's laws. Congress has two parts, the House of Representatives and the Senate. Voters elect senators and members of the House. Both the House and the Senate meet in the Capitol building.

The executive branch carries out the nation's laws. It is headed by the President, who is elected. The President lives and works at the White House.

The judicial branch includes the federal courts. It decides questions about the nation's laws. The Supreme Court is the country's highest court. It has the power to decide which laws are allowed by the Constitution.

Judges and justices in the judicial branch are not elected. They are chosen by the President and approved by the Senate.

**REVIEW** Why are there three branches of government?

### Lesson Summary

- The many people of this country are united under our government.
- Our government is based on values of liberty, equality, and justice.
- The Constitution limits the power of our government.

## Why It Matters ...

The United States government unites Americans through shared values of liberty and justice.

---

## Lesson Review

**1 VOCABULARY** Write a paragraph about the United States government that uses **representative, election,** and **citizen.**

**2 READING SKILL** How does the Constitution **solve the problem** of government becoming too powerful?

**3 MAIN IDEA: Citizenship** What is a representative democracy?

**4 MAIN IDEA: Government** What are the three branches of government?

**5 FACTS TO KNOW** What was the purpose of the Declaration of Independence?

**6 CRITICAL THINKING: Infer** Why do you think judges and justices in the national government are not elected?

**WRITING ACTIVITY** Write a "Declaration of Unity" for the United States. Describe how our government pulls us together. Explain why it is important for us to stay united.

★ ★ ★ ★ ★ ★ ★ ★ ★ ★

# National Symbols

★ ★ ★ ★ ★ ★ ★ ★ ★ ★

Americans often feel proud when they see the stars and stripes of the United States flag waving high overhead. The flag and other national symbols make Americans think about the important ideas our nation represents. These ideas include freedom, democracy, and civil rights.

## ★ The Statue of Liberty ★

The people of the United States received the Statue of Liberty as a gift from the people of France in 1885. For millions of immigrants arriving in New York, "Lady Liberty" was the first thing they saw. It suggested they could find freedom and opportunity in America. The words below are engraved at the base of the statue.

❝Give me your tired, your poor,
Your huddled masses
yearning to breathe free. . . .❞

— from "The New Colossus" by Emma Lazarus

# ★ The Washington Monument ★

In 1884, Americans finished building a monument to honor George Washington. Inside are 193 memorial stones engraved with messages. Every state sent at least one stone. Many cities, companies, and foreign nations also sent stones.

# ★ The Liberty Bell ★

The Liberty Bell arrived in Philadelphia in 1752. It was rung when the Declaration of Independence was first read in public. Later, people fighting against slavery named it "The Liberty Bell." It has become a symbol of our nation's struggle for freedom.

**Look Closely** The Liberty Bell has cracked twice. The first time, it was melted down and made again.

# Activities

1. **STEP INTO IT** Notice the torch in Liberty's hand. Talk about what this shining light might mean.

2. **DRAW IT** Draw your own memorial stone for the Washington Monument. Use words and pictures to say something important about the United States.

 **Technology** Explore more primary sources for this unit at Education Place. www.eduplace.com/kids/hmss05/

# Many Regions, One Nation

## VOCABULARY

**interdependence**
**prosperity**
**heritage**
**volunteer**

**Vocabulary Strategy**

interdependence

The prefix **inter–** means "between." **Interdependence** can mean dependence between people, or people needing each other.

## READING SKILL

**Draw Conclusions** As you read, list facts that support this conclusion.

The government helps create links between Americans.

**Making Connections** The Internet and the United States Postal Service are two systems that link Americans.

**Build on What You Know** Do you have friends or relatives who live in other parts of the country? Although you live far apart, do you feel connected? People all across our nation are connected, too.

## Linking Regions

**Main Idea** Networks of communication, transportation, and trade link people of the United States.

Americans are linked in many ways. We live in the United States. We have a national government. We share the values of liberty, equality, and justice.

Our government has always searched for new ways to link states and regions. For example, early leaders created a postal system even before there was a United States. Our nation has built roads, canals, and railroads. We have phone systems, airports, and the Internet. These links change over time, but they have always had the same goal of connecting the states and regions of the country.

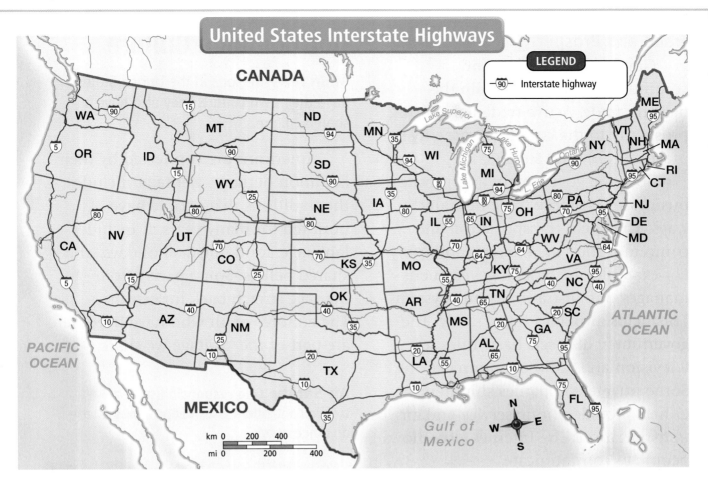

## United States Interstate Highways

**CANADA**

**LEGEND**
—90— Interstate highway

WA · OR · ID · MT · ND · MN · WI · MI · ME · VT · NH · MA · NY · RI · CT

**PACIFIC OCEAN**

CA · NV · UT · CO · WY · SD · NE · IA · IL · IN · OH · PA · NJ · DE · MD · WV · VA · KY · NC · SC

AZ · NM · OK · KS · MO · AR · TN · MS · AL · GA

**MEXICO**

TX · LA · FL

**Gulf of Mexico**

**ATLANTIC OCEAN**

Lake Superior · Lake Michigan · Lake Huron · L. Erie · Ontario

km 0 200 400
mi 0 200 400

N · S · E · W

**Interstate Highways** The Interstate Highway System has made transportation much easier.

## Interdependence of Regions

Each link that connects states and regions leads to more interdependence. **Interdependence** is a relationship in which people depend on each other. For example, think about farmers in Maryland and families living in New Jersey. Because roads connect the states, Maryland farmers can sell crops to New Jersey families who eat the farmers' crops. Both depend on each other. These kinds of links are found across the country. They help unite us and help us live better lives.

The United States government has worked hard to create these links.

Today, the United States Postal Service connects people and businesses across the country. It helps people communicate and transport goods. The mail handles billions of dollars in business every day.

The United States government has also helped build a network of roads called the Interstate Highway System. Many of these roads were built in the 1950s and 1960s. Interstate highways help people and goods move easily across the country.

**REVIEW** In what way does the United States Postal Service link different parts of the country?

315

## Trade and Prosperity

Good transportation and communication systems help the nation's trade. Active trade helps bring prosperity to the country. **Prosperity** means wealth and success.

Both the government and private businesses promote trade in many ways. They help transportation and communication systems run smoothly. For example, the federal government manages our air-traffic control system. This helps airplanes travel safely. The government also sets basic rules for television and radio communications. Some private companies ship items. Others provide phone service and air transportation. The Internet also allows people to communicate.

Another way our government helps trade is by providing a system of money and banking. This makes trade easier. Everyone agrees on how to pay for goods and services. People know what the money is worth.

## Our Common Culture

**Main Idea** Regions in the United States have their own culture. They also have a shared culture.

Americans are connected by their common heritage. **Heritage** includes the traditions that people have honored for many years. It includes language, food, music, holidays, and shared beliefs. Some parts of our heritage stretch back for centuries. The cultures of all who have lived here are part of the heritage we share.

**Air Safety** One responsibility of air traffic controllers is to keep planes a safe distance apart.

## Sharing Traditions

Holidays show our shared heritage. People in every state celebrate Independence Day. Memorial Day parades happen all across the country.

People also share a tradition of helping others. After the attacks of September 11, 2001, volunteers from around the country came to New York City. A **volunteer** is someone who agrees to provide a service without pay.

**Helping Out** These volunteers prepared food for rescue workers in New York City.

One volunteer was Timothy Mottl of Illinois. He said,

> 66 **The experience made me really look at . . . what being an American means to me.** 99

**REVIEW** In what ways do we show our shared culture?

## Lesson Summary

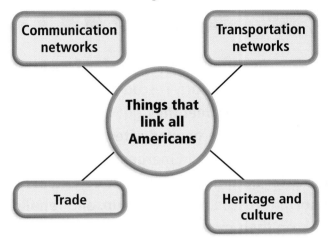

Communication networks

Transportation networks

Things that link all Americans

Trade

Heritage and culture

## Why It Matters . . .

Though each region of the United States is different, we are linked together in many ways.

## Lesson Review

1. **VOCABULARY** Write a short paragraph that shows you know what **interdependence** and **prosperity** mean.

2. **READING SKILL** What can you **conclude** about the ways government helps the economy?

3. **MAIN IDEA: Geography** List three ways the government helps link the different parts of the country.

4. **MAIN IDEA: Culture** In what ways does heritage connect people?

5. **CRITICAL THINKING: Draw Conclusions** In an emergency, why do you think people volunteer to help each other?

**HANDS ON** **ART ACTIVITY** What do you think it means to be an American? Create a poster with words and images that show our shared culture and heritage.

# VOLUNTEERS at WORK

**Why do volunteers work for free?** Whether they teach students, help seniors, rescue animals, or clean up the environment, most volunteers feel they get more than they give.

Volunteers are needed after a natural disaster, such as a flood or tornado. The Federal Emergency Management Agency does a lot to help after natural disasters, but volunteers often do much of the important rescue, relief, cleanup, and rebuilding work. They might work on their own, with church groups, or through organizations such as the Red Cross. Volunteers contribute to the common good of the nation's communities.

**Look Closely** In September of 1999, Hurricane Floyd caused the Neuse River in North Carolina to flood.

**RESCUE**

Volunteers help rescue people, pets, and livestock stranded by the floodwaters.

**RELIEF**

Volunteers help in relief centers, handing out meals and supplies and talking with flood victims.

**CLEANUP**

After floodwaters go down, volunteers help with the huge cleanup job.

**REBUILDING**

Volunteers with building skills help repair or rebuild thousands of homes.

# Activities

1. **DRAW IT** Volunteers show **civic virtue**, or the desire to do something for the common good. Draw a picture that shows an example of civic virtue.

2. **ACT IT OUT** Act out a skit of volunteers cleaning up a trail or a park.

# North American Neighbors

## VOCABULARY

**province**
**wilderness**

**Vocabulary Strategy**

province

**Province** has several meanings. All refer to parts of a larger whole. In geography, a **province** is a part of a larger country.

## READING SKILL

**Compare and Contrast**
Chart ways in which the United States is similar to and different from Canada.

**Build on What You Know**  Have you ever traveled across the United States border? How do things change when you leave our country and enter another one?

## Our Northern Neighbor: Canada

**Main Idea**  Canada and the United States have many things in common.

The United States is part of a larger region called North America. Canada makes up a large part of North America. Canada has the second largest land area of all countries in the world. The United States, however, has over nine times its population. We trade more with Canada than with any other country.

**A Vast Land**  Canada stretches from tiny fishing villages along the Atlantic to the busy city of Vancouver on the Pacific. This photo shows Peggy's Cove in Nova Scotia.

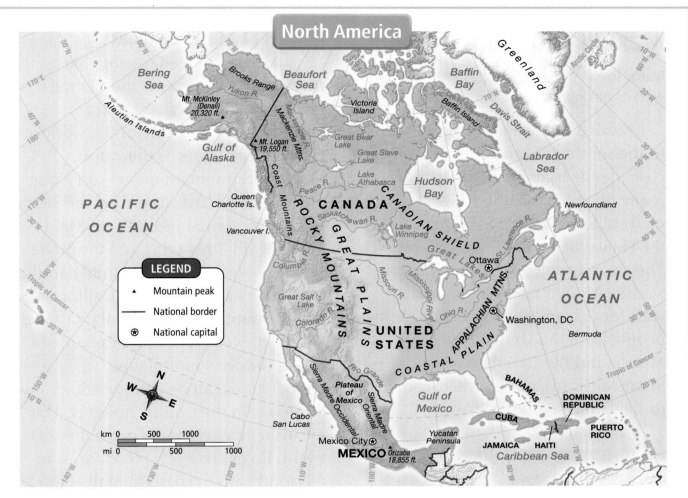

North America

Bering Sea
Brooks Range
Beaufort Sea
Greenland
Arctic Circle
Baffin Bay
Mt. McKinley (Denali) 20,320 ft.
Yukon R.
Victoria Island
Baffin Island
Davis Strait
Aleutian Islands
Mt. Logan 19,550 ft.
Mackenzie Mtns.
Great Bear Lake
Gulf of Alaska
Great Slave Lake
Labrador Sea
PACIFIC OCEAN
Coast Mountains
Peace R.
Lake Athabasca
Hudson Bay
Queen Charlotte Is.
CANADA
CANADIAN SHIELD
Newfoundland
Saskatchewan R.
Vancouver I.
ROCKY MOUNTAINS
Lake Winnipeg
Great Lakes
St. Lawrence R.
Ottawa
ATLANTIC OCEAN
Columbia R.
GREAT PLAINS
Missouri R.
Mississippi River
APPALACHIAN MTNS.
Great Salt Lake
Colorado R.
Ohio R.
Washington, DC
Bermuda
UNITED STATES
COASTAL PLAIN
Tropic of Cancer
Sierra Madre Occidental
Rio Grande
Plateau of Mexico
Sierra Madre Oriental
Gulf of Mexico
BAHAMAS
DOMINICAN REPUBLIC
Cabo San Lucas
CUBA
PUERTO RICO
Mexico City
Yucatán Peninsula
JAMAICA
HAITI
MEXICO
Orizaba 18,855 ft.
Caribbean Sea

LEGEND
▲ Mountain peak
— National border
⊗ National capital

km 0 500 1000
mi 0 500 1000

**Canada and North America** Canada makes up most of the northern part of North America.

## Climate, Land, and People

Canada extends into the Arctic Circle. Coastal mountains block warm winds that come from the Pacific. Hudson Bay, which is frozen much of the year, helps keep temperatures cool. Arctic weather sweeps down from the north. Most Canadians live along the warmer coasts and southern border.

Canada and the United States share many landforms, such as the Rocky Mountains and Great Plains. Canada has limited farmland. One major landform is the Canadian Shield, a vast area of forests and lakes. Forestry is a major industry in Canada.

American Indians have lived in Canada for thousands of years. Settlers from France and England arrived in the 1600s. In the province of Quebec, many people speak French. A **province** is a unit of government into which the nation is divided. In Canada's other nine provinces, most people speak English. Canada also has three territories. One, Nunavut, is home to Inuit and American Indian nations, though it is mostly a wilderness. A **wilderness** is a large, empty area with few people.

**REVIEW** How do Canada's population and area compare to those of the United States?

# Mexico and the Caribbean

**Main Idea** The United States shares ties with its neighbors to the south.

Mexico borders the United States to the south. Off our southeastern coast lie the islands of the Caribbean, many of which are independent nations. Some have government ties to the United States or European countries. They mostly enjoy a warm climate.

The United States trades widely with Mexico and the Caribbean. Many people from the United States visit Mexico and the Caribbean Islands. Many Mexicans and islanders come to the United States to live.

## Mexico's Land and Climate

Mexico is shaped roughly like a triangle. In the center is the Central Plateau, which has many volcanic peaks. Mexico City, one of the world's largest urban areas, is there, too.

Major mountain ranges run along Mexico's two coasts. These are the Sierra Madre Occidental (see-AIR-uh MAH-dray OK-sih-DEN-tuhl) and the Sierra Madre Oriental (OR ee EN tuhl). In the far west is Baja (BAH hah) California, a dry, mountainous peninsula. On the far eastern coast is a coastal plain.

In Mexico's mountains, temperatures can be cold. Much of Mexico is in the tropics, however. This means temperatures are generally warm. Except in a few places, such as the southeastern coast, rainfall is low.

**Antigua in the Caribbean** Mexico and the Caribbean have many different landforms. They also have people of many backgrounds.

## Languages of the Caribbean

| Islands | Languages |
|---|---|
| Aruba | Papiamento, Dutch, English, Spanish |
| Bahamas | English, Creole |
| Cuba | Spanish |
| Dominican Republic | Spanish, English |
| Haiti | French, Creole |
| Jamaica | English, Creole |
| Puerto Rico | Spanish, English |
| Trinidad and Tobago | English, Hindi, French, Spanish, Chinese |

## People and Cultures

The populations of Mexico and the Caribbean have developed in similar ways. American Indians lived in both places for centuries. Europeans began to arrive in the late 1400s. In Mexico, the Spanish conquered the mighty Aztec Empire and formed a colony. They also formed colonies on many Caribbean islands.

Other European countries set up colonies on Caribbean islands, too. European settlers included people from Great Britain, France, and the Netherlands. European settlers brought enslaved Africans to the Caribbean islands and Mexico.

Today, all of this history can be seen in the cultures of both Mexico and the islands of the Caribbean. In Mexico, Spanish is the main language.

People of American Indian and Spanish background make up much of Mexico's population. In the Caribbean, people of African background make up large parts of the population. People of European background are also present.

**REVIEW** What cultures have contributed to Mexican and Caribbean culture?

### Lesson Summary

The United States is part of North America. Its neighbors in this region include Canada, Mexico, and the Caribbean islands. The United States has much in common with these places, but each country is unique.

## Why It Matters . . .

Economic and cultural ties with our North American neighbors greatly help all of the countries on the continent.

---

## Lesson Review

**1** **VOCABULARY** Write a brief paragraph explaining what a **province** is.

**2** **READING SKILL Compare and contrast** Canada and Mexico. Think about both physical and human features of their geography.

**3** **MAIN IDEA: Economics** What country is the United States' most active trading partner?

**4** **MAIN IDEA: Geography** What landforms run along Mexico's east and west coasts?

**5** **CRITICAL THINKING: Infer** Why do you think the United States trades more with its close neighbors than with other countries?

**WRITING ACTIVITY** Write a speech for the President of the United States that tells about our relationships with our neighbors in North America.

# Early Leaders of Canada and Mexico

**Just like the United States, Canada and Mexico were once colonies.** Each struggled to unite as a nation and to gain independent political power. John Macdonald in Canada and Miguel Hidalgo in Mexico were involved in these struggles. They are two of the "founding fathers" of our neighboring countries.

## JOHN MACDONALD

1815–1891

John Macdonald came to Canada with his parents when he was five years old. In those days, Canada was made up of separate **provinces** ruled by England. Macdonald began to study law at age 15. In 1867, he wrote the British North America Act. This act explained how the provinces of Canada could become one nation. Macdonald became the first prime minister of this new nation.

Prime Minister Macdonald fought to build a strong and powerful nation. He expanded Canada's territory by adding new provinces. He also began work on a cross-country railway line. These actions made Macdonald an important person in Canada's history.

**Look Closely** In this photo, Donald Smith drives the last stake in the trans-Canadian railway in 1885.

# MIGUEL HIDALGO
## 1753–1811

Miguel Hidalgo (mee-GEHL hih-DAHL-goh) was a teacher and a priest. He was well loved by the local people. In order to create jobs, he set up workshops to make bricks, silk, wine, and leather. The colonial government had banned these activities, but Hidalgo wanted to improve people's lives.

Hidalgo and a group of others started an uprising against the government in 1810. Hidalgo led the army to some important victories, but there were also defeats. Eventually, Hidalgo was captured and executed, along with most of the other rebel leaders. The uprising did not succeed at that time, but it started something that could not be stopped. In 1821, Mexico gained independence from Spain.

**Independence Monument** This statue honors Mexico's independence from Spain.

# Activities

1. **TALK ABOUT IT** Why would John Macdonald think it was important to build a railway from one side of Canada to the other?

2. **WRITE ABOUT IT** Write a speech that John Macdonald might have given about the cross-country railroad. Explain why the railroad would be good for Canada.

 **Technology** Visit Education Place for more biographies. www.eduplace.com/kids/hmss05/

Reading and Thinking Skills

## Skillbuilder

# Draw Conclusions

▶ **VOCABULARY**
conclusion

Sometimes when you read, it is important to think about how different ideas and information go together. This is called drawing a conclusion. A conclusion is a judgment about the meaning of different facts or ideas. To draw a conclusion, you combine your own knowledge and experience along with the information provided. This can help you understand more about what you read.

## Learn the Skill

**Step 1:** Identify facts or details.

**Step 2:** Look for ways the facts and ideas might be connected to each other. For example, how might one event have caused another event to happen?

**Step 3:** Draw a conclusion by stating how you think the facts or ideas are connected.

| **Fact** Jean-Paul lives in Uranium City, located at 60°N. | **+** | **Fact** It is difficult to farm at 60°N latitude. | **=** | **Conclusion** Jean-Paul is probably not a farmer. |
|---|---|---|---|---|

About half of Canada's population has a British or French background. The rest of Canada's population includes American Indians and immigrants from other countries. In parts of Canada, many immigrants have formed large communities with others from their homeland. This has helped them keep their culture alive. For example, many immigrants from the Ukraine live on the prairies of Canada. Here the land and climate is similar to their homeland. In many Canadian cities, you can find communities of Chinese, Portuguese, and Italians where immigrants speak their native language and eat traditional foods.

## Practice the Skill

Read the paragraph above. Then answer the questions.

1 What conclusion can you draw about the land in the Ukraine? What facts or details help support this conclusion?

2 Why do you think many immigrants settle in communities with others from their homeland? What information supports this conclusion?

## Apply the Skill

Use information from Lesson 3 to draw conclusions about how immigrants have shaped the cultures of Mexico and the Caribbean. Provide details to support your conclusion.

# Central and South America

**VOCABULARY**

isthmus
rain forest

**Vocabulary Strategy**

rain forest

Two words together can make a new term. What would you expect to find in a place called a **rain forest?**

**READING SKILL**

**Compare and Contrast** Chart ways in which the United States is similar to and different from Central America.

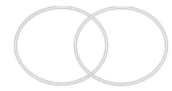

**Build on What You Know** Mexico, the United States, and Canada are parts of a region that runs from the tropics to the Arctic. Central and South America also form a region that covers a vast territory.

## Central America

**Main Idea** Although it is part of North America, Central America has many unique features.

The seven countries of Central America are also part of North America. Like Canada, Mexico, and the Caribbean, Central America shares some close ties with the United States. In the twentieth century, the United States tried to influence governments and economies in these countries. The people of Central America have not always welcomed this involvement. Today, there are still close trade links. Many Central Americans have also immigrated to the United States.

**Arenal Volcano, Costa Rica**
This beautiful volcano is one of the world's most active.

## Land, Climate, and Culture

Central America is a long, narrow region. Near the southern end is the Isthmus (IHS muhs) of Panama. An **isthmus** is a narrow strip of land that connects two larger land areas. The Isthmus of Panama is only about 50 miles wide at its narrowest point. In 1903, the United States took control of land there to build a canal. The Panama Canal opened in 1914. Today, it still allows ships to pass easily between the Atlantic and the Pacific.

Down the middle of Central America runs a series of mountains. Some are active volcanoes. The region also has many earthquakes.

Central America lies entirely in the tropics. In much of the region, rainfall is high. Rich rain forest covers many areas. **Rain forest** is dense forest that gets large amounts of rainfall every year. A huge variety of plants and animals live in the rain forest.

Central America

**Countries of Central America** The countries that make up Central America lie between Mexico and South America.

**Guatemalan Woman** Central America is home to many American Indian nations.

Central America was once colonized by Spain. Britain also colonized Belize. Spanish is still spoken in many areas. Before the Spanish arrived, American Indian nations thrived, including the Mayan Empire. Today, Central America has people of Spanish, American Indian, and mixed background.

Agriculture is a big industry in the region. Crops include coffee, sugar, and bananas. Many people survive only on the crops they can grow for themselves. Poverty is a problem.

**REVIEW** What made Panama a good place to build a canal?

# South America

**Main Idea** The geography and culture of the 12 nations of South America vary greatly.

South America is a continent that lies southeast of Central America. Together, North America and South America make up much of the land in the Western Hemisphere. South America has twelve countries, plus French Guiana (GEE ahn uh), which is controlled by France.

**North American Neighbor** Much of South America lies in the Southern Hemisphere.

### South America

LEGEND
- ▲ Mountain peak
- — National border
- ⊛ National capital

Tropic of Cancer

Caribbean Sea

Caracas · VENEZUELA
GUYANA
SURINAME
Georgetown · Paramaribo
COLOMBIA · Cayenne
Bogotá
FRENCH GUIANA
Quito · ECUADOR
Galápagos Islands (Ecuador)
AMAZON BASIN
PERU
B R A Z I L
Lima
BRAZILIAN HIGHLANDS
San Francisco R.
PACIFIC OCEAN
BOLIVIA
La Paz
Sucre · Brasília
Paraná R.
PARAGUAY
Asunción
CHILE
Mt. Aconcagua 22,834 ft. (6,960 m.)
MOUNTAINS
Buenos Aires
Santiago · URUGUAY
Montevideo
ARGENTINA
PATAGONIA
ATLANTIC OCEAN
Amazon R.
Equator
ANDES

km 0  500  1000
mi 0  500  1000

Tierra del Fuego

As with Central America, the United States has tried to influence governments in some South American countries. The United States has also prevented some other countries from influencing South America.

## Land and Climate

The Andes Mountains form a major feature of South America. Many peaks reach higher than 22,000 feet. Some are active volcanoes. South America also has a huge river system, the Amazon. Nearly one third of the continent drains into this river.

The climate of South America varies by elevation and location. Much of the continent lies in the tropics, where the climate can be wet and hot. The Amazon region has the world's largest rain forest. Even in the tropics, it can be cold in the mountains.

Parts of South America lie outside the tropics. The southern tip is near the frozen continent of Antarctica.

**Child with Llama**
The llama, a cousin of the camel, is native to South America.

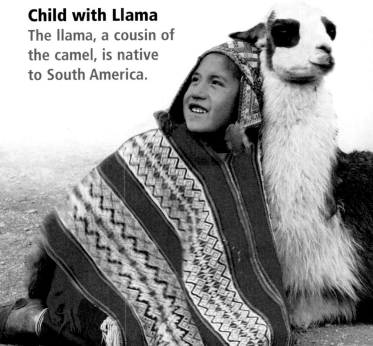

## Culture and Heritage

American Indians have lived in South America for thousands of years. One example is the Inca, who once lived in present-day Peru.

People from Spain and Portugal arrived in the 1500s. They enslaved American Indians and brought enslaved Africans to work. Later, immigrants from other parts of Europe and Asia arrived in large numbers. All of these groups help make up the population today.

Among South America's most valuable resources are its minerals. Venezuela is one of the world's top oil producers. South America is also rich in iron ore, copper, and other metals. Other resources include the huge variety of plants in the continent's large forest areas. South Americans are trying to protect this great resource.

Industry is growing in importance, especially in Brazil. However, in many large areas most people earn their living in agriculture.

**REVIEW** Name two major physical features of the South American continent.

## Lesson Summary

Central America and South America are neighbors of the United States in the Western Hemisphere. There is a great variety of land and climate, but much of the area has a tropical climate and large tropical rain forests. Central and South America share a similar historical heritage.

## Why It Matters ...

The United States needs to work closely with its neighbors on economic and environmental issues.

## Lesson Review

❶ **VOCABULARY** Write a paragraph about Central America that uses **isthmus** and **rain forest.**

❷ **READING SKILL Compare and contrast** Central America and South America in a paragraph.

❸ **MAIN IDEA: Geography** What examples show that Central and South America are lands of great variety?

❹ **MAIN IDEA: Culture** Why do many people speak Spanish in Central and South America?

❺ **CRITICAL THINKING: Generalize** Describe the populations of Central and South America today.

**HANDS ON** **RESEARCH ACTIVITY** Find information about rain forests in Central and South America. Why is it important to protect these forests? What can people do to protect them? Present your information to the class.

# The Most Beautiful Roof in the World

by Kathryn Lasky

**Scientist Meg Lowman explores one of the last frontiers of science—the rain forest canopy.** The canopy is the upper layer of leaves in a forest. To get to the canopy, Meg must climb up 60 to 100 feet. She uses a special walkway to move around the canopy.

Meg spends about five days each month in the treetops. She carefully collects samples of insects, flowers, and plants. She also spends about ten days each month studying the canopy from the rain forest floor. Meg is director of research and conservation at the Marie Selby Botanical Gardens, a rain forest research center in Sarasota, Florida. At her lab in Florida, Meg studies her samples to find out how insects affect the growth of the rain forest.

Meg wears a harness to climb to the forest canopy.

Deep in Belize, in Central America, there is a place called Blue Creek. Almost every month nearly 40 inches (102 centimeters) of rain falls. Blue Creek is considered one of the most humid places on the entire planet. In this shadowed world, pierced occasionally by slivers of sunlight, are more varieties of living things than perhaps any other place on earth. Within a 16-foot (five-meter) square, there can be upward of two hundred different species of plants.

And there are animals, too. Bats swoop through the canopy. Vipers coil among buttress roots, waiting in ambush. A rare and mysterious tree salamander slinks into the petals of an orchid. Poison dart frog tadpoles swim high above the forest floor in the tanks of bromeliads.

Meg crosses a walkway high above the forest floor.

The rain forest is a timeless, uncharted world, where mysteries abound and new or rare species appear like undiscovered islands. Within the tangled vines under the rotting bark of fallen trees, caught in the slime and mold of decaying vegetation and fungi, life teems with ceaseless energy. When a tree falls, the stump rots, bark loosens, and new creatures move in and take over the altered habitats. It is the very diversity of the rain forest that allows life to thrive everywhere, to spring back with a rush of opportunistic species to fill the gaps.

Meg walks over Blue Creek.

Viewed from an airplane, the top of the rain forest at Blue Creek looks like a field of gigantic broccoli. The bright green florets are actually the emergent growth of the very tallest trees. The crown of these trees extend above the canopy in the layer known as the pavilion. The pavilion is to the canopy as a roof is to a ceiling. From the emergent growth to the floor of the rain forest is a drop of 150 feet (46 meters) or more. Meg wants to go to the canopy, a layer below the emergent one. At Blue Creek a canopy walkway designed by specialists in rain forest platform construction has been built.

Meg is up at first light. It is drizzling but she will not wear rain gear. It is too hot. She has beans and rice for breakfast because this is all that is available. For her boys she has brought along cheese and crackers because they are tired of beans and rice. Unless the Mayan people who live in the nearby village come into the forest with chickens or melons, the menu does not vary. She kisses the boys good-bye and leaves them with her brother, Ed, who helped build the walkway. She puts on a hard hat and climbs into her safety harness. The harness has two six-foot lengths of rope attached. At the end of the ropes are Jumars, or ascenders. Jumars are used in technical rock climbing. The Metal U-shaped device has a hinged and grooved gate that allows the rope to slide up as one climbs but locks instantly with downward motion. To descend, the climber must manually push the gate open to allow the rope to slide through.

"Bye, Mom." James waves as he watches his mother begin her climb at the base of the *Ormosia*, or cabbage bark tree.

"Remember, it's our turn next," calls Edward as he watches his mom climb higher.

The boys have accompanied their mother to rain forests all over the world. Now, for the first time, Meg feels they are old enough to go up with her into the canopy. She has ordered special child-size harnesses for them. They are excited, but first their mother has work to do—traps to set for insects, leaves to tag, drawings to make, flowers to count. It will be many hours before they can join her. In the meantime, they can swim in the creek and explore a secret cave that their uncle promises to take them to.

Howler monkeys live near the top of the canopy.

# Activities

1. **TALK ABOUT IT** Discuss why scientists might want to study the rain forest.

2. **WRITE ABOUT IT** Pretend you are Meg's helper for a day. Write a journal entry describing your experience in the canopy.

# Chapter 11 Review and Test Prep

## Visual Summary

**1. – 3.** ✏️ Write a description of each item named below.

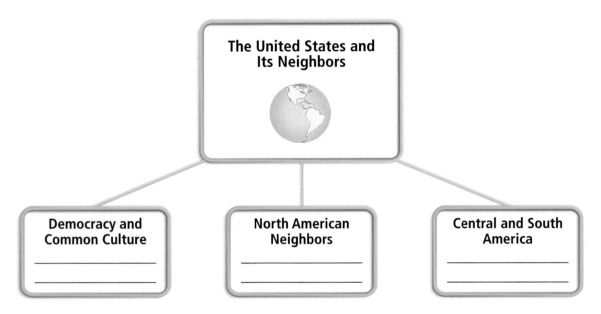

The United States and Its Neighbors

Democracy and Common Culture

_____
_____

North American Neighbors

_____
_____

Central and South America

_____
_____

## Facts and Main Ideas

✔ **TEST PREP** Answer each question below.

4. **Government** What is the executive branch of the U.S. government?

5. **Economics** In what way does interdependence help Americans live better lives?

6. **Geography** What physical features do Canada and the United States share?

7. **Culture** What countries formed colonies in the Caribbean islands?

8. **Economics** What natural resources help to support the economies of Central and South America?

## Vocabulary

✔ **TEST PREP** Choose the correct word from the list below to complete each sentence.

**constitution,** p. 310
**prosperity,** p. 316
**isthmus,** p. 329

9. _____ means wealth and success.

10. A _____ is a plan for setting up and running a government.

11. A narrow strip of land connecting two larger areas is called an _____.

✔ **TEST PREP** **Draw Conclusions**
Read the paragraph below. Then use what you have learned about drawing conclusions to answer each question.

Mexico has rugged mountains, high plateaus, low coastal plains, deserts, and even tropical rain forests. Most people in Mexico live in and around its major cities. In fact, Mexico City, the country's capital, is one of the world's largest urban areas. It is located on the central plateau, along with many of the country's largest cities.

12. What conclusion can you draw based on the facts in this passage?

   A. Most people in Mexico live along the coast.
   B. Most people in Mexico live on the central plateau.
   C. Most of the land in Mexico is rural.
   D. Most of the land in Mexico is urban.

13. Which fact supports this conclusion?

   A. Mexico City is the capital of Mexico.
   B. Mexico City is one of the world's largest urban areas.
   C. Mexico's major cities are located on the central plateau.
   D. Mexico has low coastal plains.

✔ **TEST PREP** Write a short paragraph to answer each question below.

14. **Synthesize** Why is the United States government said to be "for the people," "of the people," and "by the people"?

15. **Infer** Is it important for the United States to keep a good relationship with Canada and Mexico? Why?

# Activities

**Citizenship Activity** Make a poster that shows a way in which you might volunteer in your community. Use words and pictures.

**Writing Activity** Write a personal narrative, identifying a symbol of the United States that has meaning for you. Tell about an experience you have had that helped give that symbol a special meaning.

**Technology**
**Writing Process Tips**
Get help with your narrative at:
**www.eduplace.com/kids/hmss05/**

## Chapter 12

# Beyond the Americas

**Technology**

*e* • glossary
*e* • word games
www.eduplace.com/kids/hmss05/

## Vocabulary Preview

### vegetation

The **vegetation** of a region includes trees, bushes, grasses, and other plants. Different kinds of vegetation grow in different regions of the world. **page 341**

### alliance

An **alliance** between countries or groups can help meet goals shared by all the countries or groups. **page 348**

# Reading Strategy

**Monitor and Clarify** Check your understanding of the text using this strategy.

**Is the meaning of the text clear to you? Reread, if you need to.**

## treaty

The details of an agreement between two or more countries are written down in a **treaty.** Often, treaties are about peace or trade. **page 348**

## import

**Imports** are brought to the United States from all over the world. Americans can buy many kinds of imports, including food, electronics, and cars. **page 350**

# World Regions

**Build on What You Know** If you could visit any part of the world, where would you go? If you visited a faraway place, you would see many new things.

## VOCABULARY

**vegetation**
**dialect**

**Vocabulary Strategy**

vegetation

**Vegetation** is similar to the word vegetable. A vegetable is a plant you can eat. **Vegetation** means the plants that grow in a region.

## READING SKILL

**Categorize** List examples of different types of regions in your chart.

| Type of Region | Examples |
|---|---|
| Landform | |
| Climate | |

## Regions of the World

**Main Idea** The world has many different kinds of regions.

In this book, you have studied the major regions of the United States. Each region has some shared features. They include landforms, history, culture, and crops. Learning about a region helps you understand more about the places located there. For example, suppose you know little about Wisconsin, but you know it is in the Midwest region. You know that the Midwest has good farmland. Thus, Wisconsin probably has good soil for farming.

People divide the world into many different regions. North America and the Northern and Western hemispheres are regions that include the United States. There are also the Eastern and Southern hemispheres and six other continents.

**Torres del Paine, Chile** The mountains of Chile are part of a landform region.

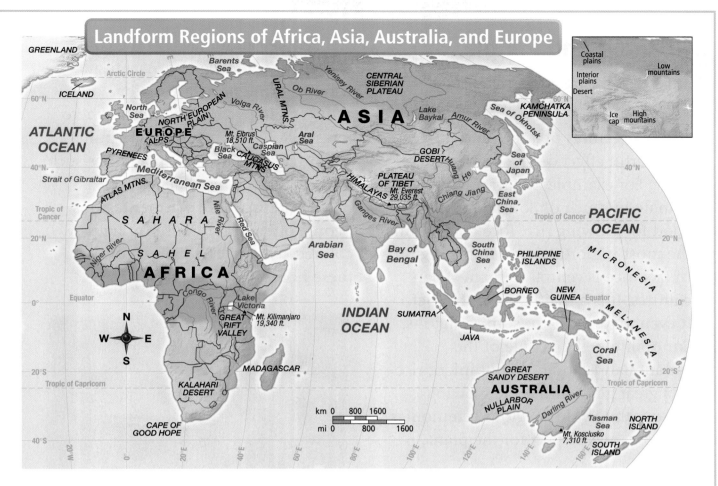

### Landform Regions of Africa, Asia, Australia, and Europe

GREENLAND

Arctic Circle

ICELAND

60°N

ATLANTIC OCEAN

North Sea

EUROPE

ALPS

PYRENEES

40°N

Strait of Gibraltar

Mediterranean Sea

ATLAS MTNS.

Tropic of Cancer

20°N

S A H A R A

S A H E L

AFRICA

Equator 0°

Niger River

Congo River

GREAT RIFT VALLEY

Lake Victoria

Mt. Kilimanjaro 19,340 ft.

W

N

E

S

20°S

Tropic of Capricorn

KALAHARI DESERT

MADAGASCAR

CAPE OF GOOD HOPE

40°S

Barents Sea

NORTH EUROPEAN PLAIN

Volga River

URAL MTNS.

Ob River

Yenisey River

CENTRAL SIBERIAN PLATEAU

A S I A

Lake Baykal

Amur River

Sea of Okhotsk

KAMCHATKA PENINSULA

60°N

Mt. Elbrus 18,510 ft.

Caspian Sea

Aral Sea

Black Sea

CAUCASUS MTNS.

GOBI DESERT

Huang He

Sea of Japan

40°N

HIMALAYAS

PLATEAU OF TIBET

Mt. Everest 29,035 ft.

Chiang Jiang

East China Sea

Ganges River

Nile River

Red Sea

Arabian Sea

Bay of Bengal

Tropic of Cancer

PACIFIC OCEAN

South China Sea

PHILIPPINE ISLANDS

M I C R O N E S I A

20°N

INDIAN OCEAN

SUMATRA

BORNEO

NEW GUINEA

Equator

0°

JAVA

M E L A N E S I A

Coral Sea

20°S

GREAT SANDY DESERT

AUSTRALIA

NULLARBOR PLAIN

Darling River

Tasman Sea

NORTH ISLAND

Tropic of Capricorn

Mt. Kosciusko 7,310 ft.

SOUTH ISLAND

km 0  800  1600

mi 0  800  1600

Coastal plains

Interior plains

Desert

Low mountains

Ice cap

High mountains

**Many Landforms** A large variety of landforms can be found on each continent.

## Types of Regions

Landform regions are based on the shape of the land. For example, mountain regions are rugged with steep slopes. Plains regions are broad and flat. Other landforms, such as hills, valleys, basins, and islands, can also define regions.

Each continent has many different landform regions. For example, the Himalayas, a mountain range in Asia, form a landform region. The British Isles in Europe and the Congo Basin in Africa form landform regions, too.

Landforms are just one kind of physical feature that geographers use to define regions. Climate is another one.

Arctic zones and the tropics are climate regions. Other regions are defined by the rain they receive. Most rain forest regions receive more than 80 inches of rain each year. We can also identify regions that share the same vegetation. **Vegetation** means the kinds of plants that grow in a region.

Human features can define regions, too. Italy, France, Spain, and Portugal form a region where people speak related languages. Egypt is part of a region where most people practice the religion of Islam. Parts of Ireland, Scotland, Wales, and France form regions where Celtic people live.

**REVIEW** What are two kinds of regions?

341

# Regions and People

**Main Idea** People in a region share some things in common but also have differences.

The features of a region can have a powerful effect on the people living there. For example, the warm and wet climate in much of Southeast Asia is good for growing rice. Rice has become the most important crop in the region. In fact, rice is central to many Asian cultures. It is a main part of the diet. It even plays a role in some religions. For example, the people of the Indonesian island of Bali think of rice as a great gift. During the growing season, they hold religious ceremonies to show their respect for the plant.

### Different Regions, Different Houses

Wooden houses are often built in forested regions. Hot, treeless regions often have light-colored adobe or cement houses.

People cannot farm in the cold climate of arctic regions. As a result, fishing and hunting are major activities. In parts of the world where forests grow, many houses are built from wood. This is true in regions such as the eastern United States and northern Europe. In warmer regions, people often build houses of light-colored cement. The light colors of these homes help people stay cool.

## Differences Within Regions

There can be variety within regions, too. In India, people share the same location. Yet there are cultural and religious differences within the country. The Hindu people of India practice different traditions than the Muslims of India. People speak dozens of different languages in Indian cities and villages, and those who speak the same language often have different dialects. A **dialect** is a regional form of a language.

One way to understand this variety is to say that different kinds of regions can overlap. A mountain region might overlap two different language regions. A language region might include part of a mountain region and part of a plains region. Learning about different world regions can help us understand our world and the people in it.

**REVIEW** How can the features of a region affect the people who live there?

**India Flower Market** India is a country of many different cultures.

## Lesson Summary

We can study the world in terms of its many regions. These include landform regions, climate regions, and language regions. Studying the features of a region can help us learn about the people who live there.

## Why It Matters ...

The same tools you use to understand the United States can also help you understand the world.

## Lesson Review

1. **VOCABULARY** Write a paragraph about regions using **vegetation** and **dialect.**

2. **READING SKILL** Landforms are one **category** of regions. Describe two other kinds of regions.

3. **MAIN IDEA: Geography** List four kinds of landform regions.

4. **MAIN IDEA: Geography** Explain how different regions can overlap.

5. **CRITICAL THINKING: Draw Conclusions** How might a warm climate influence the lives of people in a region?

**HANDS ON**

**RESEARCH ACTIVITY** What place have you always wanted to visit? Use library resources to learn about the place. What kinds of regions exist there? How have climate and other factors affected life there? Present your information to a group of classmates.

# Language Regions of the World

Our world has about 5,000 different languages. Over 200 of these languages are spoken by a million people or more. The map shows major language groups, or families of languages that developed from the same earlier language. Notice how the borders of a language group are not the same as the borders of a country.

Some languages are not a national language of any one country. For example, sign language is used by deaf people. They use hand movements and facial expressions to talk. Regions have different sign languages. American Sign Language, British Sign Language, and Japanese Sign Language are all different languages.

## Comparing Languages

| English | "One, two, three…" |
|---|---|
| Yiddish | "Eyns, tsvey, dray…" |
| Portuguese | "Um, dois, três…" |
| Indonesian | "Satu, dua, tiga…" |
| Hindi | "Ek, do, teen…" |
| American Sign Language | |

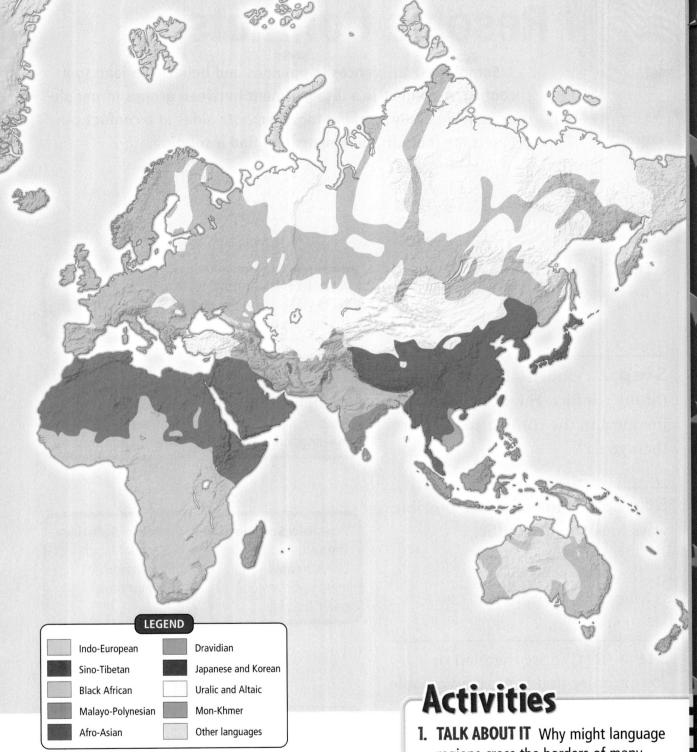

LEGEND

| | | | |
|---|---|---|---|
| | Indo-European | | Dravidian |
| | Sino-Tibetan | | Japanese and Korean |
| | Black African | | Uralic and Altaic |
| | Malayo-Polynesian | | Mon-Khmer |
| | Afro-Asian | | Other languages |

# Activities

1. **TALK ABOUT IT** Why might language regions cross the borders of many countries?

2. **PRESENT IT** Find out more about American Sign Language. Present several brief messages to the class using sign language.

345

Citizenship Skills

## Skillbuilder

# Resolve Conflicts

▶ **VOCABULARY**
conflict

Sometimes, differences in opinions and beliefs can lead to a conflict. A **conflict** is a disagreement between groups of people or individuals. By working together, both sides in a conflict can overcome their disagreements and find a solution.

## Learn the Skill

**Step 1:** Identify the conflict.

> **Conflict:** The softball team and the school band want to use the auditorium after school on Tuesdays.

**Step 2:** Understand the reasons for the conflict. Have the people involved in the conflict state their goals.

> **Goal:** The softball team wants to hold meetings on Tuesdays.

> **Goal:** The school band wants to rehearse on Tuesdays.

**Step 3:** Think of all the possible ways to solve the conflict.

> **Possible Solution:** The softball team offers to hold meetings every other Tuesday.

> **Possible Solution:** The school band offers to practice at a later time.

**Step 4:** Choose the plan or compromise that is most acceptable to everyone involved. Each side may need to compromise on its goals. A compromise is when a person or group gives up something it wants in order to move closer to an agreement.

> **Solution:** The softball team will hold meetings every other Tuesday. The band will practice in the evening on the days that the softball team has meetings.

Rain forests help keep the air clean, and they help support many plant and animal species. Rain forests also hold many valuable resources. Some people want to cut down rain forests to build houses, create farmland and sell timber. Others think that this will harm the environment. They want to keep people from disturbing the rain forest.

## Practice the Skill

Read the paragraph above. Then answer the questions.

1. Identify the conflict. What differences in opinion do people have about rain forests?
2. What are the goals of the people involved in the conflict?
3. Brainstorm ways that both groups can work together to resolve this conflict.

## Apply the Skill

Find out about a conflict that exists in your community. Learn about ways that people have tried to compromise in order to find a solution.

# Partners Around the World

## VOCABULARY

ally
alliance
treaty
free enterprise
import

### Vocabulary Strategy

ally, alliance

**Ally** and **alliance** are from the same word family. An **ally** is a partner, or someone who helps you. An **alliance** is a partnership. You and your ally agree to help each other.

### READING SKILL
**Cause and Effect**
List some effects of agreements between the United States and other countries.

| Causes | Effects |
| --- | --- |
| NATO | |
| NAFTA | |

**Build on What You Know**  Have you ever played on a sports team? If so, you know that different people can work together for a common goal. Many countries seek "teammates" around the world.

## United States Allies

**Main Idea**  The United States depends on the support of other countries for its well-being.

The United States values freedom and cooperation. We seek allies who share these ideals. An **ally** (AL eye) is a country or group that joins with another country or group for a common purpose. For example, allies can help defend each other from outside attack. The United States forms alliances for other purposes, too. An **alliance** (uh LIE uhns) is an agreement between allies to seek a common goal. Alliances for trade and scientific research are two other examples.

Often, alliances are formed by making treaties. A **treaty** is an official document that defines an agreement between nations. For example, the United States and other nations have signed a treaty against hunting whales.

**Humpback Whale**  Many nations agree that whales should be protected from hunters.

**NAFTA Allies** In 2001, Mexican President Vicente Fox, Canadian Prime Minister Jean Chrétien, and U.S. President George W. Bush showed their support for free trade in North America.

## Major United States Alliances

One example of a United States military alliance is NATO—the North Atlantic Treaty Organization. The United States and several European nations formed NATO in 1949. Its members agree to defend each other in case of attack.

The North American Free Trade Agreement, or NAFTA, is an example of a trade alliance. NAFTA allows the United States, Canada, and Mexico to trade goods with each other, usually without paying taxes or fees. The United States wants to create a free trade agreement with the rest of North and South America. In 2001, President **George W. Bush** said he wanted to see the Western hemisphere "bound together by good will and free trade."

## Allies and Partners

The United States has many allies. Mexico and Canada are NAFTA allies. European nations such as Britain, France, and Germany are some of our NATO allies. We have allies on other continents, too.

Many of our allies share our belief in free enterprise. **Free enterprise** is a system that lets people control their businesses and decide what goods to buy and sell. The United States also forms partnerships with countries that do not share these beliefs. For example, the government of China controls many Chinese businesses. Still, the United States works with China toward common goals.

**REVIEW** Why does the United States form alliances?

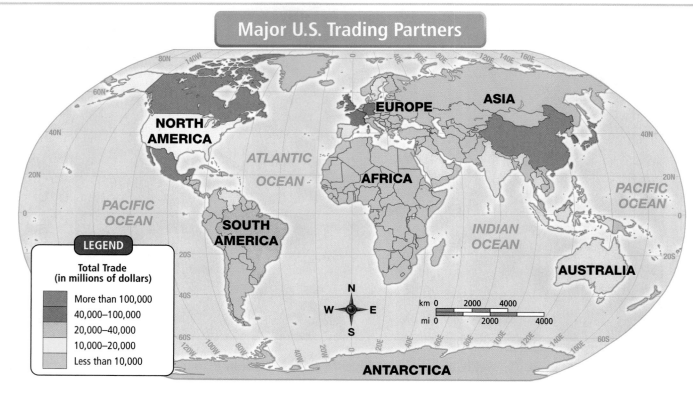

NORTH
AMERICA

EUROPE

ASIA

ATLANTIC
OCEAN

AFRICA

PACIFIC
OCEAN

SOUTH
AMERICA

INDIAN
OCEAN

PACIFIC
OCEAN

AUSTRALIA

**LEGEND**

Total Trade
(in millions of dollars)

More than 100,000
40,000–100,000
20,000–40,000
10,000–20,000
Less than 10,000

N
W — E
S

km 0    2000    4000
mi 0         2000         4000

ANTARCTICA

**U.S. Trade** The United States trades with countries around the world.

# Trading Partners

**Main Idea** Many United States alliances promote trade around the world.

The United States does a lot of trading with its allies. Our country has created many links with other countries. These links include transportation and communication. When goods, services, and information move freely between countries, trade grows. Businesses in the United States often want to increase the size of their markets. They want to sell their products anywhere in the world. Trade with foreign countries is called international trade. International means "between countries."

The United States is the most active trading nation in the world. Every year, United States businesses sell goods and services worth hundreds of billions of dollars to other countries. These exports are very important to the United States economy. Some U.S. businesses could not survive without their customers in other countries.

Consumers in the United States also spend hundreds of billions of dollars on imports each year. An **import** is a product brought in from another country. For example, every year, the United States imports billions of dollars worth of games, toys, and sporting goods.

## International Trade

Many Americans drive imported cars or wear imported clothes. Many watch television on imported sets. Some buy imported goods because they cost less than goods made here.

Many people think that free trade hurts workers. They believe that we need laws to protect jobs and the environment. Sometimes, countries pass laws that limit international trade. For example, a country may add an extra cost to imported goods. The United States has rules that protect some of its industries. At the same time, it works hard to decrease limits to free trade in other countries.

Canada and Mexico are the United States' leading trade partners. The United States also trades heavily with China, Japan, and much of Europe. Many European nations have formed an alliance called the European Union.

**REVIEW** Why is international trade important to the United States?

**Euro Coins** The European Union has created a single monetary system that most of its member nations use.

## Lesson Summary

The United States and its allies depend on each other in many ways.

The United States signs treaties with its partners and allies.

Many treaties and alliances are based on the environment, trade, and defense.

## Why It Matters...

Nations depend on each other for safety and economic success.

---

## Lesson Review

**1 VOCABULARY** Explain how an **ally** is different from an **alliance.**

**2 READING SKILL** Explain one **effect** of international trade on Americans.

**3 MAIN IDEA: Government** Why does the United States form alliances?

**4 MAIN IDEA: Economics** Why does the United States promote free trade?

**5 CRITICAL THINKING: Compare and Contrast** How is an alliance like a friendship? How is it different?

**WRITING ACTIVITY** Think of an issue that affects many nations. Write ideas for a treaty. Explain how the treaty would help all countries.

# Types of Economies

**How can you tell what kind of economy a country has?** Look at how the country makes decisions about what goods and services to produce.

The United States has a market economy. It is organized according to what goods and services consumers want and what producers are willing to provide. Since market economies allow consumers and producers to make free choices, market economies are called free enterprise systems. Market economies also use money to make it easier to buy and sell goods and services.

Some other countries have different systems. Each country must answer three basic economic questions. Its answers to these questions show what sort of economy it has. However, no economy is totally one kind. In this way, most economies are mixed economies.

## Three Basic Economic Questions

| 1 Who decides what goods and services to produce? | | 2 Who decides how to produce the goods and service |
|---|---|---|
| Consumers | + | Business owners |
| Government leaders | + | Government leaders |
| People (based on tradition) | + | People (based on tradition) |

## ③ Who decides who gets the goods and services?

| | | |
|---|---|---|
| + Consumers | = | **Market economy** |
| + Government leaders | = | **Command economy** |
| + People (based on tradition) | = | **Traditional economy** |

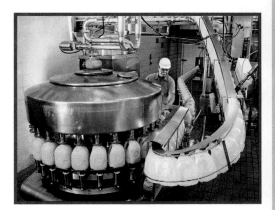

**Market Economy** A market economy encourages business owners to produce the goods and services that consumers wish to buy.

**Traditional Economy** These Mayan farmers live in Central America. In their traditional economy, they can trade with other farmers for goods such as honey and cocoa.

**Command Economy** In North Korea's command economy, people receive goods at government stores.

# Activities

1. **DRAW YOUR OWN** What goods and services do you and your family buy? Draw a picture that shows some of these.

2. **DESCRIBE IT** Describe a choice you or your family had to make in buying a good or service.

# Working Together

## VOCABULARY

**international law**
**nongovernmental**
**organization (NGO)**

**Vocabulary Strategy**

nongovernmental
organization

**Non–** means "not." A
**nongovernmental**
**organization** is a group
that does not belong to a
government.

## READING SKILL

**Problem and Solution**
Record problems that the
United Nations solves.

| Problem | Solution |
|---------|----------|
|         |          |

**Build on What You Know** When you and a friend
have a disagreement, how do you solve it? It is
important to have ways for settling disagreements.
Like people, countries also need ways to do this.

## Nations Work Together

**Main Idea** The United States and other nations have rules
to follow for handling disagreements and facing challenges.

The United States works with many other nations
toward common goals. One of the most important
goals is greater peace around the world. Toward this
goal, countries formed an organization called the
United Nations. Through this organization, nations
can face challenges in peaceful ways. This helps
prevent nations from turning to war.

**United Nations Flag** The olive branches of the
United Nations flag stand for world peace.

## The United Nations

The United Nations, or UN, was born at the end of World War II. The United States helped create the UN. Today, more than 190 countries belong to this organization. One of its goals is to build peace and friendship among the countries of the world.

In 1948, the UN adopted the Universal Declaration of Human Rights. This document protects the basic rights of people in all countries. The World Bank, a UN agency, helps countries build their economies. The United Nations also helps improve health conditions through the World Health Organization. These and other UN programs help people all over the world.

## International Law

In the United States, we have laws about how our citizens should behave. There are also rules of international law. **International law** is a set of basic rules to which the United States and many other countries have agreed. Treaties are examples of this kind of agreement. The United Nations helps nations work together to make agreements.

One area of international law has to do with war. Many countries have agreed to rules about what a country can and cannot do in war. The UN has helped organize trials for people accused of war crimes. Wars in the Balkans and Rwanda have led to trials for such crimes.

**REVIEW** When was the United Nations formed, and for what purposes?

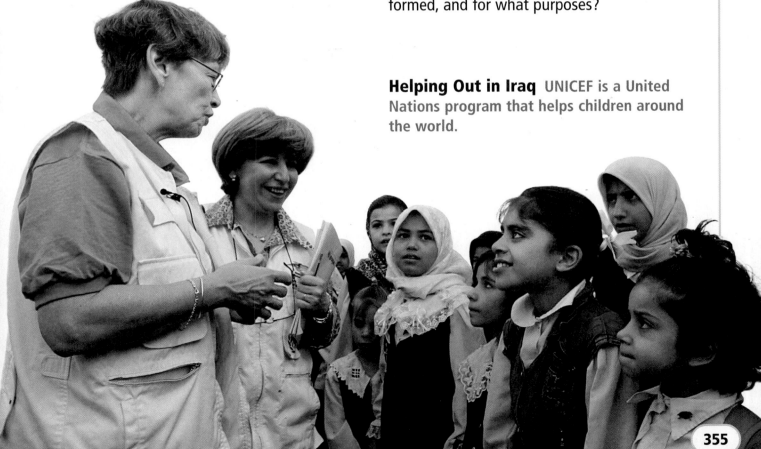

**Helping Out in Iraq** UNICEF is a United Nations program that helps children around the world.

# People Work Together

**Main Idea** Cooperation between countries takes many forms.

Many nongovernmental organizations work to build relationships across national borders. A **nongovernmental organization,** or NGO, is a group that is not part of a national government. Many NGOs work with the United Nations or with national governments to reach shared goals. These goals may include helping the poor and treating the sick.

You have probably heard of some NGOs. For example, the International Red Cross rushes to help people when disasters such as earthquakes strike. In the United States, the American Red Cross helps people give blood for others in need. Doctors Without Borders is another NGO. This group provides medical care to people who need help around the world. Other NGOs help spread useful farming techniques, protect people's rights, support democracies, and share business knowledge. There are thousands of NGOs around the world.

In general, NGOs exist for the purpose of helping people. They cross international borders in order to make the world a better place.

**Help from Outside the Government** Many NGOs give help to people wherever it is needed in the world.

## Communicating Around the World

Today, technology helps people communicate more easily and quickly than ever before. Wireless phones, the Internet, and other communication tools allow people to get in touch with each other from nearly anywhere on the planet. Sounds, pictures, and other kinds of information take only seconds to travel around the world.

In the past, people were often unable to communicate with others during difficult times. For example, after World War II, the countries of Eastern Europe were shut off from the rest of the world. The governments of these countries prevented their people from communicating with anyone in the outside world. Because of today's technology, it would be much more difficult for a government to control people's communication like this.

Some governments still try to control the information their citizens receive, but wireless phones and the Internet can connect these people to the outside world. This might help bring freedom and change to many.

**REVIEW** What are some goals of NGOs?

### Lesson Summary

- The United Nations works to keep peace and improve living conditions.

- International law helps relationships between countries work smoothly.

- Many people have built links through NGOs and through modern communications networks.

## Why It Matters ...

The nations and people of the world must find ways to resolve conflicts to make the world a better place to live.

## Lesson Review

**1 VOCABULARY** Write a paragraph telling what a **nongovernmental organization** does.

**2 READING SKILL** In what way has the United Nations tried to **solve the problem** of poor health conditions?

**3 MAIN IDEA: Government** What role do national governments play in international law?

**4 MAIN IDEA: Technology** In what ways has technology helped build links between the people of the world?

**5 CRITICAL THINKING: Analyze** Why do you think countries agree to follow international law?

**HANDS ON ART ACTIVITY** Suppose you wanted to plan an Internet site for people to learn about life in the United States. Use words and pictures to tell about your life here.

# Universal Human Rights

**What rights should every person have?** In a 1941 speech, President **Franklin D. Roosevelt** discussed four freedoms everyone should have. They were (1) freedom of speech and expression, (2) freedom of worship, (3) freedom from want, and (4) freedom from fear.

After World War II, the United Nations set up the Commission on Human Rights to protect the rights of all people in all nations. **Eleanor Roosevelt,** President Roosevelt's wife, was elected chairperson. The commission wrote the Universal Declaration of Human Rights. The declaration contains 30 articles, or brief statements, about specific human rights.

On December 10, 1948, the UN's member nations voted to adopt the declaration. It continues to guide international law today.

**Human Rights Day** December 10 is Human Rights Day. These children in India lit candles to mark the day.

# Some Articles from the Declaration

> "All human beings are born free and equal in dignity and rights. . . ."
>
> — Article 1

> "Everyone has the right to freedom of opinion and expression. . . ."
>
> — Article 19

> "Everyone has the right to take part in the government of his country, directly or through freely chosen representatives."
>
> — Article 21

THE UNIVERSAL DECLARATION OF **Human Rights**

**Eleanor Roosevelt** Eleanor Roosevelt said that respect for universal human rights begins in "small places, close to home."

# Activities

1. **TALK ABOUT IT** Eleanor Roosevelt cared about **fairness** for all people. Discuss what each article above says about fairness.

2. **DRAW YOUR OWN** Draw pictures that show each of the four freedoms from President Roosevelt's speech.

## Visual Summary

1. – 3.  Write a description of each item named below.

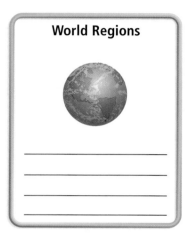

**World Regions**

_____
_____
_____
_____

**U.S. Allies**

_____
_____
_____
_____

**United Nations**

_____
_____
_____
_____

## Facts and Main Ideas

✔ **TEST PREP** Answer each question below.

4. **Economics** What effect could the features of a region have on that region's economy?

5. **Culture** In what way can learning about the regions of the world be an advantage?

6. **Government** What is free trade?

7. **Economics** Why might people buy imported goods rather than those made in their own country?

8. **History** Why do you think the United Nations was formed after World War II?

## Vocabulary

✔ **TEST PREP** Choose the correct word from the list below to complete each sentence.

**vegetation,** p. 341
**treaty,** p. 348
**free enterprise,** p. 349

9. The kinds of plants that grow in a region make up its _____.

10. In a _____ people can control their own businesses and decide what to buy.

11. Nations that make a _____ become allies.

✔️ **TEST PREP** **Resolve Conflicts** Read the newspaper article below. Then use what you have learned about resolving conflicts to answer each question.

## Nations Agree to Reduce Pollution

**KYOTO, JAPAN**—At a meeting in Kyoto, Japan, representatives from 160 nations reached an agreement to reduce global pollution by 5% before 2012. To do this, nations will decrease their own pollution output. The European Union will cut its pollution by 8%, the United States by 7%, Japan by 6%, and other countries in varying amounts.

12. What do you think were the goals of the nations involved in the conflict?

   **A.** to reduce pollution no matter what

   **B.** to reduce pollution without harming their country's industries

   **C.** to set up a future meeting

   **D.** to find out if there was actually a need to reduce pollution

13. What did the nations most likely compromise on?

   **A.** the percent each nation would cut

   **B.** the place and time of the meeting

   **C.** what nations should be involved

   **D.** how to reduce the pollution

✔️ **TEST PREP** Write a short paragraph to answer each question below. Use details to support your response.

14. **Draw Conclusions** What do you think is a main advantage of forming alliances? Give reasons to support your conclusion.

15. **Summarize** Explain the importance of nongovernmental organizations such as the International Red Cross or Doctors Without Borders.

# Activities

**HANDS ON**

**Math Activity** Use the information in the newspaper article on this page to make a graph that shows how much each nation agreed to decrease its pollution output.

**Writing Activity** Write a persuasive essay, explaining what rights you believe all children should have. Give strong reasons for your argument.

**Technology**
**Writing Process Tips**
Get help with your essay at:
**www.eduplace.com/kids/hmss05/**

## Your State and the World

Your state plays a special role in the world. People in your state may serve in the military or do business with companies overseas. They may send email to people in other countries. Where was your favorite computer game made? What goods in your state come from other countries? Find out how your state connects to the world.

### My State and the World

- **What does my state import?**
- **Where do imports come from?**
- **What countries do business with my state?**

Goods for export

Cargo ship

Many states import and export goods from Shanghai, China.

## Find Out!

### Explore how your state connects to the world.

✔ **Start with the library.**
Countries that do business with states may set up consulates in large cities or the state capital. Contact the consulates to find out about their businesses.

✔ **Read a local newspaper.**
What articles tell ways your state connects with other states, regions, and countries?

✔ **Check out international transportation and communication.**
Highways, airports, and satellite communications may link your state to the world. Try the Department of Transportation website. Or visit a local airport to find out more.

✔ **Call or visit the Chamber of Commerce.**
They might be able to tell you which nations trade with your state.

Use your state handbook to keep track of the information you find.

## Vocabulary and Main Ideas

✔ **TEST PREP** Write a sentence to answer each question.

1. Why is it important for **citizens** to vote in an **election?**

2. In what ways does **interdependence** help us live better lives? Give an example.

3. What country divides its units of government into **provinces?**

4. Give an example of how climate affects the **vegetation** of a region.

5. What are some reasons for a country to form an **alliance** with another country?

6. What do **nongovernmental organizations** (NGOs) do to build relationships between nations?

## Critical Thinking

✔ **TEST PREP** Write a short paragraph to answer each question.

7. **Draw Conclusions** Why do you think the writers of the Constitution thought it was important to limit the power of government?

8. **Cause and Effect** In what way might a mountainous region affect the lives of the people who live there?

## Apply Skills

✔ **TEST PREP** Use the bar graph below to answer each question.

**Biggest U.S. Trading Partners**
2002

Dollars (in millions): 400,000 / 300,000 / 200,000 / 100,000 / 0

Countries: Canada, Mexico, Japan, China, Germany, United Kingdom, South Korea

Country

9. Which conclusion can you draw from the graph?

   A. Spain is a U.S. trading partner.
   B. China and Germany do most of their trading with each other.
   C. Only seven countries trade goods.
   D. The U.S. trades a lot with other North American countries.

10. Which conclusion can you draw about the United States and Canada?

    A. Canada is an important U.S. trading partner.
    B. Neither country does much trading.
    C. Canada and the United States trade mostly with Mexico.
    D. They are no longer allies.

## Unit Activity

### Create a World Community Drawing

- Think about how the people in the United States work with people and nations around the world.

- Make a drawing showing one example of working together. Add a title.

- Display the drawing in your classroom.

## At the Library

**Check out this book at your school or public library.**

*Red, White, Blue, and Uncle Who?*
by Teresa Bateman
The history behind some of America's patriotic symbols is told here.

### urrent Events Project

**Create a display about how the United States works with other countries.**

- Find information about projects the United States has done with other nations.

- Pick one project and write a summary of it.

- Find or draw pictures that tell something about your project.

- Post your summary and pictures in a class display.

**Technology**
Weekly Reader online offers social studies articles. Go to :
**www.eduplace.com/kids/hmss/**

## Read About It

**Look in your classroom for these Social Studies Independent Books.**

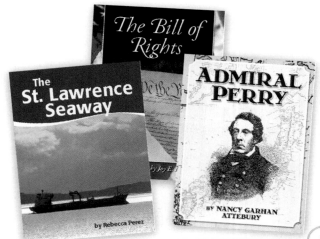

# References

## Citizenship Handbook

Citizenship Handbook

# Resources

# Pledge of Allegiance

*I pledge allegiance to the flag
of the United States of America
and to the Republic for which it stands,
one Nation under God, indivisible,
with liberty and justice for all.*

## Spanish

Prometo lealtad a la bandera de los Estados Unidos de América, y a la república que representa, una nación bajo Dios, entera, con libertad y justicia para todos.

## Russian

Я даю клятву верности флагу Соединённых Штатов Америки и стране, символом которой он является, народу, единому перед Богом, свободному и равноправному.

## Tagalog

Ako ay nanunumpa ng katapatan sa bandila ng Estados Unidos ng Amerika, at sa Republikang kanyang kinakatawan, isang Bansang pumapailalim sa isang Maykapal hindi nahahati, may kalayaan at katarungan para sa lahat.

## Arabic

ادين بالولاء لعلم الولايات المتحده الامريكيه والى الجمهوريه التي تمثلها دولة واحدة تؤمن باللة متحدة تمنح الحرية والعدالة للجميع

## Chinese

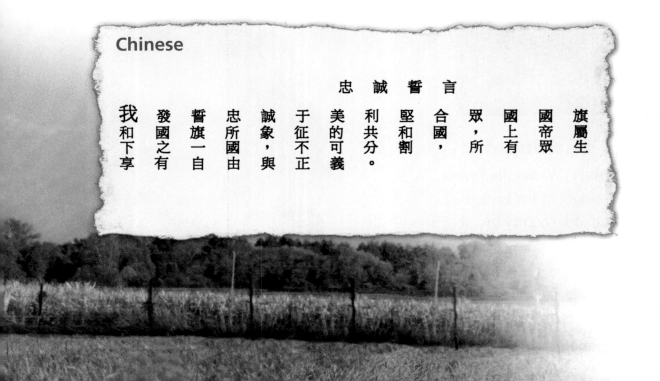

忠 誠 誓 言
合國，
國上有
眾，所
利共分。
美的可義
于征不正
誠象，與
忠所國由
誓旗一自
發國之有
我和下享
旗屬生
國帝眾

# Character Traits

Character includes feelings, thoughts, and behaviors. A character trait is something people show by the way they act. To act bravely shows courage, and courage is one of several character traits.

Positive character traits, such as honesty, caring, and courage, lead to positive actions. Character traits are also called "life skills." Life skills can help you do your best, and doing your best leads to reaching your goals.

## George Washington

**Responsibility** Washington was the first President of the United States. He led our country to freedom during the War for Independence.

## Coretta Scott King

**Fairness** King worked long and hard for fairness. A civil rights leader, she spent her life speaking out for the rights of African Americans.

**Courage** means acting bravely. Doing what you believe to be good and right, and telling the truth, requires courage.

**Patriotism** means working for the goals of your country. When you show national pride, you are being patriotic.

**Responsibility** is taking care of work that needs to be done. Responsible people are reliable and trustworthy, which means they can be counted on.

**Respect** means paying attention to what other people want and believe. The "golden rule," or treating others as you would like to be treated, shows thoughtfulness and respect.

**Fairness** means working to make things fair for everyone. Often one needs to try again and again to achieve fairness. This is diligence, or not giving up.

**Civic virtue** is good citizenship. It means doing things, such as cooperating and solving problems, to help communities live and work well together.

**Caring** means noticing what others need and helping them get what they need. Feeling concern or compassion is another way to define caring.

# Biographical Dictionary

The page number after each entry refers to the place where the person is first mentioned. For more complete references to people, see the Index.

**Baca, Elfego** 1865–1945, legendary deputy sheriff at age 19; used his bold personality to successfully pursue many other professions (p. 269).

**Bush, George W.** 1946– , became 43rd President of the United States in 2001 (p. 349).

**Clark, William** 1770–1838, explored Louisiana Territory with Meriwether Lewis (p. 206).

**Chrétien, Jean** 1934– , Prime Minister of Canada, 1993–2003 (p. 349).

**Fields, Mary** 1832–1914, first African American woman to deliver the U.S. mail; became known as "Stagecoach Mary" (p. 268).

**Ford, Henry** 1863–1947, automobile manufacturer; first to mass-produce cars on the assembly line (p. 208).

**Fox, Vicente** 1942– , became President of Mexico in 2000 (p. 349).

**Hall, Ruby Bridges** 1954– , at six years old, the first African American child to attend a white public school in New Orleans, Louisiana (p. 155).

**Hidalgo, Miguel** 1753–1811, teacher, priest, and leader for Mexican independence from Spain (p. 325).

**Jefferson, Thomas** 1743–1826, wrote the Declaration of Independence; served as third President of the United States (1801–1809); arranged for the United States to buy the Louisiana Territory from France (p. 164).

**Johnson, John H.** 1918–2005 , founder of Johnson Publishing Company, which publishes *Ebony* and *Jet* magazines; received the Presidential Medal of Freedom in 1996 (p. 153).

**King, Coretta Scott** 1927–2006, civil rights leader; married to Martin Luther King, Jr. (p. R4).

**King, Martin Luther, Jr.** 1929–1968, prominent civil rights leader; delivered "I Have a Dream Speech" in 1963 (p. 152).

**Kunin, Madeleine** 1933– , first female governor of Vermont; appointed Deputy Secretary of Education in 1993 (p. 111).

**Lewis, Meriwether** 1774–1809, explored Louisiana Territory with William Clark (p. 206).

**Lincoln, Abraham** 1809–1865, 16th President of the United States (1861–1865); issued Emancipation Proclamation in 1863 (p. 151).

**Lowell, Francis Cabot** 1775–1817, brought the power loom to the United States (p. 94).

**Meredith, James** 1933– , civil rights leader; first African American to attend the University of Mississippi (p. 155).

**Macdonald, John** 1815–1891, first Prime Minister of Canada; author of the British North America Act in 1867 (p. 324).

**Parks, Rosa** 1913–2005, civil rights leader who, in 1955, refused to give up her bus seat to a white passenger, sparking a bus boycott in Montgomery, Alabama (p. 152).

**Pinckney, Eliza Lucas** 1722–1793, successful plantation manager; introduced the indigo plant to South Carolina (p. 150).

**Pontiac** 1720–1769, Ottawa chief who fought with the French against the British during the French and Indian War (p. 205).

**Presley, Elvis** 1935–1977, popular American singer and actor who lived in Graceland, his home in Memphis, Tennessee (p. 164).

**Rice, Condoleezza** 1954– , first woman to serve as U.S. National Security Advisor (p. 153).

**Rillieux, Norbert** 1806–1894, invented the vacuum evaporator, which made sugar production cheaper and faster (p. 150).

**Rockwell, Norman** 1894–1978, American painter whose artwork appeared on the cover of *The Saturday Evening Post* for more than forty years (p. 155).

**Roosevelt, Eleanor** 1884–1962, wife of President Franklin D. Roosevelt; chairperson for the United Nation's Commission on Human Rights (p. 358).

**Roosevelt, Franklin D.** 1882–1945, 32nd President of the United States (1933–1945) (p. 358).

**Slater, Samuel** 1768–1835, built the first water-powered spinning machine in the United States (p. 94).

**Smith, John** 1579–1631, English explorer who mapped and named the New England region in 1614 (p. 106).

**Telkes, Maria** 1900–1995, inventor who explored ways to use the sun to solve energy problems (p. 30).

**Wang, An** 1920–1990, successful entrepreneur and inventor; founded computer company called Wang Laboratories (p. 111).

**Washington, George** 1732–1799, commanded the Continental Army during the Revolutionary War; first President of the United States (1789–1797) (p. 164).

**Webster, Noah** 1758–1843, wrote the first dictionary of American English (p. 110).

**Whitney, Eli** 1765–1825, invented the cotton gin, a machine that removes seeds from cotton fibers (p. 150).

# Alabama

**STATE FLAG:**

**LOCATION:**

ALABAMA

**FULL NAME:**
State of Alabama

**ADMITTED TO THE UNION (RANK):**
December 14, 1819 (22nd)

**POPULATION 2000 (RANK):**
4,447,100 (23rd)

**LAND AREA (RANK):**
50,744 square miles;
131,426 square kilometers (28th)

**CAPITAL:** Montgomery

**POSTAL ABBREVIATION:** AL

**STATE NICKNAMES:**
Yellowhammer State,
The Heart of Dixie,
The Cotton State

**MOTTO:**
*Audemus jura nostra defendere*
(We dare defend our rights)

**SONG:**
"Alabama"
(music by Edna Glockel-Gussen,
words by Julia Tutwiler)

**STATE SYMBOLS:**
**Flower:** Camellia
**Tree:** Southern longleaf pine
**Bird:** Yellowhammer
**Gem:** Star blue quartz
**Stone:** Marble
**Nut:** Pecan
**Dance:** Square dance

**ECONOMY:**
**Agriculture:** Poultry, soybeans, milk, vegetables, wheat, cattle, cotton, peanuts, fruit, hogs, corn

**Industry:** Paper, lumber and wood products, mining, rubber and plastic products, transportation equipment, apparel

State Databank

# Alaska

**STATE FLAG:**

**FULL NAME:**
State of Alaska

**ADMITTED TO THE UNION (RANK):**
January 3, 1959 (49th)

**POPULATION 2000 (RANK):**
626,932 (48th)

**LAND AREA (RANK):**
571,951 square miles;
1,481,347 square kilometers (1st)

**CAPITAL:** Juneau

**POSTAL ABBREVIATION:** AK

**STATE NICKNAMES:**
The Last Frontier,
Land of the Midnight Sun

**MOTTO:**
North to the Future

**LOCATION:**

**SONG:**
"Alaska's Flag"
(music by Elinor Dusenbury,
words by Marie Drake)

**STATE SYMBOLS:**
**Flower:** Forget-me-not
**Tree:** Sitka spruce
**Bird:** Willow ptarmigan
**Gem:** Jade
**Mineral:** Gold
**Sport:** Dog mushing
**Fossil:** Woolly mammoth

**ECONOMY:**

**Agriculture:** Seafood, nursery stock, dairy products, vegetables, livestock

**Industry:** Petroleum and natural gas, gold and other mining, food processing, lumber and wood products, tourism

# Arizona

**STATE FLAG:**

**LOCATION:**

**FULL NAME:**
State of Arizona

**ADMITTED TO THE UNION (RANK):**
February 14, 1912 (48th)

**POPULATION 2000 (RANK):**
5,130,632 (20th)

**LAND AREA (RANK):**
113,635 square miles;
294,312 square kilometers (6th)

**CAPITAL:** Phoenix

**POSTAL ABBREVIATION:** AZ

**STATE NICKNAME:**
Grand Canyon State

**MOTTO:**
*Ditat deus*
(God endures)

**SONG:**
"Arizona March Song"
(music by Margaret Rowe Clifford)

**STATE SYMBOLS:**
**Flower:** Saguaro cactus blossom
**Tree:** Palo verde
**Bird:** Cactus wren
**Gem:** Turquoise
**Stone:** Petrified wood
**Reptile:** Arizona ridgenose rattlesnake
**Amphibian:** Arizona tree frog

**ECONOMY:**

**Agriculture:** Cattle, cotton, dairy products, lettuce, nursery stock, hay

**Industry:** Petroleum and natural gas, gold and other mining, food processing, lumber and wood products, tourism

State Databank

# Arkansas

**STATE FLAG:**

**LOCATION:**

**FULL NAME:**
State of Arkansas

**ADMITTED TO THE UNION (RANK):**
June 15, 1836 (25th)

**POPULATION 2000 (RANK):**
2,673,400 (33rd)

**LAND AREA (RANK):**
52,068 square miles;
134,856 square kilometers (27th)

**CAPITAL:** Little Rock

**POSTAL ABBREVIATION:** AR

**STATE NICKNAME:**
The Natural State

**MOTTO:**
*Regnat populus*
(The people rule)

**SONG:**
"The Arkansas Traveller"
(music by Colonel Sanford Faulkner)

**STATE SYMBOLS:**
**Flower:** Apple blossom
**Tree:** Pine tree
**Bird:** Mockingbird
**Gem:** Diamond
**Insect:** Honeybee

**ECONOMY:**
**Agriculture:** Poultry and eggs, soybeans, sorghum, cattle, cotton, rice, hogs, milk

**Industry:** Food processing, electric equipment, fabricated metal products, machinery, paper products, bromine, vanadium

# California

**STATE FLAG:**

**LOCATION:**

**FULL NAME:**
State of California

**ADMITTED TO THE UNION (RANK):**
September 9, 1850 (31st)

**POPULATION 2000 (RANK):**
33,871,648 (1st)

**LAND AREA (RANK):**
155,959 square miles;
403,933 square kilometers (3rd)

**CAPITAL:** Sacramento

**POSTAL ABBREVIATION:** CA

**STATE NICKNAME:**
The Golden State

**MOTTO:**
*Eureka*
(I have found it)

**SONG:**
"I Love You California"
(music by A. F. Frankenstein,
words by F. B. Silverwood)

**STATE SYMBOLS:**
**Flower:** Golden poppy
**Tree:** California redwood
**Bird:** California valley quail
**Gem:** Bentonite (blue diamond)
**Animal:** California grizzly bear
**Fish:** California golden trout

**ECONOMY:**

**Agriculture:** Vegetables, fruits and nuts, dairy products, cattle, nursery stock, grapes

**Industry:** Electronic components and equipment, aerospace, film production, food processing, petroleum, computers and computer software, tourism

State Databank

# Colorado

**STATE FLAG:**

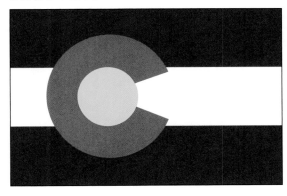

**FULL NAME:**
State of Colorado

**ADMITTED TO THE UNION (RANK):**
August 1, 1876 (38th)

**POPULATION 2000 (RANK):**
4,301,261 (24th)

**LAND AREA (RANK):**
103,718 square miles;
268,627 square kilometers (8th)

**CAPITAL:** Denver

**POSTAL ABBREVIATION:** CO

**STATE NICKNAME:**
Centennial State

**MOTTO:**
*Nil sine Numine*
(Nothing without Providence)

**LOCATION:**

**SONG:**
"Where the Columbines Grow"
(music by A. J. Fynn)

**STATE SYMBOLS:**
**Flower:** Rocky Mountain columbine
**Tree:** Colorado blue spruce
**Bird:** Lark bunting
**Gem:** Aquamarine
**Animal:** Rocky Mountain bighorn
sheep
**Fossil:** Stegosaurus

**ECONOMY:**
**Agriculture:** Cattle, wheat, dairy
products, corn, hay

**Industry:** Scientific instruments,
food processing,
transportation
equipment, machinery,
chemical products, gold
and other mining,
tourism

# Connecticut

## STATE FLAG:

## LOCATION:

CONNECTICUT

**FULL NAME:**
State of Connecticut

**ADMITTED TO THE UNION (RANK):**
January 9, 1788 (5th)

**POPULATION 2000 (RANK):**
3,405,565 (29th)

**LAND AREA (RANK):**
4,845 square miles;
12,548 square kilometers (48th)

**CAPITAL:** Hartford

**POSTAL ABBREVIATION:** CT

**STATE NICKNAMES:**
Constitution State,
Nutmeg State,
Provisions State,
Land of Steady Habits

**MOTTO:**
*Qui transtulit sustinet*
(He who transplanted still sustains)

**SONG:**
"Yankee Doodle"
(music by George M. Cohan)

**STATE SYMBOLS:**
**Flower:** Mountain laurel
**Tree:** Charter oak
**Bird:** American robin
**Mineral:** Garnet
**Animal:** Sperm whale
**Insect:** Praying mantis

**ECONOMY:**
**Agriculture:** Nursery stock, eggs, dairy products, cattle

**Industry:** Transportation equipment, machinery, electric equipment, fabricated metal products, chemical products, scientific instruments

# Delaware

**STATE FLAG:**

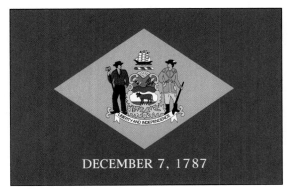

DECEMBER 7, 1787

**LOCATION:**

DELAWARE

**FULL NAME:**
State of Delaware

**ADMITTED TO THE UNION (RANK):**
December 7, 1787 (1st)

**POPULATION 2000 (RANK):**
783,600 (45th)

**LAND AREA (RANK):**
1,954 square miles;
5,060 square kilometers (49th)

**CAPITAL:** Dover

**POSTAL ABBREVIATION:** DE

**STATE NICKNAMES:**
Diamond State,
First State,
Small Wonder,
Blue Hen State

**MOTTO:**
Liberty and independence

**SONG:**
"Our Delaware"
(music by William M. S. Brown,
words by George B. Hynson)

**STATE SYMBOLS:**
**Flower:** Peach blossom
**Tree:** American holly
**Bird:** Blue hen chicken
**Animal:** Horseshoe crab
**Insect:** Ladybug
**Butterfly:** Tiger swallowtail
**Beverage:** Milk

**ECONOMY:**
**Agriculture:** Poultry, nursery stock, soybeans, dairy products, corn

**Industry:** Chemical products, food processing, paper products, rubber and plastic products, scientific instruments, printing and publishing

State Databank

# Florida

**STATE FLAG:**

**LOCATION:**

FLORIDA

**FULL NAME:**
State of Florida

**ADMITTED TO THE UNION (RANK):**
March 3, 1845 (27th)

**POPULATION 2000 (RANK):**
15,982,378 (4th)

**LAND AREA (RANK):**
53,927 square miles;
139,670 square kilometers (26th)

**CAPITAL:** Tallahassee

**POSTAL ABBREVIATION:** FL

**STATE NICKNAMES:**
Sunshine State,
Orange State,
Everglades State,
Alligator State,
Southernmost State

**MOTTO:**
In God we trust

**SONG:**
"The Swanee River
(Old Folks at Home)"
(music and words by Stephen Foster)

**STATE SYMBOLS:**
**Flower:** Orange blossom
**Tree:** Sabal palmetto
**Bird:** Mockingbird
**Gem:** Moonstone
**Stone:** Agatized coral
**Animal:** Florida panther

**ECONOMY:**
**Agriculture:** Citrus, vegetables, nursery stock, cattle, sugarcane, dairy products

**Industry:** Tourism, electric equipment, food processing, printing and publishing, transportation equipment, machinery

# Georgia

**STATE FLAG:**

**LOCATION:**

**FULL NAME:**
State of Georgia

**ADMITTED TO THE UNION (RANK):**
January 2, 1788 (4th)

**POPULATION 2000 (RANK):**
8,186,453 (10th)

**LAND AREA (RANK):**
57,906 square miles;
149,976 square kilometers (21st)

**CAPITAL:** Atlanta

**POSTAL ABBREVIATION:** GA

**STATE NICKNAMES:**
Peach State,
Empire State of the South

**MOTTO:**
Wisdom, justice, and moderation

**SONG:**
"Georgia on My Mind"
(music by Hoagy Carmichael,
words by Stuart Gorrell)

**STATE SYMBOLS:**
**Flower:** Cherokee rose
**Tree:** Live oak
**Bird:** Brown thrasher
**Gem:** Quartz

**ECONOMY:**
**Agriculture:** Poultry and eggs, peanuts, cattle, hogs, dairy products, vegetables

**Industry:** Textiles and apparel, transportation equipment, food processing, paper products, chemical products, electric equipment, tourism

# Hawaii

**STATE FLAG:**

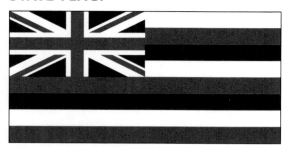

**LOCATION:**

HAWAII

**FULL NAME:**
State of Hawaii

**ADMITTED TO THE UNION (RANK):**
August 21, 1959 (50th)

**POPULATION 2000 (RANK):**
1,211,537 (42nd)

**LAND AREA (RANK):**
6,423 square miles;
16,635 square kilometers (47th)

**CAPITAL:** Honolulu

**POSTAL ABBREVIATION:** HI

**STATE NICKNAME:**
The Aloha State

**MOTTO:**
*Ua Mau Ke Ea O Ka Aina I Ka Pono*
(The life of the land is perpetuated
in righteousness)

**SONG:**
"Hawaii Panoi"
(music by Capt. Henri Berger,
words by King Kalakaua)

**STATE SYMBOLS:**
**Flower:** Yellow hibiscus
**Tree:** Candlenut
**Bird:** Hawaiian goose
**Gem:** Black coral

**ECONOMY:**

**Agriculture:** Sugarcane, pineapples,
nursery stock, livestock,
macadamia nuts

**Industry:** Tourism; food processing;
apparel; fabricated metal
products; stone, clay, and
glass products

# Idaho

**STATE FLAG:**

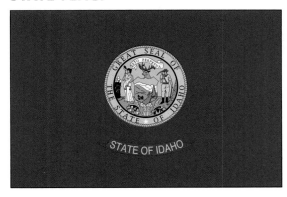

**LOCATION:**

**FULL NAME:**
State of Idaho

**ADMITTED TO THE UNION (RANK):**
July 3, 1890 (43rd)

**POPULATION 2000 (RANK):**
1,293,953 (39th)

**LAND AREA (RANK):**
82,747 square miles;
214,314 square kilometers (11th)

**CAPITAL:** Boise

**POSTAL ABBREVIATION:** ID

**STATE NICKNAME:**
Gem State

**MOTTO:**
*Esto perpetua*
(It is forever)

**SONG:**
"Here We Have Idaho"
(music by Sallie Hume-Douglas, words by
Albert J. Tompkins and McKinley Helm)

**STATE SYMBOLS:**
**Flower:** Syringa
**Tree:** Western white pine
**Bird:** Mountain bluebird
**Gem:** Star garnet
**Horse:** Appaloosa
**Folk Dance:** Square dance

**ECONOMY:**

**Agriculture:** Cattle, potatoes, dairy products, wheat, sugar beets, barley

**Industry:** Food processing, lumber and wood products, machinery, chemical products, paper products, silver and other mining, tourism

# Illinois

**STATE FLAG:**

ILLINOIS

**LOCATION:**

ILLINOIS

**FULL NAME:**
State of Illinois

**ADMITTED TO THE UNION (RANK):**
December 3, 1818 (21st)

**POPULATION 2000 (RANK):**
12,419,293 (5th)

**LAND AREA (RANK):**
55,584 square miles;
143,961 square kilometers (24th)

**CAPITAL:** Springfield

**POSTAL ABBREVIATION:** IL

**STATE NICKNAME:**
Prairie State

**MOTTO:**
State sovereignty, national union

**SONG:**
"Illinois"
(music by Archibald Johnston,
words by C. H. Chamberlain)

**STATE SYMBOLS:**
**Flower:** Native violet
**Tree:** White oak
**Bird:** Cardinal
**Mineral:** Fluorite
**Animal:** White-tailed deer
**Insect:** Monarch butterfly
**Fish:** Bluegill

**ECONOMY:**
**Agriculture:** Corn, soybeans, hogs, cattle, dairy products, wheat

**Industry:** Machinery, food processing, electric equipment, chemical products, printing and publishing, fabricated metal products, transportation equipment, coal, petroleum

# Indiana

**STATE FLAG:**

**FULL NAME:**
State of Indiana

**ADMITTED TO THE UNION (RANK):**
December 11, 1816 (19th)

**POPULATION 2000 (RANK):**
6,080,485 (14th)

**LAND AREA (RANK):**
35,867 square miles;
92,895 square kilometers (38th)

**CAPITAL:** Indianapolis

**POSTAL ABBREVIATION:** IN

**STATE NICKNAME:**
Hoosier State

**MOTTO:**
The Crossroads of America

**LOCATION:**

**SONG:**
"On the Banks of the Wabash,
Far Away"
(music by Paul Dresser)

**STATE SYMBOLS:**
**Flower:** Peony
**Tree:** Tulip poplar
**Bird:** Cardinal
**Stone:** Limestone
**River:** Wabash

**ECONOMY:**
**Agriculture:** Eggs, dairy products, cattle, soybeans, corn, hogs

**Industry:** Steel, electric equipment, transportation equipment, chemical products, petroleum and coal products, machinery

# Iowa

## STATE FLAG:

## LOCATION:

**FULL NAME:**
State of Iowa

**ADMITTED TO THE UNION (RANK):**
December 28, 1846 (29th)

**POPULATION 2000 (RANK):**
2,926,324 (30th)

**LAND AREA (RANK):**
55,869 square miles;
144,701 square kilometers (23rd)

**CAPITAL:** Des Moines

**POSTAL ABBREVIATION:** IA

**STATE NICKNAME:**
Hawkeye State

**MOTTO:**
Our liberties we prize and our rights
we will maintain

**SONG:**
"Song of Iowa"
(music by S.H.M. Byers)

**STATE SYMBOLS:**
**Flower:** Wild rose
**Bird:** Eastern goldfinch
**Colors:** Red, white, and blue
(in state flag)

**ECONOMY:**
**Agriculture:** Hogs, corn, soybeans,
oats, cattle, dairy
products

**Industry:** Food processing,
machinery, electric
equipment, chemical
products, printing
and publishing,
primary metals

State Databank

# Kansas

**STATE FLAG:**

**FULL NAME:**
State of Kansas

**ADMITTED TO THE UNION (RANK):**
January 29, 1861 (34th)

**POPULATION 2000 (RANK):**
2,688,418 (32nd)

**LAND AREA (RANK):**
81,815 square miles;
211,900 square kilometers (13th)

**CAPITAL:** Topeka

**POSTAL ABBREVIATION:** KS

**STATE NICKNAMES:**
Sunflower State,
Jayhawk State

**MOTTO:**
*Ad astra per aspera*
(To the stars through difficulties)

**LOCATION:**

**SONG:**
"Home on the Range"
(music and words by Dr. Brewster Higley)

**STATE SYMBOLS:**
**Flower:** Sunflower
**Tree:** Cottonwood
**Bird:** Western meadowlark
**Animal:** American buffalo

**ECONOMY:**
**Agriculture:** Cattle, wheat, sorghum, soybeans, hogs, corn

**Industry:** Transportation equipment, food processing, printing and publishing, chemical products, machinery, apparel, petroleum, mining

# Kentucky

**STATE FLAG:**

**LOCATION:**

**FULL NAME:**
Commonwealth of Kentucky

**ADMITTED TO THE UNION (RANK):**
June 1, 1792 (15th)

**POPULATION 2000 (RANK):**
4,041,769 (25th)

**LAND AREA (RANK):**
39,728 square miles;
102,896 square kilometers (36th)

**CAPITAL:** Frankfort

**POSTAL ABBREVIATION:** KY

**STATE NICKNAME:**
Bluegrass State

**MOTTO:**
United we stand, divided we fall

**SONG:**
"My Old Kentucky Home,
Good Night!"
(music and words by Stephen Foster)

**STATE SYMBOLS:**
**Flower:** Goldenrod
**Tree:** Tulip poplar
**Bird:** Kentucky cardinal
**Gem:** Freshwater pearl

**ECONOMY:**

**Agriculture:** Horses, cattle, tobacco, dairy products, hogs, soybeans, corn

**Industry:** Transportation equipment, chemical products, electric equipment, machinery, food processing, tobacco products, coal, tourism

# Louisiana

**STATE FLAG:**

**LOCATION:**

LOUISIANA

**FULL NAME:**
State of Louisiana

**ADMITTED TO THE UNION (RANK):**
April 30, 1812 (18th)

**POPULATION 2000 (RANK):**
4,468,976 (22nd)

**LAND AREA (RANK):**
43,562 square miles;
112,825 square kilometers (33rd)

**CAPITAL:** Baton Rouge

**POSTAL ABBREVIATION:** LA

**STATE NICKNAME:**
Pelican State

**MOTTO:**
Union, justice, and confidence

**SONGS:**
"Give Me Louisiana"
(music by Dr. John Croom,
words by Doralice Fontane),
"You Are My Sunshine"
(music and words by Jimmy Davis
and Charles Mitchell)

**STATE SYMBOLS:**
**Flower:** Magnolia bloom
**Tree:** Bald cypress
**Bird:** Eastern brown pelican

**ECONOMY:**
**Agriculture:** Seafood, cotton,
soybeans, cattle,
sugarcane, poultry and
eggs, dairy products, rice

**Industry:** Chemical products,
petroleum and coal
products, food
processing, transportation
equipment, paper
products, tourism

State Databank

# Maine

**STATE FLAG:**

**LOCATION:**

**FULL NAME:**
State of Maine

**ADMITTED TO THE UNION (RANK):**
March 15, 1820 (23rd)

**POPULATION 2000 (RANK):**
1,274,923 (40th)

**LAND AREA (RANK):**
30,862 square miles;
79,931 square kilometers (39th)

**CAPITAL:** Augusta

**POSTAL ABBREVIATION:** ME

**STATE NICKNAME:**
Pine Tree State

**MOTTO:**
*Dirigo*
(I lead)

**SONG:**
"State of Maine"
(music and words by Roger Vinton Snow)

**STATE SYMBOLS:**
**Flower:** White pine cone and tassel
**Tree:** Eastern white pine
**Bird:** Chickadee
**Gem:** Tourmaline
**Animal:** Moose
**Cat:** Maine coon cat
**Insect:** Honeybee

**ECONOMY:**
**Agriculture:** Seafood, poultry and eggs, potatoes, dairy products, cattle, blueberries, apples

**Industry:** Paper, lumber, and wood products, electric equipment, food processing, leather products, textiles, tourism

State Databank

# Maryland

**STATE FLAG:**

**FULL NAME:**
State of Maryland

**ADMITTED TO THE UNION (RANK):**
April 28, 1788 (7th)

**POPULATION 2000 (RANK):**
5,296,486 (19th)

**LAND AREA (RANK):**
9,774 square miles;
25,314 square kilometers (42nd)

**CAPITAL:** Annapolis

**POSTAL ABBREVIATION:** MD

**STATE NICKNAMES:**
Free State,
Old Line State

**MOTTO:**
*Fatti maschii, parole femine*
(Manly deeds, womanly words)

**LOCATION:**

**SONG:**
"Maryland, My Maryland"
(music from an old German carol,
words by Finley Johnson)

**STATE SYMBOLS:**
**Flower:** Black-eyed susan
**Tree:** White oak
**Bird:** Baltimore oriole
**Gem:** Tourmaline
**Crustacean:** Maryland blue crab
**Sport:** Jousting
**Boat:** Skipjack

**ECONOMY:**

**Agriculture:** Seafood, poultry and eggs, dairy products, nursery stock, cattle, soybeans, corn

**Industry:** Electric equipment, food processing, chemical products, printing and publishing, transportation equipment, machinery, primary metals, coal, tourism

# Massachusetts

**STATE FLAG:**

**LOCATION:**

MASSACHUSETTS

**FULL NAME:**
Commonwealth of Massachusetts

**ADMITTED TO THE UNION (RANK):**
February 6, 1788 (6th)

**POPULATION 2000 (RANK):**
6,349,097 (13th)

**LAND AREA (RANK):**
7,840 square miles;
20,306 square kilometers (45th)

**CAPITAL:** Boston

**POSTAL ABBREVIATION:** MA

**STATE NICKNAMES:**
Bay State,
Old Colony State

**MOTTO:**
*Ense petit placidam sub libertate quietem* (By the sword we seek peace, but peace only under liberty)

**SONG:**
"All Hail to Massachusetts"
(music by Arthur J. Marsh)

**STATE SYMBOLS:**
**Flower:** Mayflower
**Tree:** American elm
**Bird:** Black-capped chickadee
**Gem:** Rhodonite
**Beverage:** Cranberry juice
**Muffin:** Corn muffin
**Cookie:** Chocolate chip
**Dessert:** Boston cream pie

**ECONOMY:**
**Agriculture:** Seafood, nursery stock, dairy products, cranberries, vegetables

**Industry:** Machinery, electric equipment, scientific instruments, printing and publishing, tourism

# Michigan

**STATE FLAG:**

**FULL NAME:**
State of Michigan

**ADMITTED TO THE UNION (RANK):**
January 26, 1837 (26th)

**POPULATION 2000 (RANK):**
9,938,444 (8th)

**LAND AREA (RANK):**
56,804 square miles;
147,121 square kilometers (22nd)

**CAPITAL:** Lansing

**POSTAL ABBREVIATION:** MI

**STATE NICKNAMES:**
Wolverine State,
Great Lake State

**MOTTO:**
*Si quaeris peninsulam amoenam
circumspice* (If you seek a pleasant
peninsula, look around you)

**LOCATION:**

**SONG:**
"Michigan, My Michigan"
(music by William Otto Miessner
and Douglas M. Malloch)

**STATE SYMBOLS:**
**Flower:** Apple blossom
**Tree:** White pine
**Bird:** Robin
**Gem:** Isle royal greenstone
**Stone:** Petoskey stone
**Mammal:** White-tailed deer
**Wildflower:** Dwarf lake iris
**Reptile:** Painted turtle

**ECONOMY:**

**Agriculture:** Dairy products, apples,
blueberries, cattle,
vegetables, hogs, corn,
nursery stock, soybeans

**Industry:** Motor vehicles and parts,
machinery, fabricated
metal products, food
processing, chemical
products, mining, tourism

# Minnesota

**STATE FLAG:**

**LOCATION:**

**FULL NAME:**
State of Minnesota

**ADMITTED TO THE UNION (RANK):**
May 11, 1858 (32nd)

**POPULATION 2000 (RANK):**
4,919,479 (21st)

**LAND AREA (RANK):**
79,610 square miles;
206,189 square kilometers (14th)

**CAPITAL:** St. Paul

**POSTAL ABBREVIATION:** MN

**STATE NICKNAMES:**
North Star State,
Gopher State,
Land of 10,000 Lakes

**MOTTO:**
*L'Etoile du Nord*
(The North Star)

**SONG:**
"Hail, Minnesota"
(music by Truman E. Richard, words by
Truman E. Richard and Arthur E. Upson)

**STATE SYMBOLS:**
**Flower:** Lady slipper
**Tree:** Red (Norway) pine
**Bird:** Common loon
**Fish:** Walleye
**Mushroom:** Morel

**ECONOMY:**

**Agriculture:** Dairy products, corn, cattle, soybeans, hogs, wheat, turkeys

**Industry:** Machinery, food processing, printing and publishing, fabricated metal products, electric equipment, mining, tourism

# Mississippi

**STATE FLAG:**

**LOCATION:**

**FULL NAME:**
State of Mississippi

**ADMITTED TO THE UNION (RANK):**
December 10, 1817 (20th)

**POPULATION 2000 (RANK):**
2,844,658 (31st)

**LAND AREA (RANK):**
46,907 square miles;
121,488 square kilometers (31st)

**CAPITAL:** Jackson

**POSTAL ABBREVIATION:** MS

**STATE NICKNAME:**
Magnolia State

**MOTTO:**
*Virtute et armis*
(By valor and arms)

**SONG:**
"Go Mississippi"
(music and words by Houston Davis)

**STATE SYMBOLS:**
**Flower:** Magnolia bloom
**Tree:** Magnolia
**Bird:** Mockingbird
**Stone:** Petrified wood
**Land mammals:** White-tailed deer, red fox
**Water mammal:** Bottlenosed dolphin or porpoise
**Shell:** Oyster shell

**ECONOMY:**
**Agriculture:** Cotton, poultry, cattle, catfish, soybeans, dairy products, rice

**Industry:** Apparel, furniture, lumber and wood products, food processing, electrical machinery, transportation equipment

# Missouri

**STATE FLAG:**

**LOCATION:**

**FULL NAME:**
State of Missouri

**ADMITTED TO THE UNION (RANK):**
August 10, 1821 (24th)

**POPULATION 2000 (RANK):**
5,595,211 (17th)

**LAND AREA (RANK):**
68,886 square miles;
178,414 square kilometers (18th)

**CAPITAL:** Jefferson City

**POSTAL ABBREVIATION:** MO

**STATE NICKNAME:**
Show-me State

**MOTTO:**
*Salus populi suprema lex esto*
(The welfare of the people shall
be the supreme law)

**SONG:**
"Missouri Waltz"
(music by John Valentine Eppel,
words by Jim R. Shannon)

**STATE SYMBOLS:**
**Flower:** Hawthorn blossom
**Tree:** Flowering dogwood
**Bird:** Eastern bluebird
**Mineral:** Galena
**Stone:** Mozarkite
**Animal:** Mule
**Musical Instrument:** Fiddle
**Fish:** Channel catfish

**ECONOMY:**
**Agriculture:** Cattle, soybeans, hogs,
dairy products, corn,
poultry and eggs

**Industry:** Transportation
equipment, food
processing, chemical
products, electric
equipment, fabricated
metal products

# Montana

**STATE FLAG:**

**LOCATION:**

**FULL NAME:**
State of Montana

**ADMITTED TO THE UNION:**
November 8, 1889 (41st)

**POPULATION 2000 (RANK):**
904,433 (44th)

**LAND AREA (RANK):**
145,552 square miles;
376,979 square kilometers (4th)

**CAPITAL:** Helena

**POSTAL ABBREVIATION:** MT

**STATE NICKNAMES:**
Treasure State,
Big Sky Country

**MOTTO:**
*Oro y plata*
(Gold and silver)

**SONG:**
"Montana"
(music Joseph E. Howard,
words by Charles C. Cohan)

**STATE SYMBOLS:**
**Flower:** Bitterroot
**Tree:** Ponderosa pine
**Bird:** Western meadowlark
**Gems:** Montana sapphire and agate
**Animal:** Grizzly bear

**ECONOMY:**
**Agriculture:** Cattle, wheat, barley, sugar beets, hay, hogs

**Industry:** Mining, lumber and wood products, food processing, tourism

State Databank

# Nebraska

**STATE FLAG:**

**LOCATION:**

**FULL NAME:**
State of Nebraska

**ADMITTED TO THE UNION (RANK):**
March 1, 1867 (37th)

**POPULATION 2000 (RANK):**
1,711,263 (38th)

**LAND AREA (RANK):**
76,872 square miles;
199,099 square kilometers (15th)

**CAPITAL:** Lincoln

**POSTAL ABBREVIATION:** NE

**STATE NICKNAMES:**
Cornhusker State,
Beef State

**MOTTO:**
Equality before the law

**SONG:**
"Beautiful Nebraska"
(music by Jim Fras, words by Jim Fras
and Guy G. Miller)

**STATE SYMBOLS:**
**Flower:** Goldenrod
**Tree:** Cottonwood
**Bird:** Western meadowlark
**Gem:** Blue agate
**Stone:** Prairie agate
**Mammal:** White-tailed deer
**Beverage:** Milk
**Ballad:** "A Place Like Nebraska"

**ECONOMY:**
**Agriculture:** Cattle, corn, hogs, soybeans, wheat, sorghum

**Industry:** Food processing, machinery, electric equipment, printing and publishing

# Nevada

**STATE FLAG:**

**LOCATION:**

**FULL NAME:**
State of Nevada

**ADMITTED TO THE UNION (RANK):**
October 31, 1864 (36th)

**POPULATION 2000 (RANK):**
1,998,257 (35th)

**LAND AREA (RANK):**
109,826 square miles;
284,448 square kilometers (7th)

**CAPITAL:** Carson City

**POSTAL ABBREVIATION:** NV

**STATE NICKNAMES:**
Sagebrush State,
Silver State,
Battle Born State

**MOTTO:**
All for Our Country

**SONG:**
"Home Means Nevada"
(music and words by Bertha Raffetto)

**STATE SYMBOLS:**
**Flower:** Sagebrush
**Trees:** Bristlecone pine,
Single-leaf pinon
**Bird:** Mountain bluebird
**Gem:** Black fire opal
**Stone:** Sandstone
**Animal:** Desert bighorn sheep
**Metal:** Silver
**Reptile:** Desert tortoise

**ECONOMY:**
**Agriculture:** Cattle, hay, dairy products, potatoes

**Industry:** Tourism, mining, machinery, printing and publishing, food processing, electric equipment

# New Hampshire

**STATE FLAG:**

**LOCATION:**

NEW HAMPSHIRE

**FULL NAME:**
State of New Hampshire

**ADMITTED TO THE UNION (RANK):**
June 21, 1788 (9th)

**POPULATION 2000 (RANK):**
1,235,786 (41st)

**LAND AREA (RANK):**
8,968 square miles;
23,227 square kilometers (44th)

**CAPITAL:** Concord

**POSTAL ABBREVIATION:** NH

**STATE NICKNAME:**
Granite State

**MOTTO:**
Live free or die

**SONG:**
"Old New Hampshire"
(music by Maurice Hoffmann,
words by John F. Holmes)

**STATE SYMBOLS:**
**Flower:** Purple lilac
**Tree:** White birch
**Bird:** Purple finch
**Gem:** Smoky quartz
**Animal:** White-tailed deer
**Insect:** Ladybug
**Amphibian:** Spotted newt
**Butterfly:** Karner blue

**ECONOMY:**
**Agriculture:** Dairy products, nursery stock, cattle, apples, eggs

**Industry:** Machinery, electric equipment, rubber and plastic products, tourism

# New Jersey

**STATE FLAG:**

**LOCATION:**

NEW JERSEY

**FULL NAME:**
State of New Jersey

**ADMITTED TO THE UNION (RANK):**
December 18, 1787 (3rd)

**POPULATION 2000 (RANK):**
8,414,350 (9th)

**LAND AREA (RANK):**
7,417 square miles;
19,211 square kilometers (46th)

**CAPITAL:** Trenton

**POSTAL ABBREVIATION:** NJ

**STATE NICKNAME:**
Garden State

**MOTTO:**
Liberty and prosperity

**SONG:**
"I'm from New Jersey"
(music by Red Mascara)

**STATE SYMBOLS:**
**Flower:** Purple violet
**Tree:** Red oak
**Bird:** Eastern goldfinch
**Animal:** Horse
**Fish:** Brook trout
**Folk Dance:** Square dance
**Shell:** Knobbed whelk
**Colors:** Buff and blue

**ECONOMY:**
**Agriculture:** Nursery stock, horses, vegetables, fruits and nuts, seafood, dairy products

**Industry:** Chemical products, food processing, electric equipment, printing and publishing, tourism

# New Mexico

**STATE FLAG:**

**LOCATION:**

**FULL NAME:**
State of New Mexico

**ADMITTED TO THE UNION (RANK):**
January 6, 1912 (47th)

**POPULATION 2000 (RANK):**
1,819,046 (36th)

**LAND AREA (RANK):**
121,356 square miles;
314,309 square kilometers (5th)

**CAPITAL:** Santa Fe

**POSTAL ABBREVIATION:** NM

**STATE NICKNAME:**
Land of Enchantment

**MOTTO:**
*Crescit eundo*
(It grows as it goes)

**SONG:**
"O Fair New Mexico"
(music and words by Elizabeth Garrett)

**STATE SYMBOLS:**
**Flower:** Yucca
**Tree:** Pinon
**Bird:** Roadrunner
**Gem:** Turquoise
**Animal:** Black bear
**Cookie:** Bizcochito
**Vegetables:** Chili and frijol

**ECONOMY:**
**Agriculture:** Cattle, dairy products, hay, nursery stock, chilies

**Industry:** Electric equipment; petroleum and coal products; food processing; printing and publishing; stone, glass, and clay products; tourism

State Databank

# New York

**STATE FLAG:**

**FULL NAME:**
State of New York

**ADMITTED TO THE UNION (RANK):**
July 26, 1788 (11th)

**POPULATION 2000 (RANK):**
18,976,457 (3rd)

**LAND AREA (RANK):**
47,214 square miles;
122,283 square kilometers (30th)

**CAPITAL:** Albany

**POSTAL ABBREVIATION:** NY

**STATE NICKNAME:**
Empire State

**MOTTO:**
*Excelsior*
(Ever upward)

**LOCATION:**

**SONG:**
"I Love New York"
(music by Steve Karmen)

**STATE SYMBOLS:**
**Flower:** Rose
**Tree:** Sugar maple
**Bird:** Bluebird
**Gem:** Garnet
**Animal:** Beaver
**Insect:** Ladybug
**Fish:** Brook trout

**ECONOMY:**
**Agriculture:** Dairy products, cattle and other livestock, vegetables, nursery stock, apples

**Industry:** Printing and publishing, scientific instruments, electric equipment, machinery, chemical products, tourism

# North Carolina

**STATE FLAG:**

**LOCATION:**

**FULL NAME:**
State of North Carolina

**ADMITTED TO THE UNION (RANK):**
November 21, 1789 (12th)

**POPULATION 2000 (RANK):**
8,049,313 (11th)

**LAND AREA (RANK):**
48,711 square miles;
126,161 square kilometers (29th)

**CAPITAL:** Raleigh

**POSTAL ABBREVIATION:** NC

**STATE NICKNAME:**
Tar Heel State

**MOTTO:**
*Esse quam videri*
(To be rather than to seem)

**SONG:**
"The Old North State"
(music by E. E. Randolph,
words by William Gaston)

**STATE SYMBOLS:**
**Flower:** Dogwood
**Tree:** Pine
**Bird:** Cardinal
**Gem:** Emerald
**Stone:** Granite
**Mammal:** Gray squirrel
**Reptile:** Eastern box turtle
**Fruit:** Scuppernong grape

**ECONOMY:**
**Agriculture:** Poultry and eggs, tobacco, hogs, milk, nursery stock, cattle, soybeans

**Industry:** Tobacco products, textile goods, chemical products, electric equipment, machinery, tourism

State Databank

# North Dakota

**STATE FLAG:**

**LOCATION:**

**FULL NAME:**
State of North Dakota

**ADMITTED TO THE UNION (RANK):**
November 2, 1889 (39th)

**POPULATION 2000 (RANK):**
642,200 (47th)

**LAND AREA (RANK):**
68,976 square miles;
178,647 square kilometers (17th)

**CAPITAL:** Bismarck

**POSTAL ABBREVIATION:** ND

**STATE NICKNAMES:**
Sioux State,
Flickertail State,
Peace Garden State,
Rough Rider State

**MOTTO:**
Liberty and union, now and forever:
one and inseparable

**SONG:**
"North Dakota Hymn"
(music by C. S. Putnam,
words by James W. Foley)

**STATE SYMBOLS:**
**Flower:** Wild prairie rose
**Tree:** American elm
**Bird:** Western meadowlark
**Gems:** Montana sapphire and agate
**Equine:** Nokota horse
**Fossil:** Teredo petrified wood
**Beverage:** Milk
**Dance:** Square dance

**ECONOMY:**
**Agriculture:** Wheat, cattle, barley, sunflowers, milk, sugar beets

**Industry:** Food processing, machinery, mining, tourism

# Ohio

**STATE FLAG:**

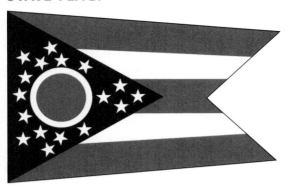

**LOCATION:**

**FULL NAME:**
State of Ohio

**ADMITTED TO THE UNION (RANK):**
March 1, 1803 (17th)

**POPULATION 2000 (RANK):**
11,353,140 (7th)

**LAND AREA (RANK):**
40,948 square miles;
106,056 square kilometers (35th)

**CAPITAL:** Columbus

**POSTAL ABBREVIATION:** OH

**STATE NICKNAME:**
Buckeye State

**MOTTO:**
With God all things are possible

**SONG:**
"Beautiful Ohio"
(music by Mary Earl)

**STATE SYMBOLS:**
**Flower:** Scarlet carnation
**Tree:** Ohio buckeye
**Bird:** Cardinal
**Gem:** Ohio flint
**Animal:** White-tailed deer
**Beverage:** Tomato juice
**Fossil:** Trilobite
**Wildflower:** Large white trillium

**ECONOMY:**
**Agriculture:** Soybeans, dairy products, corn, tomatoes, hogs, cattle, poultry and eggs

**Industry:** Transportation equipment, fabricated metal products, machinery, food processing, electric equipment

# Oklahoma

**STATE FLAG:**

**LOCATION:**

**FULL NAME:**
State of Oklahoma

**ADMITTED TO THE UNION (RANK):**
November 16, 1907 (46th)

**POPULATION 2000 (RANK):**
3,450,654 (27th)

**LAND AREA (RANK):**
68,667 square miles;
177,847 square kilometers (19th)

**CAPITAL:** Oklahoma City

**POSTAL ABBREVIATION:** OK

**STATE NICKNAME:**
Sooner State

**MOTTO:**
*Labor omni vincit*
(Labor conquers all things)

**SONG:**
"Oklahoma"
(music by Richard Rodgers,
words by Oscar Hammerstein II)

**STATE SYMBOLS:**
**Flower:** Mistletoe
**Tree:** Redbud
**Bird:** Scissor-tailed flycatcher
**Stone:** Rose rock
**Animal:** Bison
**Colors:** Green and white
**Poem:** "Howdy Folks"
      by David Randolph Milsten

**ECONOMY:**
**Agriculture:** Cattle, wheat, milk,
        poultry, cotton

**Industry:** Transportation
        equipment, machinery,
        electric products, rubber
        and plastic products,
        food processing

# Oregon

**STATE FLAG:**

**LOCATION:**

**FULL NAME:**
State of Oregon

**ADMITTED TO THE UNION (RANK):**
February 14, 1859 (33rd)

**POPULATION 2000 (RANK):**
3,421,399 (28th)

**LAND AREA (RANK):**
95,997 square miles;
248,631 square kilometers (10th)

**CAPITAL:** Salem

**POSTAL ABBREVIATION:** OR

**STATE NICKNAME:**
Beaver State

**MOTTO:**
*Alis volat Propriis*
(She flies with her own wings)

**SONG:**
"Oregon, My Oregon"
(music by Henry B. Murtagh,
words by J. A. Buchanan)

**STATE SYMBOLS:**
**Flower:** Oregon grape
**Tree:** Douglas fir
**Bird:** Western meadowlark
**Gem:** Sunstone
**Stone:** Thunderegg
**Animal:** Beaver
**Nut:** Hazelnut
**Seashell:** Oregon hairy triton
**Mushroom:** Pacific golden chanterelle

**ECONOMY:**
**Agriculture:** Cattle, vegetables, nursery stock, fruits and nuts, dairy products, wheat

**Industry:** Lumber and wood products, tourism, food processing, paper products, machinery, scientific instruments

# Pennsylvania

**STATE FLAG:**

**LOCATION:**

PENNSYLVANIA

**FULL NAME:**
Commonwealth of Pennsylvania

**ADMITTED TO THE UNION (RANK):**
December 12, 1787 (2nd)

**POPULATION 2000 (RANK):**
12,281,054 (6th)

**LAND AREA (RANK):**
44,817 square miles;
116,074 square kilometers (32nd)

**CAPITAL:** Harrisburg

**POSTAL ABBREVIATION:** PA

**STATE NICKNAME:**
Keystone State

**MOTTO:**
Virtue, liberty, and independence

**SONG:**
"Pennsylvania"
(music by Eddie Khoury and Ronnie Bonner)

**STATE SYMBOLS:**
**Flower:** Mountain laurel
**Tree:** Hemlock
**Bird:** Ruffed grouse
**Dog:** Great Dane
**Colors:** Blue and gold

**ECONOMY:**
**Agriculture:** Dairy products, poultry, cattle, nursery stock, mushrooms, hogs, hay

**Industry:** Food processing, chemical products, machinery, electric equipment, tourism

# Rhode Island

**STATE FLAG:**

**LOCATION:**

RHODE
ISLAND

**FULL NAME:**
State of Rhode Island

**ADMITTED TO THE UNION (RANK):**
May 29, 1790 (13th)

**POPULATION 2000 (RANK):**
1,048,319 (43rd)

**LAND AREA (RANK):**
1,045 square miles;
2,607 square kilometers (50th)

**CAPITAL:** Providence

**POSTAL ABBREVIATION:** RI

**STATE NICKNAME:**
The Ocean State

**MOTTO:**
Hope

**SONG:**
"Rhode Island It's for Me"
(music by Maria Day, words by Charlie Hall)

**STATE SYMBOLS:**
**Flower:** Violet
**Tree:** Red maple
**Bird:** Rhode Island red hen
**Mineral:** Bowenite
**Stone:** Cumberlandite
**Shell:** Quahog
**Colors:** Blue, white and gold
(in state flag)

**ECONOMY:**
**Agriculture:** Nursery stock, vegetables, dairy products, eggs

**Industry:** Fashion jewelry, fabricated metal products, electric equipment, machinery, shipbuilding and boatbuilding, tourism

State Databank

# South Carolina

**STATE FLAG:**

**LOCATION:**

**FULL NAME:**
State of South Carolina

**ADMITTED TO THE UNION (RANK):**
May 23, 1788 (8th)

**POPULATION 2000 (RANK):**
4,012,012 (26th)

**LAND AREA (RANK):**
30,109 square miles;
77,893 square kilometers (40th)

**CAPITAL:** Columbia

**POSTAL ABBREVIATION:** SC

**STATE NICKNAME:**
Palmetto State

**MOTTOES:**
*Animis opibusque parati*
(Prepared in mind and resources),
*Dum spiro spero*
(While I breathe, I hope)

**SONG:**
"Carolina"
(music by Anne Custis Burgess,
words by Henry Timrod)

**STATE SYMBOLS:**
**Flower:** Carolina yellow jessamine
**Tree:** Palmetto tree
**Bird:** Carolina wren

**ECONOMY:**
**Agriculture:** Tobacco, poultry, cattle, hogs, dairy products, soybeans

**Industry:** Textile goods, chemical products, paper products, machinery, tourism

# South Dakota

**STATE FLAG:**

**LOCATION:**

**FULL NAME:**
State of South Dakota

**ADMITTED TO THE UNION (RANK):**
November 2, 1889 (40th)

**POPULATION 2000 (RANK):**
754,844 (46th)

**LAND AREA (RANK):**
75,885 square miles;
196,540 square kilometers (16th)

**CAPITAL:** Pierre

**POSTAL ABBREVIATION:** SD

**STATE NICKNAMES:**
Mount Rushmore State,
Coyote State

**MOTTO:**
Under God the people rule

**SONG:**
"Hail! South Dakota"
(music and words by DeeCort Hammitt)

**STATE SYMBOLS:**
**Flower:** American pasqueflower
**Tree:** Black Hills spruce
**Bird:** Chinese ring-necked pheasant
**Gem:** Fairburn agate
**Stone:** Rose quartz
**Animal:** Coyote
**Musical Instrument:** Fiddle
**Dessert:** Kuchen

**ECONOMY:**
**Agriculture:** Cattle, hogs, wheat, soybeans, milk, corn

**Industry:** Food processing, machinery, lumber and wood products, tourism

State Databank

# Tennessee

**STATE FLAG:**

**LOCATION:**

**FULL NAME:**
State of Tennessee

**ADMITTED TO THE UNION:**
June 1, 1796 (16th)

**POPULATION 2000 (RANK):**
5,689,283 (16th)

**LAND AREA (RANK):**
41,217 square miles;
106,752 square kilometers (24th)

**CAPITAL:** Nashville

**POSTAL ABBREVIATION:** TN

**STATE NICKNAME:**
Volunteer State

**MOTTO:**
Agriculture and Commerce

**SONGS:**
"Tennessee Waltz" (music by Pee Wee King, words by Redd Stewart),
"My Homeland, Tennessee" (music by Roy Lamont Smith, words by Nell Grayson),
"When It's Iris Time in Tennessee" (music and words by Willa Waid Newman),
"My Tennessee" (music and words by Frances Hannah Tranum),
"Rocky Top" (music and words by Boudleaux Bryant and Felice Bryant),
"Tennessee" (music and words by Vivan Rorie)

**STATE SYMBOLS:**
**Flower:** Iris
**Tree:** Tulip poplar
**Bird:** Mockingbird
**Gem:** Tennessee pearl
**Animal:** Raccoon
**Horse:** Tennessee walking horse
**Wildflower:** Passion flower

**ECONOMY:**
**Agriculture:** Soybeans, cotton, tobacco, livestock and livestock products, dairy products, cattle, hogs

**Industry:** Chemicals, transportation equipment, rubber, plastics

# Texas

**STATE FLAG:**

**LOCATION:**

**FULL NAME:**
State of Texas

**ADMITTED TO THE UNION (RANK):**
December 29, 1845 (28th)

**POPULATION 2000 (RANK):**
20,851,820 (2nd)

**LAND AREA (RANK):**
261,797 square miles;
678,051 square kilometers (2nd)

**CAPITAL:** Austin

**POSTAL ABBREVIATION:** TX

**STATE NICKNAME:**
Lone Star State

**MOTTO:**
Friendship

**SONG:**
"Texas, Our Texas"
(music by William J. Marsh
and Gladys Yoakum Wright)

**STATE SYMBOLS:**
**Flower:** Bluebonnet
**Tree:** Pecan
**Bird:** Mockingbird
**Gem:** Texas blue topaz
**Stone:** Petrified palmwood
**Small Mammal:** Armadillo
**Flying Mammal:** Mexican free-tailed bat
**Dish:** Chili
**Plant:** Prickly pear cactus

**ECONOMY:**
**Agriculture:** Cattle, cotton, dairy products, nursery stock, poultry, sorghum, corn, wheat

**Industry:** Chemical products, petroleum and natural gas, food processing, electric equipment, machinery, mining, tourism

State Databank

# Utah

**STATE FLAG:**

**LOCATION:**

**FULL NAME:**
State of Utah

**ADMITTED TO THE UNION (RANK):**
January 4, 1896 (45th)

**POPULATION 2000 (RANK):**
2,233,169 (34th)

**LAND AREA (RANK):**
82,144 square miles;
212,751 square kilometers (12th)

**CAPITAL:** Salt Lake City

**POSTAL ABBREVIATION:** UT

**STATE NICKNAME:**
Beehive State

**MOTTO:**
Industry

**SONG:**
"Utah . . . This Is the Place"
(music by Gary Francis, words by Gary Francis and Sam Francis)

**STATE SYMBOLS:**
**Flower:** Sego lily
**Tree:** Blue spruce
**Bird:** California seagull
**Gem:** Topaz
**Stone:** Coal
**Animal:** Rocky Mountain elk
**Fruit:** Cherry
**Fossil:** Allosaurus
**Cooking pot:** Dutch oven

**ECONOMY:**

**Agriculture:** Cattle, dairy products, hay, turkeys

**Industry:** Machinery, aerospace, mining, food processing, electric equipment, tourism

# Vermont

**STATE FLAG:**

**FULL NAME:**
State of Vermont

**ADMITTED TO THE UNION (RANK):**
March 4, 1791 (14th)

**POPULATION 2000 (RANK):**
608,827 (49th)

**LAND AREA (RANK):**
9,250 square miles;
23,956 square kilometers (43rd)

**CAPITAL:** Montpelier

**POSTAL ABBREVIATION:** VT

**STATE NICKNAME:**
Green Mountain State

**MOTTO:**
Vermont, Freedom, and Unity

**LOCATION:**

**SONG:**
"These Green Mountains"
(music and words by Diane Martin)

**STATE SYMBOLS:**
**Flower:** Red clover
**Tree:** Sugar maple
**Bird:** Hermit thrush
**Animal:** Morgan horse
**Insect:** Honeybee

**ECONOMY:**
**Agriculture:** Dairy products, cattle, hay, apples, maple products

**Industry:** Electronic equipment, fabricated metal products, printing and publishing, paper products, tourism

# Virginia

**STATE FLAG:**

**FULL NAME:**
Commonwealth of Virginia

**ADMITTED TO THE UNION (RANK):**
June 25, 1788 (10th)

**POPULATION 2000 (RANK):**
7,078,515 (12th)

**LAND AREA (RANK):**
39,594 square miles;
102,548 square kilometers (37th)

**CAPITAL:** Richmond

**POSTAL ABBREVIATION:** VA

**STATE NICKNAMES:**
The Old Dominion,
Mother of Presidents

**MOTTO:**
*Sic semper tyrannis*
(Thus always to tyrants)

**LOCATION:**

**SONG:**
"Carry Me Back to Old Virginny"
(music and words by James A. Bland)

**STATE SYMBOLS:**
**Flower:** American dogwood
**Tree:** Flowering dogwood
**Bird:** Cardinal
**Dog:** American foxhound
**Shell:** Oyster shell

**ECONOMY:**
**Agriculture:** Cattle, poultry, dairy products, tobacco, hogs, soybeans

**Industry:** Transportation equipment, textiles, food processing, printing, electric equipment, chemicals

# Washington

**STATE FLAG:**

**LOCATION:**

**FULL NAME:**
State of Washington

**ADMITTED TO THE UNION (RANK):**
November 11, 1889 (42nd)

**POPULATION 2000 (RANK):**
5,894,121 (15th)

**LAND AREA (RANK):**
66,544 square miles;
172,348 square kilometers (20th)

**CAPITAL:** Olympia

**POSTAL ABBREVIATION:** WA

**STATE NICKNAME:**
Evergreen State

**MOTTO:**
*Al-Ki*
(American Indian word meaning
"by and by")

**SONG:**
"Washington, My Home"
(music by Helen Davis,
arranged by Stuart Churchill)

**STATE SYMBOLS:**
**Flower:** Western rhododendron
**Tree:** Western hemlock
**Bird:** American goldfinch
**Gem:** Petrified wood
**Fruit:** Apple
**Insect:** Blue darner dragonfly
**Fossil:** Columbian mammoth

**ECONOMY:**
**Agriculture:**  Seafood, dairy products,
apples, cattle, wheat,
potatoes, nursery stock

**Industry:**  Aerospace, software
development, food
processing, paper
products, lumber and
wood products, chemical
products, tourism

# West Virginia

**STATE FLAG:**

**LOCATION:**

**FULL NAME:**
State of West Virginia

**ADMITTED TO THE UNION (RANK):**
June 20, 1863 (35th)

**POPULATION 2000 (RANK):**
1,808,344 (37th)

**LAND AREA (RANK):**
24,078 square miles;
62,361 square kilometers (41st)

**CAPITAL:** Charleston

**POSTAL ABBREVIATION:** WV

**STATE NICKNAME:**
Mountain State

**MOTTO:**
*Montani semper liberi*
(Mountaineers are always free)

**SONGS:**
"West Virginia Hills"
(music by H. E. Engle, words by Ellen King),
"West Virginia, My Home Sweet Home"
(music by Col. Julian G. Hearne, Jr.),
"This Is My West Virginia"
(music by Iris Bell)

**STATE SYMBOLS:**
**Flower:** Big rhododendron
**Tree:** Sugar maple
**Bird:** Cardinal
**Gem:** Mississippian fossil coral
**Animal:** Black bear
**Colors:** Blue and gold

**ECONOMY:**
**Agriculture:** Cattle, dairy products, poultry, apples

**Industry:** Chemical products, mining, primary metals, stone, clay, glass products, tourism

# Wisconsin

**STATE FLAG:**

**LOCATION:**

**FULL NAME:**
State of Wisconsin

**ADMITTED TO THE UNION (RANK):**
May 29, 1848 (30th)

**POPULATION 2000 (RANK):**
5,363,675 (18th)

**LAND AREA (RANK):**
54,310 square miles;
140,663 square kilometers (25th)

**CAPITAL:** Madison

**POSTAL ABBREVIATION:** WI

**STATE NICKNAME:**
Badger State

**MOTTO:**
Forward

**SONG:**
"On Wisconsin"
(music by William T. Purdy, words by
J. S. Hubbard and Charles D. Rosa)

**STATE SYMBOLS:**
**Flower:** Wood violet
**Tree:** Sugar maple
**Bird:** Robin
**Mineral:** Galena
**Stone:** Red granite
**Animal:** Badger
**Dance:** Polka
**Symbol of Peace:** Mourning dove
**Domestic Animal:** Dairy cow

**ECONOMY:**
**Agriculture:** Cheese, dairy products, cattle, hogs, vegetables, corn, cranberries

**Industry:** Machinery, food processing, paper products, electric equipment, fabricated metal products, tourism

# Wyoming

**STATE FLAG:**

**LOCATION:**

**FULL NAME:**
State of Wyoming

**ADMITTED TO THE UNION (RANK):**
July 10, 1890 (44th)

**POPULATION 2000 (RANK):**
493,782 (50th)

**LAND AREA (RANK):**
97,100 square miles;
251,489 square kilometers (9th)

**CAPITAL:** Cheyenne

**POSTAL ABBREVIATION:** WY

**STATE NICKNAME:**
Equality State

**MOTTO:**
Equal rights

**SONG:**
"Wyoming"
(music by G. E. Knapp, words by C. E. Winter)

**STATE SYMBOLS:**
**Flower:** Indian paintbrush
**Tree:** Plains cottonwood
**Bird:** Western meadowlark
**Gem:** Jade
**Mammal:** Bison
**Dinosaur:** Triceratops
**Reptile:** Horned toad

**ECONOMY:**

**Agriculture:** Cattle, sugar beets, sheep, hay, wheat

**Industry:** Mining, chemical products, lumber and wood products, printing and publishing, machinery, tourism

# Geographic Terms

**basin**
a round area of land surrounded by higher land

**bay**
part of a lake or ocean that is partially enclosed by land

**canyon**
a valley with steep cliffs shaped by erosion

**cape**
a piece of land that points out into a body of water

**coast**
the land next to a sea or ocean

**coastal plain**
a flat area of land near an ocean

**delta**
land that is formed by soil deposited near the mouth of a river

**desert**
a dry region with little vegetation

**fault**
a break or crack in the earth's surface

▲ **glacier**
a large ice mass that pushes soil and rocks as it moves

**hill**
a raised area of land

**island**
an area of land surrounded by water

**isthmus**
a narrow piece of land connecting two larger land areas

**lake**
a large body of water surrounded by land

**mountain**
a raised mass of land with steep slopes

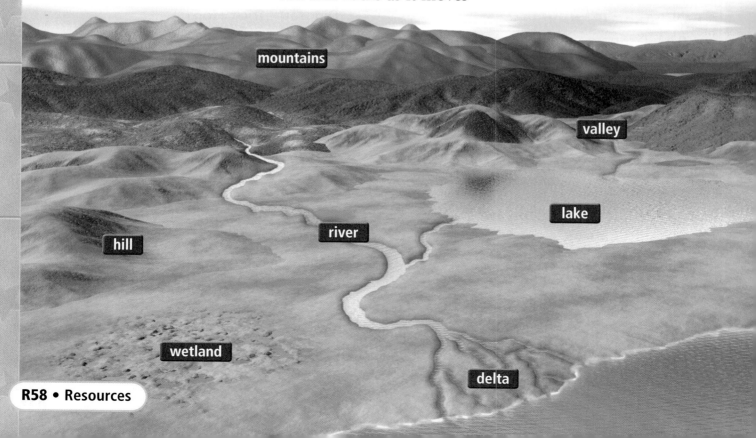

mountains

valley

lake

river

hill

wetland

delta

**ocean**
a large body of salt water that covers much of Earth's surface

**peninsula**
a strip of land surrounded by water on three sides

**plain**
a large area of flat land

**plateau**
a high, flat area of land

**port**
a sheltered part of a lake or ocean where ships can dock

**prairie**
a flat area of grassland with few trees

**rain forest**
a thick forest that receives heavy rainfall throughout the year

**river**
a body of water that flows from a high area to a lower area

**river basin**
an area that is drained by a river

**tectonic plate**
a huge slab of rock in Earth's crust that can cause earthquakes and volcanoes when it moves

**tributary**
a river or stream that flows into another river

**valley**
a low area of land between hills or mountains

▲ **volcano**
an opening in Earth's surface through which melted rock and gases escape

**wetland**
an area that is soaked with water, such as a marsh or a swamp

plateau

plain

bay

cape

peninsula

coastal plain

# Atlas

## The World: Political

ARCTIC OCEAN

GREENL
(Denm

ALASKA
(U.S.)

NORTH

CANADA

AMERICA

UNITED STATES

Bermuda
(U.K.)

NORTH
PACIFIC
OCEAN

ATLANTIC
OCEAN

Midway
Islands
(U.S.)

Hawaii
(U.S.)

MEXICO

Area of index

VENEZUELA
COLOMBIA

Galapagos
Islands
(Ecuador)

ECUADOR

SOUTH

KIRIBATI

Tokelau
(N.Z.)

Cook Is.
(N.Z.)

SAMOA

American
Samoa
(U.S.)

French
Polynesia
(Fr.)

Niue
(N.Z.)

TONGA

PERU

AMERICA

BRAZIL

BOLIVIA

PARAGUAY

Pitcairn
Islands
(Fr.)

CHILE

URUGUAY

ARGENTINA

SOUTH
PACIFIC
OCEAN

Falkland
Islands
(U.K.)

South Ge
Islands (

SOUTHERN OCEAN

UNITED STATES

GULF OF
MEXICO

BAHAMAS

ATLANTIC
OCEAN

MEXICO

CUBA

Turks &
Caicos Islands
(U.K.)

Virgin Islands
(U.S./U.K.)

Cayman
Islands
(U.K.)

HAITI

DOMINICAN
REPUBLIC

St. Martin (Fr./Neth.)
ANTIGUA & BARBUDA

JAMAICA

Puerto
Rico
(U.S.)

Guadeloupe (Fr.)

DOMINICA

BELIZE

CARIBBEAN SEA

Martinique (Fr.)

GUATEMALA

HONDURAS

ST. LUCIA
ST. VINCENT &
THE GRENADINES

EL SALVADOR

NICARAGUA

GRENADA

PACIFIC
OCEAN

COSTA RICA

PANAMA

TRINIDAD
AND TOBAGO

VENEZUELA

GUYANA

km 0    250   500

mi 0    250   500

COLOMBIA

SURINAME

FRENCH
GUIANA
(Fr.)

Atlas

ARCTIC OCEAN

RUSSIA

ASIA

ICELAND

Area of index

EUROPE

KAZAKHSTAN

MONGOLIA

GEORGIA
ARMENIA      KYRGYZSTAN
TURKEY   AZER.   UZBEKISTAN
TUNISIA   CYPRUS   SYRIA   TURKMENISTAN
         LEBANON      TAJIKISTAN      CHINA
MOROCCO   ISRAEL   IRAQ   AFGHANISTAN
         JORDAN   IRAN
ALGERIA   LIBYA      KUWAIT
WESTERN            QATAR   PAKISTAN
SAHARA    EGYPT   SAUDI   U.A.E.
(Morocco)         ARABIA   OMAN      INDIA
MAURITANIA
MALI   NIGER   CHAD   ERITREA   YEMEN
SENEGAL                  DJIBOUTI
GAMBIA   BURKINA   SUDAN
GUINEA BISSAU   FASO   NIGERIA   ETHIOPIA
GUINEA   GHANA
SIERRA   IVORY  TOGO   CEN.AFR.
LEONE   COAST  BENIN   REP.      SOMALIA
LIBERIA      CAMEROON
EQU.         UGANDA   KENYA
GUINEA   GABON   DEM.   RWANDA
SAO TOME   REP. OF   REP.   BURUNDI
AND PRINCIPE   CONGO   OF   TANZANIA
            CONGO
                  COMOROS
ANGOLA      MALAWI
      ZAMBIA   MOZAMBIQUE
      ZIMBABWE      MADAGASCAR
NAMIBIA   BOTSWANA

AFRICA

N. KOREA
S. KOREA      JAPAN

PACIFIC
OCEAN

BHUTAN
NEPAL
BANGLADESH

MYANMAR
LAOS
THAILAND
         VIETNAM
         CAMBODIA

TAIWAN

Northern
Mariana
Islands
(U.S.)                  MARSHALL
                  ISLANDS
Guam (U.S.)
FEDERATED STATES
OF MICRONESIA
                        KIRIBATI
PALAU
               NAURU

PHILIPPINES

BRUNEI
MALAYSIA

SRI LANKA
         SINGAPORE

MALDIVES

INDONESIA

EAST
TIMOR

PAPUA
NEW
GUINEA

SOLOMON
ISLANDS

TUVALU

VANUATU

New
Caledonia
(Fr.)

FIJI

INDIAN
OCEAN

MAURITIUS
Reunion
(Fr.)

AUSTRALIA

km 0   1000   2000
mi 0   1000   2000

ATLANTIC
OCEAN

NEW
ZEALAND

SOUTHERN OCEAN

ANTARCTICA

FINLAND

SWEDEN

NORWAY

RUSSIA

ESTONIA
LATVIA
LITHUANIA
RUSSIA
BELARUS

UNITED
KINGDOM

NORTH
SEA

DENMARK

km 0   150   300
mi 0   150   300

IRELAND

NETH.
GERMANY
BELGIUM
LUX.
CZECH
REPUBLIC

POLAND

UKRAINE

ATLANTIC
OCEAN

FRANCE

LIECH.   AUSTRIA
SWITZ.         HUNGARY
      SAN         SLOVAKIA
      MARINO   SLOV.
            CROATIA
            BOS. &
            HERZ.

MOLDOVA

ROMANIA

MONACO

Corsica
(Fr.)

ITALY

ANDORRA

Sardinia
(It.)

SERB. &
MONT.

MACEDONIA
ALB.

BULGARIA

PORTUGAL

SPAIN

Balearic
Islands

GREECE

TURKEY

GIBRALTAR
(U.K.)

Sicily (It.)

MEDITERRANEAN SEA

MOROCCO   ALGERIA   TUNISIA

# The World: Physical

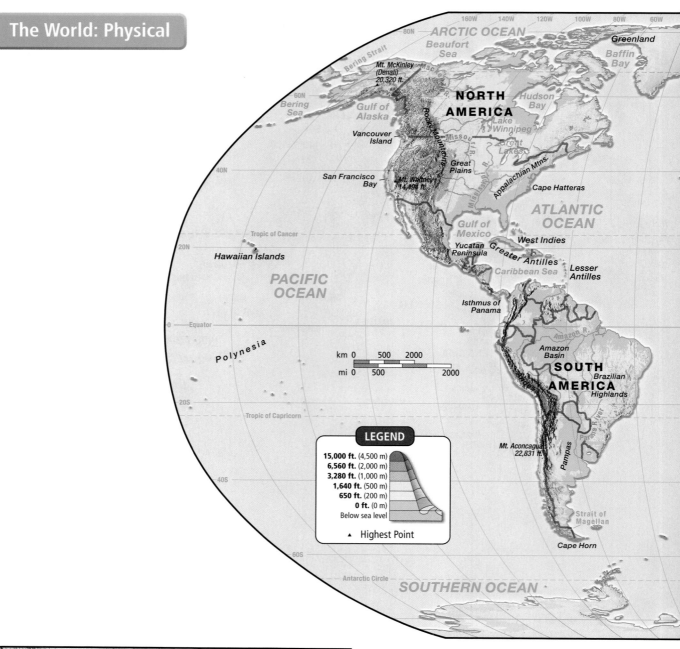

**LEGEND**

- **15,000 ft.** (4,500 m)
- **6,560 ft.** (2,000 m)
- **3,280 ft.** (1,000 m)
- **1,640 ft.** (500 m)
- **650 ft.** (200 m)
- **0 ft.** (0 m)
- Below sea level

▲ Highest Point

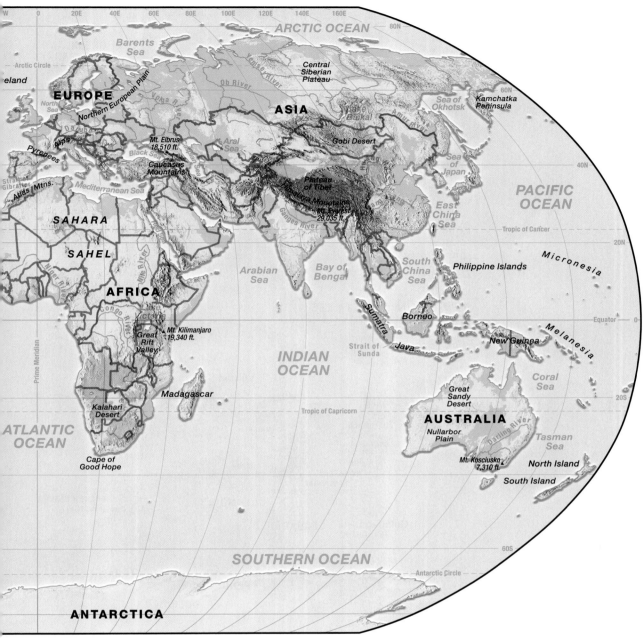

ARCTIC OCEAN

Barents
Sea

Arctic Circle

eland

EUROPE

North
Sea

Northern European Plain

Yenisey River

Ob River

Volga R.

Central
Siberian
Plateau

ASIA

Sea of
Okhotsk

Kamchatka
Peninsula

Alps

Danube

Pyrenees

Black Sea

Mt. Elbrus
18,510 ft.

Caucasus
Mountains

Aral
Sea

Gobi Desert

Amur River

Sea
of
Japan

Strait of
Gibraltar

Atlas Mtns.

Mediterranean Sea

Plateau
of Tibet

Himalaya Mountains

Mt. Everest
29,035 ft.

East
China
Sea

PACIFIC
OCEAN

40N

SAHARA

SAHEL

Nile River

Arabian
Sea

Ganges River

Bay of
Bengal

South
China
Sea

Philippine Islands

Micronesia

Tropic of Cancer

20N

AFRICA

Congo River

Lake
Victoria

Mt. Kilimanjaro
19,340 ft.

Great
Rift
Valley

Sumatra

Borneo

New Guinea

Melanesia

Equator    0

Niger River

Strait of
Sunda

Java

INDIAN
OCEAN

Madagascar

Coral
Sea

20S

ATLANTIC
OCEAN

Kalahari
Desert

Great
Sandy
Desert

Tropic of Capricorn

AUSTRALIA

Nullarbor
Plain

Darling River

Tasman
Sea

Cape of
Good Hope

Mt. Kosciusko
7,310 ft.

North Island

South Island

Prime Meridian

SOUTHERN OCEAN

60S

Antarctic Circle

ANTARCTICA

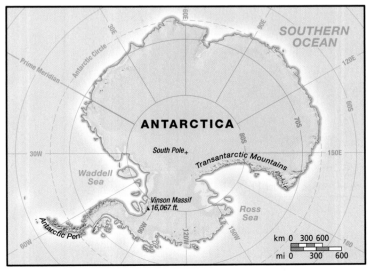

SOUTHERN
OCEAN

30E

60E

90E

Antarctic Circle

120E

Prime Meridian

60S

ANTARCTICA

South Pole +

Transantarctic Mountains

70S

80S

150E

30W

Waddell
Sea

Ross
Sea

Vinson Massif
16,067 ft.

Antarctic Pen.

60W

80W

120W

150W

180

km  0   300 600

mi  0    300   600

# Western Hemisphere: Political

ARCTIC OCEAN

140°W

Beaufort Sea

Alaska (U.S.)

60°N

GREENLAND (DENMARK)

60°W

40°W

Atlas

Hudson Bay

CANADA

Great Lakes

Labrador Sea

60°N

Ottawa

40°N

Great Salt Lake

UNITED STATES

Washington, D.C.

40°N

ATLANTIC OCEAN

Tropic of Cancer

Hawaii (U.S.)

Gulf of Mexico

BAHAMAS

Havana

MEXICO

CUBA

HAITI

DOMINICAN REPUBLIC

20°N

Mexico City

BELIZE

Kingston

U.S. VIRGIN ISLANDS

ST. KITTS AND NEVIS

GUATEMALA

Belmopan

JAMAICA

Santo Domingo

ST. LUCIA

Guatemala City

Tegucigalpa

Port-Au-Prince

BARBADOS

EL SALVADOR

San Salvador

Managua

San José

GRENADA

HONDURAS

PACIFIC OCEAN

NICARAGUA

Panama City

Caracas

VENEZUELA

Georgetown

Paramaribo

COSTA RICA

PANAMA

Bogotá

Cayenne

FRENCH GUIANA (FRANCE)

COLOMBIA

SURINAME

0°

Equator

Galápagos Is. (Ecuador)

ECUADOR

Quito

GUYANA

0°

French Polynesia (France)

Lima

BRAZIL

PERU

La Paz

Brasilia

20°S

BOLIVIA

Sucre

Tropic of Capricorn

PARAGUAY

20°S

CHILE

Asunción

N

W E

S

URUGUAY

Santiago

Buenos Aires

Montevideo

40°S

ARGENTINA

40°S

LEGEND

⊛ National capital

— National border

km 0    500   1000

mi 0    500   1000

Falkland Islands (U.K.)

South Georgia (U.K.)

60°S

60°S

140°W

120°W

100°W

80°W

60°W

40°W

# Western Hemisphere: Physical

ARCTIC OCEAN

GREENLAND

Beaufort Sea

Baffin Bay

Davis Strait

Bering Strait

Yukon R.

Mackenzie R.

Mt. McKinley (Denali)
▲ 20,320 ft.
(6,194 m)

Gulf of Alaska

Coast Mountains

Bering Sea

Hudson Bay

Labrador Sea

CANADIAN SHIELD

NORTH AMERICA

ROCKY MOUNTAINS

Coast Ranges

Great Salt Lake

Range and Basin

GREAT PLAINS

Great Lakes

Missouri R.

Mississippi R.

APPALACHIAN MOUNTAINS

Mt. Whitney
14,495 ft.
(4,418 m)

Death Valley
282 ft.
(-86 m)

Rio Grande

Coastal Plain

ATLANTIC OCEAN

Gulf of Mexico

Bahamas

Cuba

Hispaniola

Puerto Rico

Tropic of Cancer

Hawaiian Islands

Caribbean Sea

Lake Nicaragua

Lake Maracaibo

PACIFIC OCEAN

Line Islands

Galápagos Islands

Equator

Amazon R.

AMAZON BASIN

Marquesas

ANDES

SOUTH AMERICA

Society Islands

Cook Islands

Tropic of Capricorn

Atacama Desert

Mt. Aconcagua
22,834 ft.
(6,960 m)

Rio de la Plata

Valdés Peninsula
-131 ft.
(-40 m)

Falkland Islands

South Georgia

Strait of Magellan

N
W · E
S

## LEGEND

15,000 ft (45,000 m)
6,560 ft. (2,000 m)
3,280 ft. (1,000 m)
1,640 ft. (500 m)
650 ft. (200 m)
0 ft. (0 m)
Below sea level

▲ Highest Point

km 0 500 1000
mi 0 500 1000

Atlas

# United States: Political

**ARCTIC OCEAN**

RUSSIA | ALASKA | CANADA

Yukon River

Fairbanks

Anchorage

Juneau

PACIFIC OCEAN

Aleutian Islands

km 0  250  500
mi 0  250  500

N
W  E
S

WASHINGTON
Seattle
★ Olympia

Portland
★ Salem
Columbia R.

OREGON

IDAHO
★ Boise
Pocatello
Snake River

Helena ★
MONTANA
Billings •

WYOMING
Casper •

Cheyenne ★

Sacramento ★
San Francisco •

Reno •
Carson City

NEVADA

Salt Lake City ★
Provo •

UTAH

Colorado River

COLORADO
Denver ★
Colorado Springs •
Pueblo •

PACIFIC OCEAN

CALIFORNIA

Las Vegas •

Los Angeles •

San Diego •

ARIZONA

★ Phoenix

Tucson •

Santa Fe ★
Albuquerque •

NEW MEXICO

El Paso •

Rio Grande

Gulf of California

MEXICO

## LEGEND
⊗  National capital
★  State capital
•  Major city
—  National boundary
—  State boundary

Kauai
Niihau
Oahu  Kailua
Honolulu ★
Molokai
Lanai  Maui
Kahoolawe

HAWAII

PACIFIC OCEAN

Hilo •
Hawaii

km 0  50  100
mi 0  50  100

CANADA

NORTH DAKOTA
~~marck~~
Fargo

MINNESOTA

SOUTH DAKOTA
~~re~~
Sioux Falls

Minneapolis · St. Paul ★

Lake Superior

Lake Michigan

MICHIGAN
Grand Rapids ·

WISCONSIN
Madison ★
Milwaukee ·
Lansing ★

Lake Huron

Detroit ·

L. Ontario

Lake Erie

St. Lawrence River

NEW HAMPSHIRE
VERMONT

MAINE
Augusta ·
Montpelier ★
Portland ·
Concord ·
Manchester ·
Boston ·

Burlington ·

NEW YORK
Albany ★
Rochester ·
Buffalo ·

MASSACHUSETTS
Hartford ★ Providence ·
New Haven ·

RHODE ISLAND
CONNECTICUT

NEBRASKA
Omaha ·
Lincoln ·

IOWA
Cedar Rapids ·
Des Moines ★

Chicago ·

ILLINOIS
Springfield ★

INDIANA
Indianapolis ★

OHIO
Columbus ★
Cleveland ·
Cincinnati ·

PENNSYLVANIA
Harrisburg ★
Pittsburgh ·

Newark · New York ·
Trenton ★
Philadelphia ·

NEW JERSEY
DELAWARE
Dover ·
Annapolis ★
Washington, D.C. ⊛
MARYLAND

Baltimore ·

WEST VIRGINIA
Charleston ★

VIRGINIA
Richmond ★
Norfolk ·

Missouri R.

Kansas City ·
Topeka ★

KANSAS

Kansas City ·
Jefferson City ★

MISSOURI

St. Louis ·

Louisville ·
Frankfort ★

KENTUCKY

Greensboro ·
Raleigh ★

NORTH CAROLINA

Tulsa ·
Oklahoma City ·

Fort Smith ·

ARKANSAS
Little Rock ★

Memphis ·

Ohio R.

Nashville ★

TENNESSEE

Mississippi River

Columbia ★

SOUTH CAROLINA

Charleston ·

OKLAHOMA

Dallas ·

MISSISSIPPI
Jackson ★

Birmingham ·

Atlanta ★

GEORGIA

Savannah ·

ATLANTIC OCEAN

TEXAS

Austin ★
Houston ·
San Antonio ·

LOUISIANA

Baton Rouge ★
New Orleans ·

Montgomery ★

ALABAMA
⊛
Mobile ·

Tallahassee ★

Jacksonville ·

FLORIDA
Tampa ·

Gulf of Mexico

Miami ·

BAHAMAS

km 0  100  200  300  400  500
mi 0  100  200  300  400  500

CUBA

# United States: Physical

**ARCTIC OCEAN**

RUSSIA

Brooks Range

CANADA

*Bering Strait*

*Yukon R.*

Mt. McKinley
(Denali)
20,320 ft.

*Alaska Range*

Bering
Sea

Gulf of
Alaska

Kodiak Is.

Aleutian
Islands

km 0    250   500
mi 0    250   500

N
W    E
S

PACIFIC
OCEAN

San Francisco
Bay

Channel Islands

Mt. Rainier
14,410 ft.

COAST RANGE

COLUMBIA RANGE

CASCADE RANGE

COLUMBIA PLATEAU

*Columbia R.*

Mt. Hood
11,239 ft.

BITTERROOT RANGE

*Missouri River*

*Yellowstone River*

BIGHORN MTNS.

Black
Hills

Badlands

GREAT

Mt. Shasta
14,162 ft.

*Snake River*

*Sacramento R.*

SIERRA NEVADA

CENTRAL
VALLEY

*San Joaquin R.*

BASIN
AND
RANGE

WASATCH RANGE

ROCKY MOUNTAINS

*Green River*

PLAINS

Mt. Whitney
14,494 ft.

Death Valley
282 ft. below sea level

Mojave
Desert

Grand
Canyon

Painted
Desert

Colorado
Plateau

Pikes Peak
14,110 ft.

SANGRE DE CRISTO MTNS.

Sonoran
Desert

*Gila River*

CONTINENTAL DIVIDE

Llano
Estacado

Edward
Platea

*Pecos River*

*Rio Grande*

Gulf of
California

MEXICO

**LEGEND**

15,000 ft. (45,000 m)
6,560 ft. (2,000 m)
3,280 ft. (1,000 m)
1,640 ft. (500 m)
650 ft. (200 m)
0 ft. (0 m)
Below sea level

▲ Highest Point

Kauai

Niihau

Oahu

Molokai

Lanai

Maui

Kahoolawe

PACIFIC OCEAN

Hawaii

Mauna Kea
13,796 ft.

Mauna Loa
13,678 ft.

km 0   50   100
mi 0    50   100

CANADA

St. Lawrence River

Mesabi Range

Lake Superior

Lake Michigan

Lake Huron

Lake Erie

L. Ontario

Adirondack Mountains

Mt. Washington 6,288 ft.
White Mtns.

Connecticut R.

Hudson R.

ALLEGHENY PLATEAU

Catskill Mtns.

Nantucket
Martha's Vineyard

Long Island

Delaware River

Susquehanna River

Delaware Bay

Chesapeake Bay

Sand Hills

Mississippi River

Missouri River

Des Moines River

Platte River

CENTRAL PLAINS

Wabash River

Ohio R.

A P P A L A C H I A N   M O U N T A I N S

OZARK PLATEAU

Arkansas River

Red River

OUACHITA MOUNTAINS

Mississippi River

Cumberland Plateau

Tennessee R.

Mt. Mitchell 6,684 ft.

BLUE RIDGE MOUNTAINS

FALL LINE

Savannah R.

Oconee R.

ATLANTIC COASTAL PLAIN

Chattahoochee River

Altamaha R.

Tombigbee R.

Alabama R.

Pearl River

Sabine River

COASTAL

PLAIN

GULF

Brazos River

Colorado River

Galveston Bay

Mobile Bay

Pensacola Bay

Tampa Bay

Gulf of Mexico

Everglades

Florida Keys

ATLANTIC OCEAN

BAHAMAS

CUBA

km 0  100  200  300  400  500
mi 0      100      200      300      400      500

# United States: Sunshine

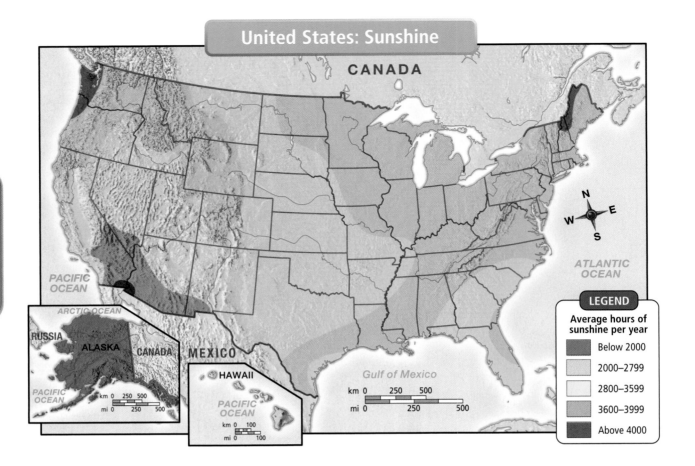

CANADA

PACIFIC OCEAN

ARCTIC OCEAN

RUSSIA

ALASKA CANADA MEXICO

HAWAII

PACIFIC OCEAN

PACIFIC OCEAN

Gulf of Mexico

ATLANTIC OCEAN

km 0 250 500
mi 0 250 500

km 0 100
mi 0 100

km 0 250 500
mi 0 250 500

**LEGEND**

Average hours of sunshine per year

| | |
|---|---|
| | Below 2000 |
| | 2000–2799 |
| | 2800–3599 |
| | 3600–3999 |
| | Above 4000 |

# United States: Vegetation

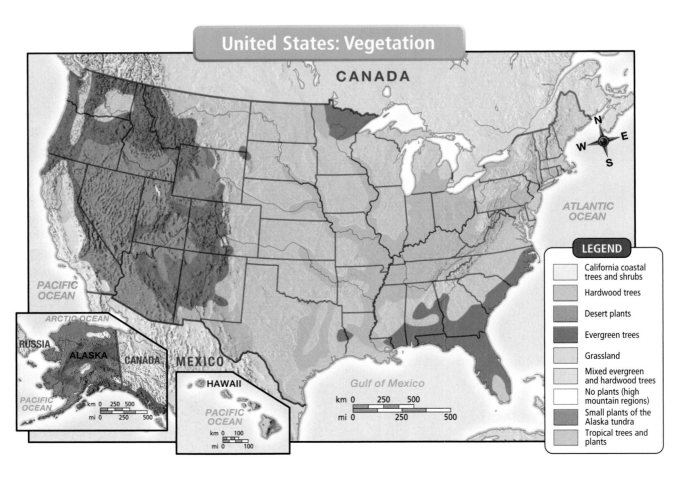

CANADA

PACIFIC OCEAN

ARCTIC OCEAN

RUSSIA

ALASKA CANADA MEXICO

HAWAII

PACIFIC OCEAN

PACIFIC OCEAN

Gulf of Mexico

ATLANTIC OCEAN

km 0 250 500
mi 0 250 500

km 0 100
mi 0 100

km 0 250 500
mi 0 250 500

**LEGEND**

| | |
|---|---|
| | California coastal trees and shrubs |
| | Hardwood trees |
| | Desert plants |
| | Evergreen trees |
| | Grassland |
| | Mixed evergreen and hardwood trees |
| | No plants (high mountain regions) |
| | Small plants of the Alaska tundra |
| | Tropical trees and plants |

# United States: Precipitation

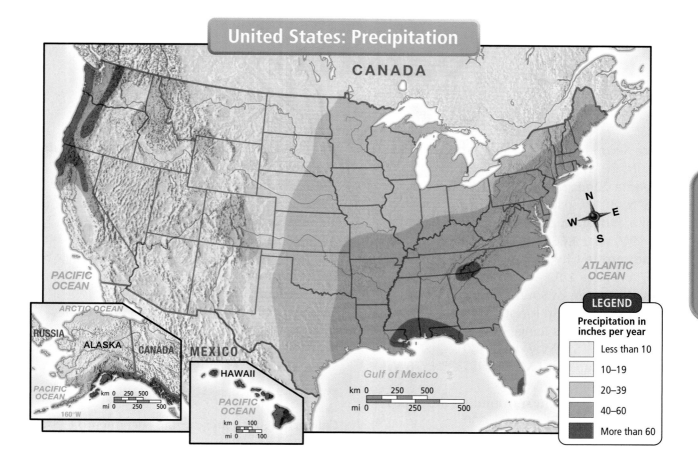

CANADA

PACIFIC OCEAN

ATLANTIC OCEAN

RUSSIA

ALASKA

CANADA

MEXICO

HAWAII

PACIFIC OCEAN

PACIFIC OCEAN

Gulf of Mexico

km 0   250   500
mi 0   250   500

km 0   250   500
mi 0   250   500

km 0   100
mi 0   100

### LEGEND

**Precipitation in inches per year**

Less than 10

10–19

20–39

40–60

More than 60

---

# United States: Population

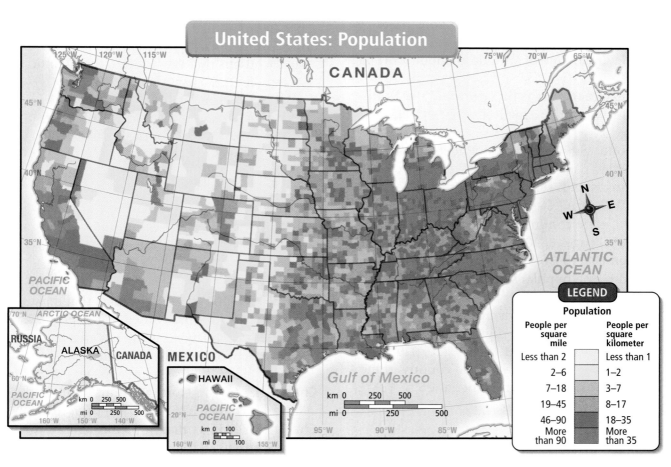

CANADA

PACIFIC OCEAN

ATLANTIC OCEAN

RUSSIA

ALASKA

CANADA

MEXICO

HAWAII

PACIFIC OCEAN

PACIFIC OCEAN

Gulf of Mexico

km 0   250   500
mi 0   250   500

km 0   250   500
mi 0   250   500

km 0   100
mi 0   100

### LEGEND

**Population**

| People per square mile | People per square kilometer |
|---|---|
| Less than 2 | Less than 1 |
| 2–6 | 1–2 |
| 7–18 | 3–7 |
| 19–45 | 8–17 |
| 46–90 | 18–35 |
| More than 90 | More than 35 |

# Gazetteer

**Africa** Second largest continent in the world (10°N, 22°E) pages 8, 107, 341

**Alabama** 22nd state; capital: Montgomery (33°N, 88°W) page R66

**Alaska** 49th state; capital: Juneau (64°N, 104°W) page R66

**Albuquerque** City in New Mexico (35°N, 107°W) page 278

**Amazon** Region in South America that has the world's largest rain forest (2°S, 53°W) page 330

**Andes Mountains** Range in western South America (13°S, 75°W) page 330

**Annapolis** Capital of Maryland (39°N, 76°W) page 116

**Antarctica** Continent surrounding the South Pole (80°S, 127°E) pages 8, 330

**Appalachian Mountains** Range stretching from Canada to Alabama (37°N, 82°W) pages 16, 17, 72, 73, 78, 190

**Arctic** Region around the North Pole, pages 55, 321, 328, 341, 342

**Arctic Circle** Line of latitude at about 66°N page 321

**Arctic Ocean** Waters that surround the North Pole; the world's smallest ocean (85°N, 170°E) page 9

**Arizona** 48th state; capital: Phoenix (34°N, 113°W) page R66

**Arkansas** 25th state; capital: Little Rock (34°N, 92°W) page R66

**Asia** Largest continent in the world (50°N, 100°E) pages 8, 107, 262, 289, 331, 341

**Aspen** City in Colorado; once a mining town and now a popular ski resort area (39°N, 107°W) page 284

**Atlantic Ocean** Extends from the Arctic to the Antarctic; east of the United States (5°S, 25°W) pages 9, 72, 79, 133, 134, 191, 320, 329

**Australia** Island continent and country in the South Pacific; capital: Canberra (25°S, 135°E) page 8

**Baja California** A dry, mountainous peninsula in western Mexico (30°N, 117°W) page 322

**Bali** An island in Indonesia (8°S, 115°E) page 342

**Balkans** Group of countries on the Balkan peninsula in southeast Europe, page 355

**Beijing** Capital of China (40°N, 116°E) page 8

**Belize** Country in South America; capital: Belmopan (17°N, 89°W) page 329

**Boston** Capital of Massachusetts (42°N, 71°W) pages 106, 107

**Brazil** Largest country in South America; capital: Brasilia (9°S, 53°W) page 331

**C**

**California** 31st state; capital: Sacramento (38°N, 121°W) page R66

**Canada** Largest country in North America; capital: Ottawa (50°N, 100°W) pages 16, 72, 190, 246, 264, 320, 321, 324, 327, 328, 349, 351

**Cape Cod** Popular tourist area in southeast Massachusetts that extends into the Atlantic Ocean (42°N, 70°W) pages 73, 76

**Caribbean** Region in the Caribbean Sea including islands and the coastal areas of Central and South America (15°N, 76°W) pages 322, 323, 328

**Cascade Mountains** Range in the United States and Canada created by volcanoes (43°N, 122°W) pages 16, 247, 290

**Central America** Group of countries in the southern part of North America between Mexico and Colombia (11°N, 87°W) pages 328, 329, 330, 353

**Central Lowlands** Flat, fertile area that makes up part of the central United States, page 228

**Central Plateau** High, mostly flat area in Mexico between the Sierra Madre Occidental and the Sierra Madre Oriental, page 322

**Chapel Hill** City in North Carolina; part of Research Triangle (36°N, 79°W) page 165

**Charles River** River that flows through Boston, Massachusetts (42°N, 71°W) page 106

**Chesapeake Bay** Inlet of the Atlantic Ocean between Virginia and Maryland (38°N, 76°W) pages 74, 116

**Chicago** Large port city on the shore of Lake Michigan in Illinois (42°N, 88°W) pages 191, 198, 218, 219, 220, 227

**China** Country in east Asia; capital: Beijing (37°N, 93°E) pages 349, 351

**Ciudad Juárez** City in Mexico just across the Rio Grande from El Paso, Texas (32°N, 106°W) page 174

**Coastal plains** Flat area east of the Appalachians extending to the Atlantic Ocean, page 133

**Colorado** 38th state; capital: Denver (40°N, 107°W) page R66

**Colorado River** River in the southwest United States; carved much of the Grand Canyon (36°N, 114°W) pages 17, 276

**Congo Basin** Large river basin in central Africa (3°N, 21°E) page 341

**Connecticut** 5th state; capital: Hartford (42°N, 73°W) page R66

**Cranberry Bay** Area near Cape Cod, Massachusetts (42°N, 71°W) page 18

**Cuba** Island nation in the Caribbean Sea; capital: Havana (22°N, 79°W) page 322

**Death Valley** Desert basin in California; lowest point in North America; holds record for hottest place in the United States (37°N, 117°W) page 248

**Delaware** 1st state; capital: Dover (39°N, 76°W) page R66

**Denver** Capital of Colorado; located on a mile-high plain east of the Rocky Mountains (40°N, 105°W) pages 51, 282

**Detroit** Large city in Michigan famous for its automobile industry (42°N, 83°W) pages 197, 208, 220, 221

**Durango** Small city in Colorado; popular with kayakers and rafters (37°N, 108°W) page 283

**Durham** City in North Carolina; part of Research Triangle (36°N, 79°W) page 165

**Egypt** Country in northeast Africa; capital: Cairo (27°N, 27°E) page 341

**El Paso** City in Texas on the Rio Grande (32°N, 106°W) page 174

**Elizabeth** City in New Jersey; part of the New York City metropolitan area (41°N, 74°W) page 39

**Endicott Mountains** Range in northern Alaska; holds record for coldest place in the United States (68°N, 154°W) page 287

**England** Region in western Europe; part of the United Kingdom (capital: London) (52°N, 2°W) pages 94, 149, 313, 324

**Europe** Continent located between the Atlantic Ocean and Asia (50°N, 15°E) pages 8, 36, 107, 114, 289, 331

**Everglades** Wetlands in southern Florida (26°N, 81°W) pages 133, 176, 177

**Florida** 27th state; capital: Tallahassee (31°N, 85°W) page R66

**France** Country in western Europe; capital: Paris (47°N, 1°E) pages 151, 205, 312, 323, 341, 349

**French Guiana** Region in South America that is controlled by France; capital: Cayenne (4°N, 53°W) page 330

**Galveston Bay** Bay on the Gulf of Mexico in Texas; connected to Houston by the Houston Ship Channel (30°N, 95°W) page 171

**Genesee River** River that flows through western New York (42°N, 78°W) page 72

**Georgia** 4th state; capital: Atlanta (33°N, 84°W) page R66

**Germany** Country in western Europe; capital: Berlin (51°N, 10°E) page 349

**Grand Canyon** Deep gorge in Arizona carved by the Colorado River and widened by wind erosion (36°N, 112°W) pages 17, 247, 276

**Great Britain** Region made up of England, Scotland, and Wales (55°N, 5°W) pages 310, 323, 349

**Great Lakes** Five freshwater lakes (Superior, Michigan, Huron, Erie, and Ontario) in the United States and Canada (45°N, 83°W) pages 18, 72, 190, 191, 192, 196, 204, 206, 219, 226

**Great Plains** In central North America; high grassland region (45°N, 104°W) pages 190, 193, 205, 207, 228, 231, 321

**Great Salt Lake** Lake in Utah; largest inland body of salt water in the Western Hemisphere (41°N, 113°W) pages 18, 248

**Greensboro** City in North Carolina; site of sit-in protest during struggle for civil rights (36°N, 80°W) page 152

**Gulf of Mexico** Body of water along the southern United States and Mexico (25°N, 94°W) pages 19, 133, 191, 194

**Hawaii** 50th state; capital: Honolulu (20°N, 158°W) page R66

**High Point** City in North Carolina; nicknamed "Furniture Capital of the World" (36°N, 80°W) page 164

**Himalayas** Mountain range in Asia; contains the world's highest peak, Mount Everest in Nepal (30°N, 82°E) page 341

**Honolulu** Capital of Hawaii; major center of tourism (21°N, 158°W) page 289

**Hoover Dam** Dam on the Colorado River; supplies power to more than one million people in the Southwest (36°N, 114°W) page 251

**Houston** City in Texas; largest city in the southern region of the United States (30°N, 95°W) pages 170, 171

**Hudson Bay** Bay in Canada that is frozen for much of the year (60°N, 86°W) page 321

**Hudson River** River in New York; major seaway for early European settlers (43°N, 74°W) pages 92, 114

**Idaho** 43rd state; capital: Boise (44°N, 115°W) page R66

**Illinois** 21st state; capital: Springfield (40°N, 91°W) page R66

**India** Country in southern Asia; capital: New Delhi (23°N, 78°E) page 343, 358

**Indian Ocean** Body of water between Africa, Asia, and Australia (10°S, 40°E) page 9

**Indiana** 19th state; capital: Indianapolis (40°N, 87°W) page R66

**Indianapolis** Capital of Indiana; transportation hub in the Midwest (40°N, 86°W) pages 198, 227

**Iowa** 29th state; capital: Des Moines (41°N, 93°W) page R66

**Ireland** Island nation in the North Atlantic; capital: Dublin (54°N, 8°W) page 341

**Isthmus of Panama** A narrow strip of land that connects Central America and South America (9°N, 80°W) page 329

**Italy** Country in southern Europe; capital: Rome (44°N, 11°E) page 341

**Jackson** Town in Wyoming; known for its outdoor activities (43°N, 110°W) page 283

**Jamestown** Historic community in Virginia; first permanent English settlement in North America (37°N, 76°W) page 149

**Japan** Island nation off northeast coast of Asia; capital: Tokyo (37°N, 134°E) page 351

**Kansas** 34th state; capital: Topeka (39°N, 100°W) page R66

**Kansas City** Largest city in Missouri; transportation hub of the Midwest (39°N, 95°W) page 198

**Kentucky** 15th state; capital: Frankfort (38°N, 88°W) page R66

**Knoxville** City in Tennessee (36°N, 84°W) page 142

**Lake Mead** Reservoir in Nevada and Arizona created by the Hoover Dam (36°N, 114°W) pages 248, 251

**Lake Michigan** One of the Great Lakes (43°N, 87°W) page 218

**Lake Superior** Largest of the Great Lakes; largest freshwater lake in the world (48°N, 89°W) pages 18, 222

**Las Vegas** Desert city in Nevada that receives about four inches of rain per year (36°N, 115°W) page 276

**Latin America** The countries of the Western Hemisphere south of the United States, page 107

**Long Beach** Major port city in California (34°N, 118°W) page 289

**Los Angeles** Large city in California; known for its movie industry (34°N, 118°W) pages 257, 289

**Louisiana** 18th state; capital: Baton Rouge (31°N, 93°W) page R66

**Maine** 23rd state; capital: Augusta (45°N, 70°W) page R66

**Marianas Trench** Located in the Pacific Ocean; deepest point in the world (12°N, 144°E) page 9

**Maryland** 7th state; capital: Annapolis (39°N, 76°W) page R66

**Massachusetts** 6th state; capital: Boston (42°N, 73°W) page R66

**Maui** One of the Hawaiian islands (21°N, 156°W) page 18

**Mauna Loa** A huge, active volcano in Hawaii Volcanoes National Park (19°N, 156°W) page 291

**Memphis** City in Tennessee; major transportation hub (35°N, 90°W) pages 162, 163, 164

**Mexico** Country in North America that shares a border with the United States; capital: Mexico City (24°N, 104°W) pages 45, 246, 264, 265, 274, 322, 323, 324, 325, 328, 349, 351

**Mexico City** Capital of Mexico; one of the world's largest cities (19°N, 99°W) page 322

**Michigan** 26th state; capital: Lansing (46°N, 87°W) page R66

**Milwaukee** Port city on the shore of Lake Michigan in Wisconsin (43°N, 88°W) page 191

**Minneapolis** Largest city in Minnesota (45°N, 93°W) pages 191, 209

**Minnesota** 32nd state; capital: St. Paul (45°N, 93°W) page R66

**Mississippi** 20th state; capital: Jackson (33°N, 90°W) page R66

**Mississippi River** Principal river of the United States; flows from Lake Itasca in Minnesota and empties into the Gulf of Mexico in Louisiana (32°N, 92°W) pages 19, 41, 133, 191, 194, 195, 208, 209, 210

**Missouri** 24th state; capital: Jefferson City (38°N, 94°W) page R66

**Missouri River** Longest river in the United States; tributary of the Mississippi River (41°N, 96°W) pages 19, 191, 208, 210, 212, 229

**Mojave Desert** Desert in the southwestern United States (35°N, 117°W) pages 248, 251

**Montana** 41st state; capital: Helena (47°N, 112°W) page R66

**Montgomery** City in Alabama; site of bus boycott during struggle for civil rights (32°N, 86°W) page 152

**Mount Jefferson** Mountain located in the Cascade Range in the northwest United States (45°N, 122°W) page 16

**Mount McKinley** Mountain in Alaska; highest point in the United States (63°N, 151°W) pages 3, 248

**Mount Rainier** Mountain in Washington state; highest mountain in the Cascade Range (47°N, 122°W) page 288

**Mount St. Helens** Volcano in the Cascade Range that erupted in 1980 (46°N, 122°W) page 21

**Mount Wai'ale'ale** Mountain in Hawaii that is one of the wettest places in the world (22°N, 159°W) page 287

**Nashville** City in Tennessee known for its music industry (36°N, 87°W) page 164

**Nebraska** 37th state; capital: Lincoln (41°N, 102°W) page R66

**Netherlands** Country in western Europe; capital: Amsterdam (53°N, 4°E) page 323

**Nevada** 36th state; capital: Carson City (40°N, 117°W) page R66

**New Hampshire** 9th state; capital: Concord (44°N, 72°W) page R66

**New Jersey** 3rd state; capital: Trenton (41°N, 75°W) page R66

**New Mexico** 47th state; capital: Santa Fe (35°N, 107°W) page R66

Gazetteer

**New Orleans** City in Louisiana; known as the birthplace of jazz (30°N, 90°W) pages 10, 50, 151, 155, 172

**New York** 11th state; capital: Albany (43°N, 78°W) page R66

**New York City** City in New York state; largest city in the United States (41°N, 74°W) pages 39, 72, 81, 114, 115, 312, 317

**North America** Northern continent of the Western Hemisphere; includes Canada, the United States, Mexico, and Central America (45°N, 100°W) pages 8, 24, 92, 114, 262, 320, 328, 340

**North Carolina** 12th state; capital: Raleigh (36°N, 82°W) page R66

**North Dakota** 39th state; capital: Bismarck (46°N, 100°W) page R66

**North Korea** Country in Asia; capital: P'yongyang (40°N, 127°E) page 353

**North Pole** Northernmost point on Earth (90°N) pages 9, 10, 74

**Nunavut** Canadian territory that is home to Inuit and other American Indian groups, page 321

**Ohio** 17th state; capital: Columbus (41°N, 83°W) page R66

**Ohio River** Tributary of the Mississippi River (37°N, 88°W) pages 19, 191

**Oklahoma** 46th state; capital: Oklahoma City (36°N, 98°W) page R66

**Omaha** City in Nebraska; starting point of Transcontinental Railroad construction (41°N, 96°W) page 229

**Oregon** 33rd state; capital: Salem (44°N, 122°W) page R66

**Pacific Ocean** World's largest and deepest ocean; mainly west of the United States (0°, 170°W) pages 9, 18, 19, 211, 212, 246, 248, 320, 321, 329

**Panama Canal** Canal across the Isthmus of Panama that connects the Atlantic and the Pacific oceans (10°N, 80°W) page 329

**Pennsylvania** 2nd state; capital: Harrisburg (41°N, 78°W) page R66

**Peru** Country on the Pacific coast of South America; capital: Lima (10°S, 75°W) page 331

**Philadelphia** Large port city in Pennsylvania (40°N, 75°W) pages 81, 82, 313

**Phoenix** Capital of Arizona (34°N, 112°W) pages 274, 275, 277

**Piedmont** Area of rolling hills between the Appalachians and coastal plains (35°N, 80°W) pages 144, 164

**Portland** Major port city in Oregon (46°N, 123°W) page 289

**Portugal** Country in western Europe; capital: Lisbon (38°N, 8°W) pages 331, 341

**Puerto Rico** A U.S. territory in the Caribbean; capital: San Juan (18°N, 67°W) page R66

Q

**Québec** Canadian province in which many people speak French (51°N, 70°W) page 321

R

**Raleigh** Capital of North Carolina; part of Research Triangle (36°N, 79°W) page 165

**Rhode Island** 13th state; capital: Providence (42°N, 72°W) page R66

**Rio Grande** River forming part of the border between Texas and Mexico (26°N, 99°W) pages 40, 133, 263, 275

**Rocky Mountains** Range in the western United States and Canada (50°N, 114°W) pages 16, 19, 190, 247, 248, 282, 321

**Rwanda** Country in Africa; capital: Kigali (2°S, 30°E) page 355

**St. Lawrence Seaway** System of canals connecting the St. Lawrence River above Montreal to Lake Ontario (49°N, 67°W) page 92

**St. Louis** City in Missouri; lies just south of where the Missouri River flows into the Mississippi (39°N, 90°W) pages 208, 230

**Salt Lake City** City in Utah; home to the nation's largest Mormon population (41°N, 112°W) page 277

**San Diego** Large city in southern California that started as a Spanish mission (33°N, 117°W) page 264

**San Francisco** Major port city and international banking center in California (38°N, 122°W) pages 255, 260, 264, 289

**Scotland** Part of Great Britain; capital: Edinburgh (57°N, 5°W) page 341

**Seattle** Major port city in Washington state (48°N, 122°W) pages 258, 288, 289

**Sierra Madre Occidental** Mountain range that runs along Mexico's western coast (25°N, 107°W) page 322

**Sierra Madre Oriental** Mountain range that runs along Mexico's eastern coast (25°N, 100°W) page 322

**Silicon Valley** Nickname for a region in California known for computer technology (37°N, 122°W) pages 43, 258

**South America** Southern continent of the Western Hemisphere (15°S, 60°W) pages 8, 328, 330, 331

**South Carolina** 8th state; capital: Columbia (34°N, 81°W) page R66

**South Dakota** 40th state; capital: Pierre (44°N, 100°W) page R66

**South Pole** Southernmost point on Earth (90°S) pages 9, 10

**Spain** Country in western Europe; capital: Madrid (40°N, 5°W) pages 45, 149, 264, 265, 325, 329, 331, 341

**Tennessee** 16th state; capital: Nashville (36°N, 88°W) page R66

**Texas** 28th state; capital: Austin (31°N, 101°W) page R66

**Torres del Paine** Mountain range in Chile (47°S, 72°W) page 340

**United States** Country that lies mostly in central North America; capital: Washington, D.C. (38°N, 110°W) pages 8, 93, 265, 266, 267, 309, 310, 315, 320, 322, 328, 329, 330, 348, 349, 350, 351, 352

**Utah** 45th state; capital: Salt Lake City (40°N, 112°W) page R66

**Vancouver** City on the Pacific coast of Canada (49°N, 123°W) page 320

**Venezuela** Country in South America; capital: Caracas (8°N, 65°W) page 331

**Vermont** 14th state; capital: Montpelier (44°N, 72°W) page R66

**Virginia** 10th state; capital: Richmond (37°N, 81°W) page R66

**Wales** Part of Great Britain; capital: Cardiff (52°N, 4°W) page 341

**Washington** 42nd state; capital: Olympia (48°N, 121°W) page R66

**Washington, D.C.** Capital of the United States (39°N, 77°W) pages 72, 114, 118, 154, 156

**West Virginia** 35th state; capital: Charleston 38°N, 81°W) page R66

**Willapa Bay Tide Flat** Coastal wildlife area in Washington state (47°N, 123°W) page 18

**Wisconsin** 30th state; capital: Madison (40°N, 89°W) page R66

**Wyoming** 44th state; capital: Cheyenne (43°N, 109°W) page R66

**York** Town in Maine; site of first sawmill in the United States (43°N, 70°W) page 82

Gazetteer

# Glossary

**adapt** (uh DAPT) to change in order to better fit the environment. (p. 135)

**adobe** (uh DOH bee) a type of clay. (p. 263)

**aerospace** (AYR oh spays) a word used to describe businesses that make airplanes. (p. 144)

**agriculture** (AG rih kul chur) the business of farming. (p. 45)

**alliance** (uh LYE uhns) an agreement between allies to seek a common goal. (p. 348)

**ally** (AL eye) a country or group that joins with another country or group for a common purpose. (p. 348)

**arid** (AYR ihd) very dry. (p. 248)

**assembly line** (uh SEHM blee lyn) a way of making products in which each worker does one small part of the job as a product moves along the line. (p. 208)

**atmosphere** (AT muh sfeer) the air that surrounds Earth. (p. 52)

**basin** (BAY sihn) an area with a low center surrounded by higher land. (p. 18)

**bay** (bay) a body of water partly surrounded by land but open to the sea. (p. 74)

**belt** (behlt) a region that has one feature stretching across a broad area. (p. 37)

**blizzard** (BLIHZ urd) a heavy snowstorm with strong winds. (p. 57)

**border** (BOR dur) a line that separates political regions, such as states or countries. (p. 37)

**boundary** (BOUN duh ree) the edge of a region. (p. 37)

**boycott** (BOY kawt) a kind of protest in which people refuse to do business with a person or company. (p. 152)

**canal** (kuh NAL) a waterway made by people. (p. 191)

**cape** (kayp) a point of land that sticks out into the water. (p. 73)

**capital** (KAP ih tl) a city where a state or country's government is located. (p. 116)

**capital resources** (KAP ih tl REE sor sihz) the tools, machines, buildings, and other equipment that a business uses to make goods or provide services. (p. 82)

**century** (SEHN chuh ree) a period of 100 years. (p. 100)

**circle graph** (SUR kuhl graf) a circle that is divided into sections to show how information is related. (p. 112)

**citizen** (SIHT ih zihn) someone who is born in a country or who promises to be loyal to the country. (p. 308)

**civil rights** (SIHV uhl rytz) the rights that every citizen has by law. (p. 152)

**climate** (KLY miht) the usual weather conditions in an area over a long period of time. (p. 53)

**coast** (kohst) the land that borders an ocean. (p. 72)

**coastal plain** (KOHST uhl playn) the flat, level land along a coast. (p. 72)

**cold front** (kohld frunt) the edge of a mass of cold air. (p. 52)

**colony** (KAHL uh nee) a settlement ruled by another country. (p. 149)

**command economy** (kuh MAND ih KAHN uh mee) a system in which the government decides what to make, who will make it, and who will get it. (p. 80)

**communication** (kuh myoo nih KAY shuhn) the exchange of information. (p. 165)

**commuter** (kuh MYOO tur) someone who travels between home and work each day. (p. 108)

Glossary

**compass rose** (KUM puhs rohz) a symbol on a map that shows direction. (p. 15)

**conclusion** (kuhn CLOO zhuhn) a judgment about the meaning of certain facts or ideas. (p. 326)

**conflict** (KAHN flihkt) a disagreement between groups of people or individuals. (p. 346)

**conservation** (kahn sur VAY shuhn) using something carefully and not wasting it. (p. 277)

**constitution** (kahn stih TOO shuhn) a plan for setting up and running a government. (p. 93)

**consumer** (kuhn SOO mur) someone who buys or uses goods and services. (p. 143)

**continent** (KAHN tuh nehnt) a large mass of land. (p. 8)

**cost of living** (kawst uhv LIHV ing) the money that people pay for food, clothing, transportation, and housing. (p. 108)

**crops** (krahps) plants that people grow and gather. (p. 26)

**culture** (KUHL chur) the way of life of a particular group of people. (p. 90)

**dam** (dam) a barrier built across a waterway to control the flow and level of water. (p. 142)

**decade** (DEHK ayd) a period of 10 years. (p. 100)

**delta** (DEHL tuh) a triangle-shaped area at the mouth of a river. (p. 133)

**demand** (dih MAND) how much of a product consumers will buy at different prices. (p. 199)

**democracy** (dih MAHK ruh see) a system in which the people hold the power of government. (p. 309)

**dialect** (DYE uh lehkt) a regional variety of a language. (p. 343)

**drip irrigation** (drihp eer ih GAY shuhn) a system that drips water very slowly at the roots of each plant. (p. 277)

**ecology** (ih KAHL uh jee) the science of the connection between living things and their environment. (p. 282)

**economy** (ih KAHN uh mee) the way the people of an area choose to use the area's resources. (p. 45)

**ecosystem** (EE koh sihs tuhm) an environment and all its living things, working as a unit. (p. 285)

**election** (ih LEHK shuhn) the way voters choose people to serve in government. (p. 309)

**elevated train** (EHL uh vay tihd trayn) a railway that runs above the ground on raised tracks. (p. 219)

**elevation** (ehl uh VAY shuhn) the height of the land. (p. 53)

**enslaved** (ehn SLAYVD) a word used to describe someone who works for no pay and can be sold as property. (p. 149)

**entrepreneur** (AHN truh pruh nuhr) a person who uses the factors of production to start a new business. (p. 83)

**environment** (ehn VY ruhn muhnt) all the surroundings and conditions that affect living things. (p. 6)

**equator** (ih QUAY tur) a line at 0° latitude that divides Earth into Northern and Southern hemispheres. (p. 9)

**erosion** (ih ROH zhuhn) a process of wearing away rock and soil. (p. 17)

**ethnic group** (EHTH nihk groop) people who share the same culture. (p. 170)

**European Union** (yoor uh PEE uhn YOON yuhn) a trading partnership in Europe that helps countries buy and sell products more easily across international borders. (p. 351)

**evaporation** (ih VAP uh ray shuhn) when water changes into vapor or steam. (p. 18)

**executive branch** (ig ZEHK yuh tihv branch) the part of a government that puts laws into action. (p. 116)

**export** (EHK sport) a product that is sent out of a country to be sold or traded. (p. 149)

**extinct** (ihk STIHNGKT) no longer existing. (p. 285)

**fact** (fakt) a statement that can be proven true. (p. 254)

**factors of production** (FAK turs uhv pruh DUHK shuhn) people and materials needed to make goods or provide services. (p. 82)

**factory** (FAK tuh ree) a building or group of buildings in which goods are made. (p. 81)

**fault** (fawlt) a break in the earth's crust. (p. 247)

**fertile** (FUR tl) filled with the materials that plants need to grow. (p. 218)

**flow resources** (floh REE sor sihz) energy sources that constantly move through the environment, such as water, sunlight, and wind. (p. 25)

**fossil fuel** (FAHS uhl FYOO uhl) an energy source formed by the remains of things that lived long ago. (p. 26)

**free enterprise** (free EHN tur pryz) a system that lets people control their businesses and decide what goods to buy and sell. (p. 349)

**fumarole** (FYOO muh rohl) a hot steam vent. (p. 285)

**geography** (jee AHG ruh fee) the study of the people and places of Earth. (p. 6)

**geothermal** (jee oh THUR ml) related to heat from beneath Earth's crust. (p. 247)

**glacier** (GLAY shur) a huge mass of slowly moving ice. (p. 17)

**globe** (glohb) a model of Earth. (p. 8)

**goods** (gudz) things that people buy and sell, including both manufactured and agricultural products. (p. 80)

**government** (GUHV urn muhnt) a system of making and carrying out rules and laws. (p. 37)

**governor** (GUHV ur nur) the official who leads the executive branch for his or her state. (p. 116)

**grain elevator** (grayn EL uh vay tur) a building used to store wheat or other grains. (p. 230)

**habitat** (HAB ih tat) the natural home of a plant or an animal. (p. 285)

**hemisphere** (HEHM ih sfeer) one half of Earth's surface. (p. 9)

**heritage** (HAYR ih tihj) the traditions that people have honored for many years. (p. 316)

**homestead** (HOHM stehd) a piece of land given to someone to settle and farm. (p. 207)

**hub** (huhb) a major center of activity. (p. 163)

**human features** (HYOO muhn FEE churz) the way people live in a particular place. (p. 8)

**human resources** (HYOO muhn REE sor sihz) the services, knowledge, skills, and intelligence that workers provide. (p. 82)

**humid** (hyoo MIHD) moist; having a lot of water vapor in the air. (p. 134)

**hurricane** (HUR ih kayn) a storm with strong and damaging winds. (p. 57)

**hydroelectric power** (hy droh ih LEHK trihk POW ur) electricity produced from flowing water. (p. 248)

**immigration** (ihm ih GRAY shuhn) the movement of people from one nation into another. (p. 95)

**import** (IHM port) a product brought in from another country. (p. 350)

**index** (IHN dehks) an alphabetical listing of the topics in a book. (p. 88)

**industry** (IHN duh stree) a business that makes goods in factories. (p. 95)

**interdependence** (ihn tur dih PEHN duhns) a relationship in which people depend on each other. (p. 315)

**interior** (ihn TEER ee ur) a place away from a coast or border. (p. 133)

**international** (ihn tur NASH uh nul) between countries. (p. 350)

**international law** (ihn tur NASH uh nul law) a set of basic rules to which the United States and many other countries have agreed. (p. 355)

**international trade** (ihn tur NASH uh nul trayd) trade with foreign countries. (p. 350)

**Internet** (IHN tur neht) a huge communications network connecting computers around the world. (p. 165)

**irrigation** (ihr ih GAY shuhn) supplying land with water. (p. 248)

**isthmus** (IHS muhs) a narrow strip of land that connects two larger areas. (p. 329)

**jazz** (jaz) American music that developed from spirituals, ragtime, and blues. (p. 172)

**judicial branch** (joo DIHSH ul branch) the part of a government that interprets, or explains, laws in the courts. (p. 116)

**landform** (LAND fawrm) a physical feature of Earth's surface, such as a mountain. (p. 8)

**latitude** (LAT ih tood) distance north or south of the equator, measured by lines that circle the globe parallel to the equator. (p. 10)

**legend** (LEHJ uhnd) a table or list that tells what the symbols on a map mean. (p. 15)

**legislative branch** (LEHJ ih slay tihv branch) the part of a government that makes laws. (p. 116)

**levee** (LEHV ee) a high river bank that stops the river from overflowing. (p. 191)

**liberty** (LIHB ur tee) the freedom from control by others. (p. 310)

**livestock** (LYV stahk) animals that people raise on farms, especially animals raised to sell. (p. 26)

**lock** (lahk) a part of a waterway that is closed off by gates. (p. 191)

**longitude** (LAHN jih tood) distance east or west of the prime meridian, measured by lines that run between the North and South poles. (p. 10)

**loom** (loom) a machine that weaves cloth. (p. 94)

**lumber** (LUHM bur) wood cut into boards. (p. 26)

**manufacturing** (man yuh FAK chur ing) making goods from other materials. (p. 108)

**map** (map) a drawing of Earth's surface. (p. 10)

**market economy** (MAHR kiht ih KAHN uh mee) a system in which people are free to decide what, how, and for whom to make products. (p. 80)

**meridians** (muh RIHD ee uhnz) lines of longitude that run north and south and measure distances east and west of the prime meridian. (p. 50)

**mesquite** (meh SKEET) a plant that grows in arid areas and has deep roots that can reach underground water. (p. 249)

**migrant worker** (MY gruhnt WUR kur) a person who moves from place to place doing seasonal work. (p. 290)

**minerals** (MIHN ur uls) natural resources that lie deep in the ground. (p. 26)

**mining** (MY ning) taking minerals from the earth. (p. 26)

**mission** (MIHSH uhn) a settlement for teaching religion to local people. (p. 264)

**NAFTA** (NAF tuh) the North American Free Trade Agreement (1992), which allows the United States, Canada, and Mexico to trade goods with each other, usually without paying taxes or fees. (p. 349)

**national park** (NASH uh nul pahrk) an area set aside by the federal government for recreational or other uses. (p. 257)

**NATO** (NAY toh) the North Atlantic Treaty Organization, formed in 1949, which is comprised of the United States and several European nations and whose members agree to defend each other in case of attack. (p. 349)

**natural resources** (NACH ur ul REE sor sihz) things from the natural environment that people use. (p. 24)

**nomadic** (noh MAD ihk) traveling from place to place. (p. 205)

**nongovernmental organization (NGO)** (non guhv urn MEHN tl or guh nih ZAY shuhn) a group that is not part of a national government. (p. 356)

**nonrenewable resources** (non rih NOO uh buhl REE sor sihz) things that nature cannot replace after they are used. (p. 25)

**nor'easter** (nohr EE stur) a storm blowing from the northeast that brings strong winds, high ocean waves, and heavy snow or rain. (p. 74)

nutrients

**nutrients** (NOO tree uhnts) materials in soil that plants need for food. (p. 279)

**opinion** (uh PIHN yuhn) an idea or a belief. (p. 254)

**opportunity cost** (awp ur TOO nih tee cawst) what someone gives up to get something else. (p. 145)

**parallels** (PAR uh lehlz) lines of latitude that run east and west and measure distances north and south of the equator. (p. 50)

**peninsula** (puh NIHN suh luh) a piece of land surrounded by water on three sides. (p. 133)

**physical features** (FIHZ ih cul FEE churz) things that are found in nature. (p. 8)

**Pilgrim** (PIHL gruhm) a person who left England to settle in Plymouth Colony. (p. 92)

**plains** (playnz) large areas of flat land. (p. 17)

**planned community** (pland kuh MYOO nih tee) a place to live that is mapped ahead of time. (p. 171)

**plantation** (plan TAY shuhn) a big farm that grows mostly one crop. (p. 150)

**plateau** (pla TOH) a high, flat area of land. (p. 132)

**point of view** (poynt uhv vyoo) the way someone looks at a topic or situation. (p. 140)

**pollution** (puh LOO shuhn) anything that makes something impure or dirty. (p. 173)

**population** (pop yuh LAY shuhn) the people living in an area. (p. 37)

**population density** (pop yuh LAY shuhn DEHN sih tee) a measure of how many people live in an area. (p. 230)

**port** (pawrt) a place along the shore of a lake or an ocean where ships can dock. (p. 289)

**prairie** (PRAYR ee) a dry, mostly flat grassland with few trees. (p. 190)

**prairie dog** (PRAYR ee dog) a rodent that belongs to the squirrel family. (p. 193)

**precipitation** (prih sihp ih TAY shuhn) water that falls to the earth as rain, snow, sleet, or hail. (p. 53)

**primary source** (PRY mehr ee sors) an account written by someone who saw an event. (p. 212)

**prime meridian** (prym muh RIHD ee uhn) a line at 0° longitude that divides Earth into Eastern and Western hemispheres. (p. 9)

**private ownership** (PRY viht OH nur shihp) a system in which individual people, not the government, own the factors of production. (p. 83)

**producer** (pruh DOO sur) someone who makes or sells goods or services for consumers. (p. 143)

**product** (PRAHD uhkt) something that is made from natural resources. (p. 26)

**profit** (PRAHF iht) in a market economy, the money left over after a business pays its expenses. (p. 80)

**prosperity** (prah SPEHR ih tee) wealth and success. (p. 316)

**province** (PRAHV ihns) a unit of government in Canada, similar to a United States state. (p. 321)

**public institution** (PUHB lihk ihn stih TOO shuhn) an organization that serves the people and communities of a country or state. (p. 117)

**pueblo** (PWEHB loh) a town made up of stone or adobe buildings. (p. 275)

**rain forest** (RAYN Fawr ihst) dense forest that gets large amounts of rainfall every year. (p. 329)

**ranch** (ranch) a farm where people raise animals, such as cattle, sheep, or horses. (p. 275)

**raw materials** (raw muh TEER ee ulz) natural resources before they are made into products. (p. 198)

**recreation** (rehk ree AY shuhn) activities done for fun or relaxation. (p. 172)

**region** (REE juhn) an area that is defined by certain features. (p. 11)

**religion** (rih LIHJ uhn) a system of faith or worship. (p. 37)

**renewable resources** (rih NOO uh buhl REE sor sihz) things that the environment can replace after we use them. (p. 25)

**report** (rih PAWRT) writing that presents information that has been researched. (p. 176)

**representative** (rehp rih ZEHN tuh tihv) a person who acts for a group of people. (p. 309)

**research** (rih SURCH) the act of studying something carefully to learn more about it. (p. 165)

**reservation** (rehz ur VAY shuhn) land set aside by the government for American Indians. (p. 210)

**reservoir** (REHZ ur vwahr) a lake that is used to store water. (p. 276)

**river basin** (RIHV uhr BAY sihn) the area that is drained by a river. (p. 42)

**rural** (RUR uhl) in a country area with few people. (p. 43)

**scale** (scayl) a ruler that shows distances on a map. (p. 15)

**scarcity** (SKAYR sih tee) a situation in which there are not enough resources to provide a product or service that people want. (p. 145)

**search engine** (surch EHN jihn) a Web site that finds other Web sites related to your key words. (p. 88)

**seasonal** (SEE zuh nuhl) happening at certain times of the year. (p. 290)

**secondary source** (SEHK uhn dehr ee sors) an account written by someone who did not witness the event. (p. 212)

**service** (SUR vihs) something a person or company does for someone else. (p. 198)

**skilled worker** (skihld WUR kur) a person who has received special training or education. (p. 259)

**skyscraper** (SKY skray pur) a very tall building. (p. 115)

**slavery** (SLAY vuh ree) an unjust system in which one person owns another. (p. 93)

**social institution** (SOH shuhl ihn stih TOO shuhn) an organization that helps the public. (p. 107)

**sod** (sahd) large chunks of soil held together by grass roots. (p. 207)

**specialization** (spehsh uh lih ZAY shuhn) making only a few kinds of goods or providing just one kind of service. (p. 258)

**suburb** (SUHB urb) a community that grows outside of a larger city. (p. 107)

**suburban** (suh BUR buhn) in a smaller town near a city. (p. 43)

**subway** (SUHB way) an underground train. (p. 107)

**summarize** (SUHM uh ryz) to tell in your own words the most important points of a piece of writing. (p. 226)

**supply** (suh PLY) how much of a product producers will make at different prices. (p. 199)

**tax** (taks) a fee paid to the government. (p. 117)

**technology** (tehk NAHL uh jee) the use of scientific knowledge. (p. 220)

**tectonic plate** (tehk TAHN ihk playt) a huge slab of slowly moving rock. (p. 16)

**temperate** (TEHM pur iht) without extremes, such as the very cold weather in the Arctic or the very hot weather near the equator. (p. 74)

**temperature** (TEHM pur uh chur) a measure of how hot or cold the air is. (p. 53)

**textile** (TEHKS tyl) cloth. (p. 94)

**tornado** (tor NAY doh) a twisting column of fast-moving air. (p. 57)

**trade** (trayd) the exchange, purchase, or sale of goods and services. (p. 81)

**transcontinental railroad** (tranz kahn tuh NEHN tl RAYL rohd) the first train system to link the eastern and western United States. (p. 267)

**transportation** (tranz puhr TAY shuhn) the business of moving people or goods from one place to another. (p. 162)

**treaty** (TREE tee) an official document that defines an agreement between nations. (p. 348)

**tributary** (TRIHB yuh tehr ee) a river or stream that flows into another river. (p. 191)

**university** (yoo nuh VUR sih tee) a school with several colleges that each focus on one area of study. (p. 107)

**unskilled worker** (uhn SKIHLD WUR kur) a person who does a job that requires no special training or education. (p. 259)

**urban** (UR buhn) in a city. (p. 43)

**vegetation** (vehj ih TAY shuhn) the kinds of plants that grow in a region. (p. 341)

**volcano** (vahl KAY noh) a place where melted rock squeezes out from underground. (p. 16)

**volunteer** (vahl uhn TEER) someone who agrees to provide a service without pay. (p. 317)

**wages** (WAYG es) the payments people receive for work. (p. 219)

**wagon train** (WAG uhn trayn) a line of wagons that carried settlers and everything they owned. (p. 266)

**weather** (WEHTH ur) the day-to-day conditions in the atmosphere. (p. 52)

**weathering** (WEHTH ur ing) the breakdown of rock caused by wind, water, and weather. (p. 276)

**wetlands** (WEHT landz) lands that have water on or near the surface of the soil. (p. 133)

**wilderness** (WIHL duhr nihs) a large area with few people and left in its natural state. (p. 321)

**zydeco** (ZY dih koh) a kind of music developed by African Americans in Louisiana. (p. 172)

# Index

Page numbers with *m* before them refer to maps.

Index

Index

Index

**Index**

# Acknowledgments

## Acknowledgments

For each of the selections listed below, grateful acknowledgment is made for permission to excerpt and/or reprint original or copyrighted material, as follows:

## Permissioned Material

"Gold," by Pat Mora, from *Home,* by Thomas Locker. Text copyright © 1998 by Pat Mora. Reprinted by permission of Harcourt, Inc.

Excerpt from the Speech, "I Have a Dream," by Dr. Martin Luther King Jr. Copyright © 1963 by Dr. Martin Luther King Jr., copyright renewed © 1991 by Coretta Scott King. Reprinted by arrangement with the Estate of Martin Luther King Jr., c/o Writers House as agent for the proprietor New York, NY.

Excerpt from *The Most Beautiful Roof in the World: Exploring The Rainforest Canopy,* by Kathryn Lasky, photographs by Christopher G. Knight. Text copyright © 1997 by Kathryn Lasky Knight. Photographs copyright © 1997 by Christopher G. Knight. Reprinted by permission of Harcourt, Inc.

Excerpt from *Rage of Fire,* by Gloria Skurzynski and Alane Ferguson. Text copyright © 1998 by Gloria Skurzynski and Alane Ferguson. Reprinted by permission of National Geographic Society.

"Sap Moon, March" and "Harvest Moon, September," from *An Algonquian Year: The Year According to the Full Moon,* written and illustrated by Michael McCurdy. Copyright © 2000 by Michael McCurdy. Reprinted by permission of Houghton Mifflin Company.

"Some Rivers," from *Sawgrass Poems: A View of the Everglades,* by Frank Asch. Copyright © 1996 by Frank Asch. Reprinted by permission of Harcourt, Inc.

Excerpt from *Storm Warriors,* by Elisa Carbone. Text copyright © 2001 by Elisa Carbone. Jacket illustration copyright © 2001 by Don Demers. Reprinted by arrangement with Random House Children's Books, a division of Random House, Inc., New York, New York.

"This is Indiana," by Rebecca Kai Dotlich. Copyright © 2000 by Rebecca Kai Dotlich. Reprinted by permission of Curtis Brown, Ltd.

Excerpt from The American Girl History Mysteries Book *Trouble At Fort La Pointe,* by Kathleen Ernst. Copyright © 2000 by American Girl, LLC. Reprinted by permission of American Girl, LLC.

"Watercolor Maine," by C. Drew Lamm, from *My America,* by Lee Bennett Hopkins. Text copyright © 2000 by Lee Bennett Hopkins. Reprinted by permission of C. Drew Lamm.

## Illustration Credits

pp. 20–21 Stephen Durke. p. 22, 65, 125, 183, 239, 301, 365 Kelly Kennedy. p. 31 Patrick Gnan. p. 32, 270 Rob Kemp. pp. 58–59 Inklink. p. 60, 102, 120, 158, 234, 258, 296, 345 Jun Park. p. 78, 175, 201, 214, 270, 274, 360 Kenneth Batelman. p. 84, 85, 86–87, 166–167, 168–169, Barbara Massey. p. 90 Susan Moore. p. 96, 97, 98, 99 Michael McCurdy. p. 108 Rob Schuster. pp. 118–119, 194–195, 286–287 Mike Saunders. p. 136, 138 Richard Waldrep. p. 148 Bernadette Lau. p. 150, 223 Andrew Wheatcroft. p. 215 Karen Minot. p. 222, 224, 225 Pleasant Publications (Betty Garvey) Reprinted with permission of American Girl, LLC from the American Girl History Mysteries book Trouble at Fort La Pointe © Copyright 2000 by American Girl. p. 250, 253, 310 Will Williams. p. 293, 295 David Bathurst.

## Map Credits

Maps by Mapping Specialists, Ltd.
Atlas maps by Maps.com

## Photography Credits

COVER (bear) © Paul A. Souders/CORBIS. (desert) © James Randklev/ Visions Of America, LLC/PictureQuest. (compass) © HMCo./Michael Indresano. (spine bear) © Paul A. Souders/CORBIS. (backcover statue) © Connie Ricca/CORBIS. (backcover nickel) Courtesy of the United States Mint. vi (tl) Kevin Anthony Horgan/Getty Images. vi (bl) Artbase Inc. vii (tl) © Bettmann/CORBIS. (br) © Michelle Garrett/CORBIS. (bl) © Richard T. Nowitz/CORBIS. viii (tl) © Bettmann/CORBIS. (bl) © Mark M. Lawrence/CORBIS. ix (tl) © Bill Ross/CORBIS. (bl) Photodisc/Getty Images. x (tl) Neal Mishler/Getty Images. (bl) Frank Siteman/PhotoEdit. xi (tl) © Jeff Greenberg/PhotoEdit. (bl) © Alan Oddie/PhotoEdit. xii (b) © Craig Aurness/CORBIS. xxii (b) © Michael Ventura/Photo Edit. 2 (bl) © Kevin Anthony Horgan/Getty Images. (bc) © Cathy Melloan Resources/PhotoEdit. (br) © Jim Wark/Index Stock Imagery. 3 (bc) © C. Partrick J Endres/AlaskaPhotographics.com. (cr) © Nancy Camel/Alamy. 4 (cl) Kevin Anthony Horgan/Getty Images. (cr) © Dale Sanders/Masterfile. 5 (cl) Artbase Inc. (cr) © David Muench/CORBIS. 7 (b) Kevin Anthony Horgan/Getty Images. 8 (b) © JP Laffont/Sygma/CORBIS. 11 (tr) © Michael Newman/PhotoEdit. 12 (bl) Ray Boudreau. 13 (tc) © Davis Barber/PhotoEdit. 15 (br) Ray Boudreau. 16 (b) Alan Majchrowicz/Getty Images. 17 (cr) Artbase Inc. 18 (cr) © CORBIS. (bl) © Layne Kennedy/CORBIS. (br) © Galen Rowell/CORBIS. (tr) © Carl & Ann Purcell/CORBIS. 19 (tr) © Cathy Melloan Resources/PhotoEdit. 20 (b) © NOAA/Handout/Reuters/CORBIS. 21 (t) © 2005 Randy Belice/NBAE/Getty Images. (b) AP Photo/Judi Bottoni. 23 (b) Ray Boudreau. 24 (b) © David Muench/CORBIS. 25 (t) © Bonnie Kamin/PhotoEdit. 26 (br) © Jim Wark/Index Stock Imagery. 27 (br) © Ed Lallo/Index Stock Imagery. (bl) © John Madere/CORBIS. 28 (cr) © Owaki-Kulla/CORBIS. (b) Glen Allison/Getty Images. 29 (tr) © David Young-Wolff/PhotoEdit. 30 (tr) © Bettman/CORBIS. 34 (cl) ©

Bill Brooks/Masterfile. (cr) J. Patton/Robertstock.com. 35 (cl) © Davd Pollack/CORBIS. (cr) © J.A. Kraulis/Masterfile. 36 (b) © Buddy Mays/CORBIS. 37 (t) © Craig Aurness/CORBIS. 39 (cr) © Thinkstock/Index Stock Imagery. 40 (bl) © Mark E. Gibson. 41 (cr) © Brian Sytnyk/Masterfile. 42 (b) © Gavriel Jecan/CORBIS. 43 (tl) © Mike Dobel/Masterfile. (cr) Artbase Inc. (tr) Jeff Zaruba/Getty Images. 44 (br) © Pete Saloutos/CORBIS. 46 (br) © Judy Griesedieck/CORBIS. 47 (tr) © Profolio Enr./Index Stock Imagery. (br) © William Ervin/Index Stock Imagery. 48 (r) © Joseph Sohm. Visions of America/CORBIS. 49 (tr) © Bill Ross/CORBIS. 52 (b) © Camerique/Robertstock.com. 53 (t) © Mark E. Gibson. 55 (tl) Gary Braasch/Getty Images. (tr) Artbase Inc. (bl) © Dale Sanders/Masterfile. (br) © Joseph Sohm. ChromoSohm Inc./CORBIS. (cl) C. Partrick J Endres/AlaskaPhotographics.com. (cr) © Lowell Georgia/CORBIS. 56 (b) © Davd Pollack/CORBIS. (cr) © Aneal Vohra/Index Stock Imagery. 68 (br) © Michelle Garrett/CORBIS. 69 (bc) © Alan Schein Photography/CORBIS. 70 (cl) © Miles Ertman/Masterfile. (cr) © Mark Richards/PhotoEdit. 71 (cr) Matthew Pippin. (cl) © Dean Conger/CORBIS. 72 (b) © Grant Heilman Photography. 74 (t) © Reuters NewMedia Inc. 75 (cr) © Joe McDonald/CORBIS. 76 (br) Tom Pantages adaptation/Courtesy NASA. 77 (bl) © Jack Stein Grove/PhotoEdit. (t) © Ernest Manewal/Superstock, Inc. 79 (tr) © Rudi Von Briel/PhotoEdit. 80 (b) © Elizabeth Hathon/CORBIS. 81 (b) © Tony Freeman/PhotoEdit. 82 (tl) © Grant Heilman Photography. 82 (bc) © Arthur C. Smith III/Grant Heilman Photography, Inc. (br) © Roy Morsch/CORBIS. (cr) Photodisc/Getty Images. 83 (tr) © David Young-Wolff/PhotoEdit. 85 (br) Ray Boudreau. 86 (sp) Ray Boudreau. 89 (b) © Chip Henderson/Index Stock Imagery. 92 (b) © David Frazier/The Image Works. 93 (b) © Bettmann/CORBIS. 100 (b) Ray Boudreau. 104 (cl) David Joel/Getty Images. (cr) © Jeff Greenberg/PhotoEdit. 105 (cl) AP/Wide World Photos. (cr) AP/Wide World Photos. 106 (b) Digital Vision/Getty Images. 108 (b) © Dennis Curran/Index Stock Imagery. 109 (cr) © Michelle Garrett/CORBIS. 110 (br) © Stapleton Collection/CORBISphoto.com. 111 (tl) Reuters, 1996. (cr) Time Life Pictures/Getty Images. 113 (br) Ray Boudreau. 114 (br) © Alan Schein Photography/CORBIS. 116 (bl) © Richard T. Nowitz/CORBIS. 118 (bl) © Adam Woolfitt/CORBIS. (br) © Tom Carter/PhotoEdit. 119 (bl) © Lee Snider. Lee Snider/CORBIS. 128 (bl) © Paul Conklin/PhotoEdit. (bc) ©Courtesy of the Tennessee Valley Authority. (br) © Bettmann/CORBIS. 129 (bc) © James A. Sugar/CORBIS. (cl) © Paul Chesley/Getty Images. 130 (cl) © Ed Bock/CORBIS. (cr) © LWA-Dann Tardif/CORBIS. 131 (cl) Ray Boudreau. (cr) © Bettmann/CORBIS. 132 (bl) J. Brian Alker/Getty Images. 134 (b) © Joe Skipper/Reuters Newmedia Inc./CORBIS. 135 (tr) © Paul Conklin/PhotoEdit. 140 (cl) Ray Boudreau. (cr) Ray Boudreau. 142 (b) Courtesy of the Tennessee Valley Authority. 143 (tr) © Inga Spence/Index Stock Imagery. (cr) © LWA-Dann Tardif/CORBIS. 144 (br) Jonathon Katnor/Getty Images. 146 (cr) Ray Boudreau. (bl) Ray Boudreau. 147 (tr)

Ray Boudreau. (cr) Ray Boudreau. 149 (tl) © Jeff Greenberg/PhotoEdit. (tr) © Jeff Greenberg/PhotoEdit. (cr) Ira Block/National Geographic Image Collection. 150 (sp) © Joseph Sohm. ChromoSohm Inc./CORBIS. 151 (cr) Louisiana State Museum. Gift of Dr. C.A. Browne. 152 © Bettmann/CORBIS. 153 (c) Kevin Lamarque, Reuters 2003. 154 (br) © Flip Schulke/CORBIS/photo.com. 155 (cr) AP/Wide World Photos. (bl) Collection of the Norman Rockwell Museum at Stockbridge, Massachusetts. (tl) © Bettman/CORBIS/photo.com. 156 (c) © Wally McNamee/CORBIS. 157 (b) Ray Boudreau. 160 (cl) © Dennis MacDonald/PhotoEdit. (cr) © Bob Daemmrich/PhotoEdit. 161 (cl) © A. Ramey/PhotoEdit. (cr) © Jim Schwabel/Index Stock Imagery. 162 (b) © Dennis MacDonald/PhotoEdit. 164 (br) © Mark E. Gibson. 165 (tr) Jim Cummins/Getty Images. 166 (sp) Ray Boudreau. 168 (sp) Ray Boudreau. 170 (b) © Rose Hartman/CORBIS. 172 (b) © James A. Sugar/CORBIS. 173 (c) © Mark M. Lawrence. 174 (bl) Paula Bronstein/Getty Images. 177 (br) Ray Boudreau. (t) © Myrleen Ferguson Cate/PhotoEdit. 182 (c) © Bettmann/CORBIS. 186 (bl) © Garry Black/Masterfile. (bc) © Bettmann/CORBIS. (br) © Steve Craft/Masterfile. 187 (bc) ©Jim Reed/Photo Researchers, Inc. 188 (cl) Jake Rajs/Getty Images. (cr) © Myrleen Ferguson Cate/PhotoEdit. 189 (cl) © CORBIS. (cr) © Bettmann/CORBIS. 190 (b) © Garry Black/Masterfile. 193 (cr) © Steve Harper/Grant Heilman Photography, Inc. 196 (b) © Al Fuchs/NewSport/CORBIS. 198 (t) © David Young-Wolff/PhotoEdit. 200 (background) Artbase Inc. 204 (b) © Michael S. Lewis/CORBIS. 207 (sp) © CORBIS. 208 (t) © Bettmann/CORBIS. 209 (cr) © Bill Ross/CORBIS. 210 (cl) © North Wind Picture Archives. (cr) © North Wind Picture Archives. 213 (br) Ray Boudreau. 216 (cl) © Pierre Tremblay/Masterfile. (cr) Artbase Inc. 217 (cl) © David Fraizer/The Image Works. (cr) Photodisc/Getty Images. 218 (b) Mark Segal/Getty Images. 220 (cr) © Steve Craft/Masterfile. (tl) © Reuters NewMedia Inc./CORBIS. 227 (bl) Photodisc/Getty Images. 228 (b) © Dennis MacDonald/PhotoEdit. 229 (tr) Jim Reed/Photo Researchers, Inc. 230 (br) Photodisc/Getty Images. 230 (tl) AP/Wide World Photos. 231 (tr) Johnny Sundby. 232 (r) © Allen Russell/Index Stock Imagery. (cl) © Bill Aron/PhotoEdit. 233 (bl) © Marilyn "Angel" Wynn/nativestock.com. 242 (bl) © Grant Heilman/Grant Heilman Photography, Inc. (bc) © Grant Heilman/Grant Heilman Photography. (bl) © Bob Rowan. Progressive Image/CORBIS. 243 (bc) © David Mendelsohn/Masterfile. (tr) © Adam Woolfitt/CORBIS. (cr) © Craig Tuttle/CORBIS. 244 (cl) © James A. Sugar/CORBIS. (cr) © Tony Freeman/PhotoEdit. 245 (cl) © Mark Richards/Photo Edit. (cr) © Tony Freeman/PhotoEdit. 246 (bl) © H. Spichtinger/Masterfile. (b) © Jan Stromme/PhotoEdit. 248 (br) Eastcott Mormatiuk/Getty Images. (b) © Grant Heilman/Grant Heilman Photography, Inc. 249 (cr) © Grant Heilman/Grant Heilman Photography, Inc. 251 (sp) Ray Boudreau. 252 (sp) Ray Boudreau. 254 (b) Ray Boudreau. 256 (bl) David R. Frazier Photolibrary, Inc. 258

(b) Loren Stanow/Getty Images. 259 (tr) David H. Smith. 260 (b) Sierra Club and its Hetch Hetchy Restoration Task Force. (tr) © San Francisco Public Utilities Commission. 261 (t) © 2000 by Anthony Dunn. 263 (sp) © Grant Heilman Photography. 265 (sp) © Tony Freeman/PhotoEdit. 266 (br) Neal Mishler/Getty Images. 268 (cr) Sister Mary Rose Krupp, Ursuline Convent Offices, 4045 Indian Rd., Toledo, OH 43606. (sp) Artbase Inc. 269 (tr) Courtesy Museum of New Mexico, neg. no. 128955 272. (cl) © Bob Rowan. Progressive Image/CORBIS. (cr) Peter Weimann/Animals Animals. 273 (cl) Mary Evans Picture Library. (cr) © Mark Richards/PhotoEdit. 274 (b) © Danny Lehman/CORBIS. 276 (b) Artbase Inc. (cr) © David Muench/CORBIS. 277 (cl) © Bob Rowan. Progressive Image/CORBIS. 278 (bl) © BAUMGARTNER OLIVIA/CORBIS SYGMA 279 (c) © Mark E. Gibson. 281 (b) Ray Boudreau. 282 (b) © Roger Ressmeyer/CORBIS. 284 (t) © Frank Siteman/PhotoEdit. 288 (b) © David Mendelsohn/Masterfile. 290 (t) © Richard Hamilton Smith/CORBIS. 291 (c) Warren Bolster/Getty Images. 304 (bc) © Bernd Obermann/CORBIS. (br) © AP/Wide World Photos. 305 (bc) © Digital Vision/Getty Images. (br) © Alamy/Artbase. 306 (cl) AP/Wide World Photos. (cr) AP/Wide World Photos. 307 (cl) © Jeff Greenberg/PhotoEdit. (cr) © Robert Estall/CORBIS. 308 (b) AP/Wide World Photos. 309 (t) AP/Wide World Photos. 312 (r) Artbase Inc. 313 (tr) Artbase Inc. (cl) © Lee Snider. Lee Snider/CORBISphoto.com. 314 (br) © Michael Macor/San Francisco Chronicle/CORBIS. 316 (cr) Jack Hollingsworth/Getty Images. (b) Artbase Inc. 317 (cl) © Bernd Obermann/CORBIS. 318 (sp) © Reuters NewMedia Inc./CORBIS. 319 (tl) Chris Todd/Getty Images. (tr) © Reuters New Media Inc./CORBISphoto.com. (bl) Dave Gatley/FEMA News Photo. (br) AP/Wide World Photos. 320 (b) © Sherman Hines/Masterfile. 322 (b) © Bob Krist/CORBIS. 324 (r) © Bettmann/CORBISphoto.com. (br) Hulton Archive/Getty Images. 325 (tr) The San Jacinto Museum of History, Houston. (bl) © Steve Vidler/Superstock, Inc. 326 (sp) Ray Boudreau. 328 (b) Margarette Mead/Getty Images. 329 (bl) © Jeff Greenberg/PhotoEdit. 330 (br) © Galen Rowell/CORBIS. 332 (tr) Christopher G. Knight. (bl) Christopher G. Knight. 333 (tr) Christopher G. Knight. 334 (t) Christopher G. Knight. 335 (cr) Christopher G. Knight. 338 (cl) © Bill Bachmann/The Image Works. (cr) © AFP/CORBIS. 339 (cl) © Brooks Kraft/CORBIS. (cr) © Don Mason/CORBIS. 340 (b) Art Wolfe/Getty Images. 342 (sp) © Sandro Vannini/CORBIS. (cr) © Amy Etre/PhotoEdit. 343 (tr) © Alan Oddie/PhotoEdit. 347 (b) Ray Boudreau. 348 (br) © Johnny Johnson/Index Stock Imagery. 349 (t) AP/Wide World Photos. 351 (tr) © Angelo Zefa. 352 (background), Artbase Inc. 353 (bl) © Tom Wagner/CORBIS SABA. (cr) Art Directors/J Sweeney. (tr) Artbase Inc. 354 (b) Digital Vision/Getty Images. 355 (b) AP/Wide World Photos. 356 (b) © Photo by Jim and Mary Whitmer. (cl) © Grothe/D.M.N./Corbis Sygma. 358 (sp) FDR Library. (bl) Reuters, 2001. 362 © HMCo/Ray Boudreau. 363 ©

Liu Liqun/CORBIS. R1 (city) © David Ball/CORBIS. (farm) © Terry W. Eggers/CORBIS. (globe) © Photo Library International/CORBIS. R2–R3 © LWA-Dann Tardif/CORBIS. R4 (l) © Museum of the City of New York/CORBIS. (r) © Reuters/CORBIS. R58 © Michael Melford/The Image Bank/Getty Images. R59 (t) © R.T. Holcomb/CORBIS.